PAPERS IN
AFRICAN PREHISTORY

PAPERS IN AFRICAN PREHISTORY

EDITED BY

J. D. FAGE

Professor of African History
University of Birmingham

AND

R. A. OLIVER

Professor of the History of Africa
University of London

CAMBRIDGE
AT THE UNIVERSITY PRESS
1970

Published by the Syndics of the Cambridge University Press
Bentley House, 200 Euston Road, London N.W.1.
American Branch: 32 East 57th Street, New York, N.Y. 10022

Library of Congress Catalogue Card Number: 74-77286
Standard Book Numbers:
521 07470 3 clothbound
521 09566 2 paperback

Printed in Great Britain by
Bookprint Limited, Crawley, Sussex

Abel

CONTENTS

LIST OF CONTRIBUTORS

A. D. H. BIVAR, *Reader in the Archaeology of the Near and Middle East, University of London.*

NEVILLE CHITTICK, *Director, British Institute of History and Archaeology in East Africa.*

J. DESMOND CLARK, *Professor of Old World Archaeology, University of California, Berkeley.*

BRIAN M. FAGAN, *Professor of Archaeology, University of California, Santa Barbara.*

MALCOLM GUTHRIE, *Professor of Bantu Languages, University of London.*

F. L. LAMBRECHT, *World Health Organisation, Botswana.*

WYATT MACGAFFEY, *Assistant Professor of Sociology and Anthropology, Haverford College, Pennsylvania.*

J. NENQUIN, *Professor, Faculty of Letters and Philosophy, University of Ghent, Belgium.*

ROLAND OLIVER, *Professor of the History of Africa, University of London.*

ROLAND PORTÈRES, *Professor, Directeur du Laboratoire d'Ethnobotanique, Muséum National d'Histoire Naturelle, Paris.*

P. L. SHINNIE, *Professor of Archaeology, University of Khartoum, Khartoum, and* MRS. M. SHINNIE.

F. J. SIMOONS, *Department of Geography, University of Texas, Austin, Texas.*

R. SUMMERS, *Director, National Museum, Bulawayo, Rhodesia.*

FRANK WILLETT, *Professor of African Art, Northwestern University.*

C. C. WRIGLEY, *Reader in African History, University of Sussex.*

Publisher's Note

All articles in this book except Chapters 3, 10, 12 and 18, and part of 14 are reprinted as they originally appeared in the *Journal of African History* with only a few minor corrections, and they have not been brought up to date. Readers will find therefore that some details, such as names of territories, refer to the conditions prevailing when the article was first written.

Chapter nos. 3, 10, 12 and 18 have been rewritten or newly translated for this volume. References in these articles are to the state of affairs when the book went to press.

INTRODUCTION

By R. A. OLIVER AND J. D. FAGE

EVER since its foundation in 1960, the editors of the *Journal of African History* have pursued a policy of inviting special contributions from Iron Age archaeologists and others working around the earlier limits of the subject, couched in the non-technical language necessary for a largely lay readership. Most of the articles reprinted in this volume have originated in this way. Between them, they embody some of the most up-to-date and forward-looking contributions to African prehistory, and it seems appropriate that they should now be presented to an audience wider than that of the *Journal*'s regular subscribers.

The author of the first two articles, Professor J. Desmond Clark, of the University of California, Berkeley, is by any account the most experienced and the widest-ranging authority on the African Stone Age. In these two magisterial surveys he presents the leading themes in the progression of African cultures, from the earliest tool-making hominids to the Late Stone Age initiators of the food-producing revolution. It is in elucidating the origins of this revolution, which made possible the settled life, and all the cultural developments that came with it, that the botanist can make his greatest contribution to African history, and this contribution is well illustrated in the article by Professor Roland Portères of the Muséum National d'Histoire Naturelle of Paris, here for the first time translated into English, which summarizes what is known from botanical evidence about the domestication of cereal food-plants in Africa north of the equatorial forests. In the two articles which follow, Mr. Christopher Wrigley of the University of Sussex puts forward in a much more tentative way the arguments for supposing that there was a parallel early development of tropical vegeculture in the woodlands south of the Congo forest which form the heart of the present Bantu Africa; while Professor Simoons, of the University of Texas, draws attention to the antiquity of another form of vegeculture in the ensete-growing region of south-west Ethiopia. Discussion on the spread of animal husbandry into Africa is not directly represented in this volume, but one of the most important conditioning factors for that spread is described in the highly original article by Dr Frank L. Lambrecht of the World Health Organisation, on the evolution and ecology of tsetse flies and trypanosomiasis, which incidentally suggests that many millions of years earlier, the tsetse fly may have created the ecological niche for the ground-living primates, and so for the evolution of man himself.

During the past twenty years, evidence from the classification of languages has come to be seen as a much more useful pointer to the nature of prehistoric African cultures than older concepts of race and culture derived from the rather unsatisfactory data of physical and cultural anthropology. In this volume the general point is made by Dr Wyatt MacGaffey of Haverford College, who concludes that in the present state of knowledge, priority should be accorded to data in the order (1) language, (2) race, (3) culture, and not the reverse. A very important contribution by a comparative linguist to the prehistory of sub-equatorial Africa is the article by Professor Malcolm Guthrie, of the School of Oriental and African Studies of London University, describing the main historical conclusions to be drawn from his life's work on the classification of the Bantu languages, now at last emerging from the press.[1] The article by Roland Oliver is an attempted synthesis, as at May 1966, of the archaeological, botanical, linguistic and historical evidence concerning the origins and dispersion of the Bantu-speaking peoples. This article is very far from being the last word on the subject; but in so far as it directs attention away from the remote and possibly insoluble problem of ultimate origins, and towards the successive stages of population growth and geographical dispersion, it may indicate the main lines of future research.

The remaining articles in the volume are by archaeologists of the Iron Age of Africa, and they present the preliminary conclusions of ongoing research. From his position at the National Museum, Bulawayo, Mr Roger Summers has been personally involved in all the major developments in Rhodesian archaeology during the last twenty years, and his article on the Rhodesian Iron Age, first printed in 1960, has been completely revised for this volume. The same is true of the article on the Iron Age sequence in the southern province of Zambia by Dr Brian Fagan, who for several years occupied a comparable vantage-point at the Livingstone Museum. Dr Fagan's article on the Greefswald sites was undertaken at the express invitation of the editors of the *Journal*, and has served a particularly valuable purpose, both in elucidating an almost unintelligible excavation literature, and in relating the conclusions to the latest findings from Zambia and Rhodesia. The southern Congo, potentially the most important region in Africa for Iron Age archaeology, has so far received only a brief series of expeditions organized by Professor Jean Hiernaux during his Rectorship of the University of Lubumbashi. The most arresting discoveries made were at the Sanga cemetery site, described in this volume by Dr Jacques Nenquin of the University of Ghent. There follow two articles by Mr Neville Chittick, for many years Director of the British Institute of History and Archaeology in East Africa. The first describes the splendid ruins first uncovered by Mr Chittick at Husuni Kubwa at the northern tip of Kilwa Island. The second reappraises the early medieval

[1] M. Guthrie, *Introduction to the Study of the Bantu Languages*. New York, Gregg, 4 vols, 1968–9.

history of the East Coast in the light of the Kilwa excavations.

The years of the *Journal*'s existence have not been the most significant ones for progress in the archaeology of the Sudan Republic, where efforts have been largely concentrated on rescue operations in connection with the flooding caused by the Aswan High Dam. Nevertheless an article by Professor Peter Shinnie and his wife Margaret presents some fresh reflections on the Christian kingdoms of Nubia in the light of the Polish excavations at Faras, and of the new analysis of Nubian pottery undertaken by Dr William Y. Adams on behalf of the Sudan Antiquities Service. Now that Professor Shinnie has taken up a post at the University of Khartoum and from there begun new excavations at the great site of Meroe, it is to be hoped that the archaeology of the Sudan will take its rightful place in the *Journal*'s pages.

Serious archaeological work, on any planned or large scale, was slower to develop in West Africa than was the case along the axis from Cairo to the Cape. Difficult working conditions were not offset by the obvious lures of unravelling the secrets of the pyramids or of Zimbabwes, or of making dramatic advances in the understanding of man's earliest history. However in the last twenty years or so, the West African situation has begun to change with ever-increasing momentum, so that today more and more archaeologists are setting to work in territories like Tchad and Cameroun, Niger and Mali, Senegal and Mauretania and, above all perhaps, Ghana and Nigeria. Some of the work done in the last few years has been truly exciting, but the field is a very wide one and, aware that there is so much more remaining to be uncovered and understood, the West African archaeologists have as yet been reluctant to generalize from what they have already achieved. Thus the survey of the archaeology of Ife by Professor Frank Willett of Northwestern University presented here must stand for the moment merely as a presage of the broader syntheses that may be expected in due course.

A final word of caution must be addressed to readers of this volume on the subject of radiocarbon dates. The articles reprinted here have been written over nearly ten years, during which the number of radiocarbon dates from Iron Age sites has been doubling approximately every year. The problem is not that the individual dates quoted have subsequently proved unreliable. It is that so many new dates have been springing up all round them that the total chronological picture has been changing dramatically from year to year. For example, Professor Clark in the second of his two articles, written in 1962, states that 'by A.D. 200 the Negro Nok Culture people were smelting iron and tin'. Since then iron-working levels in Nok Culture sites have been dated, first of all to the third, and most recently to the fifth, century B.C. Clark's statement was, and is, correct. But he would not have written it in that form today, and readers must beware of similar anachronisms throughout the volume. The editors have carefully considered whether they should try to annotate such anachronisms as of June 1968, but have decided that in view of the rate at which new information is accumulating, the additional expense involved would not be justified. Lists of, and comments on, new radio-carbon dates are published regularly in the *Journal*, and, by reference to these, new developments in any particular area of sub-Saharan African can be easily and quickly checked.

1. THE PREHISTORIC ORIGINS OF AFRICAN CULTURE

By J. DESMOND CLARK

REMARKABLE and exciting discoveries that have been made in Africa during the last five years suggest that it was here that tool-making first appeared in the geological record, and that it was then carried to other continents by hominid forms, the discovery of which has necessitated completely new thinking about the biological development of Man. In the same way the discovery, undreamed of twenty years ago, of urban centres in the Near East, dating to as early as the eighth millennium B.C., is providing unique details of life in early Neolithic times and is causing prehistorians to look back ever further into the past, almost to the close of the last glacial, for the first signs of the domestication of plants and animals and of settled village life.

Such discoveries are fundamental to the study of the origins and growth of social and economic life, and increasing use is being made of the archaeological record by the cultural anthropologist and ethno-historian, although there is still in places a lingering tendency to consider that prehistory has nothing to offer the student of present-day culture. The success of collaboration between anthropologists, linguists, historians and archaeologists has, however, already been amply demonstrated in several African countries—for example in Uganda[1] and Northern[2] and Southern[3] Rhodesia. Indeed, the archaeologist is now an indispensable part of any co-operative project to reconstruct the history of a pre-literate population.

While, therefore, it is now obvious that archaeology can provide some of the best source material for the reconstruction of cultural antecedents, population movements, and even of the origins of some social and religious practices on a factual basis, it is the new ways in which the archaeologist is using his data that render the results and potential so valuable. Today the archaeologist relies heavily on the help of his colleagues in many disciplines, particularly on those in the natural sciences. This, together with the precision resulting from improved field techniques and more meticulous observation and analysis, is providing an increasing quantity of solid scientific data, and permitting radical reassessment in

[1] M. Posnansky, 'Some archaeological aspects of the ethno-history of Uganda', in G. Mortelmans (editor), Actes du IVe Congrès Panafricain de Préhistoire (Leopoldville, 1959). Tervuren (1962), 375–80.
[2] B. M. Fagan, 'The Iron Age sequence in the Southern Province of Northern Rhodesia'. Journal of African History (1963), IV, 2, 157–77.
[3] E. T. Stokes (editor), 'Historians in tropical Africa', in Proceedings of the Leverhulme Intercollegiate History Conference (Salisbury, 1960). Salisbury, Southern Rhodesia (1962).

I

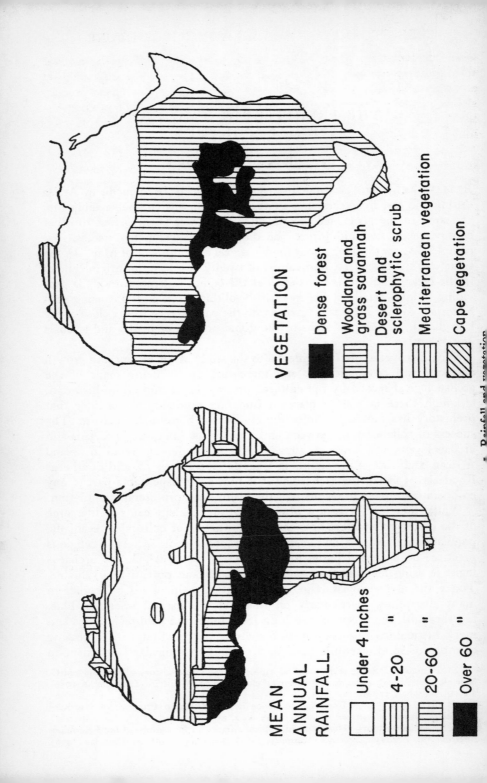

MEAN
ANNUAL
RAINFALL

Under 4 inches
4-20   "
20-60   "
Over 60   "

VEGETATION

Dense forest
Woodland and
grass savannah
Desert and
sclerophytic scrub
Mediterranean vegetation
Cape vegetation

4. Rainfall and vegetation

their interpretation. The absolute dating techniques now available have revolutionized chronologies, just as the more accurate knowledge of past environments has imparted new and vital significance to cultural remains, and permitted a deeper appreciation of the importance of the inseparable relationship there has always been between environment, culture and biological adaptation.

In addition to the close collaboration between palaeo-ecologist, physical anthropologist and prehistorian, the cultural anthropologist and ethnographer are drawn upon for help in the interpretation of the cultural evidence. Thus, on the one hand, primate behaviour studies are important as a basis for the reconstruction of life in Australopithecine times; on the other hand, ecological studies of present-day Bantu agriculturalists are a vital necessity for the interpretation of early Iron Age cultures in southern Africa, and it is necessary to study the whole continuous process of culture change in prehistoric times on a continental scale if we are to try to understand it at the regional level.

The earliest evidence of culture in the world occurs at the unique site at the Olduvai Gorge, the discovery of which is due to Dr and Mrs L. S. B. Leakey (as also is so much of our knowledge of the earliest history of man the tool-maker). Olduvai Gorge is situated in northern Tanganyika in the Eastern Rift, and cuts through some 300 feet of old lake sediments of Lower and Middle Pleistocene age. These beds are dated relatively in respect of the fossil faunas and cultural remains they contain, and absolutely by the potassium/argon method.[4] Bed I is between $1\frac{1}{2}$ and 2 million years old, and indisputable evidence of cultural activity has been found from top to bottom within it. The tool-makers camped round the edge of shallow open water near small lakes, and formed temporary camps on the mud flats exposed by seasonal fluctuations of the water level of the kind that can be seen at many of the Rift Valley lakes today. The surfaces on which the artifacts occur appear to have been covered fairly rapidly by falls of volcanic tuffs from the adjacent Ngorongoro crater.[5] The skill and patience with which these occupation areas have been uncovered have permitted the making of floor plans that show beyond any question the artificial nature of the accumulations. On these floors stones and bones are concentrated in quantity, and many of them have been artificially broken.[6] Many stones occur which, though unworked, are not natural in the area and can only have been carried in, while many others have been intentionally flaked, and bashing stones, choppers, cores, flakes and small chunks, some utilized and occasionally retouched, occur inextricably mixed with the

[4] L. S. B. Leakey, *Olduvai Gorge* (Cambridge, 1951). L. S. B. Leakey, J. F. Evernden and G. H. Curtis, 'The age of Bed I, Olduvai Gorge, Tanganyika', *Nature* (1961), CXCI, 478.

[5] R. L. Hay, 'Stratigraphy of Beds I through IV, Olduvai Gorge, Tanganyika', *Science* (1963), CXXXIX, 829–33.

[6] L. S. B. Leakey, 'A new fossil skull from Olduvai', *Nature* (1959), CLXXXIV, 491–3. 'Recent discoveries at Olduvai Gorge', *Nature* (1960), CLXXXVIII, 1050–1. 'New finds at Olduvai Gorge', *Nature* (1961), CLXXXIX, 649–50.

smashed bones of a number of different species of animal.[7] Long bones
and other bones have been broken to extract the marrow, and some of
them show unmistakable marks of having been smashed with a rounded
blunt object. The most famous of these floors is that in the upper part of
Bed I, on which were lying the remains of the Australopithecine *Zinjanthropus boisei*. Here the Leakeys found a concentration of highly com-
minuted bone some 15 feet in diameter, with larger bones on the periphery
and a mass of worked stone in and among the bone. The remains represented several different antelopes, pig, tortoise, catfish, a snake, and several
other small animals. A high proportion of the pig and antelope remains
are from immature creatures.[8] The most characteristic forms of tool are a
chopper flaked from two directions to form an irregular and usually wide-
angled cutting or chopping edge, made on a lava pebble or chunk of quartz,
and a sharp flake for cutting.

The other floors are similar, but of especial interest is one only a foot or
so above the lava on which the beds rest. Here the stone tools are, on an
average, a good deal smaller, but they are associated with various accumulations of natural stones. It is very difficult to see how these could have
got to their present position, resting on the clay, except by having been
carried there. There is certainly one, and perhaps two, concentrations in
rough semicircles, and several stones rest one upon the other as if they had
been purposely piled up.[9]

These occupation floors represent the home bases—the living quarters
—of early tool-making hominids who were in part carnivorous, obtaining
their meat by hunting and scavenging. It is probable, however, on the
analogy of modern hunter-gatherers, that quite 75 per cent of their food
was vegetable, and, in this connexion, the pebble chopper may have been
developed as a tool for sharpening sticks for digging.

Recent geological assessment of the climatic conditions under which
Bed I was formed shows that the environment must have been very like
that of the Serengeti Plains today, that is to say, semi-arid grass and park-
land, with shallow pans and lakes, and forest relics on the slopes of the
adjacent volcanic masses. The relatively sparse scatter of occupation debris
suggests that Lower Pleistocene hominids rarely stayed long in one place.

Artifacts of comparable age and form have been found at a few other
sites, notably at Ain Hanech in Algeria, at Casablanca in Morocco, in the
Albertine Rift, and at Kanam on the Kavirondo Gulf of Lake Victoria
(which yielded also an enigmatic hominid jaw fragment), as well as in
residual gravels in river and marine high terraces. It would seem that if it is
indeed in the East African tectonic region that tool-making first developed,
it was not very long before such a fundamental advance in technology
spread widely throughout and beyond the continent (fig. 2).

[7] J. D. Clark, 'Sites yielding Hominid remains in Bed I, Olduvai Gorge', *Nature*
(1961), CLXXXIX, 903–4.   [8] L. S. B. Leakey, Ibid. (6a).
[9] L. S. B. Leakey, 'Adventures in the search for man', *National Geographic Magazine*,
Jan. 1963, 132–52.

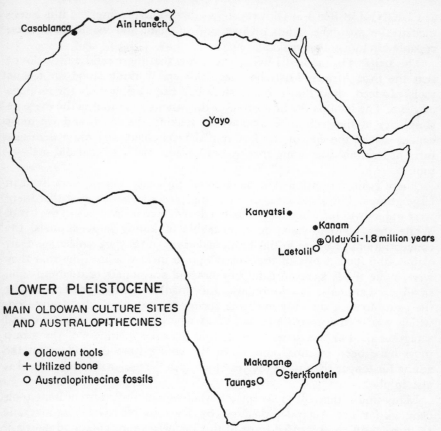

2. Distribution of Lower Pleistocene Culture and Australopithecines

No hominid more advanced than the Australopithecines is known from any of these Lower Pleistocene sediments. They are well represented by over 300 fossil remains. Two forms are known—a slenderer type (*Australopithecus africanus*), and a more heavily built type (*A. robustus*, known also as *Paranthropus*). Their membership of the family of the Hominidae is unquestionable on the evidence of their brains, teeth and jaw patterns, and because of their bipedalism and their possession of hands adapted to tool-using. Lightly built and only some 4 feet 6 inches tall, they were nevertheless able to run fast and had arms adapted to throwing.[10] In the small size of the brain and the massiveness of the face, however, they resembled the apes, with the result that they are sometimes known as the 'Man-Apes'. Napier's[11] study of the hand from the pre-Zinjanthropus horizon

[10] S. L. Washburn, 'Tools and human evolution', *Scientific American* (1960), CCIII, 3, 1–15.
[11] J. R. Napier and J. S. Weiner, 'Olduvai Gorge and human origins', *Antiquity* (1962), XXXVI, 41–7.

at FLK NNI in Bed I at Olduvai shows that though primitive, it is intermediate between the hands of apes and of man, and would have been capable of clumsy tool-making.

The artifacts in the Bed I living-sites show that there can be little doubt that the East African Australopithecines were working stone for use as tools. Indeed, their Pliocene ancestors had been using tools for millions of years. The hand is the best proof of this, though another is the extreme simplicity of the technique involved in making the tools, and we must expect that at the end of the Lower Pleistocene certainly more than one form of hominid was living that was capable of making—and did make—tools.

There is no indication that the Australopithecine tool-makers lived in large groups. The small areas of the living-places rather suggest that there were unlikely to have been more than a dozen or so individuals in the band. While they seem to have been incapable of killing large animals, the concentrations of bones in the Transvaal caves (if they are indeed, as Dart claims, the food debris of the Australopithecines) would argue that they were, none the less, resourceful hunters and scavengers of medium- and small-sized animals. No doubt, also, they made capital of the necessity for the game to seek the only available surface water during the dry season, which was in the deep limestone caves where they were ambushed and slaughtered. For this some co-operation between members of the group must have been essential and, since the young were dependent on the adults for longer than were the young of apes,[12] regular sharing of food is also implicit.

Many find it difficult to accept the wholesale manufacture of bone tools claimed for the Australopithecines by Dart in his 'Osteodontokeratic Culture', and consider that most of this material represents food debris.[13] These caves have, nevertheless, provided fairly good, though rare, evidence of the utilization of bone, as has also one of the Olduvai floors. The most impressive of these bone tools are fragments of long bones that show shallow, highly polished groovings.

Why did stone tool-making first begin in the savannah? The answer is believed to lie in economic and social necessity. The African savannah is an environment with a long dry season in which a small and very defenceless hominid, forced to protect its hunting territory and ill-equipped biologically for digging or meat-eating, had to find some way to supplement the sources of vegetable foods that would dwindle under times of climatic deterioration. It is believed that this was one of the primary reasons why these early hominids turned to meat-eating, just as baboons sometimes do today. The use of some kind of sharp cutting tool to open the skin of an antelope, or of a bashing tool to break open long bones or

[12] R. A. Dart, 'The infancy of Australopithecines', *Robert Broom Commemorative Volume* (Johannesburg, 1948), 143–52.
[13] R. A. Dart, 'The Osteodontokeratic culture of *Australopithecus prometheus*', Memoir No. 10 (1957), Transvaal Museum, Pretoria.

the shell of a tortoise, or of a sharp tool to point a stick for digging, would have meant a regular and substantial increase in the quantity and variety of food available. The hominids would also have found these tools useful for defence.

Australopithecines have been found in South and East Africa, and now in Chad, as well as in the Far East, so that it is reasonable to suppose that tool-making, this most fundamental of human inventions, spread with remarkable rapidity.

Africa abounds with pebble tools, but the earlier claim that most of these are of Lower Pleistocene age remains as yet largely unsubstantiated, and it is probable that many of these industries belong to the earlier Middle, rather than to the Lower Pleistocene. For knowledge of the cultural

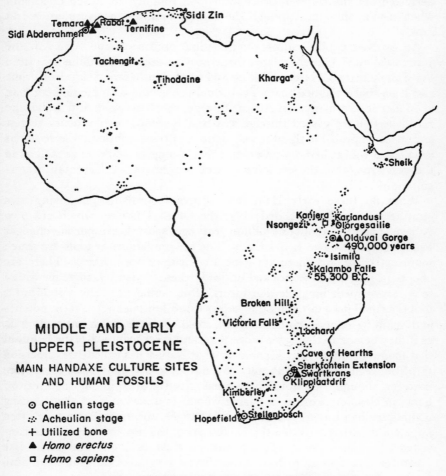

3. Distribution of Middle and early Upper Pleistocene Culture
(Chellian and Acheulian) and hominids

pattern of these times we again rely most heavily on Olduvai, for this site preserves a unique evolutionary sequence of developing stages up to the earlier part of the Upper Pleistocene. But there are now several other sites, equally well dated, though without such a long stratigraphy (fig. 3). By the beginning of the second glaciation in the northern hemisphere, there is substantial evidence that tool-making had spread throughout all the semi-arid regions of the continent and had overflowed into other parts of the Old World. The artifacts are still predominantly choppers, chopping tools and worked flakes, but they are now more shapely, show greater variety, and are generally more skilfully made, though still remaining remarkably crude in appearance. They represent the earliest stages of what is known as the Chelles-Acheul or Handaxe culture, the latter name being derived from the commonest type of tool, roughly the shape of a hand when seen in silhouette, though the earliest examples are very crude and rare.

An evolved pebble culture of this time occurs outside Africa in the Jordan valley.[14] Closely related forms may be seen in the industries from the Choukoutien Cave near Peking and from South-East Asia. In Europe also it has been claimed that a pebble culture occurs with Heidelberg man at Mauer in Germany. In Africa, Europe, the Near East, and India, the Handaxe culture passed through remarkably similar evolutionary stages, and it seems probable that the populations of those continents were not as isolated as was at first supposed and that changes in culture as well as in the genotype were the outcome of free movement, exchange and inter-communication (fig. 4).

What do these early Handaxe cultures look like? The living-sites stratified at the base of Bed II at the Olduvai Gorge, which are now believed to date to about one million years ago, show that important changes had taken place since Bed I times. The accumulations of tools are much more extensive and there are generally many more artifacts. There are choppers, polyhedral stones and utilized flakes in quantity, together with a few pear-shaped, handaxe-like forms. But perhaps the most significant tool is a small flake or chunk that shows careful retouching to form notches and scraping edges. Some of these small, delicate, informal tools look as if they belong to the Later Stone Age, and it is obvious that the hominid that made them was fully capable of what Napier has called 'the precision grip' between finger and thumb. We do not know what these tools were used for, though they would have been effective in trimming the meat off bone, in cleaning skins or in paring wood. It is also evident that hunting techniques had undergone important changes, and now it was very often large animals that provided the major part of the meat supply. These consisted of extinct forms of elephant, giraffids, and ox- and sheep-like creatures that appear to have been driven into swampy ground or into

[14] M. Stekelis, 'Recent discoveries in the Jordan valley', *South African Journal of Science* (1963), LIX, 3, 77–80.

DISTRIBUTION OF THE
HANDAXE CULTURE

4. Distribution of the Handaxe Culture in the world

open water and there butchered. This implies not only considerably improved hunting ability, but also reasonably efficient group organization.[15]

The only remains of the earliest occupants of Bed II at Olduvai are two teeth, but at Sterkfontein in the Transvaal a similar industry is found in the later, brown breccia. These pebble tools are associated with teeth of *Australopithecus*, but it is suggested that they were really made by an early form of *Homo erectus*. The somewhat later and adjacent site of Swartkrans also contained tools and the large Australopithecine *Paranthropus*, but in addition another hominid is present, previously known as *Telanthropus* and now identified with *Homo erectus*.[16]

About mid-way up in Bed II at Olduvai is a horizon known as 'the Chellean III horizon', the latest potassium/argon date for which is

[15] L. S. B. Leakey, 'Recent discoveries at Olduvai Gorge, Tanganyika', *Nature* (1958), CLXXXI, 1099–103. S. Cole, *The Prehistory of East Africa* (Macmillan, New York, 1963).

[16] J. T. Robinson and R. J. Mason, 'Australopithecines and artifacts at Sterkfontein', *South African Archaeological Bulletin* (1962), XVII, 66, 87–125.

490,000 years. Handaxes made by a stone technique are now much more common, though the pebble chopper still predominates. All the other types of tool occur, and there are now steep core-scraper forms besides, though full details have not yet been published. Associated with this cultural stage, Leakey found the greater part of a skull cap which falls within the pattern of the Pithecanthropoids, or *Homo erectus*, as this stock is now called. The Chellean III skull differs, however, in having a larger cranial capacity, and in anticipating in some measure the Rhodesioid type of man. There can be no doubt that the cultural, physical and intellectual developments that had taken place since Australopithecine times are inextricably interconnected, and the rapidity of the biological change could not have occurred without culture.

With this level at Olduvai we can correlate a 'Chellean' (Clacto-Abevillian) stage from an early marine level at Sidi Abderrahman, near Casablanca, as well as the lakeside site of Ternifine on the Algerian plateau. Here there is a somewhat more developed stone industry, and the usual bone debris from meals, together with three well-preserved jaws and a parietal bone. Arambourg has described these as belonging to an African Pithecanthropoid stock which he has named *Atlanthropus*. Thus the African representatives of this 'palaeo-anthropoid' level would be contemporary with those from China and south-east Asia.

The second half of the Handaxe culture—the Acheulian—was a time of population movement into areas where no signs of earlier occupation by man have yet been found, and it was probably a period of population increase also. The extreme richness of Africa in the stone tools of this time points to the very favourable environment in which the Acheulian was practised. It may be inferred, though it has not yet been proved, that with the advances of the polar ice-sheets in the second and third glacials, and during the Great Interglacial, there was a more temperate environment over most of the African continent, so that many areas now desert became favourable for settlement. This was also a time of great proliferation of species among the antelopes, pigs and other African mammals, so that it is to be expected that man was also quick to take advantage of the opportunities now available to him.

The Acheulian populations were, however, still confined to the savannah and, as rainfall and temperature permitted, to the drier parts of the continent. It was only later that the tropical forest zone became permanently occupied. Moreover, Man was still virtually confined in his choice of living quarters to waterside sites, probably because he had evolved no efficient means of carrying water supplies for any distance. Even more important than the richness of the stone industries of this period is the existence of a number of stratigraphically sealed and dated camping-sites, from which we can gain some idea of the manner of living of the people. Most of these occupation sites belong to later Acheulian times, from perhaps 150–50,000 years ago. There are several sites of this kind: in East Africa, at Olorgesailie, Kariandusi and Isimila; in Rhodesia, at Broken Hill and Kalambo Falls; in South Africa, at Kimberley and the Cave of Hearths; while in North Africa there are caves at Casablanca and Rabat, fossil spring sites in Egypt and the Maghrib, to mention but a few.

Acheulian man still concentrated on killing large animals, and he seems to have been much better equipped to do so than his predecessors. The handaxes are now really fine examples of the stoneworker's craft. They were made by what is known as the cylinder hammer technique, which enabled thinner and flatter flakes to be removed, and the result was most shapely tools with straight cutting edges. Another cutting tool is known as a 'cleaver', and is often U-shaped and axe-like. Balls of stone, different types of steep core-scrapers, and many varieties of small scraping and cutting tools also form an integral part of any Acheulian industry. There was already selection of raw material: the tougher, harder rocks were used for the heavy cutting and chopping tools, while the fine-grained, homogeneous rocks, capable of producing a sharp but relatively brittle edge, were used for the small tools. This must reflect differences in activity.

Some four or five variations in the cultural pattern can now be seen, though as yet no regional specialization is discernible.[17] Sometimes industries consist of high percentages of large cutting tools and low percentages of other forms. Elsewhere the large cutting tools may be completely absent (as at Hope Fountain). At yet other sites there are roughly equal percentages of both large and small tools, or industries occur with high percentages of heavy equipment—choppers, picks, core-scrapers and the like. Finally, there are the mining-sites, where the raw materials were worked up from cobbles, boulders or outcrops. This again shows that Acheulian man engaged in a number of different activities for which he used different stone tools.

Analysis of floor plans and artifact percentages, and the relationships of artifacts to each other and to the other associated material—bones, wood, natural stones that have been carried in, etc.—is helping to distinguish which groups of tools may be associated with butchering, or with hunting, with food getting, with vegetable foods and so on. But it will need a number of careful analyses before we have any data that can be considered reliable.

The sizes of the camp-sites in the open also vary—from a few feet across at Broken Hill to as much as 30 feet or more in diameter at Olorgesailie or Kalambo. In a site of this size, there will often be concentrated a large number of tools of the same kind. If the tools were all made at once, it is difficult to see the reason for such quantities; but if the site were reoccupied seasonally over several years, this profusion presents no particular problem. The same forms and profusion of tools characterize the Acheulian wherever it occurs. There is very little difference between the industries at the Cape,

[17] M. R. Kleindienst, 'Variability within the Late Acheulian assemblage in East Africa', *South African Archaeological Bulletin* (1961), XVI, 62, 35–48. 'Components of the East African Acheulian assemblage: an analytical approach', *in* G. Mortelmans (editor), *Actes du IVe Congrès Panafricain de Préhistoire* (Leopoldville, 1959), Tervuren (1962), 81–112.

in Rhodesia, East Africa, the Sahara, Egypt or Peninsular India, except in the raw materials used. The reason for this is as yet not fully understood, though it probably results from the Handaxe makers being confined largely to one type of country, namely the savannah, and to the great length of time (about 2 million years) involved. This slow development of technical ability and food-gathering practices is in turn directly related to the evolution of the genotype.

As yet, the physical type of Acheulian man is imperfectly known, whether in Africa or elsewhere, but responses to adaptation and to changes in environment appear to have produced, by genetic modification from a Pithecanthropoid ancestor, several forms. One of these must have approached the massive-browed Rhodesian man of southern Africa, another was an evolved *Atlanthropus* in the Maghrib, and yet a third was a *sapiens*-like stock, such as is represented by the smooth-browed Kanjera crania from Kavirondo.

It was not until the very end of Acheulian times in Africa that man became a regular user of fire. There are some three or four sites where evidence of fire is preserved, and all these probably date to between 50,000 and 60,000 years ago. One such site is at the Kalambo Falls, where charred logs and charcoals occur, and where man used fire to aid in sharpening sticks for digging, to shape clubs, or to make edges on knife-like tools of wood.

Thus fire-making, first known from second glacial times in the Far East, does not appear to have spread universally in Africa before the end of Acheulian times some 50–60,000 years ago, presumably because there was no need for it before. But now the climate became cooler and wetter, bringing about a considerable readjustment in the vegetation patterns and in the distribution of animal and human populations. Under a lowering of temperature of between 4° and 5°C., coinciding with the earlier part of the last glaciation in Europe, higher-living forest species replaced lowland tropical forest down to 600–900 metres below their present altitude range in sub-Saharan Africa, and a Mediterranean flora spread southwards to the southern borders of the Sahara.[18] With the vastly increased potential for food getting, technical development, and living conditions made possible by a regular use of fire, man now spread into country which he had not previously occupied—the now most favourable but formerly forest-covered regions of Equatoria. Here the routes of migration into the Congo basin and the West African rain forest must have lain along the grass-covered interfluves, and man was better able to avail himself of the opportunities offered by, on the one hand, the savannah and, on the other, the forest galleries in the adjacent valleys.

This was a time of considerable population movement and of cultural experiment. It saw the fairly rapid disappearance of the old traditional

[18] E. M. van Zinderen Bakker, 'Early man and his environments in southern Africa: Palaeobotanical studies', *South African Journal of Science* (1963), LIX, 7, 332–40.

forms of tool—the handaxe and the cleaver—in the higher rainfall, more heavily tree-covered parts of the continent. Here there developed many heavy chopping tools and smaller denticulated artifacts that are believed to have been associated with woodworking. This complex became dominant throughout the Congo and West Africa, spreading into East Africa west of the Eastern Rift and into south-east Africa down to Natal. It is known as the Sangoan culture. Elsewhere in southern and eastern Africa, in regions favourable for the preservation of the traditional type of habitat, the old handaxe tradition lingered on. This is known as the Fauresmith complex, and it is associated with pans and grasslands and an abundant ungulate and large-animal fauna (fig. 5).

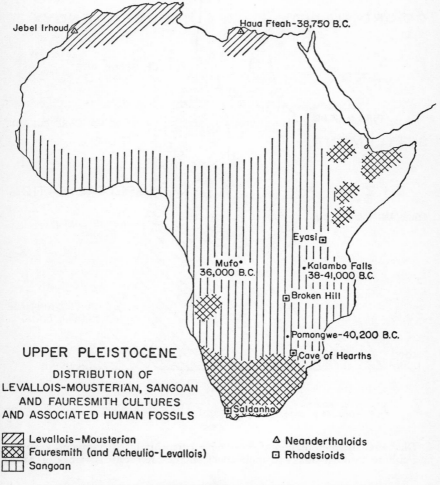

Jebel Irhoud

Haua Fteah-38,750 B.C.

Eyasi

Mufo•
36,000 B.C.

•Kalambo Falls
38-41,000 B.C.

Broken Hill

•Pomongwe-40,200 B.C.

Cave of Hearths

UPPER PLEISTOCENE

DISTRIBUTION OF
LEVALLOIS-MOUSTERIAN, SANGOAN
AND FAURESMITH CULTURES
AND ASSOCIATED HUMAN FOSSILS

Saldanha

Levallois-Mousterian   △ Neanderthaloids
Fauresmith (and Acheulio-Levallois)   ▢ Rhodesioids
Sangoan

5. Distribution of early Upper Pleistocene Culture and hominids
(Fauresmith, Sangoan, etc.)

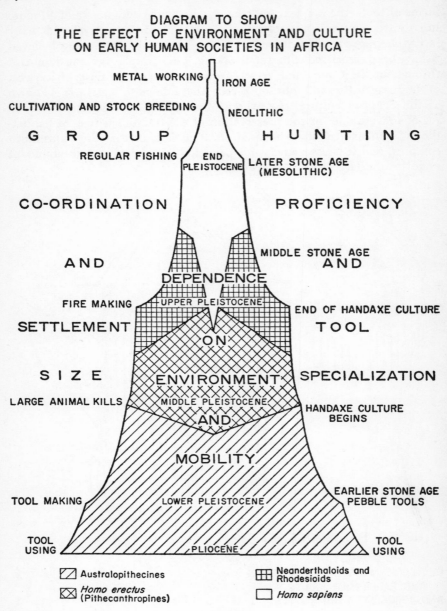

6. Diagrammatic presentation of the inter-relationship of environment, genotype and culture through time and their effect on the prehistoric societies of Africa

For the first time Man now began to occupy caves and rock shelters as regular homes, for, with his control of fire, these provided safe and more comfortable living-quarters. Furthermore, because of the regulation of the seasonal movements of the bands and the use of efficient carrying devices, he could now afford to stay in one place for much longer. Whereas the Australopithecines with their limited technology must very quickly have exhausted the sources of food available to them, the Acheulian and, later, the Sangoan and Fauresmith peoples, who were becoming steadily more proficient and inventive in their methods of food getting, were able to exploit the available resources with ever-increasing efficiency. Increase in the size of the band, more permanent residence, and ability to live in a greater variety of habitats, previously unfavourable, must have been the inevitable concomitant of increasing technical skill and mental ability, and at this time, as the distribution maps show, there were few parts of the continent where man did not penetrate. Figure 6 is an attempt to show the inter-relationship of environment, genotype and culture through time, and their effect on the prehistoric societies of Africa.

After the disappearance of the Acheulian culture from North Africa, which was contemporary with encroaching desertification, there appear, from Cyrenaica to Morocco, flake industries that are closely similar to those from the Levantine coast and the Near East generally. These are known culturally as Levallois-Mousterian and they are associated with a Neanderthal physical type. From the magnificent site of Haua Fteah in Cyrenaica, and from the newly discovered site at Jebel Irhoud in Morocco, we know that the Levallois-Mousterian people were cave dwellers, competent fire-users, and specialized in making light cutting, scraping and piercing tools from fine, thin flakes.

It is an intriguing problem whether these industries and the associated Neanderthal men were the outcome of migration into Africa from the Near East or Europe, or whether they were an autochthonous evolution from the Acheulian. The evidence is equivocal. The Kanjera type of man, if he is accurately dated, could have been ancestral to both the Neanderthal and the *sapiens* forms in Africa and, so far as the industry is concerned, the prepared-core technique is also present in the late Acheulian in North Africa. Any movement could, therefore, equally well have been out of Africa as into it. On the other hand, the closer similarities with the Near East rather than with sub-Saharan Africa, and the appearance of some representatives of the Palaeoarctic fauna in North Africa, suggest that the culture and the human stock could also be intrusive. At present the evidence is, it would seem, if anything weighted in favour of the latter alternative.

Whatever the answer, it is from this time onwards that culture in North Africa becomes differentiated from that south of the Sahara, though influences spread at favourable times in both directions (fig. 7). In the Maghrib the Levallois-Mousterian evolved into a culture—known as the

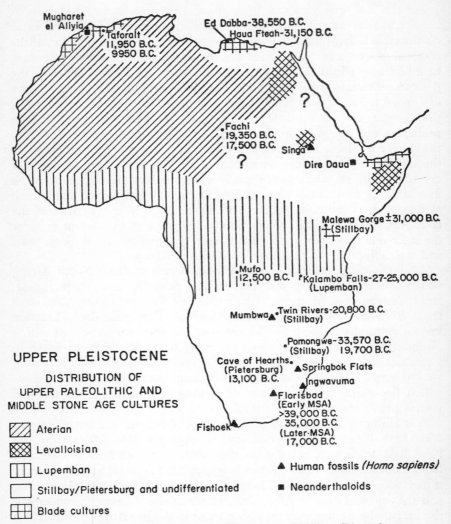

7. Distribution of the Aterian, Lupemban and Stillbay/Pietersburg

Aterian—specializing in the use of tanged flakes and points, while further east and as far south as the Horn the more generalized Levallois-Mousterian pattern was preserved. The Levallois-Mousterian was largely contemporary with the savannah-living Sangoan and the Fauresmith populations of the grasslands south of the Sahara, thus making the Neanderthalers of the north contemporary with the Rhodesian physical type in the south. This last represents the extreme development of the heavy-browed stock, and it is known from as far apart as Broken Hill and the Cape, where it represents the makers of a late Rhodesian Sangoan (or Proto-Stillbay, since these are now known to be the same thing) and of the Cape Fauresmith.

In the earlier part of the Middle Stone Age, the Rhodesioid type began to be replaced by the more efficient *Homo sapiens* forms as a result of natural selection. The Middle Stone Age proper evolved from the Sangoan and Fauresmith after about 35,000 B.C. and ended about 8–10,000 B.C. There has for long been a tendency in Europe to refer to Africa after the end of the Middle Pleistocene as a cultural backwater. This was based initially on the fact that the earliest *sapiens* stock in Europe is associated with what we know as blade and burin, or Upper Palaeolithic, industries, which rather abruptly replaced the Neanderthal populations and the Mousterian culture there about 35,000 B.C. In Africa the prepared-core technique, Mousterian if you like, continued for a further 25,000 years, and by inference drawn from the European associations it was, therefore, considered that in Africa the Middle Stone Age was made by late surviving Neanderthalers. Radiocarbon and later discoveries show that this is not the case, and there is no evidence of any such time lag in the genotype as had been postulated. The reason for the survival of the prepared-core tradition is obviously that it was the most efficient for producing the specialized equipment that was required by a hunting people in tropical and sub-tropical environments.

These Middle Stone Age cultures, as they are known in sub-Saharan terminology, though based essentially on the prepared core and faceted flake, differ in fact considerably in the nature of their end-products, so that a number of distinct variants can be identified and directly related to environmental specialization. Thus we find the Stillbay and Pietersburg variants in the savannah and grasslands of south and east Africa concentrating on light cutting, piercing and projectile tools of stone, while in the Congo forests, for example, the contemporary form, known as Lupemban, contains many axe and chopping elements and magnificent lanceolate knives or stabbing points. Whereas the tanged point was the speciality of the Aterian population, the foliate form in many varieties was that favoured south of the Sahara.

During the African Middle Stone Age there is the same evidence as in Europe for the appearance of religious beliefs. This is shown by the careful burial of the dead. Simultaneously there appear signs of an aesthetic sense in the use of paint and ornamentation. It would seem, therefore, that it was primarily the contrasting environments of glacial and tropical Africa that were responsible for the basic differences in the stone cultures.

Upper Palaeolithic blade and burin industries are found in two parts of Africa—on the Mediterranean littoral and in the East African Rift. The first appearance of Upper Palaeolithic culture in Cyrenaica[19] has been

[19] A much earlier blade industry occurs in the lower levels of the Haua Fteah cave, and is probably of an age with similar industries from the Levantine coast, where they are named Amudian and intercalate with a final stage of regional Acheulian known as Jabroudian. It is not known at present whether these early blade industries represent the ancestral form from which the Upper Palaeolithic of the Near East is derived, since they are followed in both regions by the Levallois-Mousterian.

dated to between 38 and 31,000 B.C.[20] It is considered that this may also
be the time of its earliest appearance in East Africa, though most of the
evidence there, as also in north-west Africa, belongs to later times. There
can be little doubt that these industries are intrusive from the Levant,
being introduced presumably by an early *Homo sapiens* stock which must
inevitably have hybridized with the existing populations. No human
fossils of this culture stage are as yet known, so it is not possible at present
to say whether the makers could have been the ancestors of the Erythriote
and Mediterranean longheads. There is quite a possibility that this might
have been so, for in East Africa, certainly, the later blade and burin
industries were the work of populations of this physical type, largely
identified today with the Hamites.

The close of the Pleistocene about 8000 B.C. was preceded by a cooler
and wetter climate of some 2000 years duration, during which there were
two immigrations of Caucasoid stock into North Africa, the one of Cro-
magnon type, bringing the Oranian culture to the Maghrib and the other,
probably of Mediterranean type, bringing the Et Tera culture to Cyrenaica.
At the same time there appears evidence of blade and burin industries in
the Horn, while the Aterian populations of the Maghrib were able to move
down as far as the southern and eastern Sahara and the Nile. These contacts resulted, for example, in the Congo with the final Middle Stone Age,
in the appearance of tanged projectile heads, and in South Africa and
Rhodesia in the appearance of new forms of tool made on blades. Similarly,
the bifacial foliate points of the later Aterian, the transverse arrowheads
and heavy lunate forms of the Mesolithic, and the bifaced axe element of
the Neolithic are probably the result of diffusion northwards from the
Lupemban and Tshitolian of Equatoria. This was the second major period
of cultural readjustment in Africa.

The wet phase known as the Makalian that followed the end of the
Pleistocene, which lasted from about 5500 to 2500 B.C., similarly permitted
free exchange between Mediterranean and Negroid populations that had
both moved into the Sahara with the advance of the Mediterranean flora
and the improved water supplies (fig. 8). It is from this time that waterside
habitats take on new significance. The sea coasts, rivers and lakes were now
exploited for their food sources as never before, and it was the permanent
food supply provided by the fish, shellfish and other water foods that
enabled man to remain permanently in occupation of areas where previously he had been only a seasonal visitor. The wide distribution of, for
example, the bone harpoon, the gouge and other traits of a waterside
culture throughout the southern Sahara, the Nile and the Central
African lakes, shows the rapidity with which the indigenous populations
in such favourable localities took the opportunity to improve their
economy.[21] It is useful to keep in mind this facility for readjustment

[20] E. S. Deevey, et al. (editors), *Radiocarbon* (1963), V, 37, 170–2.
[21] J. de Heinzelin, 'Ishango', *Scientific American* (1962), CCVI, 6, 105–16.

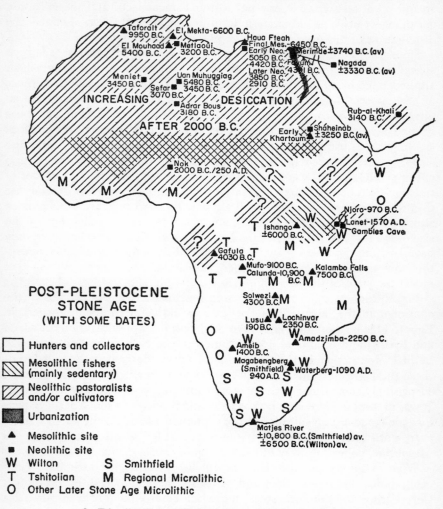

8. Distribution of Culture in post-Pleistocene times

when considering the change-over from a stone-using to a metal-working economy.

By the end of the Pleistocene, the Bush physical stock was already present in South Africa and it may be postulated that, similarly, by selective processes, the Negroid and Erythriote types had also made their appearance, though the earliest known fossils representing these types are no older than the Mesolithic or the Later Stone Age. Because of their blood group relationships, the Bushman and the Negro must be derived from the same African ancestral stock. However, only in the case of the Erythriote or Proto-Hamite does there seem to be any close tie between culture and physical stock, and it was not so much race as cultural specialization springing from long adaptation to different habitats that dictated the distribution of culture forms in the post-Pleistocene.

Since the Later Stone Age is also the period of greatest adaptive specialization, a large number of distinctive cultures can be distinguished. In the Congo basin the cultures of the plateaux differ markedly from those of the forests, though both are fairly certain to have been made by an unspecialized Negroid ancestral type. Markedly different again are those in the Albertine Rift or the Kenya Rift. In South Africa the Smithfield of the high veld, using various forms of end-scrapers made from indurated shale, is very different from the crescent-like microliths of the Wilton culture, though both were made by Bushmen and both had a number of traits in common. This specialization of equipment and the greater use that was now made of quite small animals for food is likely to have been stimulated by population increase and a corresponding reduction in the size of the hunting territory of the band. This in turn, however, could only have become possible because of the spread of new technical advances—the bow and arrow, poison, barbed fish-spears and other devices—that raised the yield of the hunting territory.

Food production and domestication first make their appearance in the continent in the later half of the sixth or early fifth millennium B.C. in Egypt. This·is, therefore, later than the beginnings of cultivation (of wheat and barley) and of animal domestication in the Near East, and there can be little doubt that in the first instance Africa derived its knowledge of these things from immigrants into the Nile Valley.[22] It took, however, a surprisingly short time for the new economy to spread across North Africa. It was present in Cyrenaica by 5000 B.C. and throughout much of the Sahara by 3500–3000 B.C. Neolithic culture is unknown south of the Sahara, however, until later, and in fact it never succeeded at all in replacing the Mesolithic, collecting, way of life throughout most of the sub-continent.

What is the reason for this cultural lag? In part it must have been geographic. But it was also, and probably more importantly, economic. Cereal crops and domestic stock in the rich environment of tropical Africa were not the necessities for permanent village life that they were in the arid and semi-arid regions in which they were first developed. This would be especially so if the primary importance of livestock was already then, as it is today in Africa, an expression of wealth rather than a source of food. The abundant vegetable and animal resources of the tropical savannah and forests provided all that was needed to maintain the Mesolithic populations at much the same level of subsistence as did the crops and stock of the Neolithic farmers, and probably with less expenditure of labour.

It was not until the Sahara began to dry up after 2500 B.C., and the consequent over-grazing forced some of the Neolithic populations there to

[22] J. D. Clark, 'The spread of food production in sub-Saharan Africa', *Journal of African History* (1962), III, 2, 211–28.

move southwards into what is now the Sudan belt, that any serious attempt at farming could have been made, though 'vegecultural' practices round the forest margins had probably been in use for some considerable time before that. Barley and wheat, however, are winter rainfall crops, and can rarely be grown in the tropics successfully except under irrigation. The high plateau in Ethiopia is one of the exceptions, but in other parts there must of necessity have been much experimentation with local potential domesticates from ± 2000 B.C. onwards. Thus several indigenous food crops were developed—rice in Guinea, sorghum and *Pennisetum* in the Sudan, tef and *Eleusine* in those parts of Ethiopia where wheat and barley were not established. This experimentation may also have stimulated the cultivation on the forest fringes of the indigenous *Dioscoreas* and of *Ensete*.

We find Neolithic cultivators in northern Nigeria, the makers of the Nok culture, between 2000 B.C. and A.D. 200, when stone began to be replaced by metal for essential tools. Neolithic pastoralists also reached Ethiopia and the Kenya Rift about 2000 B.C., and in the latter region they were not replaced by Bantu immigrants until after the sixteenth century A.D. The only other part where Neolithic industries are known, though they are all believed to be late, is the Congo basin. The whole of the rest of southern Africa remained in the collecting stage. The reason why it did so must be due, as well as to the richness of the wild food resources, to the generally inefficient equipment of Neolithic man for clearing forest and closed woodland and his inability to maintain himself in large enough communities. It was, therefore, not until the population explosion that precipitated the Bantu movements around the beginning of the Christian era that any fundamental change in the economy was feasible. What made this possible, even then, was the development of iron-working—the iron axe and spear—and, no doubt, also the introduction of the Asian food plants.

The many investigations that are going on today are steadily tracing the history of the spread of Negroid and Bantu culture into the sub-continent, and in another decade it is certain that a firm chronology will have become available. We can already trace the spread down the Central African lakes of the earliest Iron Age immigrants, the makers of the Dimple-based and Channelled ware pottery, the earliest date for which is A.D. 100 from Machili in eastern Barotseland. We know that the copper mines of Katanga were being worked and the products traded widely by the eighth century A.D.; that central Angola had been occupied by metal-users a century earlier; that trade was coming up the lower Zambezi at the same time; that by A.D. 300 there were agriculturalists living at Zimbabwe, and that by A.D. 1100 there was a flourishing centre at Mapungubwe (Bamban-dyanalo) on the Limpopo. At the beginning of the sixteenth century these earlier Iron Age cultivators were joined by other more efficiently organized groups establishing powerful political confederacies, and the process of absorption of the older populations was speeded up.

One point that needs stressing here, however, is that the coming of the Iron Age mixed farmers was not, as is all too often supposed, necessarily coincident with the disappearance of the old hunting–collecting populations. Such apparent anomalies as a Bush-Hottentot physical stock with a Negroid culture, as is found at Mapungubwe or at Inyanga and a number of other places, is surely the result of some of the old hunting populations having changed their economy. In the same way the historic Cape Hottentots were a Stone Age people who had acquired stock and become pastoralists. Moreover, from the skeletal remains from Northern Rhodesia and Nyasaland it can be seen that the Late Stone Age population was already Negroid in a number of its physical characteristics, and in the Bergdama and Hadza we can probably see surviving examples of two of the Later Stone Age populations of Equatoria.

It is, therefore, probably true to say that the origins of the older Bantu populations of these countries are most likely to be found in the Stone Age, though of course the present populations must be the results of subsequent modification by hybridization with small groups of immigrants. The fundamental change is not so much in the population as in the economy, though there is of course ample evidence to prove immigration and replacement in a number of cases. The caves and rock shelters were gradually abandoned as pressures dictated, that is, by all except the unadjustable minority of the hunting populations, and the inhabitants now settled in open villages, planted crops and herded stock. Hybridization completed the transformation that economic expediency had begun.

There is increasing proof to show that this was the pattern in many of the southern and central parts of Africa following the coming of the first groups of iron-using immigrants. The consequence is to emphasize the continuity of African culture, and to show the need to study both the prehistoric populations and their culture, since here lies the clue to the understanding of the present.

ADDENDUM

At the time of correcting the proofs of this paper Dr L. S. B. Leakey has just announced that the Pre-Zinjanthropus fossils from Bed I and new fossils from the lower part of Bed II at the Olduvai Gorge together represent a new species, *Homo habilis* (so called for his toolmaking ability), whose characteristics, it is claimed, fall outside the range of Australopithecine variability. This implies, therefore, that the species *Homo* had become genetically differentiated from the *Australopithecinae* at a time anterior to the deposition of Bed I rather than posterior to this time. If this is so it would also seem unlikely that *Homo erectus* represents a stage of human evolution directly ancestral to modern man. Some lively controversy can be expected when the full details of the new discovery are made available.

SUMMARY

The paper traces the beginnings of human culture in Africa, its evolution and spread, and shows the feedback relationship that exists between biological evolution and culture. It is demonstrated how environment is the most important factor in producing variability at the food-gathering level, and the present-day regional differences in culture are shown to have been in existence for some 40,000 years. The history of the introduction and spread of domestication is summarized, and evidence is adduced to indicate that the diffusion of Iron Age economy in southern Africa was due as much to adaptation as to immigration, thus demonstrating a real and traceable continuity up to the present day.

2. THE SPREAD OF FOOD PRODUCTION IN SUB-SAHARAN AFRICA

By J. Desmond Clark

After the end of the Pleistocene, sub-Saharan Africa seems to have been more receptive of than contributory to cultural progress in the Old World as a whole. By that time favourable localities in the sub-continent—the margins of lakes and watercourses, the sea coasts, the peripheral regions of the equatorial forest—were sometimes supporting nearly, or entirely, sedentary communities of hunting-collecting peoples who were enabled to live in this way due to the permanent presence of one or more staple sources of food: freshwater fish, water animals and plants, and sea foods; and forest foods (the *Dioscoreas*, *Elaeis guineensis*, and other oil-bearing plants), either perennial or capable of being stored. Evidence of such occupation is seen in the midden accumulations in both cave and open sites at this time.[1] Populations could thus become more concentrated and an increase in density may be inferred, the limiting factor being the maximum that any one environment could support by intensified collecting methods (fig. 1).

The two ecosystems in sub-Saharan Africa most significant in determining subsequent economic developments were the plateau grasslands and lakes of East and East Central Africa and the peripheral parts of the lowlands and montane evergreen forest zones of West and West Equatorial Africa. In the one, dependence would seem to have been predominantly on a protein diet based on game and fish, with vegetable foods of subsidiary importance, and, in the other, probably on a starch diet based on vegetable foods, supplemented to some extent by protein from fish and, to a lesser degree, from game. The introduction of cereal crops was, therefore, of the greatest importance since it permitted the sedentary, Mesolithic population to occupy, widely and permanently, territory previously capable of supporting only temporary settlement. While the introduction of agriculture would have supplemented the perennial wild plants and encouraged plant cultivation, its chief importance in the plant-tending, 'vegecultural' communities would have been to encourage *permanent* occupation of areas previously uninviting to sedentary gatherers—dry savannah and continuous canopy forest. The chief development in food production in the higher rainfall, thicker vegetation region of the west and centre probably only took place, however, after the introduction of

---

[1] Clark, J. D., 'From Food Collecting to Incipient Urbanization in Africa South of the Sahara'. In Braidwood, R. J., *Courses Towards Urban Life* (1962), Viking Fund Publications in Anthropology, no. 32. In press.

American and Asian food plants of the humid tropics and after metal-working had provided efficient tools with which to make effective inroads upon the forests.

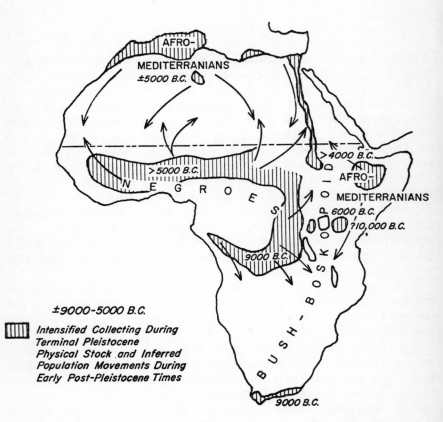

Fig. 1

Domestication of stock—cattle, sheep, and goats—may be expected to have been equally as revolutionary an innovation for human economy in both types of country. It would, however, have particular significance in providing a permanent source of protein for those occupying the forest periphery, though here its distribution must originally have been controlled by the tsetse fly.

It is well to remember with regard to agriculture that there are two factors requiring recognition: the one the cultivation of cereal crops, wheat, barley, millets, sorghum, etc.; and the other the cultivation of plant crops, *ensete*, bananas, yams, oil plants and trees, fluted pumpkins, pulses, etc. The initial 'vegecultural' stages in domesticating the latter group were almost certainly local developments south of the Sahara,[2] while, on the archaeological evidence, there can be little doubt that cereal cultivation spread to Africa from South-West Asia sometime during the fifth millennium B.C., perhaps somewhat earlier. What is believed to be the earliest Neolithic in North-East Africa is represented by the Fayum A culture dated to ±4300 B.C. by radiocarbon. By the first half of the fourth millennium Neolithic culture had spread to the upper Nile at Khartoum, where the Khartoum Neolithic at Es Shaheinab dates to ±3200 B.C. Arkell, however, considers that these dates are unreliable and would make the initial introduction into Lower Egypt earlier and the spread to the Sudan more rapid.[3] Some confirmation for Arkell's suggestion is found in the radiocarbon dating for three Saharan Neolithic industries with pottery occurring in rock shelters with paintings of cattle scenes in the Tassili. If the paintings can be associated with the industries, it would indicate that cattle were already domesticated in North Africa by the sixth millennium B.C.[4a, 4b]

The staple cereals cultivated in the lower Nile at this time were barley and emmer wheat, and the silos of the Fayum A peasants contained 80 per cent barley and 20 per cent wheat.[5] The bifacially worked serrated sickle blade is an intimately related tool, and it seems probable, therefore, that the extent of the distribution of all forms of sickle blades in Africa may perhaps provide some indication of the extent of wheat and barley cultivation, and so of the use of these crops as staples in the continent in prehistoric times. In this distribution area can be included the Nile Valley, the Mediterranean coast west to Cyrenaica, the eastern oases of the Sahara, and perhaps the Western Sudan and the Tigré plateau of Ethiopia.

From the sixth to the third millennium B.C. the Makalian Wet phase in Saharan and sub-Saharan Africa, which would seem to be the equivalent of the Atlantic stage in Europe, permitted movement of human and animal populations from the Mediterranean littoral southwards, and from the savannah of West and Central Africa northwards. Such a favourable habitat enabled Later Stone Age Mesolithic hunters and fishers, with their improved methods of food getting, to populate the Sahara to an extent never before possible, and must have rendered these communities particularly receptive of and quick to adopt the new practices of cereal and

[2] See n. 1 above.
[3] Arkell, A. J., 'Khartoum's Part in the Development of the Neolithic', *Kush* (1957), v, 8–12.
[4a] Lhote, H. Personal communication.
[4b] Mori, F., *Arte preistorica del Sahara Libico* (De Lucca, Rome, 1960).
[5] Cole, S., 'The Neolithic Revolution', British Museum (Natural History) (London, 1959), 11.

crop cultivation and domestication of animals (especially the latter) when
these were diffused (fig. 2).

The material culture of the Mesolithic/Neolithic populations of the
Southern Sahara, from Mauritania in the west to the Nile at Khartoum
in the east, indicates a way of life based on hunting and fishing. This
is shown especially in the bone harpoons, fish-hooks, and bifacially worked
stone projectile points, and implies a reasonably well-watered and bush
covered terrain that was very different from the desert conditions that exist
there today.[6] It would seem not improbable that the inhabitants of the settlements grouped round the pans and river courses of such sites as Asselar,
Taferjit, Tamaya Mellet, and In Guezzam were Negroids whose spread had
been made possible by the northward displacement of the Sudan and Sahel
belts. Skeletal remains of Negro-type have been found at Asselar, Tamaya
Mellet, Early Khartoum, and several other sites in the central Sahara.

Contact with populations living to the south of the desert during these
millennia, and the later movement out of the desert that must have been
forced on some of the inhabitants by the post-Makalian dry phase after
the middle of the third millennium B.C., are likely to have been the causes
whereby knowledge of and experiment in cereal crop cultivation passed to
the sub-Saharan populations.

Dambo and waterside sites and the fringes of forests must have seen
the first attempts at tropical agriculture and plant cultivation. Much
surface material and a very few stratified sites together with one or two
radiocarbon dates tend to confirm this. In tropical West Africa (Guinea,
Mali, Mauritania,[7] the Ivory Coast, Dahomey, Ghana,[8a, 8b] and Nigeria
(Nok Culture)),[9a, 9b] two stages of Neolithic culture were present or can be
inferred, the main distinguishing feature being the absence of pottery from
the earlier stage. In the north-eastern and north-western parts of the Congo
basin only one stage has so far been distinguished.[10] Almost nothing is
known about the settlement patterns of any of these West African and
Congo forest and savannah cultures except where rock shelters were used,
but it can be inferred that the usual form was an open village consisting of,
for Neolithic groups in the forest, a fair-sized population.

[6] Monod, T., and Mauny, R., 'Découverte de nouveaux instruments en os dans l'Ouest
Africain'. In Clark, J. D., and Sole, S., *Proceedings of the 3rd Pan-African Congress on
Prehistory, Livingstone, 1955* (Chatto and Windus, London, 1957), 242–7.
[7] Vaufrey, R., 'Le Néolithique paratumbien: une civilisation agricole primitive du
Soudan', *La Revue Scientifique* (1947), no. 3, 267, 205–32.
[8a] Davies, O., 'Neolithic cultures from Ghana', *C.R. 4th Pan-African Congress, Leopoldville, 1959* (1962). In press.
[8b] Shaw, C. T., 'Report on excavations carried out in the cave known as "Bosumpra"
at Abetifi, Gold Coast Colony', *Proc. Prehist. Soc.* (1944), X, 1–67.
[9a] Fagg, B. E. B., 'An outline of the Stone Age of the Plateau Minesfield', *Proc. Int.
West African Conference* (1949).
[9b] Willett, F., 'Investigations at Old Oyo, 1956–7: An Interim Report', *J. Hist. Soc.
Nigeria* (1960), II (1), 59–77.
[10] Mortelmans, G., 'La préhistoire du Congo Belge', *Revue de l'Université de Bruxelles*
(1957), 2–3.

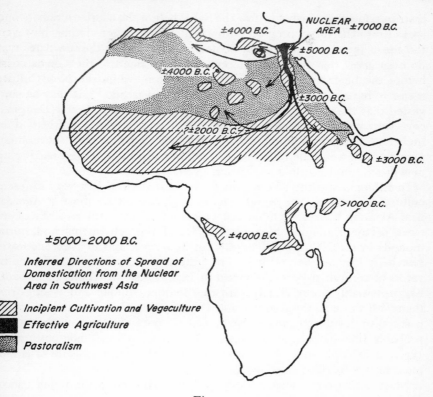

Fig. 2

If Vaufrey[11] is correct in supposing that a proportion of the polished celt-like artifacts from Aouker and Hodh (15–17°N: 5–10°W) were used as hoes, it will imply that some incipient cultivation at least was being practised in this now desert region at some time during the Sahara Wet Phase (i.e., before 2000 B.C.) when suitable terrain for cultivation may be expected to have existed there. Alternatively, these hoe-like celts may have been nothing more than the working ends of digging sticks for collecting wild vegetable foods. If, indeed, some of these celt-like tools are hoes and the absolute dates are in any way reliable, it would seem that experimentation with yam and millet cultivation, which had been under way from the fifth to the third millennium, had, by the time of the Nok Figurine culture in the first millennium B.C., resulted in the appearance, firstly of incipient, and then, of full food-producing communities on the fringes of the forest and in the savannah.

These Neolithic communities were all equipped with wood-working tools, the axe and the adze, and, it would seem, with the hoe also. Their

[11] See n. 7 above.

distribution covered what is now the Sahel belt of the southern Sahara and spread into the forest proper. Without adequate carbon dating, however, the age of these cultures cannot be determined, though the few dates that do exist show that the Neolithic had not penetrated to the Ghana coast before the beginning of the fourth millennium, while the Nok Culture seems to have lasted from ±918 B.C. to about A.D. 200.[12] It may be suggested that the soft stone hoe was the implement used for yam (*Dioscorea cayenensis* or other indigenous *Dioscoreas*) and sorghum cultivation in higher rainfall zones where a more broad-bladed tool than the pointed digging stick would be required for mound cultivation or for breaking up new ground under a thick vegetation cover.

In Ethiopia and the lake region of the East African Rift very different cultural assemblages are found. The most significant are those at Agordat near Axum in Eritrea,[13] Quiha and Tuli Kapi on the northern and western parts of the Ethiopian high plateau,[14] and the settlements and burial mounds in the Nakuru-Naivasha basin in Kenya, and in Ngorongoro in Northern Tanganyika.[15a, 15b, 15c] The cultural associations of the hoe cultivators of central Abyssinia reported by Père Azais[16] in Woolega and Kaffa lie, presumably, more closely with the Southern Sudan and West Africa than with those of the Agordat and Gregory Rift Cultures, among which pastoralism seems to have assumed greater importance. It would seem also probable that there is an association between the stone hoe cultures of Western Ethiopia and *ensete* cultivation, since there is a measure of agreement in the distribution of both.

Most of the other East African Neolithic cultures made much use of obsidian for their smaller percussion flaked tools, knives, scrapers, burins, and projectile barbs. This suggests a somewhat more mobile hunting and pastoral form of livelihood. Some writers have suggested that the whole cattle complex of the Sahara Neolithic peoples was derived from Arabia via the Horn. The archaeological evidence, however, lends no support to this hypothesis, and the rock art in particular indicates that the pastoral groups depicted therein came *from* the Sahara or Nubia *to* the Horn, and not the other way round.[17] Other than the pecked and ground stone axes, of which several distinctive types are found, these assemblages lack

---

[12] Deevey, S. E., *et al.*, 'Yale natural radiocarbon measurements III', *Science* (1957), CXXVI, 908–19.

[13] Arkell, A. J., 'Four occupation sites at Agordat', *Kush* (1954), II, 33–62.

[14] Clark, J. D., *The prehistoric cultures of the Horn of Africa* (Cambridge University Press, London, 1954).

[15a] Leakey, L. S. B., *The Stone Age Cultures of Kenya Colony* (Cambridge University Press, London, 1931).

[15b] Leakey, M. D., 'Report on the excavations at Hyrax Hill, Nakuru, Kenya Colony', *Trans. Roy. Soc. South Africa* (1945), XXX, iv, 271–409.

[15c] Leakey, M. D., and Leakey, L. S. B., *Excavations at the Njoro river cave* (Oxford University Press, London, 1950).

[16] Bailloud, G., 'La Préhistoire de l'Ethiopie'. In *Mer rouge—Afrique orientale. Cahiers de l'Afrique et de l'Asie* (Paris, 1959), 15–43.

[17] See n. 14 above, 295–315.

the heavy wood-working equipment of the forest and savannah cultures. The most characteristic domestic equipment consisted of stone bowls and palettes of various kinds, usually made from lava, together with flat grindstones and deep, bag-shaped pottery, sometimes with handles and spouts. In some instances, evidence of permanent dwellings (Hyrax Hill) and settlements (Lanet) suggests a different cultural tradition with a fairly long history and probably some form of incipient agriculture. Cattle were present in the northern part of the Horn by the second millennium B.C., if we can accept the evidence of the Deir-el-Bahari bas reliefs, and some of the later Kenya Neolithic peoples are known to have owned cattle (Hyrax Hill). Among this last, the zebu strain has been identified, so that it is likely to have been acquired sometime after the first half of the first millennium B.C. when, it is believed, this stock began to be diffused across the straits from Southern Arabia.

The grindstones and bowls strongly suggest some form of crop cultivation. In Eastern Ethiopia these crops may have been wheat, barley, and *teff*,[18] while in the Gregory Rift area the plants are more likely to have been primarily finger millet (*Eleusine* sp.), with the addition of various sorghums and *Pennisetum*. The length of time during which these Neolithic communities occupied East Africa and Ethiopia is not known, but a carbon date of 1063 ± 80 B.C.[19] for a late phase of the Stone Bowl Culture suggests that they were already established there in the second millennium B.C., while another date of A.D. 1584 ± 100 for the late settlement site at Lanet probably represents the upper limit.[20]

Arkell has suggested that the stone work and some of the pottery from the Jebel Kokan settlements at Agordat indicate possible association with the late C Group people of Lower Nubia, while certain two-lugged polished stone axe-heads, which are believed to be contemporary, recall forms found in 17th Dynasty tombs in Egypt. The Agordat settlements may, therefore, he further suggests, be evidence of movements of C Group peoples southwards from Lower Nubia, perhaps some time near the beginning of the third millennium B.C. (*c.* 2000 B.C.), either as a result of the military occupation of Nubia by the Egyptian Pharaohs of the 11th Dynasty or because of the continued desiccation of Lower Nubia.[21] In this connection also it is possible that the first appearance of the C Group peoples in Nubia, between *c.* 2240 and 2150 B.C., may have been brought about by the same process of dessication which terminated the Makalian Wet Phase about the middle of the third millennium, and which caused some of the Southern Saharan Neolithic groups to move north-west

---

[18] Simoons, F., 'Some questions on the economic prehistory of Ethiopia'. Paper read at the Third Conference on African History and Archaeology, School of Oriental and African Studies, July 1961, University of London (1961).

[19] Leakey, L. S. B., *Annual Report of the Coryndon Museum* (Nairobi, 1956).

[20] Deevey, E. S., 'Yale natural radiocarbon measurements, V', *Amer. Journ. of Science* (1960), Radiocarbon Supplement II, 58.

[21] Arkell, A. J., *A History of the Sudan* (Athlone Press, London, 1961), 46–54.

down the Wadi Howar to the Nile. There are stone tumulus graves in the
western part of the Southern Sahara reminiscent of those built by the C
Group peoples in Nubia,[22] and it would seem possible that this ethnic
group was originally living in the southern fringes of the Sahara. If this
is indeed the case, then they may be expected to have contributed to similar
movements southwards into the West African Sudanic zone (as also into
the Horn) about this time.

These food-producing cultures occupied only a comparatively limited
part of sub-Saharan Africa. In the greater part of the sub-continent the
populations continued to live by hunting and gathering, and the degree of
permanence of the settlement was dependent on the habitat and biome
(fig. 2).[23a, 23b]

On archaeological evidence, the economic distribution pattern in the
sub-continent by the beginning of the present era would seem to have been
one of Neolithic food-producing peoples in a few parts of the savannah
and peripheral forest zones of West and East Africa, with hunter-gatherers
over the greater part of the continent south of the Sahara. Generalizations
are always most dangerous, especially when based on foundations as
insecure as those which are all that are available at present. Bearing
in mind this reservation, however, it may be tentatively suggested that
the Neolithic hoe and axe cultures were the product of predominantly
negroid peoples, while the East African stock-raising communities are
associated more with populations of Mediterranean stock. All these prehistoric cultivators and stock owners must, however, have relied extensively
on collecting and hunting to supplement their diet.

The Negro, as stated above, was already present in fossil form in post-
Pleistocene times in the Southern Sahara, well north of the forest zone.[24]
This last, because of the generally acid nature of the soils, is, unfortunately,
universally unfavourable to the preservation of fossils. There is, however,
reason to suppose that the origin of the Negro physical stock and its
distribution in Africa is linked with the forest and woodland savannah
regions of the west and centre. In the east, 'proto-Hamitic', long-
headed, long-faced peoples, believed to be intrusive into the continent
from South-West Asia, had been established since at least the terminal
stages of the Pleistocene.[25] The southern and drier parts of Eastern
Africa were occupied by the Old Yellow-Skinned (Bush-Boskopoid)

[22] Monod, Th., 'Sur quelques Monuments lithiques du Sahara Occidental', *Actas y
Memorias de la Sociedad Espanola de Antropología, Etnografía y Prehistoria* (Madrid,
1948), XXIII, nos. 1–4, 12–35.
[23a] Cole, S., *The Prehistory of East Africa* (Penguin Books, Harmondsworth, 1954),
215–46.
[23b] Clark, J. D., *The Prehistory of Southern Africa* (Penguin Books, Harmondsworth,
1959), 189–93.
[24] Briggs, L. C., 'The living races of the Sahara Desert', *Peabody Museum Papers*
(Cambridge, Mass., 1958), XXVIII, no. 2, 12–15.
[25] Leakey, L. S. B., *The Stone Age Races of Kenya* (Oxford University Press, London,
1935).

populations, whose origins lie in the proto-Australoid (Rhodesioid) forms of the early Upper Pleistocene.[26] Contrary to what has sometimes been said, archaeological evidence shows that there is as yet no sign of a true Bush (as distinct from Boskopoid or Bush-Boskopoid) stock before the beginning of post-Pleistocene times, and its appearance would seem, therefore, to be the outcome of environmental and social or cultural selection pressures during the closing part of the Pleistocene.[27] The African Negro may well have been the product of other such selection pressures, operative this time in an equatorial environment, and which had brought about a different modification of the ancestral Rhodesioid stock.

The archaeological record as yet provides no confirmation for the belief that an independent centre of cereal crop domestication existed in West Africa as suggested by Portères and Murdock,[28, 29] or in Ethiopia, though it must be admitted that much of the latter region is unknown prehistorically. Moreover, the known distribution of the various food plants used in sub-Saharan Africa is confirmatory evidence that local experimentation and adaptation in these zones followed, but did not precede, the transmission of a knowledge of cereal cultivation from across the desert, and also that this transmission took place at several points at once. Thus, in West Africa, *Digitaria* and *Oryza* were the staple and did not spread farther east or south. On the Ethiopian high plateau, wheat and barley are the most important crops, perhaps transmitted by C Group immigrants from Nubia, but again did not spread widely, perhaps because of their general unsuitability without irrigation in the tropical savannah region. The sorghums, on the other hand, are very widely distributed.[30] They are cultivated in all except the evergreen forest and would seem to have been domesticated first in the central Sudanic zone south of the Sahara. The wide distribution of sorghum and *Eleusine* as the dominant crops in sub-Saharan Africa suggests that it was this central Sudan zone from Nigeria to Western Ethiopia that was the most significant for the spread of food production into South Central and Southern Africa at a time confirmed by the archaeological record as having been about the beginning of the present era.[31]

This fundamental change in the economy of the Southern African peoples was brought about by population movement in the first instance and it is

[26] Tobias, P. V., 'New evidence and new views on the evolution of man in Africa', *South African Journal of Science* (1961), LVII, no. 2, 25–38.

[27] Tobias, P. V., 'Bushman Hunter-gatherers: A Study in Human Ecology'. In *Ecology in South Africa* (1960). In press.

[28] Portères, R., 'Vieilles agricultures de l'Afrique intertropicale', *L'Agronomie Tropicale* (1950), no. 5, 489–507.

[29] Murdock, G. P., *Africa; its peoples and their culture history* (McGraw Hill, New York, 1959).

[30] Schell, R., *Plantes alimentaires et vie agricole de l'Afrique noire* (La Rose, Paris, 1957).

[31] Fagan, B. M., 'Radio-carbon dates for sub-Saharan Africa I', *Journ. Afr. Hist.* (1961), II (1), 137.

likely, but not certain, that the first immigrants may also have been metal users. Distribution (fig. 3) suggests that the main route for diffusion was down the high ridge country that forms the central spine of the continent on either side of the Rift Valley. The reason for this is likely to have been the

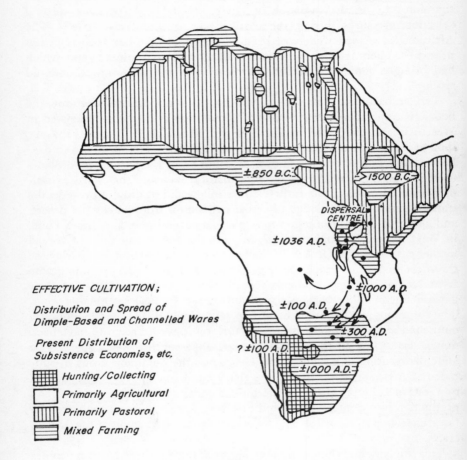

EFFECTIVE CULTIVATION;

Distribution and Spread of
Dimple-Based and Channelled Wares

Present Distribution of
Subsistence Economies, etc.

Hunting/Collecting

Primarily Agricultural

Primarily Pastoral

Mixed Farming

Fig. 3

need for a stock-owning people to find a tsetse-free route with ease of movement. The migration may be considered to have taken place at a time when the climate was temporarily somewhat drier than it is today[32] and when, therefore, the tsetse belts were likely to have been more restricted. A regular knowledge of metal-working techniques could have spread to the

[32] Mitchell, B. L., 'Ecological aspects of game control measures in African wilderness and forested areas', *Kirkia* (1961), 1.

Neolithic populations of the southern Sudan zone from about 500 B.C., both from across the Sahara in the west[33] and from Meroe in the east.[34]

The earliest food producing population of Southern Africa (as distinct from East and West Africa) of which we have knowledge were the authors of a very characteristic pottery tradition. This comprised decoration involving channelling, grooving, incised hatching, and sometimes stamping on globular pots and deep and shallow bowls. It is referred to in East Africa[35] and also in Ruanda Urundi[36] and the Kasai[37] as Dimple-based pottery. In Rhodesia it is known as Channelled ware north of the Zambezi[38] and Bambata ware[39] south of the river. The uniformity of this pottery in Uganda, Ruanda, Kavirondo, and the Katanga indicates that its initial dispersal may have been quite rapid. A Dimple-based pot from Nsongezi rock shelter in Uganda has been dated to A.D. 825±150.[40] Channelled ware has been dated to c. A.D. 100±212 in Eastern Barotseland where it occurs on a buried land surface.[41] A late and variant form, known as Gokomere ware, was present in A.D. 330±150 on the Zimbabwe acropolis, and the typical Channelled ware occurs again at the Kalambo Falls[42] where a late phase dates to A.D. 1080±180. This last date probably marks the end of this culture as such, since by A.D. 1085±150 it had been replaced at the Zimbabwe acropolis by pottery of a quite different tradition.[43] In modified form it seems to have lingered in the Rhodesias and southern Tanganyika until fairly recent times.

No evidence of working iron or other metal has yet been found with the earliest Channelled and Bambata wares (Bambata, Zimbabwe, Zambezi Valley, and Machili), but it is present at the Mabveni settlement excavated by Robinson,[44] the date of which is, however, not yet known. Worked iron occurs with the Dimple-based ware in Uganda and Kenya; iron slag and tuyères are also present at the Kalambo Falls, and in Ruanda remains of furnaces have been found.[45] It would not be altogether inconsistent,

[33] Mauny, R., 'Histoire des métaux en Afrique occidentale', Bull. I.F.A.N. (1952), XIV, no. 2, 546–95.

[34] Wainwright, G. A., 'Iron in the Matapan and Meroitic Ages', Sudan Notes and Records (1945), 5–36.

[35] Leakey, M. D., Owen, W. E., and Leakey, L. S. B., 'Dimple-based pottery from Central Kavirondo', Coryndon Museum Occasional Paper, no. 2 (Nairobi, 1948).

[36] Hiernaux, J., and Maquet, E., 'Cultures préhistoriques de l'âge des métaux au Ruanda Urundi et au Kivu, Congo Belge', Acad. roy. des sciences d'Outre mer; Classe des sciences nat. et méd., New Series (1960), LX, no. 2, 1–102.

[37] Nenquin, J., 'Dimple-based pots from Kasai, Belgian Congo', Man (1959), 242.

[38] See n. 23b above, 287–9.

[39] Summers, R. F. H., 'The Southern Rhodesian Iron Age', Journ. Afr. Hist. (1961), II (1), 1–13.

[40] Posnansky, M., 'Pottery types from archaeological sites in East Africa', Journ. Afr. Hist. (1961), II (2), 177–98.

[41] See n. 31 above.

[42] See n. 39 above.

[43] See n. 39 above.

[44] Robinson, K. R., 'An early Iron Age site from the Chibi District, Southern Rhodesia', S. Afr. Arch. Bull. (1961), XVI, no. 63, 75–102.

[45] See n. 36 above.

therefore, if the earliest groups of this migration to enter Southern Africa were still largely stone using, and had acquired their knowledge of metal working by diffusion down the north-south highway from later immigrants of the same racial stock, and perhaps also from the South-East African coast, to which the knowledge was communicated by traders coming from across the Indian Ocean in search of gold.

Little is known of the settlement patterns or dwellings of these Dimple-based/Channelled ware peoples, but in Uganda, as also at Bambata and perhaps at Gokomere, rock shelters were sometimes occupied.[46a, 46b] The usual type of settlement must, however, have consisted of free standing dwellings in the open. Of considerable importance, therefore, are Robinson's Mabveni excavations which show that the settlement there consisted of a small open village comprising several huts made of pole and daga with similarly constructed grain bins.

Nothing is known either about the physical characteristics of the Dimple-based/Channelled ware population, though the Stamped ware tradition south of the Zambezi is associated with a Bush-Boskopoid stock. North of the river no skeletal remains have been found with Channelled ware but later Iron Age remains show both Bush-Boskopoid and negroid features together with hybrids.[47a, 47b] Afro-Mediterranean characteristics are apparent also in some of the Later Stone Age populations in Rhodesia and South Africa.[48] Their presence in the south in association with certain cultural traits strongly suggests a movement of East African long-heads into the sub-continent in late prehistoric times. Such a movement would seem most likely to have taken place about the beginning of the present era, and to have been responsible for transmitting to the historic Hottentots their stock and characteristic pottery. Whether or not such a movement was connected with, or quite separate from the Channelled ware population is unknown, though it is thought most likely to have been separate. Channelling is a characteristic motif for decoration of some Hottentot pottery, but, apart from that, the two traditions have little in common. The general shape, and the pointed base form of the Hottentot pots, the lugs and spouts, are much more closely linked with the Neolithic Stone Bowl cultures of the Gregory Rift.

Such population movements, bringing with them fundamental improvements in food getting, must have profoundly affected the Later Stone Age inhabitants of Southern Africa, and, in fact, all hunter-gatherers with whom

[46a] Lowe, C. van Riet, 'The Pleistocene Geology and Archaeology of Uganda, Part II, Prehistory', *Geol. Survey of Uganda Mem.* (1952), VI.

[46b] Gardner, T., Wells, L. H., and Schofield, J. F., 'The recent archaeology of Gokomere, Southern Rhodesia', *Trans. Roy. Soc. S. Africa* (1940), XXVIII, 219–53.

[47a] Tobias, P. V., 'Skeletal remains from Inyanga'. In Summers, R. F. H., *Inyanga* (Cambridge University Press, London, 1958), 159–72.

[47b] Tobias, P. V. Unpublished report on skeletal remains from Northern Rhodesian sites.

[48] Wells, L. H., 'Late Stone Age human types in central Africa', *Proc. 3rd Pan-African Congress on Prehistory* (1957), Clark, J. D., and Cole, S., 183–5.

the Neolithic and Iron Age farmers came into contact. It has generally been assumed that there was a sharp cultural break between the Stone and Iron Ages in sub-Saharan Africa, with the proviso that some peoples at the Stone Age level persisted in their way of life living in symbiosis with Iron Age food producers until quite late times—where some Bushman, Pygmy, and other groups are concerned, for example, until the present day. Ample evidence exists, as has for long been appreciated, for this overlap and contemporaneity of stone- and metal-using peoples, but what has not been appreciated is the potential and degree to which cultural adaptation must sometimes have taken place, thus enabling some of the Later Stone Age food-gathering populations to change their economy and so to compete favourably with the metal-using immigrants. Such a change would generally mean the abandonment of sites favourable for hunter-collectors and the settlement of others more suitable for stock raising and cultivation. That such changes did not, however, come about all at once is evident both from the archaeological record and from oral tradition,[49] which indicate that processes of acculturation leading to economic revolution had been under way from the beginning of this era up to the present day. It might, therefore, be expected that some of these successful communities may have evolved into Bantu tribal groups we know today, and that these would show to a varying degree evidence in their physical composition of their Bush-Boskopoid ancestry. Indeed, this is precisely what we do find in those parts of South Central Africa where skeletal remains of proto-historic times have been studied.[50a, 50b, 50c]

So far as the writer is aware, no skeletal remains have as yet been found associated with the Dimple-based pottery and Channelled ware complex, so that it is impossible to know to what physical type the makers of these cultures belonged. They may, possibly, have been Nilotic Negroes, since the region of their dispersal is believed to lie in the area of the western Rift and the upper reaches of the Nile (fig. 3). If this were the case, it might in part account for the long-headed element in the proto-historic populations of some southern regions. On the other hand, the wide dispersal of the pre-Bush ('Boskopoid') stock in later Pleistocene times, as indicated by the Singa skull,[51] suggests that 'Bush-Boskopoid' peoples might still have been occupying the northern parts of Central Africa in proto-historic times and so could have been the authors of the Dimple-based wares. Certainly the late prehistoric metal-using pastoralists

[49] Clark, J. D., 'A note on the pre-Bantu inhabitants of Northern Rhodesia and Nyasaland', *S. Afr. Journ. Sci.* (1950), XLVII, no. 3, 42–52.

[50a] Wells, L. H., 'Fossil man in Northern Rhodesia'. In Clark, J. D., *The Stone Age Cultures of Northern Rhodesia* (South African Archaeological Society, Cape Town, 1950).

[50b] See n. 47a above.

[50c] Galloway, A. (ed.), 'Symposium on human skeletal remains from the northern and eastern Transvaal', *S. Afr. Journ. Sci.* (1935), XXXII, 616–41.

[51] Wells, L. H., 'The fossil human skull from Singa'. In *The Pleistocene Fauna of two Blue Nile sites* (1951), British Museum (Nat. Hist.), 'Fossil Mammals of Africa', no. 2, 29–42.

of the Masai steppe seem to have been of this type, but there is as yet no indication that they were connected with the Dimple-based pottery complex.

The intermingling of Negroid and Bush-Hottentot characteristics in the physical make-up of the present Bantu populations in Southern Africa can give some indication of the degree to which hybridization has taken place. Only the archaeological record, however, is likely to show whether the original culture and physical stock was basically Negroid, Bush-Hottentot, or other. In A.D. 1055 ± 65 the proto-historic population of Bambandyanalo on the Limpopo was essentially Bush-Boskopoid, though certainly they were settled pastoralists and perhaps agriculturalists also. Some slight Negroid admixture can be seen to have taken place at nearby Mapungubwe by the fourteenth century.[52] The same would seem to have been the position in Southern Rhodesia, where prior to the fifteenth century the population was also apparently of Bush-Boskopoid stock. It was not until the coming of the B_2 peoples into Southern Rhodesia, most probably from the Southern Congo, that Negroid features became common.[53]

Archaeological evidence in support of this successful economic revolution among some of the Later Stone Age groups is as yet slight; but up to now it has not been looked for very closely. The obviously symbiotic and friendly relationship that existed between the Stone Age populations and the earliest Iron Age immigrants in South Central Africa implies that there can have been few conflicts over ownership of territory or water.[54] These immigrants are likely to have possessed sheep[55] and cattle[56] and, since their numbers were sufficiently small and their dependence on hunting and collecting, while considerable, neither so great nor so essential as in the case of the autochthonous hunter-gatherers, they were able to live peacefully among these last since their stock as well as crop cultivation had rendered them partially independent of their environment.

Caves in Uganda[57a, 57b, 57c] and Ruanda[58] and the Nachikufu and Kasama caves[59a, 59b] in Northern Rhodesia, to mention but a few, show that shortly

[52] Galloway, A., *The Skeletal Remains from Bambandyanalo* (Witwatersrand University Press, Johannesburg, 1959).   [53] See n. 39 above.

[54] Cooke, C. K., 'Rock art in Matabeleland'. In R. F. H. Summers, ed., *Rock Art of Central Africa* (National Publications Trust, Southern Rhodesia, 1959).

[55] Goodall, E., 'The rock paintings of Mashonaland'. In R. F. H. Summers, ed., *Rock Art of Central Africa* (National Publications Trust, Southern Rhodesia, 1959).

[56] Robinson, K. R., *Khami Ruins* (Cambridge University Press, London, 1959).

[57a] O'Brien, T. P., *The Prehistory of Uganda Protectorate* (Cambridge University Press, London, 1939).   [57b] See n. 46a above.

[57c] Posnansky, M., 'Excavation of a rock shelter at Hippo Bay, Entebbe'. In Brachi, R. M., *Uganda Journal* (1960), XXVI, 62–71.   [58] See n. 36 above.

[59a] Clark, J. D., 'The newly discovered Nachikufu Culture of Northern Rhodesia and the possible origin of certain elements of the South African Smithfield Culture', *S. Afr. Arch. Bull.* (1950), V, no. 19.

[59b] Fagan, B. M., 'A Nachikufu site at Kasama cave, Northern Rhodesia' (n.d.). In press.

before their disappearance the microlithic industries had sometimes undergone important modification in the general falling out of the formal tool element. For example, a much lower percentage of microliths is usually, though not always, recorded while the debitage remains the same. The lithic industry is accompanied by pottery acquired by exchange with the agriculturalists, by iron and copper, and by evidence also of the smelting of metal. The 'degeneration' of the stone element seems to be at the same rate as the increase in the other traits, and may be interpreted as the replacement of stone by iron for the working parts of tools and weapons. This process is completed by the final abandonment of the caves and rock shelters which were only used again as refuges in much later times. Acculturation of this kind was actively under way from the time of the earliest pottery traditions (i.e. Bambata ware, Gokomere ware, Dimple-based ware), all of which have been found in association with microlithic industries, and probably reached a peak during the tenth century. After that time it still continued, however (e.g. at Nachikufu and Bimbe wa Mpalabwe, etc., in Northern Rhodesia), until as late as the sixteenth century. Those groups which had not become hybridized or changed their economy by that time, perhaps because of the unsuitable nature of their territory or for other reasons, seem largely to have lost the opportunity to do so, and remained as hunter-gatherers until they were absorbed or eliminated in the last century. The reason for this is unknown, but is possibly one of the effects of an over-all population increase during the sixteenth century and of movements from the Congo basin which began about the same time.

Though systematic investigation of the proto-historic field has as yet barely begun, archaeology can provide some indication of the time range during which metal-working peoples penetrated the sub-continent. By A.D. 200 the Negro Nok Culture people were smelting iron and tin and there is no indication that this was brought about by any population change. In the Kenya Rift, Neolithic long-heads, in the later stages metal users also, continued until quite late times, and in the Nakuru Basin seem to have been replaced by Iron Age peoples—probably Bantu Negroids—by the sixteenth century A.D. The BaKongo in the lower Congo were still using stone up to the end of the fourteenth or early fifteenth century, when iron smelting was introduced,[60] and when presumably the incipient cultivators whom the BaKongo subjected on their arrival in that region were also still using stone. The BaLuba had iron weapons when they moved into the Sankuru Basin at the end of the fifteenth century, but the people whom they defeated had not.[61] On the other hand, the Kuba, who were fishers, hunters, and collectors as well as cultivators

[60] Cavazzi da Montecuculo, *Istoria descrizione de'tre regni Congo, Matamba e Angola* (Bologna, 1687), F. Alamandini, ed.
[61] Bequaert, M., 'La préhistoire du Congo Belge'. In *Encyclopédie du Congo Belge* (Brussels, 1952), 47–9.

of millet and bananas, are said to have learnt the art of smithing from one of the groups already settled in the lower Kasai when the Kuba arrived before 1568.[62] The distinctive Kisalian Culture shows that there were certainly agricultural communities in the Katanga by the eighth and ninth centuries[63] making extensive use of copper and with an elaborate pottery tradition. Whether, however, the Kisalian can be taken as characteristic of the pre-Luba people in the Kasai is not known, nor is the origin of this culture. Since the Channelled ware complex occupies the country to the east, it is likely that the antecedents of the Kisalian should be sought in the north-west—in the lower Congo, Gabon, or Cameroons.

During the earlier part of the Iron Age in Southern Africa (A.D. ?–1450), the importance of metal was for weapons and not for agricultural tools, and tradition not infrequently ascribes the success of one tribal group or another to their possession of iron for spears and arrow-heads. Only during the sixteenth century and later does iron appear to have been worked extensively for other kinds of equipment also—utilitarian, ornamental, and ceremonial. Stone continued in use, however, for some purposes in some regions until quite late times. For example, there is reason to think that it was being used for axes in Ghana until the last century,[64] and to about the same time by the Herero in South West Africa.[65] Stone scrapers were still used until recently by the Lungu peoples in North-Eastern Rhodesia,[66] and the survival of typical Later Stone Age techniques for the manufacture of gun flints from *grès polymorphe* and quartz in North-Eastern Angola shows that the tradition must have been kept alive by one or more late hunting and gathering groups, now, no doubt, forming a clan or clans within an existing Bantu tribal unit.[67]

The same process of acculturation can be seen also in East Africa. In this connexion we may cite the cairn burials in Northern Tanganyika of people who were physically Bush-Boskopoid and culturally were metal-using pastoralists.[68a, 68b] It can be seen to have taken place also fairly recently among at least one click-speaking group (the Sandawe), while others (the Hadza) remain essentially collectors. The Iraqw, on the other hand, are

[62] Vansina, J., 'Recording the oral history of BaKuba: II, Results', *Journ. Afr. Hist.* (1960), I (2), 257–70.

[63] Nenquin, J., 'Une collection de céramique Kisalienne au Musée royale du Congo Belge', *Bull. Soc. Roy. Belge, Anthrop. et Préhist.* (1958), LXIX, 151–210.

[64] See n. 8b above.

[65] van Reenen, W., *Diary of a Journey north of the Orange River in 1797.* (Van Viebeeck Society Publications, 1935), 317.

[66] Clark, J. D., 'Certain industries of notched and strangulated scrapers in Rhodesia, their time range and possible use', *S. Afr. Arch. Bull.* (1958), XIII, 50, 56–66.

[67] Clark, J. D., 'Prehistoric cultures of north-east Angola and their significance in tropical Africa' (1962), Chap. x. In press.

[68a] Galloway, A., 'The Nebarara skull', *S. Afr. Journ. Sci.* (1933), XXX, 585–96.

[68b] Fosbrooke, H. A., 'Prehistoric wells, rainponds and associated burials in northern Tanganyika'. In Clark, J. D., and Cole, S., *Proceedings of the 3rd Pan-African Congress on Prehistory, Livingstone 1955* (Chatto and Windus, London, 1957), 321–35.

probably basically a Neolithic group, though changed by hybridization and contact with Bantu Negroids. In South Africa the best example of this kind of acculturation is that of the Hottentots, who acquired livestock and other traits (but not crop cultivation) from pastoral neighbours, perhaps the intrusive Kakamas peoples of long-headed Afro-Mediterranean stock.[69] As Wells, and several authors subsequently, have pointed out, the closest connexions of the Kakamas people, who must have been in South West Africa before A.D. 1500 lie with the Neolithic/Stone Bowl cultures of the East African Rift.[70]

Summarizing, therefore, it can be seen that only in Southern Rhodesia has systematic archaeological investigation of proto-historic sites been carried out for any length of time. In other regions, investigations have begun only during the past decade, and in others they still remain to be initiated. Stratified cultural material from excavations is very rare and that from the surface must always be of only doubtful value. At this stage, therefore, any interpretation and synthesis of this material must remain tentative in the extreme. The broad pattern is beginning to appear, however, especially when the cultural material is used in conjunction with the botanical, ethnographic, and linguistic evidence. It should be remembered, however, that while these last can provide most important pointers to origins and movements, they can never become a substitute for the direct cultural evidence which can only be obtained from excavation of occupation sites.

Knowledge of cultivation of cereal crops was, on the existing available archaeological evidence, transmitted across the Sahara from South-West Asia via the Nile and perhaps the Maghrib, and with this agricultural knowledge must have come domestic stock—long- and short-horned cattle, sheep, and goats. The sedentary hunters and fishers, as also the 'vege-culturalists' of the savannah dambos and forest fringes, were not slow to develop by experiment and adaptation their own domesticates, and to occupy territory which formerly had permitted only temporary settlement. This change in the economy and accompanying movement of populations seems to have begun during the second millennium at the latest. The continued dessication of the Sahara, the transmission of the knowledge of metallurgy to West and South Central Africa, and also, no doubt, the conquests of the Axumite empire in Ethiopia, caused a further movement of stock owners and cultivators from the Sudanic belt and the Horn southwards into the Congo Basin, South Central, and Southern Africa. Here symbiotic existence of hunters and cultivators resulted, it is suggested, in many of the former forsaking their nomadic life and becoming semi- or fully-sedentary cultivators and pastoralists. Most of them must have conducted their lives on a simple pattern of transhumance, as did the

[69] Wells, L. H., 'Recent and Fossil Human Types in South Africa', *Roy. Soc. S. Afr.* (1948), Robert Broom Commemorative Volume ,133–42.
[70] See n. 25 above.

Bantu and Hottentot communities of the south-east coastal regions in the sixteenth and seventeenth centuries.[71]

The introduction of metallurgy helped considerably to speed up and intensify this process of transformation from a collecting to a food-producing economy, which in most areas must have been completed by the end of the sixteenth century. What proportion of the present Bantu populations of the sub-continent arose in this way, through hybridization and acculturation, cannot as yet be assessed. Up to the time of the Ngoni invasions and tribal movements initiated by the Zulu chief Chaka during the first half of the last century, there must have been many groups occupying territory which had been their traditional home from the time when they were hunter-gatherers.

[71] Boxer, C. R., *The tragic history of the sea, 1589–1622*, Hakluyt Society (1957), Second Series, CXII.

3. PRIMARY CRADLES OF AGRICULTURE IN THE AFRICAN CONTINENT*

By ROLAND PORTÈRES

LONG-DISTANCE travel and transfers of cultivated plants from continent to continent have had extremely important repercussions upon the development of civilizations through their direct action on the prosperity of their agriculture and on their dietary habits. It is not necessary to do more than to recall the role played by the potato in temperate countries, and by maize in the tropics. The role of both was to *break famine and to conquer shortages*.

Certain regions have provided the world's agriculturalists with much more than others. The leaders are Asia and America. At first sight, Africa has contributed little and late. It had gifts lavished on it from the two continents mentioned through the Arab expansion of the eighth to tenth centuries and the Iberian voyages of discovery in Asia from the fifteenth to the sixteenth centuries and in America from the seventeenth to the nineteenth centuries.

If Africa appears to have provided little for other continents, it is because Africa is only just beginning to be known, and because it is a continent hard on man, and for a number of reasons, exhausted and extremely difficult to rehabilitate. It is also the case that much confusion has reigned and still reigns about the origin of some major plants used for food. Nevertheless, Africa gave the world coffee, oil palms, the cereal sorghums, the Bulrush or Pearl millets (*Pennisetum* spp.) etc.

Africa is divided into a number of regions based on latitude. This division, a distinguishing feature of the continent, is many-sided, and affects climate, vegetation, soil, man and agriculture. Each climatic zone has its own specific peculiarities. Altitude has exerted a great effect. On either side of the Congo-Nile backbone, it has created a high altitude world in East Africa and a sloping-plain world in west Africa.

A further small axis, a cretaceous upheaval, running from O Principe almost up to L. Chad, again subdivides Africa in all respects.

Present dietary habits are of two kinds:

(a) the equatorial forest type, with agriculture based on digging and mound making, and producing only starchy food from fruits, tubers, rhizomes and roots, with an important contribution from edible leaves;

(b) the tropical savannah type, with steppe agriculture producing only cereals (sorghums, finger millets, pearl millets, eleusine) and leguminous seeds.

* This is a translated and slightly revised version of the paper 'Berceaux agricoles primaires sur le continent Africain', published in *J.A.H.* III, 2 (1962), pp. 195–210.

Historically speaking, men of the first dietary type were at a very low level of civilization by contrast with those of men at the cereal savannah stage. Everything at present known of Africa's human societies, linguistics, folklore, physical anthropology, ethnography, agricultural skills, and variations in the collection of plants cultivated, leads to the conclusion that *forest type agriculture* is a very recent phenomenon. In the West African forest area the only agricultural civilization to be found is that of the yam, an indigenous product. The ancestral branches of the many peoples on the equatorial area had in the past certainly been familiar with a steppe-style agriculture similar to that now found in the tropical area properly so-called. Perhaps, but not certainly, these ancient forebears of the present forest dwellers to a large extent created the cereal agriculture from which their descendants are so far removed today. One example can be given in rice cultivation.

Cereal agriculture people, forced back by nomads, who in their turn followed a sedentary life in agricultural cradles which they viewed as already prepared for them, did not know what to do with their ancestral knowledge and their steppe agricultural skills when fate forced them to live for centuries in equatorial forests where the cereals they had bred could not grow.

They thus found themselves forced back upon gathering and collecting food, then on attempting gradually to cultivate starchy root crops.

Forest peoples have always been regarded as backward examples of human evolution; everything points to the fact that they are survivals of a well developed race which has been plunged back into the darkness of primitive human life. Comparison between Africa's equatorial and tropical zones shows that, broadly speaking, only the former has benefited from the introduction of Asian and American cultivated food plants (bananas, taro, Caribbean cabbage, manioc, sweet potatoes). By contrast, the steppe area has not assimilated any new basic cereal, but only sometimes a specific additional food (Asiatic rice).

The equatorial zone properly so called produced no ancient agricultural civilization. The tropical zone gave birth to a few, but their distinguishing features now seem hard to trace. These civilizations often disappeared or perished because they themselves ruined the land which had given them birth and prosperity.

These vanished agricultural civilizations can be rediscovered through seeking the geographical cradles of ancient agricultures. Folklore and linguistics can supply some evidence, but it is hard to interpret. Africa is a poor source of documents or inscriptions, or of durable materials to provide witnesses *in situ* of human work in the agricultural field.

The research technique discovered and developed by Vavilov makes it possible, when applied to Africa, to rediscover these cradles. The technique is based on a dynamic and interpretative use of genetic science.

A cradle of agriculture represents a superimposition of areas with numerous and different cultivated crops, each characterized by variation in one cultivated species. Determination of the *centre of origin* of this species is of no more than secondary interest, since this centre cannot but agree with that of the area of variability brought about by cultivation. The *focus* or *primary variation centre* is defined by a highly diversified variation with a concentration of dominant characters (genes). The existence of an area of primary variation attests some degree of agricultural development. Extension on the borders of the area of primary variation determines the appearance and maintenance (to bring about later evolution) of recessive genetic characters which were hidden within the *primary variation area overloaded with dominant characteristics*. There thus arose *secondary variation areas* where the recessive characteristics were liberated. When a series of variation areas are superimposed, i.e. when successive civilizations have continued to operate for a long period in the same region, there are legitimate grounds for supposing that some degree of agricultural civilization developed there. This then becomes a *cradle of agriculture*. Each one of the homes of agriculture detected through this method by Vavilov coincides geographically with one of the great civilizations evolved by humanity throughout the ages starting from Neolithic times.

*   *   *   *   *

Vavilov has demonstrated the existence throughout the world of eleven cradles of agriculture:

In Asia: *the Chinese, Hindu, Indo-Malayan, Central Asian, West Asian.*

In America: *the Central American, Peruvian-Ecuadorian-Bolivian, Chilean* (from Chiloe), and *Brazilian-Paraguayan.*

In Africa: *the Mediterranean* and *Abyssinian.*

In Europe: none.

The *Mediterranean cradle* does not seem to have played an important part in inter-tropical Africa. None of the species originating from this centre spread to inter-tropical Africa except for the Saharan fringes.

SPECIES OF RICE CULTIVATED IN AFRICA

Oryza Barthii A. Chev. (hardy rice) and *O. breviligulata* A. Chev and O. Roer. are both, and particularly the former, species of rice gathered and collected.

Two other species are cultivated in Africa:

(*a*) *O glaberrima* Steudel, West African rice.
(*b*) *O. sativa* L., a rice introduced from Asia.

The ancestor of *O. glaberrima* seems to have been *O. breviligulata*, but *O. Barthii* may have played a part in the diversification of African cultivated rice.

The area covered by *O. breviligulata* extends over the Sudan and Sahel from the Atlantic to Oubangui-Chari. At the present time the primary centre of varietal diversification is found in the delta of the middle Niger. The forms occurring there show exclusively *genetically dominant characteristics:* deciduous spikelets, anthocyanin pigmentation of the vegetative and flowering parts, purple colouration of the seed coats, coarse stiff panicles; the habitat is aquatic, and all the forms are described as 'floating', being able to extend their haulms progressively as the water level rises.

This *centre of primary variation on the Niger* is situated at the heart of the area occupied by *O. breviligulata.*

There is also a *secondary* centre of variation which covers an area on either side of the Gambia, bounded on the north by the River Sine and on the south by the River Casamance. This *senegambian* centre of variation contains forms derived from the preceding ones, but which have acquired *recessive genetic characters*: the absence of anthocyanin pigmentation, white caryopses, spikelets retained to maturity, loss of the 'floating' characteristic, more supple and finer panicles.

On the mountainous backbone of Guinea is found a *secondary* centre of variation which is in process of emancipation, with loss of the floating characteristic, a tendency to the disappearance of anthocyanin pigmentation and to the whitening of the caryopses, softening of the panicle, loss of the 'floating' character.

This *secondary Guinean* centre is only in process of liberation: its varietal populations are still not independent, since the recessive characters found are surrounded with groups of dominant characters; nevertheless, they very clearly tend to free themselves of them.

In among the three centres which have been described, there are found throughout the whole of the extreme west of West Africa cultivated forms which are very highly evolved as compared with those of the Niger primary centre in respect of the panicle, pigmentation, the 'floating' characteristic, and the deciduousness of the spikelets. These acquisitions are, however, always few and always partial. No general trend towards recessivity can be observed which affects the whole of the characteristics mentioned.

In West Africa, *O. glaberrima* has about 1,500 cultivated varietal populations. They are grouped into thirteen botanical varieties comprising forty-one botanical forms.

Comparison of the variations between *O. glaberrima* and *O. sativa* reveal a very close parallelism. It is, however, of limited extent, since crosses between forms from the primary and secondary centres have not occurred in *O. glaberrima* with the vigour and complexity found in *O. sativa.*

There is also found in *O. glaberrima* types which have a spreading panicle during growth, and which have markedly elongated spikelets reminiscent of *O. sativa*, sub-species *indica*. It must be presumed that these forms arose through crosses from *O. Barthii* and *O. glaberrima* (perhaps also originally *O. breviligulata*).

Dextrin-like properties (sticky rice) largely predominate in the primary centre, and elsewhere tend to disappear or have already done so. Many mixed forms are found with starchy-dextrinous properties.

West Africa thus possesses a rice-growing cradle of agriculture peculiar to itself and anterior to the arrival of Asiatic rice, with two important areas of varietal diversification already complete, and another in course of liberation. The general picture is one of a relatively high degree of evolution with populations no longer demanding flooding or irrigation.

The names for rice in this rice-growing cradle are not borrowed from Asian originals. They are *malo, maro, mano* or some derivative of them. It can be shown that *-lo, -ro, -no*, are roots meaning 'food, nourishment', and that *ma-* is a prefix of Bantu origin applied to foods or liquids with the meaning of 'bulk'.

Linguistic study of the word for 'rice' leads to the following hypothesis. The Bantu were familiar with rice as a cereal which could be gathered or collected. Negritos appear to have been the people who started cultivation. Mande peoples apparently developed it.

Furthermore, the Senegambian secondary centre encompasses a specific and geographically well-defined collection of megalithic sites, made up of circles of (phallic ?) laterite steles, set upright and carefully sited (solar cult ?). They mark ancient watercourses. It may be thought that this megalithic civilization cultivated rice, as it is now cultivated along the present-day watercourses. This civilization long antedates the arrival of the Mande (twelfth to thirteenth century).

It is at present difficult to date. If this Senegambian megalithic civilization is to be dated somewhere between 1500 and 800 B.C., and taking account of the variations within *O. glaberrima*, it may be assumed that rice-growing on the middle Niger must have been well developed by 1500 B.C., which would mean that it has now been in existence for 3500 years.[1]

In the delta of the middle Niger, rice-growing has hardly progressed beyond the techniques of traditional agriculture. This stagnation is normal when agriculture continues in a centre of primary variation burdened by dominant genes. The Senegambian secondary centre, in its present condition, appears to be a survival.

It seems unlikely that rice-growing in West Africa could have come into being through a chain of cultural contacts with Asia, or that the idea of invention could have been a counterpart of rice-growing in Asia. African rice-growing came into being from habits of gathering and collecting, from the existence of a delta and of local species. The local names for rice also provide a strong presumption in favour of a spontaneous rice

[1] EDITORIAL NOTE: Professor Portères was writing in 1962. Since then, a single C-14 date for a Senegambian stone circle has been published: it is A.D. 750±110. (See *J.A.H.*, X, 1 (1969), 150–1).

culture which developed historically with no knowledge of any other cradle of rice-growing.

*   *   *   *   *

Analytical study of the forms and varietal types of rice make it possible to define small hereditary units (known as Jordanian species or Jordanons). This Jordanian analysis applied to West Africa and transposed onto the geographical plane makes it possible to delimit the area occupied by the cultivation of *O. glaberrima* before the sixteenth century.

Prior to the arrival of Asian rice in the interior of west Africa, rice-growing was known from C. Verde to L. Chad, but did not reach the Atlantic except between the R. Senegal and the R. Bandama, with sporadic cultivation to as far as Axim (Ghana). Thus, when Asian rice reached the West African coast, all the generic names for African rice were given to it. On the other hand, wherever African rice was not known, one finds names derived from *Arroz*, *Riz*, *Rijst*, *Rice*, etc., which have been taken from the Arabic *Eruz*, *Erruz*, etc. All the coastlands and countries of Africa where African rice was not known in antiquity use these new names in a more or less mangled form. In the area in which African rice was known in the sixteenth century, these names are unknown.

This ancient rice-growing region immediately adopted all the varieties of rice introduced from Asia. Elsewhere, Asian rice was not taken over, since the pursuit of rice-growing presupposes populations relatively skilled in handling rice fields and in the techniques of cultivation. Here, then, rice was totally unknown as a food.

Rice cultivation in West Africa was therefore not promoted by the Portuguese; they did no more than introduce varieties of a different species. Nevertheless, the far richer choice of varieties provided by the Portuguese resulted in the intensified cultivation of rice, and particularly of forms with white caryopses.

Jordanian analysis, as conceived by Alexis Jordan, and then used genetico-geographically by Vavilov, makes it possible to study varietal diversification within a single species. It becomes of much greater significance when it is associated with the geographical concept, as was done by Vavilov. It was this method which we have used in the study of *O. glaberrima*, which has been summarized above. For the study of *O. sativa* which has been introduced into West Africa, a novel *prospective method of agrarian companionship* has been worked out, based on the data established and confirmed by Jordan and Vavilov. This method makes it possible to pinpoint where a varietal population was introduced (no matter how many centuries have since elapsed) and where later it spread geographically.

By this means it is possible, with very great accuracy, of the order of ±25–50 kilometres, to localize the point of introduction of an original (primitive) varietal population and to ascertain from what introduction any specific population derives, no matter what its morphological impoverishment or its enrichment by subsequent *population mutations*.

Taken as a whole, two particularly important zones are found where Asiatic rice arrived and in which it expanded on the Atlantic coast of West Africa:

(*a*) between the R. Cacheo and the R. Casamace.
(*b*) between Conakry (Guinea) and Grand Bassa (Liberia).

Arrival and expansion are necessarily two linked concepts. Many introductions were made elsewhere (particularly outside the original rice growing area) but, for the reasons stated earlier, they never made any headway.

These digressions were necessary to show what are the methods applicable to geo-biological research into cultivated species.

In East Africa, Asian rice, when introduced, was also not spontaneously adopted, except at the actual places where strangers to the continent were active. It was the Arabs who introduced rice (eighth to tenth centuries), and then later spread it into the interior (nineteenth century).

In Madagascar, Indo-Malayans appear to have introduced rice growing during the fifteenth century. The names and varieties cultivated in the island appear to come from the south of the Indian peninsula.

THE LARGE MILLETS, OR
SORGHUMS (GUINEA CORN)

Since Schweinfurth (1891), Egyptologists and present-day Egyptian botanists have agreed in thinking that the cultivation of sorghum *Durra* (originating from *Sorghum aethiopicum* Rupr.) could go back no further than the Roman-Byzantine era, since the most ancient grains known were of the Coptic period (sixth and seventh centuries A.D.).

A. de Candolle (1883) could not accept India as the homeland of the cereal sorghums and favoured a tropical African origin, though at the time he had no real basis to support him in this argument. Vavilov (1935) thought that the sugar sorghums spread from the Ethiopian centre, and that the Indian centre had bred the cereal sorghums. However, Snowden (1936) demonstrated by Jordanian analysis the unchallengeable African origin of the cereal sorghums, and showed that the sugar sorghums could have arisen independently in both India and Africa.

The present writer (1950) re-examined the question using the material supplied by Snowden, and advanced the view that the African cereal sorghums had an independent botanico-geographical origin, that their birth took place both in many places and with many species, that there were different regions in which they were developed from one wild species, and that the forms arising from it were still cultivated in the area where each of the species occurred spontaneously.

(1) *Sorghum arundinaceum* Stapf is a wild species with a distribution area covering the equatorial and wet tropical zone from C. Verde and the

Atlantic to the Indian ocean. In ancient times it was exploited solely by West Africans, who obtained from it many varieties belonging to Jordanian species: *S. aterrimum* Stapf, *S. nitens* Snowd., *S. Drummondi* Millsp. and Chase, *S. margaritiferum* Stapf, *S Guineense* Stapf, *S. gambicum* Snowd., and *S. exsertum* Snowd. The cultivation of all these species is confined to West Africa. Nevertheless, still within the area where *S. arundinaceum* occurs spontaneously today, there are two specific Jordanian species cultivated in East Africa: *S. conspicuum* Snowd. (from Tanzania to Rhodesia and Angola) and *S. Roxburghii* Stapf. (Uganda, Kenya, Rhodesia, South Africa and Madagascar). These two species might well come from crossing the Jordanian species arising from *S. arundinaceum* and *S. verticilliflorum*, all of which, and particularly *S. Roxburghii*, are widely cultivated in India and in Burma.

(2) *Sorghum verticilliflorum* Stapf is a wild species peculiar to East Africa, with a growth area extending from Eritrea to South-East Africa. Ancient peoples raised from it a first group of varieties of the 'Kaffir' type, such as *S. caffrorum* Beauv., *S. coriaceum* Snowd., *S. dulcicaule* (sugar Sorghum), forming a group confined to South-East Africa; the second group belongs to the Nile-Chad region, from the Nigerian Sudan to Eritrea, with *S. nigricans* Snowd. and *S. caudatum* Stapf.

(3) *Sorghum aethiopicum* Rupr. occurs spontaneously in Eritrea and in Abyssinia. This is the stock from which originated the cultivated species: *S. rigidum* Snowd. in the valley of the Blue Nile; *S. durra* Stapf, cultivated from L. Chad to India and in all the semi-desert areas; *S. cernuum* Host., *S. subglabrescens* Schw. and Asch., cultivated in the Nilotic region; and *S. nigricum* with a secondary settlement in the delta of the middle Niger.

Cultivation of *S. durra* is known from the eastern Sudan to India, in Asia Minor and from Mesopotamia to Iran and to Gujerat.

GENERAL POST BETWEEN AFRICA AND INDIA

We have just seen that the cultivated sorghums resulted from crossing between Jordanons deriving from *S. arundinaceum* or from *S. verticilliflorum*, all cultivated in East Africa and in India, and *S. durra*, cultivated in North-East Africa and Asia. This presupposes the pre-existence of a current of migration between East Africa and India. This problem of ancient exchanges, with long periods of cultivation, is still more complicated.

Sorghum bicolor Moench is a unity the Jordanian species of which appear to have been produced by crossing the cultivated form of *S. aethiopicum* with the wild species *S. sudanense*, all African species. The following Jordanons are found: *S. Dochna* Snowd., widely cultivated in India and in Burma, which later spread to subtropical eastern Asia (Arabia) and was more recently reintroduced into Africa and into Europe; *S. bicolor* Moench (in the strict sense), probably cultivated in Arabia, which spread over India and Burma and is now cultivated throughout the world; *S.*

miliforme Snowd., from North-East India and recently introduced into Kenya; *S. simulans* Snowd. of Malawi; *S. elegans* Snowd. in Tanzania, with some forms discovered in Togo and in Dahomey; *S. notabile* Snowd. of the eastern Sudan, Chad and Nigeria.

Similarly *S. nervosum* Bess. has cultivated Jordanons which derive at once from *S. aethiopicum* (particularly *S. durra*) and from *S. bicolor*. This great tertiary circle of races includes *S. membranaceum* Chiov., with numerous races cultivated in the eastern Sudan, in Eritrea, in India, in China, in South Africa and in South-East Africa; *S. nervosum* (in the strict sense) from eastern Asia (particularly in China), but nevertheless represented in India, and recently arrived in North America from Manchuria; *S. Ankolib*, cultivated from Eritrea to Somaliland, and from Egypt to the eastern Sudan; *S. melaleucum* Stapf, cultivated in Egypt and the eastern Sudan; and *S. splendidum* Snowd., known to be cultivated only in Burma, Thailand, Indonesia, the Philippines and Hawaii. All these cultivated Jordanons appear to have arisen from contact between the cultivated African types and the Asiatic types which were either wild or, perhaps, formerly cultivated.

All this leads to the conclusion in respect of these Jordanons that relations between East Africa and Asia must go very far back into the past.

The cereal sorghums thus originate from three independent seats of varietal diversification:

(1) West Africa
(2) Nile-Ethiopia
(3) East Africa, with rebounds from India

Thus Africa created cereal sorghums long before India, which used African types as parents.

The standard linguistic interpretation derives the Italianate *sorgo* from the latin *surgo* 'I arise', an allusion to this cereal's great height. The present writer has shown that the term was borrowed from the Hamitic languages, in which it meant no more than 'the durra with the bent ear'. The following words similar to the term *durra* can be quoted: Arabic and Aramaic *dura*; eastern Arabic *zoora*, *zurut*; Sanscrit *zurna*, *zoorna*; Nabathian *dhsura*; Nilotic *zor*, *got*, *djor*.

THE PENICILLARY MILLETS
(BULRUSH, PEARL MILLET, ETC.)

The penicillary millets (Candle millet, African millet, Small millet, Bulrush millet, Pearl millet) are also products of Africa which are very widely cultivated both there and in India.

Without expatiating on the score or so of known Jordanons, the existence of the following centres should be noted:

(1) West African, with *Pennisetum pychnostachyum* Stapf and Hubb.,

P. nigritanum Dur. and Schinz, *P. Leonis* S. and H., *P. gambiense* S. and H., *P. cinereum* S. and H.

(2) Chad, with *P. ancylochaete* S. and H., *P. gibbosum* S. and H., *P. Maiwa* S. and H.

(3) Nilotic, with *P. orthochaete*, *P. perspeciosum*, *P. vulpinum*, *P. niloticum* (all Stapf and Hubb.). This centre's salient features are above all the deciduous spikelets, grain hidden between flowering glumes, hollow haulms.

(4) East African, with *P. echinurus*, *P. malacochaete*, *P. albicauda*, *P. typhoides* (which reached Arabia and India), *P. spicatum* Koern. of Tanzania, which is also found in North Africa and in Spain.

These millets again show the same distribution of centres of origin, and the role played in East Africa in their dissemination towards India and the Red Sea.

ELEUSINE MILLET

Finger millet is a cultigen (produced under cultivation), which is usually related ancestrally to *Eleusine indica* Gaertn. All the *Eleusine* species appear to have been produced in Africa.

Eleusine Coracana Gaertn. is cultivated from Eritrea to L. Chad and in Natal, Arabia, Ceylon and India. De Candolle gave the mountainous parts of India as its country of origin; Vavilov thought that the Abyssinian high plateaux could be the possible seat of origin.

The cultivated varieties appear more or less identical in Africa and in India. The agricultural techniques used are very similar. Except in very recent times, no term used to designate this cereal has been more or less common to India and Africa.

Burkill considers that its cultivation goes back in India to at least about 1300 B.C., the period of the arrival of the first Aryans.

Various Sanscrit names are known: *raji, rajika, rajikay*, which are still used throughout the whole of India, and *ragi, raga*, etc. . . . The present writer has shown that the origin of the term is Dravidian, and its meaning 'red', referring to the colour of the grain. The Singhalese term *Kurakan* means 'dark-coloured grain'; the names *natchini, nachani* on the Coromandel and Malabar coasts (as well as in Sanscrit) signify 'China grass'. The only evidence this provides is to show that the plant arrived after another millet called *China, Cheni (Panicum miliaceum)*; it was nevertheless believed in southern India that Panic millet originated in Arabia or Egypt (where however it is called *rumi*).

In Abyssinia a list of terms, *dagussa, daguja, tocusso, tokshin, tankah*, can have the meaning of 'beer', because eleusine is everywhere used to prepare a drink. This suggests a close relationship with the Tigrinya *dagussa, detch*, for 'mead'; the Semitic *gurage dagasam*, 'prepare for the feast', *deges*, 'feast'. The meaning may also be equated with the Temacheq, *dakno* 'mead', and the Semitic, *dochn* 'sugar sorghum'. *Dagussa* is the grain used in the preparation of beers drunk at feasts and ceremonies as a 'poor man's mead'.

The present writer has also put forward another hypothesis which would allow the ultimate origin of cultivation to be placed among the Nubians. The Arabian-African names for 'eleusine' are *telebum, telbum, talban*, in Abyssinia, in the Nilotic Sudan, in Oubangui-Chari; this accounts for *tamba* in Haussa.

This probably relates to TRB (= TLB), a Nubian root for 'to cultivate' (see Murray).

On the whole, the semantic evidence suggests more likelihood of an African than an Asiatic origin until such time as more complete botanical and genetic research has been done.

ABYSSINIAN TEFF

Abyssinian millet, *Teff, Tief* (*Eragrostis Tef* Trotter), is cultivated for its grain only on the Ethiopian High Plateaux. Many plants resembling it are also known locally as *Teff*; some of them are in addition cereals which are collected (e.g. *E. pilosa* P.B.). Apart from very recent times, this cereal has not penetrated elsewhere.

The present writer has shown that the term *teff* was not of Semitic but rather of ancient Egyptian origin. While the ancient Egyptians do not appear to have been familiar with the cultivation of Abyssinian *teff*, they made use of *Eragrostis pilosa* in exactly the same way as is done today in the valley of the Nile and North-East Africa (Barth, 1858, and Kotschy, 1862). Unger (1866–67) found grains of it in the Dassur Pyramid (3359 B.C., Fourth Dynasty) and in blocks of clay from the ancient town of Ramses (1400–1300 B.C.) built at the beginning of the New Empire.

As a name, *Teff*, (*Tief*) appears to come from the Egyptian *t'ef* '*provisions, food*'.

THE WEST AFRICAN FINGER MILLETS (FONIO, ETC.)

West Africa supplies two further millets:

(1) *Digitaria Iburua* Stapf or *Iburu*, very little cultivated apart from localized cultivation in Dahomey and Bauchi.

(2) *Digitaria exilis* Stapf or *Fonio, Fundi*, cultivated from C. Verde to L. Chad, with the greatest number of forms in the Upper Senegal-Niger region.

These two millets appear to derive respectively from *D. ternata* Stapf and *D. longiflora* Pers., wild species with a growth area from C. Verde to India.

Other cultivated Digitaries are known in Europe and in India, but they are very different.

Fonio or Fundi plays a very important part as food in West Africa.

THE PRIMARY CRADLES OF AGRICULTURE OF AFRICA

A long list of cultivated plants could be given which originated in Africa. The foregoing examples, given merely as a preview, make it quite clear that ancient African agricultures rose progressively by their own efforts, and from their own roots, to a very high level before receiving the support of other non-African agricultures. A study may now be made of the *primary cradles of agriculture* in Africa.

A. WEST AFRICAN COMPLEX

I. *Tropical sector*

(*a*) Senegambian subsector

Sorghums: *Sorghum gambicum, S. cernuum* (secondary centre).

Millets: *Pennisetum pychnostachyum, P. nigritanum, P. leonis, P. gambiense.*

Millets: *Digitaria exilis, Brachiaria deflexa* var. *sativa.*

Rice: *Oryza glaberrima* (secondary centre).

Oil seeds: *Polygala butyracea.*

(*b*) Central Nigerian subsector

Sorghums: *Sorghum margaritiferum, S. guineense, S. mellitum, S. exsertum, S. nigericum.*

Millets: *Pennisetum cinereum.*

Rice: *Oryza glaberrima* (primary centre).

Geocarps: *Kerstingiella geocarpa* Harms.

Karite: *Butyrospermum Parkii* is well represented in West Africa.

Rhizomes and Tubers: *Coleus Dazo* A. Chev. and *C. dysentericus* (both have a secondary centre for some special forms).

Toxic plants: *Mundulea sericea* A. Chev.

(*c*) Chad-Nilotic subsector

Sorghums: none.

Millets: *Pennisetum ancylochaete, P. gibbosum, P. Maiwa.*

Oil seeds: *Ceratotheca sesamoides* Endl., *Sesamum radiatum* Sch. (in part).

II. *Sub-equatorial sector*

Yams: This sector has produced many cultivated yams all of west African ancestry. Two major species have been abundantly in evidence: *Dioscorea dumetorum* Pax and, above all, *D. cayenensis* Lamk. with a varietal group differing from the typical populations: *D. rotunda* Poir. To these the following should be added as having also provided cultivars: *D. bulbifera* L., *D. macroura* Harms, *D. prehensilis* Benth., *D. colocasifolia* Pax, *D. hirtiflora* Benth.

Oil seeds: *Telfairia occidentalis* Hook f., *Elaeis guineensis* Jacq. (in part).

Toxic plants: *Tephrosia Vogelii* Hook.

Stimulants: *Cola nitida* A. Chev.

More recently, cultivation has been extended to *Coffea abeocutae* Cramer, *C. canephora* Pierre (numerous regional Jordanons), *C. stenophylla* (various Jordanons), *C. liberica*.

B. NILE-ABYSSINIAN COMPLEX

(*a*) Nilotic sector
  Sorghums: *Sorghum durra, S. rigidum, S. cernuum, S. subglabrescens.*
  Millets: *Pennisetum orthochaete, P. perspecium, P. vulpinum, P. niloticum.*
  Oil seeds: *Sesamum indicum* L., *S. alatum* Thonn., *S. radiatum* Sch. and Thonn.
(*b*) Abyssinian sector.

This is responsible especially for *Teff* (*Eragrostis abyssinica*), *Dagussa* (*Eleusine Coracana*), *Hordeum distichum* L. var *zeocriton* L., or fan barley with a compact ear, *H. distichum* subspecies *abyssinicum* Stol. (secondary centre of Emmer wheat), *Triticum durum* Desf. subspecies *abyssinicum* Vav. (secondary centre), *Triticum turgidum* subspecies *abyssinicum* Vav. (secondary centre), *T. polonicum* L., grex *abyssinicum* Vav. There also originated in Ethiopia, as indigenous secondary cultivars, special forms of *Secale cereale* L., *Pisum sativuum* L., *Vicia sativa* L., *Lathyrus sativa*.

Other species very special to Abyssinia also originated from this sector: *Catha edulis* L. (Kat, or Arabian tea), the coffee bush *C. arabica* L., *Carthamus tinctorius* L. (Safflower), *Ricinus communis* (known to the Egyptians as far back as the 4th millenium B.C.), *Brassica carinata* (Mustard), *Lepidium sativum* (garden cress), *Ensete edulis* or *Musa Ensete* L. (Grain or fibre banana), *Guizotia abyssinica* ('Niger' with oleaginous seeds), etc.

C. EAST AFRICAN COMPLEX

This is particularly responsible for:
  Sorghums: *S. caffrorum, S. coriaceum, S. dulcicaule, S. caudatum* (secondary centre), *S. subglabrescens* (secondary centre).
  Millet: *Pennisetum echiurus, P. malacochaete, P. albicauda* (from Angola), *P. typhoides, P. spicatum.*

D. CENTRAL AFRICAN COMPLEX

Originally this supplied very little:
  Voandzeia subtrannea Thon. (groundnuts), *Coleus Dazo* and *Coleus dysentericus* Bak (primary centres), *Elaeis guineensis* Jacq. (in part).
  In modern times: *Coffea canephora* Pierre (in part).
  This note ignores the Mediterranean cradle of agriculture with which Africa is partly concerned, the Egyptian unit which in fact appears to have been nothing other than a European-African-Asiatic secondary centre, and the Saharan network of oases, which is only a collection of trans-plantings from the other adjacent agricultural centres.

GENERAL SURVEY

Viewed as a whole, the African continent provides two major general complexes which gave birth to two different kinds of agriculture.

(1) *The Seed Agriculture Complex*, peculiar to open country (unforested), analogous to more or less steppe-like regions. It is characterized by the sowing of grain as the preparation for cultivation. Peoples possessing this agriculture incessantly extended it by clearing the forest zone which restricted them. These are true cereal agricultures, and it developed cradles of origin whose influence spread rapidly from West Africa to Abyssinia.

The seed agriculture complex creates a field-type landscape without gardens and without orchards. This explains the use of the plough when, by reason of the altitude, the climate is particularly suitable for the rearing of animals and their employment for draught work.

(2) *The Vegeculture Complex*, which is peculiar to the forest regions, and gave rise to small-sized cradles of agriculture in which rhizomes and tubers were developed as cultivars. It is particularly favourable for the creation of gardens and orchards close to dwelling places, and the field-type landscape is thus extremely rare. No tool other than the hoe is used. It is expressed in practice by the planting of cuttings, rhizomes, tubers, shoots, etc., as the preparation for cultivation.

Over recent centuries these differences have tended to be evened out.

SUMMARY

A search for the geographical cradles of agriculture of ancient times throws some light on the poorly dated past of the African continent. The present note studies only the *primary cradles* of the African continent's agriculture. Viewed as a whole, three separate centres are found: one in Abyssinia, one in West Africa, another in East Africa. These primary cradles still continue to be more or less independent, whereas the plants introduced later into Africa tend to cover the whole continent, wherever ecology or the economy are favourable. The Mediterranean and Egyptian cradles produced virtually nothing of their own. They are essentially secondary centres.

Within the primary cradles, the *seed agriculture group* covers the open regions, the *vegeculture group* (shoots, rhizomes, roots) spreads over areas which are or were covered by forests.

BIBLIOGRAPHY

Bois, Daniel, *Les Plantes alimentaires chez tous les Peuples et à travers les Ages* (Paris, 1927, 1929, 1934), 3 vols.

Burkill, I. H., *A Dictionary of the Economic Products of the Malay Peninsula* (London, 1935), 2 vols.

Dalziel, J. M., *The Useful Plants of West Tropical Africa* (London, 1937).

De Candolle, A., *Origine des Plantes cultivées* (Paris, 1883).

Ficalho, Condé de, *Plantas Uteis da Africa Portugueza* (Lisbonne, 1884).

Greenway, P. J., 'Origins of some East African food Plants', *The East Afr. Agri. Jour.* (1945).

Haudricourt, A. G., et Hédin, L., *L'Homme et les Plantes Cultivées* (Paris, 1943).

Jacques-Felix, Henri, 'Pour une enquête sur le Voandzou (*Voandzeia subterranea* Thou)', *L'Agronomie Tropicale* (1950), v, n⁰ 1–2, 62–73.

Murdock, George Peter, *Africa; its peoples and their culture history* (New York, 1959).

Perrier de la Bathie, H.,' Les Plantes introduites à Madagascar', *Rev. Bot. Appl. Agric. Trop.* (1931), XI, 719, 833, 920, 991; (1932), XII, 48, 128, 213.

Portères, Roland, 'Vieilles Agricultures africaines avant le XVIᵉᵐᵉ siècle. Berceaux d' Agriculture et Centres de variation', *L'Agronomie Tropicale* (Sept.–Oct. 1950), v, n⁰ 9–10, 489–507.

Portères, Roland, 'Sur la ségrégation géographique de gènes de l'*Oryza glaberrima* Steudel dans l'Ouest-Africain et sur les Centres de culture de cette espèce', *C.R. Acad. Sc. Paris* (séance du 30 Juillet 1945), t. 221, 152–53.

Portères, Roland, 'L'Aire culturale de *Digitaria Iburua* Stapf, céréale mineure de l'Ouest-African', *L'Agronomie Tropicale* (Nov.–Dec. 1946), 1, n⁰ 11–12, 589–92.

Portères, Roland, 'Une céréale mineure cultivée dans l'Oust-Africain *Brachiaria deflexa* C. E. Hubb. var *sativa* nov. var.)', *L'Agronomie Tropicale* (Janv.–Fév. 1951), VI, n⁰ 1–2, 38–42.

Portères, Roland, '*Eleusine Coracana* Gaertner. Céréale des humanités pauvres des pays tropicaux', *Bull. Inst. Franç. Afr. Noire* (Dakar, Janv.–Mars 1951), XIII, 1–78.

Portères, Roland, 'Géographie alimentaire—Berceaux Agricoles et Migrations des plantes cultivées en Afrique Intertropicale', *C.R. Soc. Biogéographie* (Paris, 1951), n⁰ 239, 16–21.

Portères, Roland, 'L'Introduction du Maïs en Afrique', *J. Agric. Trop. et Bot. Appl.* (1955), II, n⁰ 5–6, 221–32.

Portères, Roland, 'Historique sur les premiers échantillons d'*Oryza glaberrima* St. recueillis en Afrique', *J. Agric. Trop. et Bot. Appl.* (1955), II, n⁰ 10–11, 535–6.

Portères, Roland, 'Un Problème d'Ethnobotanique: relations entre le Riz flottant du Rio-Nunez et l'origine medinigerienne des Baga de la Guinée Française', *J. Agric. Trop et Bot. Appl.* (Oct.–Nov. 1955), II, n⁰ 10–11, 538–42.

Portères, Roland, 'Présence ancienne d'une variété cultivée d'*Oryza glaberrima* en Guyane Française', *J. Agric. Trop. et Bot. Appl.* (1955), II, n⁰ 12, 680.

Portères, Roland, 'Nouvelles variétés agrobotaniques de Riz Cultivés (*Oryza sativa* L. et *O. glaberrima* Steudel)', *J. Agric. Trop. et Bot. Appl.* (1955), II, n⁰ 12, 575–99.

Portères, Roland, 'Taxonomie Agrobotanique des Riz Cultivés (*O. sativa* L. et *O. glaberrima* Steud.)', *J. Agric. Trop. et Bot. Appl.* (Juillet à Dec. 1956), III, n⁰ 7 à 12, 341–84, 541–80, 627–700, 821–56.

Portères, Roland, 'Compagnonnage agraire et Génétique biogéographique chez les Riz Cultivés', *C.R. Soc. Biogéographie* (Paris, 1957), 68–99.

Portères, Roland, 'Les Appellations des Céréales en Afrique', *J. Agric. Trop. et Bot. Appl.* (1958), v, n⁰ 1 à 11 (16–34, 311–64, 454–86, 732–61); (1959), VI, n⁰ 1–2 et 4 à 7 (68–76, 189–233, 290–340).

Snowden, J. D., *The Cultivated Races of Sorghum* (London, 1936).

Stapf, O., 'Iburu and Fundi, two Cereals of Upper Guinea', *Kew Bull.* (1915), n⁰ 8, 381–6.

Vavilov, N. I., *Bases théoriques de la Sélection des Plantes*, t. 1: 'Sélection Générale' (Moscow-Leningrad, 1935), XVII + 1043 pp.

Watt, Sir George, *Dictionary of the Commercial Products of India* (London, 1908), 1 vol.

Wrigley, Christopher, 'Speculations on the Economic Prehistory of Africa', *Journal of African History* (1960), 1, 2, 189–203.

4. SPECULATIONS ON THE ECONOMIC PREHISTORY OF AFRICA

By CHRISTOPHER WRIGLEY

Apart from relatively late Semitic influence . . . the civilizations of Africa are the civilizations of the Hamites, its history the record of these peoples and of their interaction with the two other African stocks, the Negro and the Bushman, whether this influence was exerted by highly civilized Egyptians or by such wider pastoralists as are represented at the present day by the Beja and Somali. . . . The incoming Hamites were pastoral 'Europeans'—arriving wave after wave— better armed as well as quicker witted than the dark agricultural Negroes.

THESE propositions, taken from the late Professor C. G. Seligman's *Races of Africa*, are perhaps the most notorious expression of the racialist interpretation which dominated studies of the African past during the first half of the twentieth century. It is deplorable that they should have been allowed to appear in the third, posthumous edition, issued in 1957 with the blessing of most of Britain's leading Africanists and clearly intended to serve as the standard British text-book on African ethnology. The idea of negro Africa as savagery modified by the influence of European or quasi-European intruders is clearly no more than an extrapolation from the situation which has existed in very recent times; and sufficient knowledge has been accumulated to make it no longer legitimate to theorize *in vacuo* about 'waves' of invasion. Although tropical Africa has certainly received major cultural imports from time to time, the archaeological record suggests, on the whole, continuous indigenous development rather than a succession of external impacts; and the palaeontological record makes it clear that people of caucasoid type, so far from being invaders, were resident, at least in East Africa, from the remotest times with which we need concern ourselves.

The point to which I would draw attention here, however, is that the negroes were described as 'agricultural'. Nor was Seligman alone in conceding the most important of human arts to the dim-witted aboriginals. Stuhlmann had assigned the introduction of cultivation to the earlier, negro waves of imigration from Asia.[1] Baumann's 'palaeonigritic' peoples were likewise cultivators.[2] It is at first sight surprising that writers who were so firmly convinced that tropical Africa owed all the rudiments of civilization to foreigners should have been prepared to admit that it possessed the basis of all civilized life before it came under the influence of caucasoid

[1] *Beiträge zur Kulturgeschichte von Ostafrika* (Berlin, 1909), 824–8.
[2] H. Baumann and D. Westermann, *Les Peuples et les Civilisations de l'Afrique* (Paris, 1948).

59

intruders. Part of the explanation, no doubt, lies in the deep-rooted north
European upper-class prejudice which made it easy to associate tillers of
the soil with inferior status and capacity. A more important point, however, is that in Seligman's day the historic significance of the development
of agriculture had not yet been fully appreciated. It was even commonly
believed that hoe-cultivation was the oldest of all forms of economy.[3]
Given this premise, there was no problem. In so far as the question was
discussed at all, it was merely assumed that the negroes had brought their
hoe-culture with them from their supposed homeland somewhere in Asia,
whence they had emigrated before the evolution of the superior white race
and of its superior plough-culture.

But with the progress of prehistoric archaeology in the Middle East
during the inter-war years a new picture was taking shape. Gordon Childe,
especially, taught us[4] to believe that the emergence of a food-producing
economy was the great divide in human history; that this change took place
in the Middle East quite abruptly in the fifth or sixth millennium B.C.;
that it was closely linked with a number of other technical innovations,
notably pottery and polished stone implements; and that this 'neolithic'
complex was subsequently diffused to other areas of the world. Now in
Africa south of the Sahara assemblages of the classical neolithic type have
been found only in Ethiopia[5] and Kenya[6], and unequivocal evidence for the
practice of agriculture is lacking except in Iron Age sites. There is thus a
consensus of opinion among archaeologists, not only that the agriculture of
tropical Africa derives from the example of the Middle East, but also that
in this part of the world Middle Eastern influence was feeble and belated.
On this point, Alimen's summing up may be taken as representative.

La profonde révolution de l'économie humaine qu'est le Néolithique, appor-
tant l'agriculture et la domestication, ne se marque vraiment que dans l'Afrique
septentrionale, la seule à vrai dire qui, comme l'Europe, soit assez facile à
cultiver. Dans de nombreuses portions d'Afrique, les conditions désertiques ou
tropicales ont été, pour les premiers cultivateurs, un trop grave handicap.... La
civilisation néolithique apparait donc comme étrangère au continent africain,
où elle pénètre par le N.[7]

Childe's concept of the 'neolithic revolution', followed at the close of the
fourth millennium by the 'urban revolution', was too obviously inspired
by the nineteenth-century (and especially the Marxist) scheme of sharply
defined historical stages to carry complete conviction; and recent dis-

[3] See for instance M. Weber, *General Economic History* (London, 1923), 1.
[4] V. Gordon Childe, *New Light on the Most Ancient East* (London, 1934); *What Happened in History* (Harmondsworth, 1942).
[5] G. Bailloud, 'La Préhistoire de l'Ethiopie', in M. Albospeyre and others, *Mer Rouge— Afrique Orientale* (Paris, 1959), 24.
[6] L. S. B. Leakey, *The Stone Age Cultures of Kenya Colony* (Cambridge, 1931); Sonia Cole, *The Prehistory of East Africa* (Harmondsworth, 1954).
[7] H. Alimen, *Préhistoire de l'Afrique* (Paris, 1955), 496–7. This statement is not free from ambiguity, and I have therefore left it in the original rather than use the English translation by A. H. Brodrick, *The Prehistory of Africa* (London, 1957), 427.

coveries have made rather drastic modifications necessary. In the first place, the date of the transition to agriculture has been pushed further and further back into the past, until the excavations at Jericho have brought it back to the eighth millennium at least.[8] Moreover, this first Jericho, which came into existence four thousand years or more before the 'urban revolution', was already, by any ordinary standard, a town. Secondly, the neolithic complex has tended to disintegrate. Pottery, for example, which was formerly regarded as an integral part of the complex, has turned up in non-neolithic contexts in the Ertebølle culture of northern Europe, in the Khartoum mesolithic[9] and in the upper Capsian of Kenya.[10]

Meanwhile, the idea of agriculture as a relatively late and revolutionary development in human history has been opposed from a quite different quarter. The arguments of American ethnobotanists such as Ames, Anderson and Sauer[11] have made almost no impact on prehistorical thinking in Britain, which is virtually monopolized by archaeology. They nevertheless appear to deserve very serious consideration. Most of the world's crop plants were already in use by 3000 B.C., some of them in highly evolved forms which imply a very long prior history. Nor is it likely that the main staples of modern agriculture were the first to be developed, for in out-of-the-way places there are still to be found a number of inferior crop plants, such as 'Job's tears' and the grain amaranths, which would hardly have been taken into use when wheat or rice or maize was already available. The botanical evidence, in fact, points to the conclusion that the flowering of the neolithic economy in the Middle East was preceded by a long period of rudimentary and experimental agriculture, the beginnings of which may go back well into the Pleistocene epoch. Nor were these beginnings necessarily in the Middle East, or concerned with cereals. Sauer believes that tropical gardening, based on the propagation of fruit and tuber plants, is ancestral to the sowing of field crops, and that its origins lie in south-east Asia.

Professor G. P. Murdock has now applied similar botanical arguments to the problem of the origins of agriculture in tropical Africa.[12] Pointing out that the crop plants of this region are quite different from those of the Middle East, and that many of them—notably the millets (*Sorghum vulgare*, *Eleusine coracana* and *Pennisetum typhoides*), simsim (*Sesamum orientale*), certain pulses (*Vigna sinensis*, *Cajanus cajan*) and the Guinea yam (*Dioscorea cayenensis*)—are certainly or probably indigenous, he makes the forthright assertion that agriculture was initiated in the upper Niger area by the ancestors of the Mande-speaking peoples about 5000 B.C., and that they took this step independently of, though somewhat later than, the peoples of south-western Asia.

Murdoch

[8] K. M. Kenyon, *Digging up Jericho* (London, 1957).
[9] A. J. Arkell, *Early Khartoum* (London, 1949).　　　　[10] Leakey, op. cit. 103.
[11] Oakes Ames, *Economic Annuals and Human Culture* (New York, 1939); Edgar Anderson, *Plants, Man and Life* (New York, 1952); Carl O. Sauer, *Agricultural Origins and Dispersals* (New York, 1952).
[12] *Africa: Its Peoples and Their Culture History* (New York, 1959), 64ff.

For such precision of date and place there does not appear to be any adequate justification. Nor is it, on the whole, likely that the starting-point of African agriculture was in the western Sudan. Murdock's main argument for this choice is based on plant distribution: certain crops, such as fonio (*Digitaria exilis*) are peculiar to West Africa. But this hardly proves his point, for such plants might well have been added by West Africans to the stock of cultigens which they had received, or brought with them, from the east. We might even turn the argument about, and ask why, if sorghum and pearl millet spread from west to east, fonio should have failed to accompany them. A secondary argument, founded on the wide extension of the 'Nigritic', or Niger-Congo language-family, and especially of its Mande branch, is even less convincing. The dispersion of Mande languages can more plausibly be attributed to empire-building and trading activities at a very much later date. The Sudanic language-family, centred on the upper Nile area, has ramifications hardly less wide than those of Niger-Congo; and it is in the region of the eastern Sudan and western Ethiopia that the birthplace of most African crop plants is probably to be sought. Botanists have long regarded Ethiopia as a major centre of agricultural evolution—not merely, as Murdock suggests, because this was the only part of tropical Africa to be visited by Vavilov, but because its wide range of soils and climates makes it ideally suited to plant variation and ennoblement.

Whereas criticisms may be made of his more specific hypotheses, Murdock's main contention, that the antiquity of African agriculture is much greater than archaeologists have been willing to concede, is surely well founded. Not only is the continent the original home of a large number of cultivated plants, but some at least of these species have proliferated into a great many different races and varieties,[13] clearly indicating a history that cannot reasonably be fitted into the two-thousand-year span of the African Iron Age. Many of them, moreover, recur in India; and, again, the number of Indian varieties, as well as their concentration in the interior of the sub-continent, suggests that their introduction cannot have been at all recent. The most concrete evidence, however, comes from the study of the cotton plant.

The cultivated cottons of the Old World belong to two species, *Gossypium herbaceum* and *G. arboreum*. The latter, which is fairly certainly the more recently evolved, is known to have been woven at Mohenjodaro in the third millennium B.C. Varieties of the older *herbaceum* species are widely distributed in northern Africa, Persia and central Asia, but until recently its original centre was believed to have been in or near southern Arabia. It is well established that the wild ancestor of the true cottons was *G. anomalum*, a desert shrub which grows only on the fringes of the Sahara and the Kalahari. Between this plant and the most primitive cultivated plants, however, there is a morphological as well as a geographical gap. Sir Joseph Hutchinson (to whom I am indebted for much patient tuition on this subject) argued that the former could be filled only by *G. herbaceum* race

[13] See J. D. Snowden, *The Cultivated Races of Sorghum* (London, 1936).

africanum, a crude but lint-bearing cotton which is found growing wild in a belt running across southern Africa from Ngamiland to Mozambique.[14] The geographical gap remained, and could be bridged only by one of two very improbable hypotheses. Either, as Hutchinson himself suggested, seeds of the wild *africanum* were gathered and taken home by Arabian seafarers, who must therefore be supposed to have reached southern Africa at least as early as 3000 B.C. Or cotton spread northwards across East Africa under cultivation, so that agriculture must be supposed to have been practised in *southern* Africa at an equally early date. Now, however, an alternative theory has been proposed. It is suggested that a primitive *herbaceum*, ancestral both to the *africanum* race and to the known cultivated cottons, was developed in south-west Ethiopia.[15] However this may be, the combined evidence from cotton genetics and Indian archaeology leaves no reasonable escape from the conclusion that cotton was being cultivated in Africa before 3000 B.C.—and probably long before, since the plant had to undergo considerable evolutionary change before being used in the Indus Valley civilization. Further, although cotton may have been grown for its oil long before its lint was spun, it is not likely to have been among the first African plants to be domesticated.

The theory of the high antiquity of African agriculture receives additional support—more nebulous perhaps, but also, in my view, convincing—from the linguistic configuration of the continent. The languages of tropical Africa are legion, and, apart from Bantu, there are no large groups having an indisputable common descent. Nevertheless, on the most widely accepted view, the great majority of languages do belong to three main stocks: the Hamito-Semitic family, including the Chadic and Cushitic groups; the Niger-Congo family, comprising most of the languages of West Africa together with Bantu; and the Sudanic family, occupying most of north-central Africa.[16] The Hamito-Semitic family extends over north Africa and western Asia, but the other two stocks are confined within, and clearly indigenous to, the regions south of the Sahara.[17] This configuration seems to me to be radically inconsistent with the view that until about two thousand years ago these regions were inhabited only by a few primitive hunters. Are we to suppose that peoples equipped with a knowledge of metallurgy and agriculture, and presumably multiplying and expanding with great rapidity, would everywhere have adopted the speech of the scanty groups of aboriginals whom they found in the land? Common sense forbids, and so does analogy. On the contrary, many of the surviving

[14] J. B. Hutchinson, 'Evidence on the origin of the Old World Cottons', *Heredity* (1954), VIII.

[15] G. Edward Nicholson, 'The Production, History, Uses and Relationships of Cottons in Ethiopia', *Economic Botany* (1960), XIV, 3.

[16] J. H. Greenberg, *Studies in African Linguistic Classification* (New Haven, 1955). We learn from Murdock (op. cit. 14) that Greenberg now tentatively includes in the Sudanic family most of the minor groups which he formerly classed as independent.

[17] Bantu has been related, by one student or another, to nearly every language-family of the Old World, except Indo-European. These theories, however, are sheer fantasy.

independent hunters—such as the Pygmies, the Ndorobo and the Bergdama—speak the language of their agricultural or pastoral neighbours.
Yet, if the first cultivators did not thus lose their language, the orthodox
conception of African prehistory cannot be reconciled with the range of
African linguistic variation. What we should expect, if agriculture were a
recent innovation, would be a wide network of closely related languages.
This is just what we do find in the Bantu third of Africa, but elsewhere
we are confronted by wide networks of languages which are only very
remotely related. The more ambitious claims of glottochronology may or
may not command conviction, but on no reasonable concept of relative
linguistic distance can a period of less than several millennia be allotted
to the differentiation which has taken place within the Niger-Congo and
Sudanic stocks. And it seems at least a plausible assumption that this
differentiation accompanied the spread of an agricultural economy.

Against these arguments are arrayed the negative inferences from
archaeology. In the first place, there is the rarity in tropical Africa of
assemblages that are strictly comparable with those of Middle Eastern and
European neolithic sites. It is, however, not true that neolithic tools are
absent, for the characteristic ground stone axe has been found sporadically
in almost every part of the continent. It is admittedly possible, even probable, that neither these implements nor the more elaborate neolithic
assemblages of Ethiopia and Kenya belong to a period which antedates the
Iron Age by any very wide margin. On the other hand, although polished
stone tools and the cultivation of the soil are so closely linked in the minds
of archaeologists that the term 'neolithic' has virtually come to *mean*
'food-producing', there is in reality no universal or necessary connexion
between these two techniques. Even in the last century, many thoroughly
agricultural African tribes did not use either iron or stone hoes. Moreover,
in the equipment of 'neolithic' Jericho there was an 'almost complete
lack . . . of picks or hoes for working the soil'.[18] An agriculture sufficiently
advanced to support a town of perhaps three thousand people was apparently carried on by means of the stone-weighted digging-stick, such as was
used by many prehistoric African peoples who have not been accorded
neolithic status.

A much more serious difficulty is the absence of direct evidence for
agriculture, in the form of actual grains or of grain-impressions on potsherds. For this reason Arkell has rejected the view that the authors of his
Khartoum mesolithic culture were agriculturalists, even though their
equipment included not only pottery but also large numbers of grinding-
stones. He assumes that the sole function of the latter was the preparation
of ochre, with which indeed many of them were stained. It is not for a
layman to dispute this conclusion. Yet I am inclined to think that it should
not weigh decisively against the botanical and linguistic evidence for the
great antiquity of African agriculture.

[18] Kenyon, op. cit. 57.

To affirm that the cultivation of the soil has a long history in tropical Africa, however, is not necessarily to affirm, as Murdock does, that it had no historical connexion with developments in the Middle East. The fact that the Middle Eastern crops do not occur in negro Africa is not in itself conclusive, for in few parts of negro Africa can they be grown with satis-factory results. As cultivating peoples moved southwards they might have discarded wheat and barley in favour of tropical grasses better suited to their new environment, much as in northern Europe these plants were partially displaced by oats and rye.[19] A variant on this would be a theory of 'stimulus diffusion': a tenuous culture-contact might have induced the peoples south of the Sahara to seek out and utilize their own cultivable grasses.

The case for the derivation of tropical African agriculture from the Middle East would be strengthened if it could be shown that the pottery associated with the Khartoum mesolithic and with the Upper Capsian of Kenya was, or could have been, similarly derivative. This is largely a matter of dating, and here, unfortunately, we are in an area of complete uncertainty. The neolithic site of Shaheinab in the Sudan has been dated by radio-carbon to c. 3300 B.C.; and McBurney suggests that the Khartoum mesolithic preceded it by no more than five hundred years, so making it possible to attribute the earliest Sudanese pottery to the influence of neolithic Egypt (Fayum, c. 4400 B.C.).[20] This short dating, however, seems hardly reconcilable with the marked climatic change which Arkell showed to have occurred in the interval. In Kenya, the Upper Capsian culture belongs to the latter part of the Gamblian pluvial, which Leakey equated with the last glaciation of Europe. This correlation has been seriously questioned, and a considerably lower date has been postulated for the Kenya Capsian.[21] Yet it is difficult to reduce the chronology sufficiently for the purpose now in view, for the Elmenteitan culture, which suc-ceeded the Capsian after an interval, and which produced *fine* pottery, has been dated by the varve method to about 5000 B.C.[22] On balance, therefore, it still seems likely that pottery was being made in parts of tropical Africa before it was being made in Egypt, and at least as early as it was being made anywhere in the Middle East.

On the other hand, there are indications of a different kind which tend to support the diffusionist hypothesis. I have elsewhere adduced evidence for the former presence in Uganda of myth and ritual which have Middle Eastern and Aegean affinities and which, in my view, clearly go back to the very beginnings of agricultural civilization.[23] And the first Jericho seems

[19] The analogy is not exact, however, for oats and rye were themselves originally Middle Eastern plants.
[20] C. B. M. McBurney, *The Stone Age of Northern Africa* (Harmondsworth, 1960), 244.
[21] F. E. Zeuner, *Dating the Past* (London, 4th edn., 1958), 249ff. Alimen, op. cit. 249–50. McBurney, op. cit. 59–60.
[22] Alimen, op. cit. 251.
[23] C. C. Wrigley, 'Kimera', *Uganda Journal* (1959), XXIII, 38.

to be linked to the lacustrine region of central Africa by its beehive huts and, more specifically, by the curious custom of removing the jawbones of the dead.[24]

The whole question of diffusion and independent development in relation to agriculture seems to need re-examination. I believe, indeed, that the basic idea of putting seeds (or tubers) back into the ground was a genuine and unique invention. For it is hard to accept that man should have lived on the earth for tens of thousands of years, during which this idea occurred to no-one, and that it should then have occurred to several people independently at what was, prehistorically speaking, almost the same moment. On the other hand, we have to account for the existence in different parts of the world of agricultural systems based on entirely different sets of cultigens and showing no definite trace of historical connexion. These considerations can be reconciled by accepting both the antiquity and the gradualness of agricultural development. The first crucial step having been taken, there ensued, not a revolutionary change in the ways of human life, but a period of several thousand years, in which, over steadily widening areas of the world, people were practising a very rudimentary and part-time agriculture, collecting seeds of all kinds and sometimes re-sowing them. Eventually, in each region, certain of the plants so assisted became productive enough to be used to the exclusion of all others, and to provide the main instead of the subsidiary source of food. The period of collection and experimentation then came to an end, and regular agriculture began.

It is even conceivable that, in this limited sense, the agriculture of tropical Africa is original and that of the Middle East derivative. For this there can be no kind of proof, but certain general considerations may be adduced. It was formerly supposed that agriculture arose in the Middle East as a response to a shift in the storm-track, the Saharan or Arabian hunters deciding that as the game supply was giving out they had better go down into the valley and grow wheat instead. It is not difficult to see the essential implausibility of this theory. The Industrial Revolution may indeed be looked on as a response to the challenge presented by rapid population growth and, indirectly, by exhaustion of the timber supply. But it could have been carried out only by a society that was already exceptionally wealthy, well organized and technically proficient. And in the same way it is likely that agriculture was initiated by a culturally advanced people living in a favourable setting; it was probably not cultivation but irrigation that was forced on the peoples of Egypt and western Asia by an increasingly unpropitious climate.

Now, if a high chronology can be accepted for the Khartoum mesolithic and the Kenya Capsian, we have in tropical Africa, at the relevant period, societies of high technical capacity, proved by their pottery to have attained the sedentary condition which is the basic pre-condition of agriculture.

[24] Kenyon, op. cit. 62. Cf. J. Roscoe, *The Baganda* (London, 1911), 109.

And from the ecological aspect I must take issue with Alimen's condition that, apart from its northern fringe, the African continent was ill-suited to cultivators. Much the greater part of Africa is neither desert nor jungle, and its wide savannahs, with their easily worked soils and rapid vegetation growth, surely provided an environment that was *better* suited to a primitive agriculture than either the arid sub-tropics or the cold dark forests of the temperate zone. It is true that tropical soils are mostly poor and that agriculture did not possess here the rich potentialities that belonged to it in some other regions. But those potentialities were realized only by a long effort of adaptation, organization and invention. The agricultural systems of tropical Africa remained primitive precisely because they were in the first place so easily established.

Besides the agriculture of the savannahs, there is also the fundamentally different system which prevails in the forest and woodland zone of Africa. And whereas Murdock claims an independent and ancient origin for the former, he believes the latter to be exotic and relatively recent. Some of the most important of the forest-zone crops are undoubtedly native to south-east Asia: the banana or plantain, at least two species of yam (*Dioscorea alata* and *D. esculenta*)[25] and taro or cocoyam (*Colocasia antiquorum*), as well as sugar-cane. Murdock's view is that the forests of west and central Africa could not have been effectively occupied by cultivating peoples until after the introduction of these 'Malaysian' plants, an event which he dates, mainly on lexicostatistical grounds, to the first centuries of the Christian era. The manner of their coming he describes as follows.[26]

People of southern Borneo, having become active in maritime trade, made their way round the shores of the Indian Ocean and arrived on the East African coast. Thence some of them set out to colonize Madagascar, where their language is still spoken. Meanwhile their crop plants had been adopted by the Cushitic peoples who were already practising the savannah type of agriculture both in Kenya and in Uganda. From Uganda they were transmitted to the central and western Sudan. Thus equipped, the West African cultivators began to move into the Guinea forest zone. One tribe, however, whose language formed the Bantu sub-sub-sub-group of the Niger-Congo family, advanced into the Congo basin, eventually emerging on to the savannah to occupy most of central and south-eastern Africa. Here, however, a problem arises. During their sojourn in the forests the Bantu had inevitably lost their savannah crops. How then did they re-acquire them? Answer: some of them went first to Uganda, where they borrowed sorghum and eleusine millet from the Cushites and passed them on, together with monarchical institutions, to their brethren in the Congo, who were then able to press on with the occupation of the lands to the east and the south.

This account is almost entirely conjectural, unnecessarily complicated

[25] *D. bulbifera* is often added to this list, but the attribution of certain African yams to this Asiatic species is not certain.

[26] Op. cit. 207 ff.

and intrinsically improbable. These drought-hating plants would have had great difficulty in crossing the arid wilderness of eastern Kenya. It would be much better, as well as simpler, to bring them straight across the ocean to Madagascar, where an Indonesian invasion is attested by the incontrovertible testimony of language, and then to ferry them over to the Zambezi valley, whence they could spread without difficulty over central and west Africa. In addition, the assumption that tropical gardening, the cultivation of fruits and tubers, began in Africa only with the advent of the Malaysian plants is very much open to question. It is evident that the Indonesians did not themselves colonize the mainland in any numbers, or they would have left definite ethnic and linguistic traces of their presence. Their crops must therefore have been adopted and diffused by the indigenous population. This is unlikely to have happened, at any rate with the speed with which it must have happened, unless the aborigines had already been familiar with a similar form of agriculture. Now Murdock's main reason for selecting a more northerly and roundabout route is his belief that archaeology denies the existence at this time of any kind of agriculture southward of northern Tanganyika, and, secondly, his total and literal acceptance of Greenberg's theory of the derivation of the Bantu languages from the Niger-Congo family. As to the second, the recent work of Bantu linguists in England suggests that, while the ultimate derivation of Bantu from Niger-Congo may be accepted, there was nevertheless a secondary fanning-out of Bantu peoples from a dispersal area situated towards the south-centre of their present sphere. As to the first argument, the evidence is not unambiguous. There are definite traces of a prehistoric 'vegeculture' in central and south-central Africa, though it has been suggested that its practitioners, in spite of their wholly lithic equipment, may have been contemporary with iron-using peoples.[27] The botanical evidence points in the same direction. Not all the forest-zone crops of Africa are exotics. The 'Kaffir potato' (*Coleus spp.*) and the Guinea yam are undoubtedly native; and in central as well as west Africa there are a number of other yam species which are found both in wild and in cultivated forms.[28] These, being of inferior quality, are now rarely used. But they exist, and their existence shows that some sort of forest gardening could have been and probably was practised before the coming of the banana and the Asiatic yams. It is also perhaps significant that in a great number of languages, distributed across the continent from Tanganyika to Guinea, the word for 'yam' contains the element *ku*.[29] This element is undoubtedly indigenous, being identical with a common West African verb meaning 'to dig'. In Bantu languages it occurs in a variety

[27] J. Desmond Clark, *The Prehistory of Southern Africa* (Harmondsworth, 1959), 191–6

[28] See articles in the *Revue Internationale de Botanique Appliquée et d'Agriculture Tropical* by A. Chevalier, xxxii (1952), H. Jaques-Felix, xxxvii (1947), and A. Walker, xxxii (1952)

[29] E.g. Mende, Nalu, Avatime *ku*; Teke, Chagga, Kikuyu *-kwa*; Kamba *-kwatsı* Taveta *-likwa*; Mabea *nankwa*; Zigua *-kudumbe*; Ruanda *-tuku*; perhaps Bemba *-rungwa* Shambala, Luba *-lungu* (< *-rukwa*, *-luku*?). See D. Westermann, *Die Westliche Sudansprachen* (Berlin 1927), 233 and H. H. Johnston, *A Comparative Study of th Bantu and Semi Bantu Languages* (London, 1923), II, 421.

of compound forms, which cannot be derived from a single ancestor. In central and east Africa, therefore, the use of these words, and of the plant they denote, must have preceded the migrations of the Bantu. Thus it appears that the Malaysian plants, though very valuable acquisitions, did not have quite the revolutionary significance that Murdock has assigned to them, that there was already an ancient province of yam culture, extending over the whole forest and woodland zone of Africa.

Whatever may be said about agriculture, it is quite certain that animal husbandry did *not* develop independently in Africa south of the Sahara where the fauna does not and did not include possible ancestors of the domestic cow, sheep or goat. As to the time and manner of their coming there is very little direct evidence. Sheep and goats were present at Shaheinab in the late fourth millennium,[30] cattle and sheep in the Kenya Neolithic, probably not much later. Domestic animals are not attested archaeologically in other areas until quite recent times, but it seems highly improbable that, having crossed the main geographical barrier, they should not soon have spread over the remainder of the continent. The original route of entry almost certainly led from Egypt by way of the Nile valley. The other route sometimes suggested, from Arabia across the Horn, is ruled out by the absence of all but the most primitive cultures in south Arabia until the first millennium B.C.[31] and in Somalia until the Christian era.[32] Moreover the word for 'cow', in a great variety of Sudanese and East African languages, can be referred to the Nubian form, *ti*.[33]

Murdock makes in this connexion an extremely important and original point. Stock-keeping in Africa is by no means co-extensive with the practice of milking. In West Africa, notably, cattle are milked only by the Fulani and in areas of Fulani influence. From this he infers that the Nubians borrowed cattle from Egypt 'without the associated milking complex'.[34] The argument might, I think, be taken further: the Nubians acquired cattle before the practice of milking had begun. It is noteworthy that the un-milked cattle of the West African forest zone and pockets of central Africa are dwarf shorthorns of the species *Bos brachyceros*.[35] Their distribution in the least accessible parts of the continent (where they have lived long enough to acquire immunity from trypanosomiasis) implies that they were among the first, if not the first, arrivals. Yet *Bos brachyceros* is generally believed to have been evolved later than the humpless longhorn, *Bos primigenius*, and to have reached Egypt only in early dynastic times. These

[30] A. J. Arkell, *Shaheinab* (London, 1953), 17.

[31] G. Caton Thompson, *The Tombs and Moon Temple of Hureidha* (London, 1944).

[32] J. Desmond Clark, *The Prehistoric Cultures of the Horn of Africa* (Cambridge, 1954).

[33] E.g. Moru-Madi *ti*; Interlacustrine Bantu *-te*; Mbugu *dee*; Temein *nteng*; Shilluk *dyang*; Nandi *tany*, pl. *tic*; Merarit *te*. The numerous West African forms in *ni* perhaps have the same origin. These data were kindly supplied to me by Professor A. N. Tucker and Miss Bryan, who are not responsible for the linguistic and other inferences drawn.

[34] Op. cit. 19, 44.

[35] J. Boettger, *Die Afrikanische Haustiere* (Jena, 1958); Colonial Office, *The Indigenous Cattle of the British Dependent Territories in Africa* (London, 1957).

assumptions, however, may need revision. The first cattle to reach north-west Europe, in the third millennium, were shorthorns, said to bear a close resemblance to those of West Africa.[36] Moreover, in association with the pre-neolithic Sebilian culture of upper Egypt there are bones both of *primigenius* and of *brachyceros* cattle.[37] The Sebilians are assumed to have been a purely hunting people and the bones to be those of wild animals. But is it not possible that they were in fact the domesticators of cattle, and that tropical Africa acquired its first stock from this source in the fifth millennium or earlier?

It has generally been believed hitherto that the pastoral and agricultural economies of Africa were originally quite distinct; that pastoralism was a racial characteristic (Baumann, for instance, used cattle-herding as irrefragable evidence for the presence of his Eastern Hamites); and even, absurdly, that the pastoralists were responsible for the transmission of the elements of higher culture to the Negro peoples and for the original construction of complex political systems. Murdock's argument, as he sees, completes the work of destruction that Greenberg began when he severed the supposed link between a pastoral economy and Hamitic forms of speech. The extensive dairying of such peoples as the Fulani, the Masai and the Herero, so far from being an original trait, must be a secondary and comparatively recent development. Cattle, in Africa as elsewhere, must have been originally the property of agricultural peoples.

The innovation, moreover, was a disastrous one. The fourth chapter of Genesis is an impudent libel, for Abel, not Cain, has always been the killer. It is one of Murdock's chief achievements to have seen the herdsmen of Africa, from the Masai to the Hilalian Arabs, for the destructive barbarians that they were—chief disturbers of the peace of the continent, and, we may add, chief spoliators of its soil.

Up to the end of the Egyptian Neolithic we have assumed that tropical Africa was in tenuous contact with Egypt and, through Egypt, with western Asia. In the case of agriculture and pottery, contact is only probable, and the direction of movement uncertain. In the case of domestic animals neither the fact of contact nor its orientation can be in any doubt. Towards the end of the fourth millennium, however, the general picture undergoes a sharp, and for tropical Africa a disastrous, change. Just at the time when the northern peoples were constructing urban civilizations, characterized by large-scale social organization, metallurgy and writing, it seems that insuperable geographical obstacles arose to sunder them from the peoples of the south. For tropical Africa had no bronze or copper age; and, although this deficiency might possibly be accounted for by the scarcity of the relevant mineral deposits, the most likely inference is that between the fourth and the first millennium it was totally out of contact with the north. This period of isolation, in the post-Makalian dry phase, was probably the

---

[36] D. Hill, 'The Origins of West African Cattle', *Ibadan* (1957), no. 1.
[37] Alimen, op. cit. 126; D. M. A. Bate in A. J. Arkell, *Early Khartoum*, 272–3.

most crucial in the whole long history of the region. It was then that it fell decisively behind North Africa and most of Eurasia, and acquired that character of technical and cultural backwardness which even the advent of the Iron Age could not entirely alter.

The technique of iron-working did succeed in crossing the Sahara without any very undue time-lag, reaching Nigeria shortly before and south central Africa shortly after the time of Christ. There seems little reason to doubt that the mediators of this technique were the people of Meroe in upper Nubia. It is, however, doubtful whether it spread directly southward into central Africa. The tribes of the southern Sudan, who might have been expected to have experienced the earliest and most intensive influences of Nile Valley civilization, notoriously remained among the most primitive, from the point of view of material culture, in the entire continent; and it seems that the swamps of the Bahr-al-Ghazal and the arid steppes lying between the upper Nile and the mountains of Ethiopia long acted as a barrier to the passage of iron-age cultures, which were forced to penetrate southward by a more devious route.

The immensity of the area covered by the closely related group of Bantu languages calls out for explanation. Behind these vast and evidently quite recent movements there must have been a powerful dynamic. Murdock's theory, that the dynamic was provided by the acquisition of bananas, fails to account for the Bantu penetration of large areas in which the banana could have been of little or no use; and his solution of this difficulty is too involved to be readily accepted. Moreover, it could be valid only on the assumption that the banana reached central Africa from the north-west, and that it entered a land which was previously devoid of crops. I have argued, however, that bananas arrived first in south-east Africa, which is certainly not the homeland of the Bantu, and that they were adopted by people who were already cultivators. If these things are so, it might be a reasonable hypothesis that the acquisition of bananas by the Bantu when some of them were already settled in the latitude of the Zambezi might have produced important secondary migrations into favourable areas, but we must still look elsewhere for the asset which enabled the first Bantu-speakers to impose themselves and their language on these pre-existent agricultural societies. I do not see what that asset could have been unless it were the iron spear. Plausible *a priori*, this theory finds support in the fact that the early iron-using Nok culture impinges on the central Benue valley, which Greenberg has selected as the probable homeland of the Bantu.[38] Thus I see these people, not as agriculturalists spreading out over a virtually empty land, but as a dominant minority, specialized to hunting with the spear, constantly attracting new adherents (as many east and central African traditions actually affirm) by their fabulous prestige as suppliers of meat, constantly throwing off new bands of migratory adventurers, until the whole southern sub-continent was iron-using and Bantu-speaking.

[38] Greenberg, op. cit. 116.

This story, however, is probably an over-simplification, for it is necessary also to account for the distinction, clearly visible in the archaeological record of southern Africa, between the peaceful, unstratified society of its Iron Age A and the complex warlike states that succeeded them.[39] It is possible that there were two 'waves' of Bantu immigration, or that the Bantu civilization of Rhodesia underwent a profound internal change as the result of the development of the gold trade. There are, however, some indications, especially from the associated pottery, that the 'A' cultures derived from the north-east, perhaps ultimately from the 'Azanian' coast, and were therefore not Bantu.[40] If so, the later Bantu ascendancy would be attributed, not to metallurgy as such, but to the military organization and ethos which arose from the full exploitation of the iron spear.

The coming of iron technology must indeed have brought about far-reaching changes in every branch of African life. But if there is any substance in the arguments presented in this paper there can be no warrant for the common assumption that it made for a complete break with the past, and that the history of Africa is virtually coterminous with the Iron Age—as is implied, for example, in Mr Basil Davidson's recent book.[41]

The orthodox picture of African prehistory presents, indeed, a curiously unconformable appearance. Up to a point, the record is one of extraordinary continuity. From the first chipped pebbles to the cultures of almost modern times there is unbroken linear evolution—with one possible interruption represented by the blade-using cultures of late pluvial times. Even the Kenya Neolithic shows clear links with what had gone before. But as we approach the threshold of history this continuity is abruptly shattered. The whole of Africa's enormous past is bundled off into the Kalahari with the Bushmen, and the stage is cleared for the enactment of a new story with a new cast. First, we are told, the Negro appears from nowhere and takes possession of the land. Later, a ghostly horde of civilized Hamites, having apparently no connexion with the 'proto-Hamites' long resident in the land, marches across eastern Africa, constructing roads and terraces and irrigation systems and founding elaborate political systems.[42] These then disappear into the mists from which they came, and their civilizations fade into the light of common Bantu day.

All this is very odd. There is really no need to make a mystery of the emergence of 'the Negro'. The various physical traits which make up this concept were presumably gradual deviations, for the most part environmentally determined, from the less specialized forms of *Homo sapiens* which occupied Africa in the pluvial epoch. (Though not visible in the archaeological record until perhaps ten thousand years ago, this evolutionary trend may have begun much earlier in the forest zone, where

[39] J. Desmond Clark, *The Prehistory of Southern Africa*; R. F. H. Summers; *Inyanga* (Cambridge, 1957). [40] Murdock, op. cit. 210.
[41] *Old Africa Rediscovered* (London, 1959).
[42] Cole, op. cit. 275 ff. Cf. H. A. Wieschoff, *The Zimbabwe-Monomotapa Culture* (Wisconsin, 1941).

evidence is lacking.) Nor is there anything specially mysterious about the outburst of engineering activity that clearly took place in many parts of east and central Africa between 500 and 1500 A.D. It was the product of iron tools and of the political organization associated with the iron spear— both, I have suggested, brought thither from the west. Nor, again, need we be puzzled by the disintegration of most of the Bantu states and the dereliction of their works, or attribute these disasters to that *diabolus ex machina*, the slave trade. A 'dark age', after all, is a familiar historical phenomenon, signifying merely that organization has broken down. The cause of the breakdown here was undoubtedly again the iron spear. It is not for nothing that Ogun, god of smiths, is also god of war. Unlike Bronze Age kingdoms, whose rulers could easily monopolize the raw materials of military power, the kingdoms of the Early Iron Age are almost necessarily ephemeral, for in these conditions every young man can say with Archilochus, *mutatis mutandis*: 'My spear wins bread, my spear wins Thracian wine.' Where this is said, the centre cannot hold. The sackers of cities soon gain ascendancy over the builders. Nor was there here an active commerce such as made the dark age of post-Mycenean Greece a relatively brief interlude. Indeed, the misfortune of most parts of eastern Africa was not that they had to endure the slave trade but that they had no trade at all. Where commercial possibilities did exist, as on the coast and in the region of the Rhodesian gold-field, Bantu civilization was exceptionally vigorous and long-sustained.

5. ASPECTS OF EVOLUTION AND ECOLOGY OF TSETSE FLIES AND TRYPANOSOMIASIS IN PREHISTORIC AFRICAN ENVIRONMENT

By FRANK L. LAMBRECHT[1]

Introduction

THE history of human populations has been wrought by geographical and geological factors, the effects of natural selection and, later, by complex social interaction. An important biological factor in the evolution of hominid forms must have been their susceptibility to pathogenic organisms. Each time new animal forms arise, they start building up increasingly complex parasitic associations. Their survival will depend on how they will react to this challenge, as well as to other factors of the environment in which they elect to live. Interaction between parasite and host may theoretically take the following courses: (1) the parasite is rejected because the host is resistant, i.e. offers an environment unsuitable for development, or (2) the parasite finds conditions suitable for multiplication, in which case further developments form a spectrum, with excessive multiplication leading to a high mortality of the host at one end, and multiplication slowing down and leading either to rejection of the parasite (e.g. through acquired immunity) or to a balance in which the parasite becomes a commensal, possibly becoming dangerous again when conditions upset the physiology of the host. In course of time, a parasite population and its host population tend to adapt to each other, the parasite ceases to be harmful, and a balance may be reached where parasite and host become mutually beneficial. Classical examples of the latter stage are the specialized cellulose-digestive protozoa in the gut of termites and the bacterial flora in the rumen of cattle. This gradual development of mutual adaptation between parasite and host is accepted as a general rule although it cannot be accepted as being without exceptions.

The degree of tolerance, resistance or susceptibility of a certain animal regarding a given parasitic infection is not necessarily transferred to its phylogenetic successors. Also, parasitic organisms have their own evolution during which new forms and species appear and against which existing immunity mechanisms may be ineffective. Certain viruses may very well be such a new type of parasites. On the other hand, our body

[1] Part of this work was indirectly supported by a grant for the study of endoparasites of Oriental primates by the U.S. Armed Forces Epidemiological Board (Contract DA-49-193-MD-2291).

is probably destroying scores of micro-organisms of which we are not aware.

In many instances parasitism, in conjunction with predation, helps to control excessive growth of animal and plant populations.

Because of superior technology developed only in the last two hundred years or so, man has been able to upset the 'natural' weeding-out of the human population through parasites. Without the application of modern medicine, the human population would be far less than the present-day figure. The longevity of the Neanderthal man was, according to Deevey,[2] about 29 years; in medieval times it was about 35 years, and, for the U.S.A. in 1950, 70 years. There is not much difference between the longevity of the Neanderthal man of about 100,000 years ago and that of the medieval man of barely 500 years ago. The amazing recent increase in the span of life dates from recent advances in scientific medicine and hygiene.

Infectious diseases have been known as long as written history. Evil spirits, bodily 'humours', miasmas, filth and the like were said to be the cause until Pasteur, Lister and other microbiologists began to realize that man, and other animal forms, were constantly challenged by organisms too small for the naked eye to see. Among the diseases known to be caused by protozoa, malaria was feared from very long antiquity. Although many African tribes believed that the disease was caused by the bite of the mosquito, Westerners believed it to be due to poisonous air rising from swamps—until at the end of the last century Ronald Ross discovered it was transmitted by the mosquitoes living in the swamps. It was later found that the *Plasmodium* parasite went through a complex life cycle, partly in mosquitoes which ingested infected blood, partly in the liver and blood-cells of the vertebrate host. It has been found that a number of mammal hosts have their own forms of malaria.

Transmission of pathogens by insect vectors was soon discovered to be very common throughout the tropics and subtropics, and even in temperate countries. One of such diseases in Africa became known as 'sleeping sickness' because of the lethargy it produced in the sick person during the later stages of the infection. It was discovered that the disease was caused by a microscopic flagellate of the genus *Trypanosoma*, and that the parasite was transmitted by the biting flies of the genus *Glossina*, commonly called tsetse flies.

Both trypanosomes and glossinas must have been present in Africa since very remote times. Glossinas are at present confined to the African continent. However, fossil impressions of flies belonging to this group have been found in the Miocene beds in North America.[3] If we eliminate

[2] Deevey, E. S. 1960. 'The Human Population', *Scientific American*, CCIII (3), 194–204.

[3] Cockerell, T. D. A. 1907. 'A Fossil Tsetse Fly in Colorado', *Nature, Lond.*, LXXVI, 414; 1909. 'Another Fossil Tsetse Fly', *Nature, Lond.*, LXXX, 128; 1919. 'New Species of North American Fossil Beetles, Cockroaches and Tsetse Flies', *Proc. U.S. Nat. Mus.*, LIV, 301–11.

the very slight possibility of glossinas having arisen from two independent focal origins, then the flies must have had a far wider distribution in prehistoric times. Their disappearance from areas other than the African continent may be the result of a combination of climatic changes, natural barriers and glaciations. Proof of the antiquity of glossinas in Africa is provided by their presence during the Miocene period in North America and their survival in the African continent.

Protozoa Flagellates, grouped in the family Trypanosomatidae, are known to be of considerable geological age. The speculations on the evolution of this family have been recently reviewed in a detailed paper by J. R. Baker.[4] In this review, the question is debated whether the trypanosomes originated in invertebrates and then later transferred to vertebrate hosts, (a) by the ingestion of the insect, (b) at the time when certain groups of insects became bloodsuckers; or whether trypanosomes developed in the tissues of vertebrates and became adapted to insects. There are strong reasons for accepting the first hypothesis of primary development in insects.[5]

Africa has left very little in the way of recorded history, except, of course, for Egypt, an area well outside the distribution of glossinas and sleeping sickness. Also little is known about the history of trypanosomiasis, but, under the circumstances, this is no proof that the disease did not exist during historic and prehistoric times. Nevertheless, based on the evidence, outlined above, of the great antiquity of both vector and parasite, it can be assumed that trypanosomes were most probably parasitic in certain animal forms at the time of the branching-off of the Primates, and certainly of the Hominids. As such, there is little doubt that glossina-borne trypanosomes circulated in the very areas archaeological discoveries have proved to be the sites of the first human occupations. Whenever they came into contact with infected flies, the first hominids were exposed to infections in the same way as other animal forms. It is impossible to postulate how soon this exposure gave rise to potent infections and what the effect of these infections might have been upon the first human populations. The point we want to make is that man in Africa was exposed to possible trypanosome infection at his very remote origin. As such, there seems to be no reason why human trypanosome strains should not have developed early during our evolution and that, consequently, sleeping sickness may well be a very old disease.

Origin of Trypanosomes in man

Somewhere during the late Miocene or the Pliocene, certain branches of the primate order in Africa left the forest environment and took to

[4] Baker, J. R. 1963. 'Speculations on the Evolution of the Family Trypanosomatidae Doflein, 1901', *Exper. Parasitol.*, XIII, 219–33.

[5] Another possibility, considering an even older phylogenetic origin, would be that of flagellates circulating in plant-sap, then adapting themselves to insects feeding on these plants, and later developing in vertebrates when some of the insect groups began feeding on blood. Certain plants, like some *Euphorbia* species, do harbour phytoflagellates and lend some support to this possibility.

the savannah.[6] There they developed the unspecialized but highly successful characteristics which would give rise to species of the family Hominidae, one of which was to become *Homo sapiens*.

One of the factors that may have been favourable in allowing certain primates to become ground-dwellers is, I believe, the availability of an assortment of ground-level niches left unoccupied by the elimination of large groups of animals which were susceptible to the circulating trypanosomes in that region. The baboon is a surviving example of another successful ground-dwelling primate in Africa. Significantly, these monkeys are socially highly organized and, from that point of view, are more closely related to man than any other primate.

By choosing to live on the ground, these primates came into contact with parasites to which they were unaccustomed and towards which they had no native resistance. Various animal trypanosome strains, carried around by tsetse flies, must certainly have been inoculated in the early hominids as they were in other animal forms living at ground-level. Some of these strains may have been adaptive enough to develop within the new host and to give rise to genuine infections. These may have been severe at the onset, and mortality among early hominids very high. They may even have been the cause of the regression and disappearance of certain hominid species which otherwise could have progressed in their evolution as well as *Homo sapiens*, or maybe even more successfully.

Trypanosoma gambiense and *T. rhodesiense*, the two African trypanosome species infective to man, belong to what is known as the *T. brucei*-group, which includes a third member: *T. brucei*. All three trypanosomes look identical, but differ markedly in their behaviour in the vertebrate host. *T. gambiense* is mostly transmitted from man to man by *Glossina palpalis* and allied flies living in the forest and forest galleries; it causes a chronic disease, ending in death after one or more years. *T. rhodesiense* induces an acute disease in man, often fatal within a few months after the onset of the infection. Whereas *T. gambiense* is essentially a man-to-man transmitted disease, the maintaining hosts of *T. rhodesiense* are antelopes of the savannah; man is only occasionally infected because the savannah happens to be the habitat of flies of the *morsitans*-group for which man is only a transient host, the staple food of these flies being mainly game. The third member of the group, *T. brucei*, is not infective in man. It circulates in wild animals, without apparent ill-effect, but it is very pathogenic for most domestic animals. It is suggested that the creation of the two trypanosomes responsible for human sleeping sickness was the outcome of their evolution in two distinct and ecologically separated biotopes, one in the forest and one in the savannah, and that this fact is still responsible for

[6] Clark, J. D. 1959. *The Prehistory of Southern Africa*. Penguin Books, Harmondsworth, Middlesex; 1960. 'Human Ecology during Pleistocene and later Times in Africa South of the Sahara', *Current Anthropology*, 1, 307–24; Washburn, St. L. 1961. *Social Life of Early Man*. Viking Fund Publ. in Anthropology, no. 31.

keeping the two trypanosomes as biologically distinct species. The trypano-somes of the *brucei*-group probably arose from a common ancestral strain parasitic in prehistoric faunas. The sequence of evolution might have been as follows:[7]

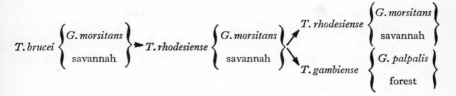

The idea that *T. rhodesiense* arose before *T. gambiense* is supported by the following:

1 If, as is for good reasons assumed, the hominid species had their origin in the savannah,[8] then their contact with trypanosomiasis must have been through *morsitans*-type flies and animal-carried trypanosomes. Such trypanosomes as would infect the hominids under these circumstances would probably assume characteristics of a partially adapted parasite, such as *T. rhodesiense*.

2 *T. gambiense* is characterized by transmissions in permanent human settlements or at frequented river-sites, as the strain needs the constant man–*palpalis* contacts to be maintained. These circumstances were certainly not existing at the time of genesis of the hominid species.

The establishment of the two human trypanosome strains can be described as follows:

1 *T. rhodesiense* may have evolved from intermittent transmissions as early as the late Miocene or Pliocene, when hominid-types were exposed to certain strains of the *T. brucei*-group trypanosomes at the first stages of their occupation of the savannah. The parasite failed to become well adapted, and remained virulent in man owing to:

 a little and irregular contact between the hominid host and the vectors, *G. morsitans* and other flies of the savannah.

 b low densities and scattered distribution of early hominid populations.

 c rapid mortality in victims, decreasing chances for further trans-mission.

 d low infection rates of tsetse flies with the trypanosome.

2 *T. gambiense* evolved from *T. rhodesiense* by mutation and subsequent adaptation when hominids began to invade forest environment and became a choice host of tsetse flies of the *palpalis*-group (primarily

[7] Van Den Berghe, L. and Lambrecht, F. L. 1963. ' The Epidemiology and Control of Human Trypanosomiasis in *Glossina morsitans* Fly-Belts ', *Amer. J. Trop. Med. & Hyg.*, XII, 129–64.

[8] Clark, 1959 and 1960; Washburn, 1961.

crocodile tsetses) dwelling in the same environment. The strain became truly man-adapted because:

  a the vector, *G. palpalis* and allied flies, feed readily on man.
  b regular contact and transmission was assured because *G. palpalis* and related species congregate where man tends to gather for his daily activities.
  c persons afflicted with *T. gambiense* are still well enough for many months to carry out daily routines, and the trypanosomes have a good chance to be picked up and further transmitted by large numbers of flies.
  d sources of constant new infections are provided by 'healthy carriers' —persons infected with *T. gambiense* without apparent ill-effect.

Over long periods, large numbers of early hominids may have fallen victim to the virulent *T. rhodesiense*, but the factors regulating its transmission prevented real epidemics during those times. Infrequent contact was, and still is, the reason why this strain never adapted to man. Though hunting in the savannah, early hominids returned often to the forest edge or to certain places in the dense vegetation cover along rivers and lakes:[9] mutation of *T. rhodesiense*-like strains into the relatively milder *T. gambiense* was the outcome of frequent contacts with stenohygric tsetse fly species of the *palpalis*-group, for which the dense streamside vegetation is the typical habitat. Certain suitable spots along the water-banks became regular gathering places for resting, drinking and bathing, especially where paths forded streams, resulting in a very close man–fly host-relationship. Very sick members, afflicted by trypanosomiasis, may have been left there to die in the shade of the trees. These, and other infected hominids, brought increasing numbers of human savannah trypanosomes into the forest habitats and into contact with *G. palpalis*. Later, contact between fly and man increased further when man began to travel and to settle along the water edge. In this close environment, transmission of the human trypanosome became more frequent and regular than in the savannah. As genetic resistance began to develop as a result of prolonged contact with a single host species, in this case human, so did the strain become increasingly adapted to man. The relatively mild *T. gambiense*, as we know it today, is the result.

Other trypanosomes, maybe even more acutely infective to man, may have arisen during prehistoric times. Such virulent strains would have been weeded out because, by killing the victim more rapidly, they had less chance to be picked up again by the insect vectors. Milder strains, circulating for longer periods in living carriers, had a far better chance to be ingested and further transmitted into new hosts by the tsetses.

The study of infectious diseases has shown that parasites often evolve in parallel adaptations to their host. As antibody mechanisms develop within

[9] Clark, 1959; Washburn, 1961.

the host, so will the parasite tend to become less virulent by mutation and adaptation. The trypanosomes discussed evolved through the agency of an invertebrate vector. The ecology of the vector is therefore all-important and decisive in determining whether the parasite remains in one type of host or spreads to other animal groups. This in turn will influence the degree of adaptation of the parasite to certain hosts.

The differentiation of T. gambiense *and* T. rhodesiense *in natural biotopes*

The taxonomic position of *T. gambiense* and *T. rhodesiense* in relation to each other and to *T. brucei* has been discussed by many authors.[10, 11] Are *T. gambiense* and *T. rhodesiense* one and the same species, or is the former merely a milder form of the latter? For the present it is more convenient to call them by their generally accepted separate species names. The question becomes more than academic however, when, as certain authors imply, it would be possible for one strain to change into the other, depending on whether the strains are transmitted by *palpalis*-group flies or by *morsitans*-group flies. Differences in virulence have been reported as proof that transformations from one strain into the other do occur. But degrees of virulence are reported for many pathogenic organisms, and should not be taken as proof that they are on their way to becoming something else. Also, sometimes the word 'virulence' is used in a misleading way, when 'speed of establishment' (or 'onset of parasitaemia'), 'rate of infection' (or 'successful infection-rate per given number of bites or inocula'), 'infectivity' (or 'minimal infection dose') or 'incubation time' would indicate more specifically what is meant. For instance, a highly virulent strain can have a low infectivity when large numbers of the organism are required to start the infection. In contrast, a parasite may be highly infective but of low virulence when infections can be started by few organisms but cause an infection of low pathogenicity.

According to Willett,[12] man becomes infected by *T. rhodesiense* only when a single inoculation contains not less than 20,000 trypanosomes. *G. pallidipes*, a fly of the *morsitans*-group, delivers large numbers of trypanosomes at the moment of bite; *G. morsitans* and *G. swynnertoni* somewhat less, and *G. palpalis* only few. Willett suggests that since *G. pallidipes* delivers more trypanosomes this would tend to increase the virulence of the strain. On the other hand, in studies by Van Hoof,

[10] Baker, 1963.
[11] Ashcroft, M. T. 1959. 'A critical Review of the Epidemiology of Human Trypanosomiasis in Africa', *Trop. Dis. Bull.*, LVI, 1073–93; 1963. 'Some Biological Aspects of the Epidemiology of Sleeping Sickness', *J. Trop. Med. & Hyg.*, LXVI, 133–6; Hoare, C. A. 1950. *Handbook of Medical Protozoology*. The Williams & Wilkins Company, Baltimore; 1957. 'The Classification of Trypanosomes of Veterinary and Medical Importance', *Veterinary Reviews and Annotations*, III, 1–13; Willett, K. C. 1956. 'The Problem of *Trypanosoma rhodesiense*, its History and Distribution, and its relationship to *T. gambiense* and *T. brucei*', *East African Med. J.*, XXXIII, 473–9.
[12] Willett, K. C. 1956. 'An Experiment on Dosage in Human Trypanosomiasis', *Ann. Trop. Med. & Parasit.*, L, 75–80.

Henrard and Peel,[13] *G. palpalis* provoked infections with *T. gambiense* by injecting few of these trypanosomes. This would indicate that *T. gambiense* is more infective than *T. rhodesiense* which, according to Willett, needs large numbers to start an infection. If the infectivity of the two species were relatively constant, this would constitute another important biological difference between them. This difference could be expressed as follows:

T. rhodesiense has a *high virulence* for man, but a low infectivity: infections occur only at a minimum dose of 20,000 trypanosomes delivered in one infection, but pathogenicity is high because the organism kills the host in about six weeks.

T. gambiense has a relatively *low virulence* for man but is highly infective: relatively few trypanosomes can start an infection, but it is chronic, the victim may survive for three years or more, or even become a 'healthy carrier'.

From the above postulations it would follow that flies of the savannah, especially *G. pallidipes*, will be good carriers of *T. rhodesiense* because they inoculate sufficient numbers of trypanosomes at one blood-meal. *G. palpalis* is an inefficient carrier of *T. rhodesiense* because it does not inject the required numbers of trypanosomes to start an infection by that parasite.[14]

Let us suppose that a mixture of *T. rhodesiense* and *T. gambiense* is released in hypothetical uninfected areas of forest and savannah. In the forest, transmission of *T. rhodesiense* will presumably be damped down to extinction because, for various reasons explained above, *G. palpalis* is an ineffective vector of this trypanosome. In the savannah, *G. morsitans* can carry both trypanosomes, but *T. gambiense* will be damped down or 'weeded out', the fly feeding mainly on game, which are poor carriers of *T. gambiense*.

The system of selection in operation today was probably also responsible for the creation of the two strains. The maintenance of the highly infective but mildly virulent *T. gambiense* became possible through the agency of *G. palpalis* and the presence of man, as part of the forest environment. The transmission requirements of *T. rhodesiense* made it a prisoner of the savannahs where *G. pallidipes*, and other *morsitans* flies, together with the wild animals, became suitable intermediate hosts.

In fig. 1 the 'filtering out' is represented schematically. As noted, it would seem possible to find *T. gambiense* strains in the savannah under

[13] Van Hoof, L., Henrard, C. and Peel, E. 1937. 'La Piqure de la Glossina infectieuse', *Ann. Soc. Belg. Med. Trop.*, XVII, 59–62.
[14] There is strong evidence to believe that there is a marked difference in the anti-coagulant properties of the salivary gland excretions between flies of the *morsitans*-group and those of the *palpalis*-group. In the latter, the very strong anticoagulant action enables these flies to feed on the nucleated blood of reptiles and birds without danger of blocking their mouthparts. The difference in the properties of the salivary gland fluid may partially be responsible for regulating the number, or forms, of the trypanosomes it harbours.

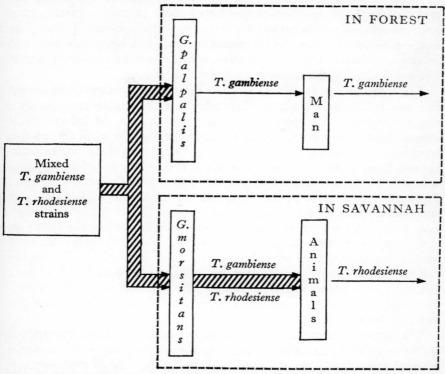

Fig. 1. The 'filtering-out' mechanism and strain separation of a mixture of *T. rhodesiense* and *T. gambiense* according to whether it develops in *G. palpalis* or in *G. morsitans*

certain circumstances. This may explain strain variations and mixed virulences sometimes found.[15]

Fly ecology in relation to infection rates

Today's flies can be divided into two major ecological groups: those having their habitat in rain-forest type of vegetation (*fusca*- and *palpalis*-groups) and those that have their habitat in the drier woodland savannahs (*morsitans*-group). In order to survive and breed, the tsetse flies depend on suitable habitats in which vegetation communities are important, especially in the case of savannah flies. A fairly accurate *Glossina* distribution pattern can be imposed on a map of plant communities and some information on seasonal meteorological conditions and fluctuations. Assuming that *Glossina* habitat requirements have not changed during the last million years, the same thing could be done for each period of the Pleistocene. Development of savannah tsetses may well be directly linked

[15] Lester, H. M. O. 1933. 'The characteristics of some Nigerian Strains of the Poly-morphic Trypanosomes', *Ann. Trop. Med. & Parasit.*, XXVII, 361–95.

to successful occupation of the vast plains by ungulate groups during the
general drought of the Pliocene that lasted about 10 million years, a time
long enough, indeed, to permit the evolution and adaptation of tsetse flies
in these environments and of trypanosome cycles in both vertebrate and
invertebrate hosts. This long association explains the complete tolerance
of most wild African animals towards these infections.

The epidemiology of sleeping sickness may have varied markedly during
the various Pleistocene stages independently of fly distribution. Indeed,
the development of trypanosomes within the fly, and its infectivity, is
affected by environmental temperatures, not only of the adult fly but also
temperatures to which the pupae were exposed during their incubation in
the soil. Temperatures not only affect speed of development of the trypanosomes in the fly, but also the proportion of flies that will become infected.
Prolonged rains would curtail fly populations because water-logging of
soil would cause high mortality in the pupae. The twenty-two known
Glossina species are found in areas generally falling within the following
limits: temperatures between 20° and 28°C., relative humidity between
50 and 80 per cent, and a rainfall between 25 and 60 in. (Rainfall limits are
difficult to indicate; it is clear that an 80-in. rainfall distributed all year
round in a sandy soil would be less harmful than the same rainfall concentrated during three months on impermeable loam.) The present fly-
belts are between latitudes 15°N. and 29°S.

The climatic alternations of the Pleistocene must have had a tremendous
influence on the distribution of tsetse fly species and also on the infection
rates of these flies. Take the case of *G. pallidipes*, a fly of the *morsitans*-
group. This fly is a very effective transmitter of sleeping sickness of the
Rhodesian type owing to the large numbers of trypanosomes it injects. In
contrast with *G. morsitans*, essentially an open woodland fly, *G. pallidipes*
is found mainly in thicket-like vegetation. This leads us to suppose that
at periods of intense thicket cover, and thus of maximum *G. pallidipes*
distribution, more potential *T. rhodesiense*-carrying flies would be
circulating than at periods of more open savannahs. In addition, more
thicket cover would encourage the spread and numbers of bushbuck
(*Tragelaphus scriptus*) and of the common duiker (*Sylvicapra grimmia*),
two antelopes known to be very suitable reservoirs of *T. rhodesiense*. We
conclude that periods of maximum *T. rhodesiense* circulation would
probably have coincided with periods of maximum thicket cover. If it
were possible to compose the landscape for the various Pleistocene periods
in Africa, either from fossil plants or from fossil remains of the two
antelopes, then it would equally be possible, with a reasonable amount of
accuracy, to indicate whether they were correlated with high or with low
sleeping sickness incidences. Fossil records indicate that forms of both
Sylvicapra grimmia and *Tragelaphus scriptus* became widely distributed in
southern Africa during the Middle Pleistocene.[16] The genus *Sylvicapra*

---

[16] Wells, L. H. 1963. Personal communication.

may have derived from the genus *Cephalophus*, a forest duiker, as a form adapted to the savannah environment.[17] In East Africa, *T. scriptus* is recorded in Olduvai Bed IV, which would date it at Late Middle or Early Upper Pleistocene. The Olduvai Gorge deposits are also the site of the discovery by L. S. B. Leakey of *Zinjanthropus boisei* and other 'ape-man' fossils. One is tempted to speculate that *T. scriptus*, and possibly *S. grimmia*, were the original source of trypanosome infections in early hominids.

Four major pluvial periods are recognized in Africa during the Pleistocene, though further correlation and mapping are necessary to establish the existence of the earlier three. Periods of high rainfall favoured development and spread of forests. We do not know, however, what would be the rate of growth and spread of the forest under various circumstances. Moreau and others have correlated present isolated faunal distribution to continuous forest belts in the past. Vegetation communities have no doubt changed extensively, both in composition and in spread, in relation to the changing climate of various Pleistocene periods, and this in turn changed fly distribution and fly infection rates. R. Summers, who has studied environmental changes during the past in Southern Rhodesia, concludes that rainfall was reduced to 50 per cent of today's averages between the Middle Stone Age and the First Intermediate Stone Age. In contrast, rainfall was twice today's averages during the First Intermediate Stone Age. His vegetation maps for these periods indicate that during the high rainfall period the north-eastern part of Southern Rhodesia was covered by forest extending, presumably, all the way from the Congo basin rain forest. This is corroborated by the brief appearance of Sangoan culture implements in that part of Rhodesia, normally known from the Congo forest.[18] Possibly during that period *G. palpalis* had advanced with the forest environment, and *T. gambiense* followed. During the very dry period between the First Intermediate Stone Age and the Middle Stone Age, flies of the savannah type must have been restricted to the north-east, the rest of the country being under desert-like conditions. As the extremely dry period subsided, suitable savannah fly vegetation spread south, and this extensive fly-belt must have formed a very effective barrier against southward thrusts of human populations.

In regard to temperatures, it is said that at certain stages of the Pleistocene they may have been 5° C. lower than they now are.[19] This would restrict infected flies to a considerably smaller area than the one they occupy today, an area located, presumably, at the latitude of the warmer tropics. Present regions of human sleeping sickness may have been free of the disease during these cold periods. In regard to distribution of infection rates, Ford and Leggate found that for a number of savannah tsetses the rates

[17] Ibid.
[18] Summers, R. 1960. 'Environment and Culture in Southern Rhodesia: A Study in the "Personality" of a Land-Locked Country', *Proc. Amer. Phil. Soc.*, CIV, 266–92.
[19] Moreau, R. E. 1933. 'Pleistocene Climatic Changes and the Distribution of Life in East Africa', *J. Ecol.*, XXI, 415–35.

increase with the distance from the median at 7°S., which they call the 'Glossina equator'.[20] This they correlate with the prevailing mean annual temperatures. Of reported Rhodesian sleeping sickness cases 90 per cent are south of the equator. This correlation may also have been in operation during Pleistocene times, though *Glossina* equators and even geographic equators may have been slightly different at certain periods. It is also tempting to postulate that the southern distribution of Rhodesian sleeping sickness is correlated to the generally southern distribution of *G. pallidipes*.

RELATIONSHIP BETWEEN CERTAIN AFRICAN TRYPANOSOMES AND THEIR 'ESCAPE' OUTSIDE GLOSSINA BELTS

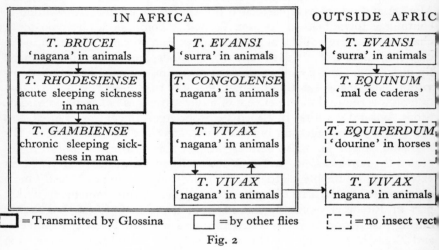

Fig. 2

In later stages of organization, man faced another, economically more important encounter with trypanosomiasis when he introduced domestic animals. These animals showed themselves to be very susceptible to trypanosome strains which circulated without ill-effect in the maintaining wild animals. In domestic stock most of these trypanosome species cause an acute and mostly fatal infection called locally *nagana*. This disease is produced by three different trypanosome species: *T. brucei*, *T. congolense* and *T. vivax*. The diagram in fig. 2 gives an idea of what the relationship between various African trypanosomes might be. It will be noted that some trypanosomes have dispensed with the need of cyclic development in the tsetse fly, and have thus been able to escape the African continent to which the genus *Glossina* is confined, by developing the ability of mechanical transmission through other biting flies and, in the case of dourine, even by contact.

[20] Ford, J. and Leggate, B. N. 1961. 'The Geographical and Climatic Distribution of Trypanosoma Infection Rates in *G. morsitans*-group of Tsetse Flies', *Trans. R. Soc. Trop. Med. & Hyg.*, LV, 383–97.

Trypanosomiasis and early food-gatherers

The influence of trypanosomiasis on man's history during the Pleistocene can only be guessed, and the guess can be only as accurate as the scanty information on these early human populations. Information on vegetation, animal distribution and meteorological data is needed to compose a picture of the disease in early times. Lacking all this information, the epidemiology of human sleeping sickness of the past can be presented only in broad outline with the hope that details can be filled in later as more information on prehistoric ecological environments becomes available.

SCHEMATIC REPRESENTATION OF THE EVOLUTION OF HUMAN TRYPANOSOMIASIS

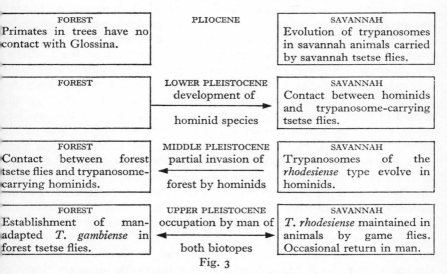

FOREST	PLIOCENE	SAVANNAH
Primates in trees have no contact with Glossina.		Evolution of trypanosomes in savannah animals carried by savannah tsetse flies.
FOREST	LOWER PLEISTOCENE development of hominid species →	SAVANNAH
		Contact between hominids and trypanosome-carrying tsetse flies.
FOREST	MIDDLE PLEISTOCENE partial invasion of ← forest by hominids	SAVANNAH
Contact between forest tsetse flies and trypanosome-carrying hominids.		Trypanosomes of the *rhodesiense* type evolve in hominids.
FOREST	UPPER PLEISTOCENE occupation by man of ← → both biotopes	SAVANNAH
Establishment of man-adapted *T. gambiense* in forest tsetse flies.		*T. rhodesiense* maintained in animals by game flies. Occasional return in man.

Fig. 3

It is possible that early savannah-dwelling hominids began to recognize that certain vegetations were irritating to man because of biting flies. Though they may not have connected this with the fatal disease that followed, they may nevertheless have avoided places where fly concentrations were particularly high. If they did, this may well have saved them. Camp sites may be expected to be found outside the main fly-belts for each of the periods to which they belong.

Other diseases, such as malaria, of course influenced human settlements and destiny. The very high incidence of the sickle-cells trait found in many African populations, the result of long-standing selection-pressure by hyperendemic malarial infections in favour of a trait which is otherwise somewhat deleterious to the individual, is proof how intimately the disease was tied with the evolution of these populations. But the fact that such a genetic trait has developed is also proof that the population remained in contact with malarious areas. As such, one wonders whether human population movements, settlements and distribution were much influenced by the disease.

Sleeping sickness, however, is a very acute disease at all ages and rapidly fatal in the case of *T. rhodesiense*. Human populations were not merely hampered by it, but their numbers may have suffered severe losses, and places where the disease was prevalent were probably avoided as much as possible. Extensive fly-belts with particularly high fly densities may have formed a barrier to their occupation by human groups or destroyed those who tried to penetrate them. The extent of the fly-belts, and of other restricting conditions, must have changed during the slowly evolving climates of the Pleistocene; the localization of prehistoric sites may vary accordingly for each period.

Human trypanosomiasis may have played a selective role as human groups began to specialize. Those, such as hunters, whose occupation called for activities in the savannah, faced the dangers of *T. rhodesiense* more than those whose activities kept them away from the fly-belts. Permanent occupation of certain areas must have changed the development and relationship between parasites and man. Intestinal infections by helminths, for instance, must have increased rapidly as human groups settled in villages. Anopheles adapted to breeding places in the environments created by man's various activities. These settlements became the logical feeding-grounds for the adult mosquito, and human malaria must have become rampant. With respect to human trypanosomiasis, the results of the human sedentary mode of life were different in the forest communities from those in the savannah. Occupation of the forest and forest galleries did not adversely affect *G. palpalis*. On the contrary, it increased contact between man and fly; the active occupation of parts of the savannah, and the change in the vegetation this brought about, disturbed *G. morsitans* populations, and chased away the game animals on which this species depended for its food. The outcome was that increasing human settlements in the forest created more niches for *T. gambiense* and activated spread of Gambian trypanosomiasis; in the savannah, on the contrary, human occupation depleted both game and fly populations, thus decreasing the chances of *T. rhodesiense* transmissions. The adaptation of *T. gambiense* to man must have been especially active during more specialized hunting/ collecting stages when people moved in and began to settle in forest areas and when they began to spend more time in fishing. The general increase of human populations in Africa, and more intensive occupation of the two major ecological entities, forest and savannah, widened the gap between the biological differences of *T. gambiense* and *T. rhodesiense*, the former becoming more man-adapted. While *T. rhodesiense* acted like a spearhead in the evolution of human trypanosomiasis, it was *T. gambiense* which spread into vast areas and became man-specific. These areas advanced or retreated in accordance with the shrinkage or expansion of the specific habitats of the vectors.

Trypanosomiasis and pastoralists

Domestication of stock must have been a revolutionary step in human economy, but the distribution of this new economy must have depended on fly-free areas. Paintings in rock-shelters indicate that cattle were already domesticated in the Sahara by 3500–3000 B.C. and perhaps even by the sixth millennium B.C.[21] Domesticated cattle of Euro-Asian humpless longhorn *Bos primigenius* stock were brought into Africa via the Sinai peninsula and can be traced in Egyptian settlements by about 5000 B.C. In North Africa they interbred with the indigenous *Bos opisthonomus*. Another type of cattle, a humpless shorthorn or *Brachyceros*, entered Egypt in the same way. Descendants of the humpless longhorn and the humpless shorthorn survive today in a few places in North and West Africa.[22] They have acquired a certain tolerance to trypanosomiasis which enables them to resist the local strains. This immunity, however, breaks down in the presence of new strains or under conditions of stress, for example food shortage. Ford describes the routes taken by five successive waves of cattle and their owners along their migrations into various parts of Africa.[23]

A fundamental change in the economy of the African people accompanied population movements, especially the migrating pastoralists. Some of these first migrants may have been metal users.[24] The main route for diffusion was down the high ridge country on either side of the central Rift valley.[25] The reason for this is likely to have been the need for stock-owning people to find a tsetse-free route. Fuller[26] and later Dicke,[27] among others, give accounts of the struggle of stock owners due to fly-belts in South Africa. In his narrative of explorations and discoveries in South-Western Africa between the years 1850 and 1854, Anderson[28] mentions how a party of Englishmen and their horses, accompanied by natives and their cattle, had to turn back from a journey to the north of Lake Ngami. The party lost most of the horses, one man thirty-six of them, and also sustained heavy losses in cattle, victims of the tsetse flies which infested the areas through which they had to travel.

Fly-belts have more effectively restricted movements of pastoralists than of non-pastoralists. Cattle owners must have realized at an early stage that their herds would face heavy losses when travelling through *Glossina*

[21] Ford, J. 1960. *Distribution of African cattle*. Proc. 1st Sci. Congress, Salisbury, S. Rhodesia, pp. 357–65.

[22] Ibid.

[23] Ibid.

[24] Clark, J. D. 1962. 'The Spread of Food Production in Sub-Saharan Africa', *J. Afr. Hist.*, III, 211–28.

[25] Ibid.

[26] Fuller, C. 1923. 'Tsetse in the Transvaal and Surrounding Territories; an Historical Review', *Trop. Dis. Bull.*, XXI, 785.

[27] Dicke, B. H. 1932. 'The Tsetse Fly's Influence on South African History', *S. Afr. J. Sci.*, XXIX, 792–6.

[28] Anderson, Ch. J. 1857. *Lake Ngami: Four Years Wanderings in the Wilds of South Western Africa.* (1850–4.) Hurst & Blackett, London.

zones. To avoid this, caravans began to follow the same routes through fly-free corridors. Resting-places and water-holes may have become occupied permanently along these roads. Certain trades may have developed along these migration lines, or market places where goods were exchanged. Fly-free grasslands became favourite stopping-places and the site of permanent settlements. In this way, the movement and the areas occupied by these early pastoral tribes may give us a realistic pattern of fly-free areas during these times.

The penetration of cattle from North Africa farther south was subject to the existence of natural fly-free corridors, and those created by man himself. Agricultural tribes have taken advantage of the fertile soil of relatively high productivity and the adequate water supply of the forest fringes. They have created a wedge between the forest fly habitats and those of the savannah. These fly-free areas have been exploited by the pastoralists, not only as a migration route, but often as permanent settlements. Such is the story of the Sanga cattle in Ankole and Ruanda and Urundi when Nilotic cattle owners arrived there some 500 years ago to find open grass-land created by their cultivating predecessors. In Ruanda and Urundi, the pressure of these pastoral overlords (Batutsi) has compelled the agriculturists (Bahutu) to hew new fields at the expense of the forest edge, which at one time they were destroying on a wide front at the rate of a kilometre every year.[29] The chain of events has created new situations. Because of the degradation in the pastoral overlordship in its relation to other groups, and for various additional reasons, open grasslands have become invaded by pyrophitic wooden plant species, and they have changed to tree savannahs suitable for *G. morsitans*. This invasion is happening very rapidly in western Uganda[30] and in Ruanda and Urundi.[31] Ankole cattle are now being pushed farther south and west by *G. morsitans* advancing both from the West African fly-belt coming down from the north and by the East African-belt coming in around the south and west of Lake Victoria. During the last 50 to 70 years the gap between the two belts has closed from over 300 miles to less than 50.[32] And unless modern man finds some way to deal with this new situation, the fly is once again shaping Africa's history.

Trypanosomiasis in recent times

The first medical reports from Africa, during the later 1800s and early 1900s, revealed that sleeping sickness was spreading: that *T. gambiense*

[29] Cited in Ford, 1960.
[30] Ford, J. and Hall, R. de Z. 1947. ' The History of the Karagwe, Bukoba District', *Tanganyika Notes and Records*, XXIV, 3–27.
[31] Van Den Berghe, L. and Lambrecht, F. L. 1956. ' Étude biologique et écologique des Glossines dans la région du Mutara, Ruanda', Acad. R. Sci. Col., mémoire T.IV, fasc. 2 pp. 1–101; 1962. 'Étude biologique et écologique de *Glossina morsitans* West, dans la région du Bugesera, Rwanda', Acad. R. Sci. d'Outre-Mer, mémoire T.XIII, fasc. 4, pp 1–116.
[32] Ford, 1960.

was being dispersed from West African areas, southwards along the Atlantic Coast and also in central and eastern parts of the continent. At present, the disease is found as far south as central Angola and east along the shores of Lake Victoria. Its distribution is that of *G. palpalis* and allied flies in lowland rain forest. *T. rhodesiense* was first described from the Luangwa valley in Northern Rhodesia. From there the disease seems to have spread northwards and westwards. It is now reported in many scattered places in eastern African savannahs, north up to the Sudan and west to just inside the Ruanda–Urundi border. Its distribution matches that of the savannah tstse flies.

No doubt, as human populations increased and more people began to travel, so infectious diseases were likely to become distributed more widely and more frequently. It is hard to believe, however, that both *T. gambiense* and *T. rhodesiense* remained confined for untold centuries each in its particular focus of origin, and that their dispersion occurred conveniently to be witnessed at the time of the arrival of the first scientific observers. The dispersion of the disease may have been one of several such propagations in the past. It will be shown in specific examples later on how, in many cases, man's actions have borne directly on the epidemiology of sleeping sickness. Frequent travelling would certainly favour its dispersion. It should not be taken for granted, however, that the advance of the disease witnessed by the early explorers and survey teams was the first one in the history of the infection, or that it was due primarily to the use of trade routes. Well travelled trade routes, criss-crossing many parts of central and southern Africa, had existed for many centuries before they began to be used by explorers from outside.[33] It is also possible that the idea of the advance of sleeping sickness, as recorded by earlier surveys, was not the advance of the disease at all, but was the outcome of the advance of survey teams with more adequate knowledge and equipment as they penetrated deeper into remote parts of Africa.

A few written records indicate that sleeping sickness was known in remote times. The first mention of the possible implication of (tsetse) flies in diseases is, according to a report by P. Glover,[34] the one from the Bible (Isaiah vii. 18–19: 'And it shall come to pass in that day, that the Lord shall hiss for the fly that is in the uttermost part of the rivers of Egypt. . . . And they shall come . . . all of them in the desolate valleys, and in the holes of the rocks, . . . and upon all bushes.')

According to H. H. Scott,[35] in the *Egyptian Gazette* of December 1931 H.R.H. Prince Omar Tussim quoted a passage in ancient Arabic literature by Al-Qualquashandi about the rulers of the Mali Kingdom. Referring to Mari Diata II (fourteenth century), he states: 'His end was to be over-

[33] Curtin, P. D. 1963. Personal communication.
[34] Glover, P. E. 1961. *The Tsetse Problem in Northern Nigeria*. Printed for the Colonial Office by Patwa News Agency (E.A.) Ltd., Nairobi, Kenya.
[35] Scott, H. H. 1939. *A History of Tropical Medicine*. The Williams & Wilkins Company Baltimore.

taken by the sleeping sickness (*illat an-nawm*) which is a disease that frequently befalls the inhabitants of those countries, and especially their chieftains. Sleep overtakes one of them in such manner that it is hardly possible to awake him. He (the King) remained in this condition during two years until he died in the year 775 A.H. (A.D. 1373–4).'[36]

'A disease that frequently befalls the inhabitants' indicates that the disease was well known and widespread in the area. That the disease lasted two years indicates that it was caused by *T. gambiense*.

The Arabs were the early colonizers of Africa. It is thought that the reason they did not extend their sphere of influence more widely was the difficulty of transport through the fly-belts.

During the sixteenth century, the Portuguese launched large expeditions into the interior of East Africa, but they were beaten back when large numbers of their horses and camels fell victim to the tsetse flies and trypanosomiasis.

The history of Africa would have been very different had not the western explorations from the fifteenth century on been confined to coastal areas, owing to the hazards of trypanosomiasis and other disease in the interior.

The steps to the discovery of the trypanosomes as pathogenic organisms and their transmission by the tsetse flies can be chronologically summarized:

1742 Atkins described 'negro lethargy' on the Guinea Coast among slaves from the interior.

1803 Winterbottom commented on the disease as he saw it near Sierra Leone and mentioned that slave-dealers would not buy those with enlarged glands.

1846 Trypanosomes were first described from fishes.

1849 Robert Clarke described the disease on the Gold Coast.
     Trypanosomes were described in rats by Lewis in Bombay.

1880 Trypanosomes were found in the blood of horses in Madras by Evans.

1890 Trypanosomes were seen for the first time in man by Nepveu, but their significance was not known.

1895 Bruce showed 'nagana' in animals to be due to a trypanosome, *T. brucei*.

1901 Forde and Dutton found trypanosomes in a man suffering from sleeping sickness, in Gambia. The parasite was called *T. gambiense*.

1902 Castellani found trypanosomes in the cerebrospinal fluid of patients in Uganda.

1903 Bruce and Nabarro showed that trypanosomiasis is carried by *G. palpalis*.

1910 Trypanosoma in a white man who had travelled in the Rhodesias was described by Stephens and Fantham as being caused by a new trypanosome species: *T. rhodesiense*.

1912 Yorke and Kinghorn showed that *T. rhodesiense* is transmitted by *G. morsitans*.

Man has changed many disease patterns: he, as much as disease itself, is part of the environment. The following examples illustrate cases in which man's action has increased and spread trypanosomiasis.

[36] Cf. Levtzion, N. 'The Kings of Mali', *J. Afr. Hist.*, IV, 3 (1963), 350.

During the previous century, slave-traders broke up large settlements into smaller communities by actual raids or by inciting fear. In the savannah, the decreasing human densities no longer held back *G. morsitans* populations, nor game animals, and contact with fly and *T. rhodesiense* became more frequent. Slave caravans, no doubt, also spread the disease by taking persons infected with trypanosomiasis into uninfected areas along the road to the coastal slave markets. (In Northern Rhodesia, however, the slave trade had the opposite effect. Small scattered villages were abandoned and the inhabitants began to gather in larger, stockaded agglomerations which could be better defended against the raiders.)[37]

It is said that Stanley's porters, some carriers of trypanosomes, introduced the disease in certain parts of Central Africa. However, in Martinique, Guerin, as early as 1869, observed that the disease must be widespread in the Congo when he found many infected slaves among those imported from that country. Mense also reported many infections in the Congo basin in the end of the nineteenth century. Bloss estimates about half a million deaths by sleeping sickness in that area between 1896 and 1906.[38] Rodhain, leader of the first Belgian medical research team, visiting areas along the Lualaba river in 1911, found few survivors after a Gambian epidemic. In some villages the remaining survivors were too sick to bury the dead.[39] All this evidence, especially the earlier portions, certainly suggests that sleeping sickness was well established in the Congo basin at the time, or very soon after, Stanley's party reached the river during his second expedition (1879–84).

The scope of sleeping sickness epidemics is shown by the one north of Lake Victoria due to *T. gambiense*, between 1902 and 1905, when the disease carried away 200,000 people out of a population of 300,000.

Ford gives a dramatic example of how an apparently wise reorganization changed the destiny of a whole human population in the Semliki valley after the start of the Belgian administration in that part of the Congo.[40] The valley was described by Lugard in 1893 as grassland; a flourishing agricultural population lived on the western slopes of Mount Ruwenzori, and owned cattle that grazed in the valley. Belgian administrators changed the land use, and the native population was moved down from the slopes to the valley floor along the banks of the Semliki river. This increased and established permanent contact between man and the *G. palpalis* population of the forest gallery lining the river. By 1920 most of the human population was either dead, had fled, or had been hospitalized. The Gambian sleeping sickness spread to the shores of Lakes Edward and George, where the Uganda government was forced to evacuate many thousands of people and their cattle from areas that they had occupied for the preceding 300

[37] Clark, J. D. 1963. Personal communication.
[38] Bloss, J. F. E. 1960. 'The History of Sleeping Sickness in the Sudan', *Proc. R. Soc. Med.*, LIII, 421–6.
[39] Van den Berghe, L. and Lambrecht, F. L. 1963.
[40] Ford, J. 1960.

to 400 years. The abandonment of the grasslands resulted in the growth of thickets, allowing *G. pallidipes* to reach and occupy these valleys from higher-level forests, where they had been confined by agricultural settlements. From this area, *G. pallidipes* spread eastward and was finally halted about 100 miles east from where the fly started some fifty years earlier. In 1921 some Uganda cattle owners returned to their old pasture land with about 120 head of cattle. Three years later all the cattle were dead, presumably because of trypanosomiasis transmitted by *G. pallidipes*.

Specialists think that bush country and wooded savannahs have increased, at least during the present century, and probably before. One of the reasons may be the increasing cultivation by native methods in which fields are abandoned every few years. In addition, some European concepts, related to the period of grass burning, likewise have made it possible for tree-cover to develop in previous grassland. All this has increased areas of vegetation suitable for savannah flies.

The actual invasion by *G. morsitans* of a previously uninfected tsetse fly area was witnessed in the Bugesera region of Ruanda–Urundi in 1953. It was thought that the fly advanced from an established fly-belt in adjacent Tanganyika, and that this advance was made possible by the development of shrub and woodland savannah in former grassland after the decline of cattle-owners' settlements and partial abandonment of these areas due to political changes and to rinderpest.[41] In 1954 an epidemic of Rhodesian sleeping sickness occurred, induced probably by increasing contact between fly and scattered mixed-farm settlements. It was also suggested tentatively, that *G. morsitans* in that region had become a potentially more active *T. rhodesiense* carrier because anti-warthog campaigns had forced it to feed more on bushbuck and duiker and man himself, to make up for the decreasing numbers of its choice host.[42]

During the last decades, the number of Gambian sleeping sickness cases has decreased, due mainly to new and better methods of controls of the vectors, and of medical care.

The number of Rhodesian cases has remained almost at the same level. The lesser success of the action against this infection is due to the difficulty of control of the *morsitans*-group flies over the vast territories they occupy. Therapeutic action against the infection itself is not always successful.

Natural fluctuations in the number of sleeping sickness cases have been recorded. They may be related to changing annual temperatures and variations in the duration and severeness of seasons, affecting fly densities and dispersion and their rate of infection by trypanosomes. Decrease and even disappearance of flies from the savannah following the dramatic decrease of game populations after the severe rinderpest epidemic at the end of the last century have been described from a number of regions.[43]

[41] Van den Berghe, L. and Lambrecht, F. L. 1962.   [42] Ibid. 1963.
[43] Fuller, C. 1923.

Decrease of *G. morsitans* densities and Rhodesian sleeping sickness often follows the opening up of infested areas by new roads, mining activities, large agricultural layouts and other industries which would tend to affect the surrounding vegetation and game populations drastically.

Elimination of game and subsequent eradication of fly has been achieved by the shooting out of game in certain parts of Africa. More peaceful methods of eradication of savannah flies have been accomplished in other areas. The control scheme organized by Swynnerton and his colleagues for and with the help of the Basukuma people around Shinyanga, Tanganyika, will remain a classic example: 2000 to 3000 square miles were reclaimed from tsetse bush by clearing, a local government was better organized, health improved and wealth increased mainly because cotton could then be grown as a cash crop.[44] Another successful example is the 'Anchau Settlement Scheme': an area of about 700 square miles in Northern Nigeria was reclaimed from *palpalis*-group flies, making possible the settlement of about 50,000 people out of danger of trypanosomiasis.[45] The fight against *G. palpalis* and Gambian sleeping sickness has become increasingly successful through the use of selective clearings and of insecticides. A significant example of this is the achievement in the Kuja-Migori rivers system, where *G. palpalis* has been exterminated over large areas east of Lake Victoria.[46] Direct action against the infection of either type of sleeping sickness has been possible, of course, by moving away threatened human populations, and by continuous medical surveys and care.

In spite of the vast knowledge of the epidemiology of both man and animal trypanosomiasis, the fly still restricts and guides today's planning and denies the full use of hundreds of square miles of African country. Inasmuch as trypanosomiasis has been part of the history of Africa, so it will be of its future. It has been realized that trypanosomiasis forms an integral part of the problems facing modern Africa; that of the evaluation of its resources, of the precise use of its land, of the proper conservation of its wildlife and of the stabilization of its social, economic, and cultural systems.

The task of the tsetse and trypanosomiasis research worker leads him, sooner or later, to study all the aspects of the African environment. In the control of tsetse flies, much more thought has been given to land-use and especially to the conservation of wildlife.[47] Recent studies show not only that wildlife can be a source of important financial income through the tourist trade, but also that the utilization of wildlife can be more reasonable

[44] Buxton, P. A. 1955. *The Natural History of Tsetse Flies*. Lond. School of Hyg. & Trop. Med., memoir no. 10. H. K. Lewis, London.
[45] Glover, P. E. 1961.
[46] Glover, P. E., Le Roux, J. G. and Parker, D. F. 1958. 'The Extermination of *Glossina palpalis* on the Kuja-Migori River Systems with the Use of Insecticides', *Intern. Sci. Comm. Trypanosomiasis Res. Comm. Techn. Coop. Afr.*, Brussels 1958, Publ. no. 41, 331–42.
[47] Van den Berghe, L. and Lambrecht, F. L. 1963.

and profitable than that of the introduced domestic animals. Domestication of certain indigenous animals, such as the eland, resistant to trypanosomiasis, is another promising possibility of orienting African resources to an economy well adapted to the African environment. These, and other aspects of trypanosomiasis research, may lead to fascinating new possibilities of better control of the disease, and of the more rational use of the land.[48]

SUMMARY

Exposure to and invasion by parasitic organisms may play an important part among many other intrinsic factors that guide the evolution of animal forms. Trypanosomes, two species of which cause African sleeping sickness today, are blood parasites of great antiquity. Their presence in Africa at the time of the first stages of human evolution may have been of great consequence, at first acting as a discriminating agent between resistant and non-resistant types of hominids, and later also in shaping migration routes and settlement patterns. As a possible clue as to why man arose in Africa, the author postulates that trypanosomes may have precluded the development of certain ground-dwelling faunas, allowing certain more resistant primates to fill the empty ecological niches. Some of these primates, thus becoming ground-dwellers, became the precursors of the hominid branch. The evolution of T. gambiense and T. rhodesiense, the two human parasites, and their development in the tsetse fly, are debated. The epidemiological aspects and patterns of the disease are examined under the changing climatic conditions of the Pleistocene and during later times, when Africa was opened up by Western exploration.

[48] I should like to express my sincere appreciation to Dr J. D. Clark, Professor of Anthropology at the University of California (Berkeley), for his encouragement and advice; to Dr Philip D. Curtin, Professor of History at the University of Wisconsin, for his critical review and valuable suggestions; to Dr L. H. Wells, Professor at the University of Cape Town, South Africa, for his information on fossil antelopes and to Drs J. R. Audy, F. L. Dunn and D. Heyneman of the Hooper Foundation staff who have given time for reading and discussing the manuscript.

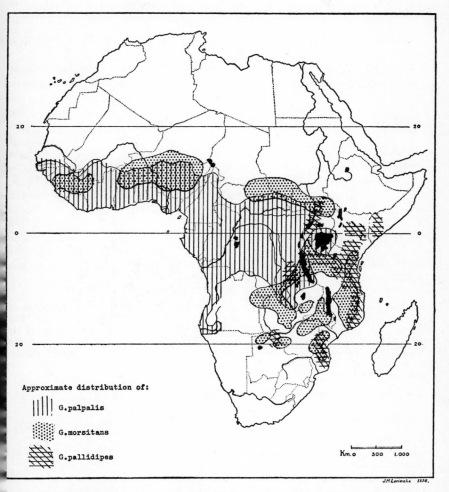

Fig. 4. Distribution of important sleeping sickness vectors. (After Leeson 1953, cited by Buxton 1955.)

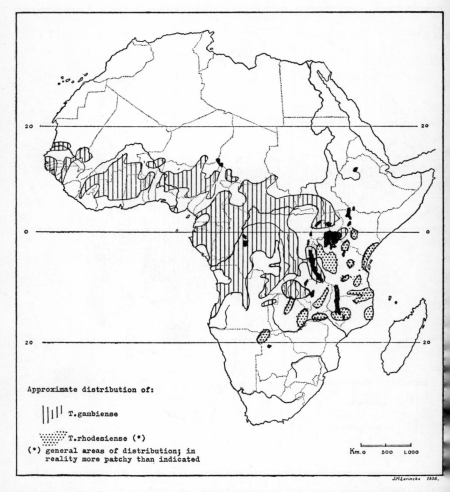

Fig. 5. Distribution of the two kinds of human sleeping sickness. (After Leeson, cited by Buxton 1955.)

6. CONCEPTS OF RACE IN THE HISTORIOGRAPHY OF NORTHEAST AFRICA[1]

By WYATT MACGAFFEY

MODERN histories of pre-colonial Africa make effective use of relatively new sources of data, including some which were once the exclusive concern of physical anthropology. Indeed, the field of race history has been virtually abandoned by anthropologists, who are represented (in English) by little else besides G. P. Murdock's *Africa* and the revised third edition of C. G. Seligman's *Races of Africa*, itself a survival from an earlier phase of African studies.

This withdrawal by anthropology has been encouraged by new developments in the study of race since the 1930's, seriously questioning earlier assumptions regarding the identity of races, the means of identification, and the relationship between race and culture. It appears that a like scepticism has not occurred to all historians of Africa. A number of hypotheses advanced in recent years incorporate dubious assumptions about race and political development. Examination reveals a consistent pattern in these ideas and the uses they serve, and suggests a sociological interpretation of their curiously anachronistic persistence.

The bulk of the data considered in this essay comes from accounts of events falling in the twilight zone sometimes called proto-history. Their authors are collectively described for convenience as historians, although many are not in fact primarily historians by profession and training. The focus of concern is northeast Africa, selected because of its critical importance in the history of immigration to the continent and not because the ideas to be discussed are peculiar to writers on that area. Ideas and their interpretation are the principal topic of the paper, which is only secondarily concerned with history itself.

The results of the discussion will not solve an historian's problem for him, but may help him to deal more critically with concepts of race.

IDEALISM AND PSEUDO-DARWINISM

In the last two decades of the nineteenth century, the structure of industrial nationalism in Europe and the structure of imperial relations abroad assumed their modern form. Both called for an ideology which sanctioned as natural and necessary a polarization of the rulers and the ruled, the

[1] An earlier draft of this paper was presented at a seminar conducted by Raymond Mauny at the University of California, Los Angeles. I am grateful to Professor Mauny, Professor J. B. Birdsell and members of the African Studies Center, U.C.L.A., for their advice and encouragement.

bearers and the receivers of culture. Contemporary sociological trends facilitated the development of such an ideology.

In Germany in particular, idealistic sociology interpreted the diversity of empirical facts by relating them to systems of logically interrelated idea types. In this approach, events occurring in space and time are assigned meanings which make them congruent with an eternal, i.e. timeless, system Talcott Parsons's discussion of the development of the method suggested the terms 'idealism' and 'idealistic analysis' used here to refer to it.[2]

Concurrently we find the development of pseudo-Darwinian sociology exemplified in extreme form by Gumplowicz.[3] The method of this school differs from the idealistic in its search for causal relations among empirical phenomena. Its principal assumptions include the polygenetic origin of mankind and the predominance of conquest and class conflict in processes of political development. Both schools employ contradistinctive model for empirical and analytical processes alike. F. Toennies, *Gemeinschaft und Gesellschaft*, 1887, exemplifies the idealistic use of such a model.

In simplified and also more rigid forms, these concepts were applied to the ethnography of northeast Africa as it was developed in the first decade of the twentieth century by such scholars as Meinhof in linguistics and Seligman in anthropology. The influence of idealism is seen in their attribution of absolute value to the Caucasoid and Negroid types. These absolute values and their relations are treated as social universals, and are believed to be represented equally in the biological, linguistic, cultural and political aspects of man. This means that evidence of the dichotomy may be transferred from one aspect to another to make up for the lack of fact there. As J. H. Greenberg has observed, only partly in jest, the method at its worst results in treating cattle as a linguistic trait. Racial and cultural phenomena are regarded as Negroid or Caucasoid, or as a mixture of these two; the mixture, however, remains a mixture and does not constitute a new type.

The pseudo-Darwinian influence is seen in the ranking of the two types and of their attributes. Physically, long heads, aquiline noses, ortho gnathism and other features are regarded as Caucasoid and as indicating superior capacities. Linguistically, morphological systems regarded as more complex than others are treated as evidence of more sophisticated distinction of categories and hence, again, of superior capacities. Above all centralized and especially autocratic systems of government are believed to show clearly superior political capacity and hence the infusion of Caucasoid ideas, if not actually of a Caucasoid genetic element. These assumptions recur in more specialized fields, such as the history of art and architecture

The foregoing matters are already familiar; I have reviewed them only to specify certain features of the tradition of thought in which the historical debate has taken place. Nor may we assume that the old way of thinking

---

[2] Talcott Parsons, *The Structure of Social Action* (Glencoe, Ill., 1949), 473–87.

[3] L. Gumplowicz, *The Outlines of Sociology* (trans. Moore, Philadelphia, 1899).

has vanished. It is true that pseudo-Darwinism is in decline, on the whole, but since World War II its existence has been prolonged by subtle infusions, as I hope to show. And idealism, which is not as vulnerable to moral and political objections, is still powerful.

THE BROWN RACE

In 1880, Lepsius suggested that the indigenous populations of Africa could be reduced to two stocks, the Hamitic in the north and the Negro in the south; the Sudan represented a zone of intermixture. This view is still current, but instead of the Hamitic we find the Brown or Mediterranean race.[4] The Brown race concept has a dual ancestry. It was originally invented by G. Sergi, but substantially modified by Elliot Smith. Since Sergi's formulation was first published in 1895, long before the application of genetics or even statistics to physical anthropology, it is a curiosity of great interest that he should be directly cited in the present decade as an authority on race.[5]

Sergi sought to counter the Aryan ideology associated with growing German influence in Europe, and rejected all classifications of races which did not fix a great gulf between the Italians and the Germans. In his view the Aryans were Eurasiatic barbarians, responsible for the destruction of the great Mediterranean civilizations. Although Europeans speak Indo-European languages, they belong essentially to the Eurafrican species, which includes the African, Mediterranean and Nordic branches.

According to Sergi, only the skeleton, and especially the skull, can provide systematic indices of race. Cranial form is hereditary and immutable; in hybrids we find not a fusion of traits to produce an intermediate type, but a juxtaposition of traits retaining their racial identity.[6] Skin colour and hair form are 'external' traits without diagnostic value because they are subject to environmental influence; this explains the wide variation among Eurafricans, from blond Nordics to dark WaTussi, all of whom, however, are definitely set apart by their cranial form from the Eurasiatics and the Negroes.

Consequently, 'the Brown race' is something of a misnomer for Sergi's concept, which is properly the Eurafrican or Hamitic race, with brown as its typical skin colour. Of this group, the Mediterranean is a subdivision:

La stirpe mediterranea, quindi, è una parte della camitica, molto diffusa in Africa... e comprende i Camiti dell'Africa settentrionale, e quelli dell'Europa meridionale... La stirpe mediterranea insieme col resto della camitica in Africa è bruna con variazioni grandi... ma con caratteri osteologici communi, uniformi dagli Wahuma ai Baschi, dagli Egiziani agli Italici, agli Iberici.[7]

[4] A. J. Arkell, *A History of the Sudan from Earliest Times to 1821* (London, 2nd ed. 1961), 22–4.
[5] K. M. Barbour, *The Republic of the Sudan; a Regional Geography* (London, 1961), 74; G. Sergi, *The Mediterranean Race* (London, 1901).
[6] Sergi, *Antropologica della stirpe camitica* (Turin, 1897), 10.   [7] Ibid. 395.

Elliot Smith, though basically in agreement with Sergi, was inclined to accord independent status to the Nordic or Teutonic race, or races, and wanted to add to the Eurafricans the ancient Sumerians, the Arabs, the Dravidians, and other dwellers on the shores of the Indian Ocean, forming a new but very loosely defined entity called the Brown Race 'in reference to the distinctive colour of their skin'.[8] The Mediterraneans and Hamites are subgroups of this race. Neither in Sergi's nor in Elliot Smith's scheme are Brown and Mediterranean equivalent terms.

The term Hamitic is to be rejected as a racial label not, as Arkell suggests, because it is properly a linguistic label, but because the racial category which it designates, and the entire theory of race with which it is associated, is inadequate. Consequently, the substitution of Brown or Mediterranean is no improvement. It would be more correct, and less quaintly archaic, to say White or Caucasian; this is Seligman's understanding of Sergi's concept.[9]

It is clear that 'the Brown or Mediterranean race' is an extremely imprecise concept. Its survival is to be attributed to its ideological usefulness, no small part of which lies in its ambiguity. In a word, it is a myth. In his study of myths, Lévi-Strauss observes that their structure is a dual one, purporting simultaneously to describe past events and everlastingly recurrent patterns.[10] Mythopoeic thought begins with ideas which the myth makers apprehend as antithetical, and seeks to resolve the contradiction by developing mediators between the opposed pairs. Mediating ideas are typically ambiguous, as their logical function demands.

The properties of the Brown race concept are clearly revealed by the use made of it by Cheikh-Anta Diop.[11] Diop seeks to exalt African culture, although his conclusions are intended to contradict those of traditional European historiography, his methods are identical.

When Diop observes, on the subject of the races of Egypt, that 'Mediterranean' is an anthropologist's euphemism for 'Negroid', he is very nearly right, in the sense that the term represents an effort to associate a whole range of peoples and their achievements with the Caucasian ideal, while glossing over their dubious correspondence with the Caucasoid physical type. Similarly, he is correct in saying:

Les anthropologues ont inventé la notion ingénieuse, commode, fictive du 'vrai Nègre' qui leur permet de classer au besoin tous les Nègres réels de la terre

---

[8] G. Elliot Smith, *The Ancient Egyptians* (London, 1923), 67–9.

[9] C. G. Seligman, 'Some aspects of the Hamitic problem in the Anglo-Egyptian Sudan', *J. R. Anthrop. Inst.* XLIII (1913), 595; and 'Psychology and racial differences' in J. A. Hadfield (ed.), *Psychology and Modern World Problems* (New York, 1936), 55; see also Carleton S. Coon, *The Races of Europe* (1939).

[10] C. Lévi-Strauss, 'La structure des mythes', in *Anthropologie structurale* (Paris, 1958), 227–56.

[11] C-A. Diop, 'Histoire primitive de l'Humanité; évolution du monde noir', *Bull. IFAN*, XXIV B (1962), 449–541; and 'Réponses à quelques critiques', ibid. 542–74.

CONCEPTS OF RACE IN NORTHEAST AFRICA 103

comme de faux Nègres, se rapprochant plus au moins d'une sorte d'archétype de Platon, sans jamais l'atteindre.[12]

On his part, he is confident that the ancient Egyptians were Negroes; even if, as the centuries passed, they grew steadily lighter in colour, they remained none the less Negroes. Indeed,

La seule conclusion scientifique conforme aux faits est que la première humanité, c'est-à-dire les tout premiers *Homo sapiens*, étaient des 'négroïdes'.[13]

His authorities, not surprisingly, include Sergi and Elliot Smith. He supports his view by drawing attention to portraits of negroid Egyptians, chiefly of the predynastic period but also of later times, even the New Empire. Such pictures have been a source of some embarrassment to Egyptologists. One solution has been to stress differences of social rank and to emphasize that 'superior classes' show profiles 'of smoothly contoured, fine Mediterranean form'.[14] Although the nobility often had Negro wives, the most nearly Egyptian of the mixed offspring always assumed the superior social roles.[15]

In ordinary usage, given individuals or populations may be described as Negro, Caucasian, or whatever, as long as the relevance of the term to their external appearance is clear. Inevitably, the criteria of relevance vary somewhat from one cultural context to another; where ambiguity results, other descriptive terms should be chosen. Similarly, if Mediterranean is intended to imply a general physical type common to the shores of the Mediterranean, no difficulty arises, although the usefulness of the term is limited by the extent of agreement on its signification. As has already been indicated, in the context of northeast Africa this extent is narrow.

A different logic is at work when Mediterranean indicates a racial category and an author is at pains to allocate a people to it and not to some other category. Thus A. J. Arkell:

Physically both [the A and C groups] belonged to the Brown or Mediterranean race, and despite published statements to the contrary, there were only the lightest negroid characteristics in any of the C group skulls.[16]

Arkell cites H. Junker, the Austrian Egyptologist, as an authority. Junker's article, 'The First Appearance of the Negroes in History' (1921), is a far-fetched attempt to show not only that the Egyptians were entirely Hamitic but that neighbouring populations were not Negro either. This requires him to challenge the interpretation put upon the evidence by Derry, Smith, Meyer, Breasted, MacIver, Reisner, and others, whose published statements may be the ones Arkell mentions. Proceeding from figure to figure, he argues that people in Egyptian art who look like Negroes are really something else; in a particular case, 'The hair might be that of

[12] Ibid. 461. [13] Ibid. 452.
[14] Coon, *Races of Europe*, 96.
[15] G. A. Reisner, *Excavations at Kerma*, Harvard African Studies, VI (1923), 557.
[16] Arkell, *History of the Sudan*, 46.

Negroes, but just as well, and more probably, Hamitic hair.'[17] The 'foreign-looking' traits of the XII Dynasty and the contemporary C group stimulate him to masterpieces of sophistry.

It is generally agreed that from the beginning of the Predynastic period the population of Lower Egypt was a general Mediterranean type specifically similar to all subsequent populations of that area; and that at some point to the south this type gave way to an African Negro type. Argument centres on the nature and location of the boundary, whether the Upper Egyptian populations at different periods were substantially indigenous and what were their relations with Nubia. These questions are important not only for Egyptian history but also for the investigation of Egyptian influence on the rest of Africa, and vice versa, at different periods.

The archaic A group and B group series are virtually indistinguishable and nobody has any difficulty in regarding them as Mediterranean. Trouble arises over the C group, who seem intrusive, and who show features which may be negroid. Their measurements also indicate relationship with the Meroitic and X group series, to which the same doubt applies.

The analytical approach employed by Derry, Elliot Smith and others of the osteometric persuasion, has probably been taken to its ultimate refinement by Batrawi, whose study is not listed in Arkell's bibliography. Batrawi wants to show that Egypt was continuously inhabited by the same people, with the implication that Egyptian culture was indigenous and not to be credited to alien immigrants. By applying the coefficient of racial likeness, a device which represents a refinement of Sergi's method, he believes he is able to prove his point, but he is forced to include various uneasy arguments explaining the nature of the 'negro influences' which his figures reveal; specifically, the C group, Meroitic and X group series show a higher nasal index than the others. Like Elliot Smith before him, Batrawi explains the discontinuity between the C and D groups as the result of the removal of negroid influence; he is evidently happier to accept its removal than its initial arrival, but he does not deny its existence.[18]

Arkell extends his eccentric view to the X group,[19] and indeed to all the historical populations of Nubia: 'The inhabitants of the Dongola Reach were not negroes in Dynastic times any more than they are today.'[20] This conclusion is by no means the obvious one. Most writers accept Seligman's account, which speaks of the ebb and flow in Nubia of Egyptians from the north and Negroes from the south. Seligman speaks of Negroes who resembled the modern Nubians pressing upon pre-Ptolemaic Egypt, and of the Nubians represented in New Kingdom art as unmistakably full

[17] H. Junker, 'The first appearance of the negroes in history', *J. Egypt. Archaeol.* v (1921), 128n.

[18] A. Batrawi, 'The racial history of Egypt and Nubia', *J. R. Anthrop. Inst.* LXXV (1945), 81–101; LXXVI (1946), 131–56.

[19] Arkell, review of L. P. Kirwan, *The Oxford University Excavations at Firka, Sudan Notes Rec.* XXIII (1940), 360.

[20] Arkell, *History of the Sudan*, 86.

blooded Negroes.[21] The evidence from the more isolated parts of Nubia, and from other sources, is that the Nubians before the coming of the Arabs were more negroid than the modern population, of whom Keane says: 'The Nubian (Barabra) type is obviously Negroid'.[22] Kirwan says, 'The chief characteristic of the X group is their strikingly negroid aspect', which is more marked than in the C group and Meroitic remains.[23]

The point of these citations, selected from an extensive literature which affords many more, is not to decide by a sort of ballot whether the population of Nubia at any given period was or was not Negro, or whether 'the Hamitic element predominated'. The point is to show the extent of disagreement among competent authorities, even among those who share the view that races are either 'pure' or 'mixed'. Dogmatic assertions that a people are 'really' Negroes or 'really' something else evidently cannot be based, in this case at least, on the ostensible facts. In a more general context, all such statements must be regarded as inherently incapable of proof, and as dependent for their meaning upon the idealistic assumption.

RACE AND CULTURE

The argument about race, as conducted by Junker, Seligman, Diop, and others who share the same conceptual framework, is ultimately about culture and, in particular, about government. From the European point of view, the classification of races and specification of their attributes served, directly or indirectly, to sanction the colonial enterprise (there are, of course, many other aspects both of race theory and of colonialism). The superiority of the Caucasoids centred on their political capacity. Knowledge of government was contrasted with another ideal construct, absence of knowledge of government, which was attributed to the opposite pole of the system. If these attributes were innate and immutable, government by those who knew how of those who did not was a reasonable and natural consequence. It is only recently that Seligman's Hamites, 'better armed and of sterner character', have been replaced by Huntingford's Hamites, who live by the plough.[24]

The idea of government, according to this approach, appears in Africa as Divine Kingship. Since good government—for reasons which were more obvious before World War I than they are now—is not only centralized but authoritarian, African kings with divine trappings but without authority, such as the Reth of the Shilluk, are placed willy-nilly in the same category with those of Bornu and Ghana. The emergence of such kingships is attributed to Caucasoid if not Egyptian influence, and usually to the

[21] Seligman, 'Some aspects of the Hamitic problem...', 617–25; see also H. A. MacMichael, *A History of the Arabs in the Sudan*, 1, ch. 2 (Cambridge, 1922).
[22] A. H. Keane, 'Ethnology of Egyptian Sudan', *J. R. Anthrop. Inst.* XIV (1885), 103.
[23] L. P. Kirwan, *The Oxford University Excavations at Firka* (Oxford, 1939), 36, 40.
[24] G. W. B. Huntingford, 'The peopling of East Africa by its modern inhabitants', in oland Oliver and Gervase Mathew, *History of East Africa*, 1 (Oxford, 1963), 58–93.

founders of Caucasoid dynasties, since the idea of government is mor
effectively transmitted by genetic than by other means.

From the historical point of view, certain difficulties arise. Seligman
one of the originators of the thesis, held that, if divine kingship diffused from
Egypt, it began to do so not later than 3,000 B.C.[25] Since the ritual aspect
of this so-called kingship are highly patterned, a common fount is no
unlikely; moreover, their content is such that they could well have been
diffused in association with the neolithic agricultural economy. However
ritual ideas are quite a different matter from government, let alone authori
tarian government. As Goody says ' "Kingship" itself is much too vague
And to add the epithet "divine" does little to help'.[26] For the upholder
of the Hamitic theory there remained a problem faced also by Diop,[27] tha
of explaining why Egyptian civilizations did not spring up all over Africa
The solution has been to give the diffusion a relatively recent date, an
attention has focused on the kingdom of Meroe.

Diop gives the date 500 B.C. for the arrival in West Africa of tall Negroe
from Egypt. This may in fact be a good date for the diffusion of iron int
West Africa, with accompanying population movements. Iron-workin
flourished in Meroe from the sixth century onwards. Livingstone advance
the attractive hypothesis that such migrations, facilitated by the use of iro
in agriculture, resulted in environmental changes which in turn explai
the distribution of the sickling gene in West Africa.[28] But it is most un
likely that migrants of this period were the first Negroes to appear in Wes
Africa.

Then there are the upholders of the Sudanic civilizations thesis, currentl
represented by Oliver and Fage[29]; and Arkell.[30] They differ in that, whil
Arkell confines himself to speculations on Meroitic influence, Oliver an
Fage also speculate about Yemeni influence. They share the merit of draw
ing attention to the importance of the east–west route from various point
on the Nile, through the Wadi el Melk or El Obeid to the Jebel Marra i
Dar Fur and thence to Lake Chad. This route corresponds, in its souther
branch particularly, to a natural ecological zone, and deserves more atten
tion than it has received.

If, as seems likely, this route was well travelled in Meroitic times, iron
working could perhaps have spread to West Africa by 500 B.C. 'Kingship
might also have passed the same way but, according to Arkell, it had to wa
for suitable bearers, 'scions of the royal family of Meroe', fleeing to the wes
with the secret of kingship. 'The royal family' here makes good sense i
terms of the pseudo-Darwinian thinking we have been investigating;

[25] Seligman, *Egypt and Negro Africa* (London, 1934), 60.
[26] J. Goody, 'Feudalism in Africa?', *J. Afr. Hist.* IV (1963), 15.
[27] *Bull. IFAN*, XXIV (1962), 554.
[28] F. B. Livingstone, 'Anthropological implications of sickle cell gene in West Africa
Am. Anthrop. LX (1958), 533–62.
[29] R. Oliver and J. D. Fage, *A Short History of Africa* (Harmondsworth, 1962), 44–5
[30] Arkell, *A History of the Sudan*, 177.

is completely unnecessary from any other point of view. But the story as told has caught the imagination of historians, and already occupies almost the same mythological status as the fall of Constantinople, that other disaster whence sweetness and light diffused to a barbarian continent.

It is inevitable, in the present state of knowledge of Africa, that hypotheses should bulk rather large in historical accounts. But we may require such hypotheses to be economical, central to the data, and consistent with relevant theory in other fields; in practice, these requirements turn out to be one and the same. P. M. Holt has recently shown that Arkell's tentative identification of a Bornu prince as the founder of the Funj dynasty is based upon a forced interpretation of dubious material.[31] This is an instance in which the requirements for sound hypotheses have been neglected because of prior assumptions about the nature of cultural and political processes.

If Negroes are confined above the fifth or sixth cataract of the Nile, a corridor is preserved for the transmission of the ideas which gave rise to every manifestation of superior culture in Negro Africa. For similar reasons, the Teda, Tama, Meidob, Barya, Daju and other modern peoples may be gratuitously credited with Caucasoid forebears of Hamitic speech. Where Meroe fails, Bornu may be invoked as the source of 'organization' and 'the tradition of ruling'.

Another cultural problem which arises is that of African influence on Egypt. Mass burials of retainers, as found at Kerma in Nubia during the New Kingdom and in the X group cemeteries of the same region at the end of the Meroitic period, are said by archaeologists to be un-Egyptian. Various sources of this alien influence have been suggested, with 'Central Africa' favoured, apparently on the grounds that suttee burial is barbaric and 'Central Africa' is the home of barbarism. Lest the influence be interpreted as amounting to a serious modification of the Egyptian race, Reisner offers the following explanation:

The female in such primitive communities remains in a much more backward state than the man. Her functions approach more nearly to those of an animal, and she clings with ignorant and uncomprehending obstinacy to the practice of her neolithic ancestors...The influence of an old negress from Central Africa in a hareem of such females might have started the *sati*-custom in the Egyptian colony [Kerma]; the influence of half a dozen such women would have made it endemic.[32]

This idea is so far-fetched that there may seem to be little value in quoting it. But it is merely an extreme example of the assumption that structurally significant changes in behaviour can be adequately explained by new notions casually introduced. Moreover, in a somewhat popularized but

[31] Arkell, 'More about Fung origins', *Sudan Notes Rec.* xxvii (1946), 87–97; *A History of the Sudan*, 208; and P. M. Holt, 'Funj origins: a critique and new evidence', *J. Afr. Hist.* iv (1963), 39–56.
[32] Reisner, *Excavations at Kerma*, 557–8.

entirely serious book published recently we find the following literal acceptance of Reisner's view:

> The number of Africans in these princely harems was very large and their normal way of life may have included a total acceptance of the idea that their role in daily life involved an eventual journey with their lord to the 'other world'.[33]

Similar defences of the Hamitic homeland are given by Sergi and Batrawi; indeed it would be tedious to list all the historical speculations which owe their lives to these harem women.

THE GENETICAL CONCEPT

The idealistic assumption is that the observed physical variety of peoples can be explained as the consequence of mixture between a limited number of ideally and historically discrete types or races. This assumption enters into the substance of inferences from skeletal measurements, and it is only in terms of such an assumption that many of these inferences have meaning. Anthropologists of this way of thinking have discovered negro skeletons in some of the least likely places,[34] and are prone to disagree strongly among themselves regarding the proper classification of a given specimen. The Asselar and mesolithic Khartoum remains are said to be undoubtedly Negro; historical hypotheses are based upon this classification, and our attention is drawn to the 'striking problem' that the Kenya Capsian and the Khartoum Mesolithic are technologically similar but 'racially' distinct.[35] An authority such as Carleton Coon, however, finds the Asselar skull ambiguous and the Khartoum skull to resemble that of a modern local Sudanese, a mixture of Hamite and Negro.[36]

At the close of the nineteenth century an alternative methodology was already challenging idealism. Beginning in the physical sciences, and increasingly in social sciences, the units of analysis ceased to be regarded as concrete and irreducible but as systems of relations whose boundaries were determined by their internal structure and by the structure of the wider systems of relations to which they belonged.[37] The rediscovery of Mendelian genetics at about the same time effected a similar transformation in biology. In a recent review, Dobzhansky offered a geneticist's view of race:

> A biological species can be likened to a cable consisting of many strands; the strands—populations, tribes and races—may in the course of time subdivide, branch or fuse; some of them may fade away and others become more vigorous and multiply. It is, however, the whole species that is eventually transformed

[33] W. A. Fairservis Jr., *The Ancient Kingdoms of the Nile* (New York, 1962), 115.
[34] J. B. Birdsell, 'The origin of human races', review of C. S. Coon, *The Origin of Races, Quart. Rev. Biol.* XXXVIII (1963), 185.
[35] Arkell, *Early Khartoum* (Oxford, 1949), 31–3, and *A History of the Sudan*, 24–8; Oliver and Fage, 20–1.
[36] Coon, *The Origin of Races* (New York, 1963), 650–1.
[37] E. A. Cassirer, 'Structuralism in modern linguistics', *Word*, I (1945), 99–120.

into a new species. The populations, or races, in which these evolutionary inventions have occurred then increase in number, spread, come in contact with other populations, hybridize with them, form superior new gene patterns that spread from new centres and thus continue the process of change.[38]

This view of race does not preclude the use of osteometric data, but by emphasizing variability and adaptation it rules out what is here being called the idealistic assumption. Apparent continuities and discontinuities in phenotypical distributions of all kinds are studied for the information they afford on the genetic structure of particular places and periods, and not to fill out a taxonomic scheme. The potentially greater empiricism of this approach, and the possible uses of genetic models to reconstruct past processes[39] recommend it to historians.

Genetic data for Africa are not yet abundant, but at least the genetical concept warns us not to be confident that a given skull, when measured in a sufficient number of dimensions, can be assigned to one of a limited range of types, or to a specific intermediate position indicating a mixture of types; it follows that it is still more difficult to regard such a skull as representative of an ethnic group which may be similarly classified, and to base historical reconstructions upon this classification. Moreover, the difficulties exist in regard to genetic as well as to morphological data, though perhaps not to quite the same degree. It has even been suggested that the notion of race be dispensed with entirely.[40] At least we can be sure that the dichotomous Lepsian view of the population of Africa is inadequate, though it is still offered. Indeed, even in 1885, Keane rejected it.

The transition to the new logic required by modern theory has been imperfectly accomplished in physical anthropology and still less adequately in disciplines which draw upon its conclusions. Idealistic thinking has persisted even among geneticists, some of whom still seek to classify races; a genetic coefficient of racial likeness has even been developed. Among non-geneticists, it has frequently been assumed that serological analysis will provide the sure indices of race that the most sophisticated osteometry failed to provide. Thus we find:

The value of the evidence which blood groups and sickle cells may be able to provide when the material is much more abundant and methodical will lie in its application as a test of traditional history. The sickle-shaped red blood cell is normal in Negroes. African ethnic groups which have mixed with Negroes, however, show traces of sickling which vary according to the amount of Negro blood they have.[41]

Not only is this not true; it contradicts the fundamental logic of genetics. And it seriously distorts the views of Huntingford's principal authority,

[38] T. Dobzhansky and Ashley Montagu, 'Two views of Coon's *Origin of Races*', *Current Anthrop.* IV (1963), 365.
[39] Birdsell, 'Some implications of the genetical concept of race in terms of spatial analysis', *Cold Spr. Harb. Symp. Quant. Biol.* XV (1950), 259–314.
[40] Livingstone, 'On the non-existence of human races', *Current Anthrop.* III (1962), 279–81. [41] Huntingford, 58.

H. Lehmann.[42] Huntingford's own views represent an extreme case of the idealistic fallacy. He cites the Kordofanian Nuba and similar peoples in Dar Fung as the only surviving representatives of the Negro in East Africa; and even they 'are certainly not "pure" types'. This alleged racial status of the Nuba seems even more remarkable when the continent is considered as a whole; sickling rates are highest in East Africa, which may therefore be the place of origin of the Negro,[43] but decline steadily to the west and south. Rates for the Nuba are not mentioned, any more than the question of selection, but these groups are deemed to show 'some of the main features of what may be called Negro culture'.

Lehmann's opinion, in the article cited, is that sickling is a Veddoid trait which entered the continent relatively late. 'While measurements of R_0 frequency may be used as a "tracer" of African ancestry, the sickle cell trait can obviously not be used for this purpose'.[44] He notes the importance of environmental pressures, including malaria and social structure. Since the article was written, a considerable literature on sickling has grown up, but most conclusions remain tentative. N. A. Barnicot, concluding a recent joint report on 'A survey of some genetical characters in Ethiopian tribes', observes:

It need hardly be stressed that although certain morphological features and certain genes are particularly frequent in Africa there is considerable regional variability and any tendency to think in terms of some hypothetical ancestral group in which all these features were maximal should be resisted.[45]

According to Huntingford,

We have to deal with three 'foundation stocks' in East Africa: Bushman, Negro, and Hamite, with probably a leavening of Stone Age blood...These stocks have in turn given rise to the other ethnic groups of East Africa, groups which may be called hybrid in that they are formed from the mixture of two or more dissimilar stocks.[46]

The modern cultural picture is seen as the result of a parallel hybridization. The difficulty of accounting for it satisfactorily in terms of the interaction of a limited number of primordial groups is met by supposing an indefinite series of hypothetical ethnotypes within the basic unity of each race; permutations of these can conjecturally explain any degree of ethnographic diversity. The introduction of political and social organization on a wider scale than the tribe is credited to the Hamites, although

It should perhaps be made clear that the position which it appears proper to assign to the Hamites is not due to a mere 'belief in the inherent superiority of

---

[42] H. Lehmann, 'Distribution of the sickle-cell gene. A new light on the origin of the East Africans', *Eugen. Rev.* XLVI (1954), 101–31.

[43] Huntingford, 64.   [44] Lehmann, 128.

[45] N. A. Barnicot, in 'A survey of some genetical characters in Ethiopian tribes', *Am. J. Phys. Anthrop.* XX (1962), 208A.

[46] Huntingford, 83.

the Hamite element', as Greenberg puts it, but to their actual and potential abilities as demonstrated by factual evidence.[47]

Any ethnotypes which lack chiefship or Hamitic patriliny may be excluded from consideration as civilizers: the Sidamo and Galla, rather than the Egyptians, are to be regarded as the source whence 'ideas of political growth spread westwards'.[48]

THE USES OF LINGUISTICS

The point of this essay is to suggest that certain modes of thought, as applied to the racial history of northeast Africa, govern the methods of investigation and, very largely, the results. This is not an original point, nor surprising in itself, although the persistence of these particular modes of thought in contemporary writing is remarkable and calls for some explanation. It may be found in the colonial relation and the idealistic tradition in science, which are sociological factors in the historiographic environment. I am not suggesting an explanation in terms of the personal attitudes and intellectual habits of the individual authors; nor am I interested in an anti-colonial crusade.

It is noteworthy that in the last fifty years the products of idealistic dialectical analysis have become established as collective representations with a life of their own. Even for Seligman the Hamitic hypothesis was ostensibly no more than that, but since World War II it has taken on the sanctity of established doctrine. Scholars who are not themselves concerned with racial taxonomy seize upon it to help them in diverse and highly specialized researches. Thus an archaeologist, studying the distribution of a certain kind of stone axe in West Africa, finds reason to believe it may have some connexion with the C group, and thus 'a strain of ultimately western European (or western Mediterranean) origin seems present'.[49] At this stage our hypothesis has become a virus.

If the Negroid–Caucasoid polarity is dispensed with, the historical question of racial distributions and cultural diffusion takes on a new form. Simple logical analysis shows that the approach being reviewed attributes priority to data elements in the order: culture, race, language. This order should be reversed. Only in language do we have at the moment both the information and the method which permit classifications in which we can have some degree of confidence and from which relationships can be traced. This remains true even if Greenberg's more controversial classifications are wrong.

We have to do with two entirely different language families, Niger-Kordofanian and Nilo-Saharan, besides Afro-Asiatic.[50] Such divisions

---

[47] Huntingford, 83, n.2.   [48] Huntingford, 71.
[49] R. A. Kennedy, 'A necked and lugged axe from Nigeria', *Bull. IFAN*, XXII B (1960), 209.
[50] J. H. Greenberg, *The Languages of Africa*, pub. 25 of the Indiana University Research Center in Anthropology, Folklore and Linguistics (Bloomington, 1963).

imply distinct communities which we would also expect, particularly at the neolithic technological level, to display different adaptive modes and to occupy distinguishable ecological zones. Physical differences would also be expected, though not necessarily at the racial level; some differences have in fact been repeatedly noticed, though not in the present frame of reference, and are mentioned below for what they are worth. It goes without saying that each 'community' or ethnic group, at the level being considered, would show considerable internal differentiation; that specific correlations between linguistic and cultural or physical patterns do not necessarily persist; and that particular tribes may change their linguistic or cultural affiliation, or both, relatively rapidly.

In the Niger-Kordofanian language family the principal substocks are Niger-Congo and Kordofanian. Whereas the former has diffused over most of West and Central Africa, apparently in relatively recent times, the latter has been progressively confined to the refuge of the Nuba Hills in southern Kordofan. The Nuba correspond to the conventional Negro type; that is, they 'are unanimously described by Russeger, Petherick, Lepsius and other intelligent observers as emphatically a Negro race'.[51] Similar people live or have lived in Dar Fung and elsewhere to the north and east of the Nuba Hills.[52] Greenberg's association of their languages with those of West Africa agrees with earlier observations that they look like West Africans and have cultural affinities with Nigeria.[53] The implication of the linguistic distribution is that the Niger-Congo branch moved westward.

Nilo-Saharan includes Koman, Fur, Maban, Saharan (Teda, Zaghawa), Songhai and Chari-Nile. The distribution of the first five branches suggests an archaic radiation of peoples speaking these languages and it corresponds, as C. Wrigley has noted, to a Sudanic zone, formerly much more habitable.[54] In Chari-Nile, the family relevant to the present consideration is Eastern Sudanic, which includes Nubian, Barya, Tabi, Nyima, Temein, Tama and Daju, all within the Egyptian vicinity (Nilotic is the principal remaining branch of Eastern Sudanic[55]). The speakers of all these languages differ sufficiently from the negro stereotype for many observers to impute to them a degree of Hamitic or 'non-negroid' ancestry; the range of such speculation is indicated by the racial labels which have been applied to the Teda.[56] Most of the Eastern-Sudanic-speaking peoples have traditions of dispersal from the Nile valley in or near Nubia,[57] confirming the linguistic indication

[51] Keane, 103.

[52] E. E. Evans-Pritchard, 'Ethnological observations in Dar Fung', *Sudan Notes Rec* xv (1932), 55.

[53] E.g. C. G. and B. Z. Seligman, *Pagan Tribes of the Nilotic Sudan* (London, 1932), 15 and Lucy Mair, in A. Phillips (ed.), *Survey of African Marriage and Family Life* (London 1953), 115.

[54] C. Wrigley, 'Linguistic clues to African history', *J. Afr. Hist.* III (1962), 272.

[55] Greenberg, 85.

[56] P. Huard and M. Charpin, 'Contributions à l'étude anthropologique des Teda d Tibesti', *IFAN*, xxii B (1960), 180–7.

[57] Arkell, *A History of the Sudan*.

of a secondary radiation of this group in relatively recent times, possibly early in the present era.

A conservative list of the language groups relevant to the history of Egyptian relations with the south and west must include Kordofanian, Eastern Sudanic (excluding Nilotic), Saharan, and perhaps Fur, besides the Afro-Asiatic languages Berber and Beja. Only remote links, if any, exist between them, and a corresponding list of distinguishable ethnic groups is implied. Cultural and political relations in northeast Africa are therefore to be studied historically as relations separately involving the groups on such a list, and not as relations between Hamites and an un-differentiated mass of 'Negroes'. Familiar problems can thus be posed in a new way. This is not the place to advance new hypotheses with supporting data, and a sketch of some of the possibilities must suffice.

Such scanty clues as the C group affords point to an affiliation with Eastern Sudanic speakers rather than with any other modern peoples.[58] A considerable body of archaeological evidence exists to suggest that cattle-owning peoples related to the C group entered the Sahara from the east in a zone and at a time consistent with the linguistic evidence, mentioned above, for a radiation of Nilo-Saharan speakers. Much of the archaeological evidence has been presented by P. Huard, who refers to the immigrants as Eastern Hamites and links them with such Nilotes ('demi-Hamites') as the Shilluk.[59] It should be clear that the Hamitic label simply creates difficulties. Whatever the remote ancestry of the Shilluk may have been, in the present state of anthropological knowledge it is quite unwarranted to describe them as a mixture of Negro and Hamite. It may be necessary to recognize the existence in this area, in neolithic times, of a substantial population which does not correspond to the Caucasoid or the Negroid stereotype, and which cannot meaningfully be reduced to a mixture of the two in any given proportions. In any case, once the supposed link between race and culture is abandoned, the problem of racial typology loses much of its significance. Its solution must await adequate clinal analysis of physical characters along the Nile valley axis.

Evidence suggests that peoples corresponding physically to the modern Nuba constituted a second major ethnic group at this approximate time level, i.e. in the last three millennia B.C. The predominant adaptive mode for this group was apparently agricultural. It might be expected that Kordofanian speakers would furnish some sort of cultural link between Egypt and West Africa, but no evidence of this has been advanced. The hypo-thetical linguistic unity of Kordofanian and the apparent historical con-nexion between the Nuba Hills and Dar Fung remain to be substantiated.

If the provisional identification of these two groups can be sustained, analysis of the affiliations of such celebrated Nubian enigmas as the X group

[58] Ibid. 49–53.
[59] Huard and Charpin, 'Contribution à l'étude...'; and P. Huard 'Figurations d'ani-maux à disques frontaux', *IFAN*, XXIII B (1961), 476–517.

and the Black and Red Nuba gains a new dimension.[60] So far as I know, the possibility that Meroitic is a Kordofanian language has not yet been seriously entertained;[61] scarcity of facts is evidently only one factor at work here. The evidence may remain insufficient for some time to come. At present it appears to indicate that Meroitic is not Nubian and not Hamitic; however, one should beware of Vycichl's argument that it must therefore be 'a negro language'.[62] Another question relates to the date of the introduction of Nubian into Nubia; the need to assume that this language is Hamitic has obscured the fact that there is no real reason to suppose it was introduced before the end of the Meroitic era.[63] In any case, the grounds for supposing an ethnic link between the C group, X group, Noba and even Shilluk are stronger than those for attributing Hamitic affiliation to any of them.

SUMMARY

Recent accounts of the proto-history of Africa use data from physical anthropology, but also concepts of race which physical anthropologists in general have abandoned as unsatisfactory; thé paper seeks to explain this phenomenon sociologically. Late nineteenth-century political and sociological trends helped to produce patterns of thought which can no longer be regarded as affording adequate explanations of social processes. These patterns combined idealism, or the method of contrasting ideal types, with pseudo-Darwinism, which sought the origins of political development in the interaction of differently endowed groups. In African ethnography of the early twentieth century such concepts led to the view that the continent was inhabited by two groups, Caucasoids and Negroids, and by mixtures of the two which remained mixtures, to be analysed as such. The Caucasoid and Negroid types were regarded as absolute and universal, represented equally in the biological, linguistic, cultural and political aspects of man.

Recently the term Hamite for the Caucasoid ideal has fallen into disfavour, but certain authors speak of the Brown Race. This concept is without scientific value, and must be regarded as a myth with specific ideological functions related to the colonial situation. These authors find that adequate explanation of the occurrence of political centralization consists in adducing the possibility of a Caucasoid (Hamitic or Brown) genetic intrusion. Distorted hypotheses of ethnic migrations result.

Idealistic racial classification has now been displaced in physical anthropology by the genetical concept, which emphasizes adaptation and variability and studies the genetic structures of particular places and periods with little or no reference to racial taxonomy. This approach is inherently more useful to historians than the idealistic approach. However, the genetical concept has been subordinated to idealistic schemes by those who allege, for example, that the sickling gene affords an index of absolute racial classification.

[60] Kirwan, 'A survey of Nubian origins'.
[61] W. Vycichl, 'The present state of Meroitic studies', *Kush*, v (1957), 74–81.
[62] Ibid. 88.
[63] W. MacGaffey, 'The history of negro migrations in the northern Sudan', *SWest. J. Anthrop.* XVII (1961), 178–97.

In the present state of knowledge of Africa, logical priority should be accorded to data elements in the order: language, race, culture, instead of the reverse. Linguistic distributions, despite the uncertainties of classification, afford the best clues we have at present to the migrations of the past. Once the Negroid–Caucasoid polarity is dispensed with, several well-known enigmas in the history of northeast Africa take on a new form. Correlation of linguistic and archaeological data suggests a westward migration of Nilo-Saharan speakers at approximately 3,000 B.C. It may be necessary to recognize the presence, at this time level, of a distinct ethnic group contrasting specifically with the 'Hamites' and with the speakers of Kordofanian languages, who are 'Negroes'. Whether this be true or not, the influence of Egypt on Africa, and vice versa, must be studied in terms of a plurality of discrete, autonomous groups instead of the undifferentiated Negroes and Hamites of the traditional approach.

7. SOME QUESTIONS ON THE ECONOMIC PREHISTORY OF ETHIOPIA[1]

By Frederick J. Simoons

BECAUSE of a meagre archaeological record, the economic prehistory of Ethiopia has been largely a matter of speculation. In this speculation, Ethiopianists have understandably directed considerable attention to South Arabia, whence came the ancestors of the politically dominant Amhara and other Semitic peoples of Ethiopia. Perhaps stemming from this focus, certain writers have credited various innovations to the Semites without supporting evidence. It is the purpose of this paper to question certain widely held assumptions, especially those respecting the origin of ensete culture, which is important today in parts of southern Ethiopia, and the characteristic cereal-plough agriculture of the north, which was supposedly introduced by the Semitic invaders.

THE ENSETE AND ENSETE CULTIVATION

In Ethiopia, recognized by Nicolai Vavilov as a minor cenre of plant domestication, one of the most striking of the locally domesticated food plants is the ensete (*Ensete edule*; formerly *Musa ensete*), which bears a striking resemblance to the banana and is thus sometimes referred to as the 'false banana' (see fig. 1). Until modern times, when it spread widely round the world as an ornamental, the ensete was cultivated only in Ethiopia. Today Ethiopia is still the only place where it is grown for food. With the ensete it is not the fruit (which is leathery and has large seeds and little pulp), but the false stem and young shoots which principally serve as food. They may be boiled and eaten as a vegetable, or pounded, buried, fermented, and either boiled into porridge or baked into a 'bread' which is comparable in food value to manioc flour and similar starchy tropical products. Unlike the cultivated banana, the cultivated ensete is a highland plant which grows at elevations of from 5000 to about 10,000 feet. According to Hugh Scott, in the Gughé Mountains of the south ensete is able to grow higher than all crops, except barley, in places subject to seasonal frost.[2] This makes it a competitor with the temperate land cereals for agricultural land.

---

[1] A first draft of this paper was presented at the third Conference on History and Archaeology in Africa, held at the School of Oriental and African Studies, University of London, in July 1961.

[2] Hugh Scott, 'Journey to the Gughé Highlands (Southern Ethiopia), 1948–9; Bio-geographical Research at High Altitudes', *Proceedings of the Linnean Society of London*, 163, pt. 2 (1952), 131.

Fig. 1. The ensete, from James Bruce, 1790

Even more interesting than the plant itself is the fact that in some
regions of central and southern highland Ethiopia, especially among
various Cushitic groups, the ensete almost completely overshadows other
food plants, and forms a monoculture. The ensete areas, with their thick
plantations, are reputed to have among the most dense rural population
of Ethiopia (180 to 450 per square mile).[3] In addition the ensete cultivators have been more secure than if they had cereals. In the first place
the Semitic conquerors of the north look down on ensete as food. Further

[3] Helmer Smeds, 'The Ensete planting culture of eastern Sidamo, Ethiopia', *Acta
Geographica*, 13, no. 4 (1955), 34.

more, the ensete is too difficult to prepare for eating or to carry away to be an attractive prize to raiders. And finally, the plantation itself is difficult to destroy.

Who domesticated the ensete?

This brings us to the question of the domestication of the ensete, and by whom it may have been brought about. W. Stiehler suspects that the ensete-planting culture goes back to Negroid or even Pygmoid peoples, whom he views as the ancient inhabitants of the southern Ethiopian Plateau.[4] The existence of Pygmoid people in ancient Ethiopia can be dismissed as fanciful. Even the assertion that Negroes were the original inhabitants of Ethiopia has been cast out; instead, physical anthropologists contend, Caucasoids were solidly in possession of the area from the eastern Sudan to the former British East Africa from Late Pleistocene times into the Neolithic.[5] The Negroes of Ethiopia are thus late arrivals. Of course, it is still possible that ensete was domesticated by them after their arrival. On the other hand, neither the present-day Negro tribes of southern Ethiopia[6] nor those of the north cultivate ensete (admittedly most of them live at low elevations and in areas that may be unsuited to it), which suggests that they are not responsible for its domestication.

This leaves the various Cushitic groups, the early inhabitants of highland Ethiopia, as possibilities. Investigation of them reveals a remarkable concentration of ensete cultivation among the Sidama people of the south (see fig. 2, based on Stiehler, 1948), who also have elaborate methods of using the plant. The Sidama would thus seem likely candidates. The claim that the Galla brought the ensete with them on their initial migration into the highland can be dismissed, for they presumably came from an arid lowland home where the ensete is not known.

Was the ensete cultivated in ancient Egypt?

One early idea about the former extent of ensete cultivation was that of James Bruce, who conjectured that the ancient Egyptians grew ensete for food until finally it was displaced by wheat.[7] Though ignored at the time, his notion has recently been revived by the botanist Vivi Laurent-Täckholm. She argues that the ensete was known to the ancient Egyptians and was probably cultivated by them for food. This she supports by pointing to the similarity in form between the ensete and a common plant design on Middle Predynastic (c. 3500–3100 B.C.)[8] pottery found at

---

[4] W. Stiehler, 'Studien zur Landwirtschafts- und Siedlungs-geographie Äthiopens', *Erdkunde*, 11 (1948), 267.

[5] William W. Howells, *Mankind in the Making* (Garden City, N.Y.), 1959, pp. 311–12.

[6] N. W. Simmonds, 'Ensete cultivation in the southern highlands of Ethiopia; a review', *Tropical Agriculture*, 35 (1958), 307.

[7] James Bruce, *Travels to discover the source of the Nile* (London, 1790), 5 vols., v, 40–1.

[8] Dating for Egypt and Nubia is based on the tables prepared by W. C. Hayes and M. B. Rowton for *The Cambridge Ancient History*, revised edition.

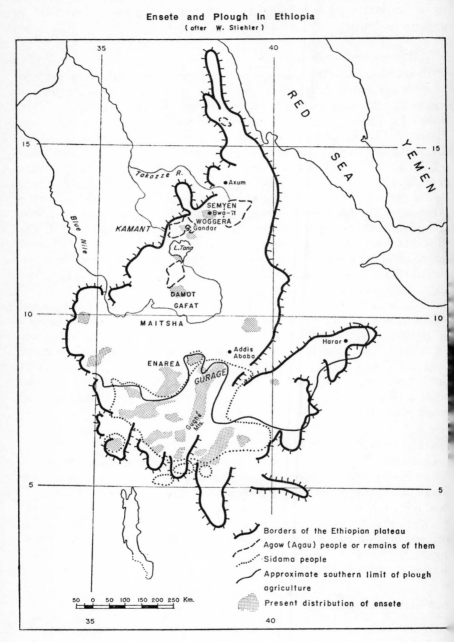

Fig. 2

Naqada in Upper Egypt.[9] The plant design (see fig. 3) appeared in a scene of daily life, which suggested that it was important to the people. Additional support is claimed in the hieroglyphic sign known to the Egyptologists as 'The Plant of the South', which is characterized 'by a pendant top and

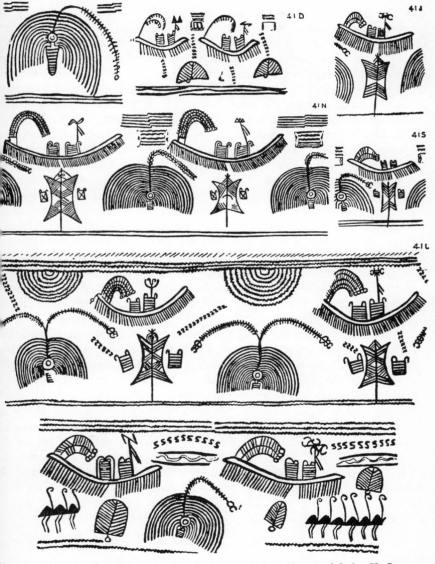

Fig. 3. Naqada pottery designs with plant identified as *Ensete edule* by V. Laurent-Täckholm. (From W. M. F. Petrie, *Prehistoric Egypt*)

[9] Vivi Laurent-Täckholm, 'The plant of Naqada', *Annales du Service des Antiquités de l'Egypte*, 51 (1951), 299–312.

usually 2 pairs of basal leaves', and which in sculpture is frequently shown
with a somewhat swollen base.[10] The principal objections to Mrs Laurent-
Täckholm's suggestion have been: (1) That both the plant design or
Naqada pottery and the hieroglyph 'Plant of the South' actually represent
other plants. The pottery design is generally viewed as depicting an aloe
and the hieroglyph a *Juncus* or *Scirpus*. (2) That even if both signs do
represent the ensete, it would prove only that the people had knowledge
of the plant. It may be that they had contact with the ensete areas of
Ethiopia directly or through intermediaries. More puzzling is the occurrence of the pottery design in scenes of daily life. (3) That the ensete could
not have survived under the climatic conditions and in the marshy riverine
habitat postulated for it in ancient Egypt. The fact that it was successfully
introduced to Egyptian gardens in the last century suggests that climatic
conditions would not exclude it. Moreover, the suitability of the ensete
for a marshy habitat is not altogether certain. Helmer Smeds has argued
that in Ethiopia it is not a plant of such places.[11] On the other hand
Baker and Simmonds list the occurrence of *Ensete edule* in moist and open
places, 'mainly on river sides, swamp margins and forest clearings'.[1]
James Bruce also heard that ensete in Ethiopia sometimes grew under
swampy conditions.[13] Thus it is not certain that the ensete would be out
of place in the swampy margins of the Nile in Egypt; in fact, the opposite
seems reasonable. (4) That no remains of the ensete plant have been found
in Egyptian archaeological deposits. The latter objection is difficult to
answer, but Laurent-Täckholm and Drar have introduced the possibility
that certain Predynastic fibres, whose identity has not yet been finally
decided, are from the ensete.[14]

Despite the fact that the evidence presented is far from convincing, the
possibility that the ensete was cultivated in Egypt should not be discarded.
If the people of Jarmo had trade contact with the Persian Gulf and with
Lake Van in Turkey, why should not the Middle Predynastic Egyptians
a later and more advanced people, have had contact with highland
Ethiopia, and brought back some of the readily transported ensete seeds
It may be that ensete seeds and fibre are somewhere preserved and awaiting
discovery in Egypt. Should cultivation of ensete be established for Egypt
all sorts of further interesting questions would come up about the
economic relations between Egypt and Ethiopia in ancient times. At
the present, however, the evidence is simply not sufficient to state
definitely, as a few writers have, that ensete was cultivated by the ancient
Egyptians.

[10] V. Laurent-Täckholm and Mohammed Drar, *Flora of Egypt*, III (Cairo, 1954
537–8.
[11] Smeds, op. cit. 28.
[12] R. E. D. Baker and N. W. Simmonds, 'The genus Ensete in Africa', *Kew Bulletin*
1953, p. 416.
[13] Bruce, op. cit. v, 26–37.
[14] Laurent-Täckholm and Drar, op. cit. 538–41.

Was ensete once cultivated extensively in northern Ethiopia by Cushites as a food plant?

In the late eighteenth century a tradition existed that the Galla, during their later migrations in which they moved northward across the highland, brought the ensete from Enarea and Maitsha to the Agow and to the Damot region.[15] This would make ensete a fairly recent introduction in the north, perhaps from the sixteenth century. This tradition, however, is opposed by W. Stiehler, who argues that the isolated sections of ensete cultivation in northern Ethiopia represent the remains of an earlier wider cultivation in pre-Semitic times.[16] According to him, this cultivation, which was spread northward to the 'Takazze line' by Cushites, was finally displaced by cereal-plough agriculture with the southward advance of the Semites.[17]

Stiehler's claim is based on: (1) the existence in Bruce's time of ensete cultivation among the Agow-speaking peoples of Godjam (Gojjam), who were descendants of the ancient pre-Semitic inhabitants of northern Ethiopia, and (2) the existence of islands of ensete cultivation elsewhere in the north. There is incontrovertible evidence that plantations of ensete existed just south of Lake Tana in the late eighteenth century, and that it was the main food of the Agow people living there.[18] It is the existence and character of the other islands, north of Lake Tana, that is in question. On his map, Stiehler (1948: Karte 1) located two present-day areas of cultivation near Gondar and another in Semyen (Semien). My field investigations in 1953–4, however, showed only that ensete grows occasionally in gardens and round churches near Gondar, not that it is common in the area or that it is used for food. Nor have I uncovered evidence that it was widely cultivated for food in this region in the past. It may even be that the garden and churchyard ensete are derived from the local wild plants which still are found here and there in the countryside. The Semyen area of ensete cultivation is interesting, because Semyen is a rough mountain area (Ras Dedjen rises to more than 15,000 feet) and contains one remnant group of Agow in the isolated region of Sahalla along the River Takazze. This is just the sort of place in which one expects to find ancient survivals. Walter Plowden's description a century ago of many villages on the west side of Bwa-īt (Buahit) Mountain almost hidden by (cultivated?) ensete[19] may seem like strong support, but actually it is exceptional. The Portuguese travellers, as well as Charles Jacques Poncet and James Bruce, for example, do not seem to have noted it in Semyen. Hugh Scott in 1952–3 noticed only a few ensete in the area, and these in Woggera in farm enclosures built during Italian times.[20] Josef Werdecker did not observe ensete on

[15] Bruce, op. cit. III, 584.
[16] Stiehler, op. cit. 266–7.
[17] Ibid. 267–8, 273–4, 277–80, Karte 1.
[18] Bruce, op. cit. III, 584.
[19] Walter C. Plowden, *Travels in Abyssinia and the Galla Country* (London, 1868), 395.
[20] Hugh Scott, 'Biogeographical research in High Simien (Northern Ethiopia), 1952–53', *Proc. Linn. Soc. Lond.*, 170, pt. 1 (1958), 52.

either of his pack trips in Semyen, the later of which, in 1955, involved seven weeks in the area.[21] Nor did I see it cultivated during a month-long mule trip through Semyen in 1953–4, though I gathered information about it. My informants who knew the ensete from near-by villages distinguished two plants: *gunaguna* and *enset*. The *enset*, they said, is reproduced from segments of the root, since it does not flower and fruit or put out offshoots; thus it is entirely dependent on man for reproduction. Elsewhere in Ethiopia, cultivated ensete is similarly dependent. The *gunaguna*, on the other hand, will grow wild, and can propagate itself through seed. Both plants are cultivated in gardens, but their principal use is for wrapping goods and for fibre. In certain villages, it is asserted, the ensete is used as a scarcity food, but in others not. All this suggests that we are dealing with two plants in Semyen, one, the *gunaguna*, a local wild plant, and the other, the *enset*, an introduced plant which cannot flower and may thus have come from some warmer region. Since the term used for it is *enset*, the same word used by the Sidama of South Ethiopia for the plant, it may have been introduced from the south.

Even more curious is the fact that in Semyen the ensete is cultivated less by the Agow, who might be expected best to preserve ancient elements, than by the Amhara. Elsewhere in the area, the pagan Kamant (Kemant, Qemant), the most conservative Agow-speaking group of the north, cultivate no ensete either. All this lends little support to the assertion that ensete was once widely cultivated in northern Ethiopia for food. It seems likely that there may have been an ancient use of the local wild plant in the north as an ornamental, a fibre plant, and perhaps a scarcity food, but that food use was important in early times only in southern Ethiopia, though subsequently it spread north to the southern shores of Lake Tana.

DID THE SEMITIC INVADERS INTRODUCE THE PLOUGH TO ETHIOPIA AND FIRST DEVELOP CEREAL-PLOUGH AGRICULTURE THERE?

If, as suggested above, the Cushites of northern Ethiopia did not cultivate ensete in pre-Semitic times, one may ask, what was their means of subsistence? This brings us to the question of North Ethiopian cereal-plough agriculture and its origins. There is no doubt that North Ethiopians, whether Semitic or Cushitic, have a curious fixation on cereals, pulses, and oil plants, to the neglect of fruit trees, green vegetables, and roots and tubers. It is also true that the plough is associated with this system of agriculture. The Semitic Amhara, it should be noted, look down on ensete eaters, and have encouraged cereal cultivation in certain conquered areas of the south, where the ensete and other vegetatively reproduced plants cultivated with hoe and digging stick have traditionally been important. From this and similar material, certain writers have concluded that the Semitic-speaking invaders from Yemen, who conquered and settled

[21] Josef Werdecker, personal communication, 5 April 1956.

northern highland Ethiopia from 1000 to 400 B.C., introduced the plough from Arabia, and that it was they, too, who modified the local cultivation into cereal-plough agriculture.[22]

Though at one time or another I have been attracted by these assertions, I am becoming increasingly wary of them. They seem to focus on diffusion by migrating peoples to the exclusion of the less spectacular, slow diffusion by other means, as from one group to another along trade routes. It almost seems as if scholars were dazzled by the ruins of Semitic temples, palaces, and tombs at Axum and elsewhere, and without further grounds ascribed to their builders other cultural innovations as well. In the Mediterranean world and in Mesopotamia also, it was the treasures of art and architecture that so filled the minds of the traditional European archaeologist that he ignored the less spectacular sites, the humble villages in which agriculture developed and which gave the landscape a character that has persisted until the present day. At one extreme were W. J. Perry and his followers who, apparently overcome by the glories of Egypt, gave that land and people too important a role in advancing culture. I am suggesting here that we may be dealing with a similar phenomenon in Ethiopia; that, by ignoring the less dramatic data, we have given the Semites credit for innovations for which there is no proof, archaeological or otherwise.

Indeed, there is some evidence, however sketchy, that the Cushites had developed cereal-plough agriculture before the Semitic invasion. It is generally accepted, for example, that t'eff was cultivated in Ethiopia before the Semitic invasions, for there is no evidence that it was ever used in South Arabia. Moreover, sorghum and finger millet, presumably African domesticates, would have been available to the Cushites, and probably even certain types of wheat and barley.[23] George P. Murdock, it is true, states that the Semites presumably brought with them (introduced?) wheat

---

[22] Stiehler, op. cit. 264–5.

[23] Stiehler, relying on earlier Russian work which made Ethiopia a centre of origin of cultivated wheats and barley, argues that these two cereals were used by the Cushites in their field agriculture in pre-Semitic times (Stiehler, op. cit. 269, 274). The present consensus, however, agrees with Elisabeth Schiemann ('New results on the history of the cultivation of cereals', Heredity, v, 1951, 312–13) that Ethiopia is a centre of diversity, but not a centre of origin of wheats and barley. The centre of wheat domestication is placed by Hans Helbaeck in the fringes of the Fertile Crescent, and of barley in the region stretching from Morocco to Turkestan (Hans Helbaeck, 'Domestication of food plants in the Old World', Science, 130, no. 3372 (1959), 365). Though Nicolai Vavilov himself as long ago as 1937 reputedly gave up Ethiopia as a centre of wheat and barley domestication (Naum Jasny, The wheats of classical antiquity (Baltimore, 1944), 29), the idea shows surprising persistence, appearing even in a recent publication of my own (Frederick Simoons, Northwest Ethiopia: peoples and economy (Madison, 1960), 104, 105).

The striking variability among Ethiopian hard wheats, according to Edgar Anderson's suggestion, may derive from the Ethiopian pattern of mixing wheats of various kinds in the same field, which encourages crossing and diversity (Edgar Anderson, 'The evolution of domestication' in Sol Tax, The evolution of life (Chicago, 1960), 75–6). Schiemann has suggested that temperature shock and ultra-violet light also favour mutations in mountainous areas (Schiemann, op. cit. 309, 311).

and barley,[24] but a Semitic introduction (if this is what he means) appears unlikely for the following reasons. Emmer wheat and barley were known very early in other centres of civilization in the Old World—in Mesopotamia by 7000 B.C. (Jarmo)[25] and in Egypt by about 4500 B.C. (Merimde). Moreover, the existence of considerable contact among the ancient centres is increasingly known and documented. Though direct contact between highland Ethiopia and Egypt has not been proved for times pre-dating the Semitic invasion, it is a real possibility. Already about 2600 B.C., the Pharaoh Sneferu dispatched to Phoenicia a fleet of forty vessels to obtain cedar logs,[26] which indicates a considerable skill in navigation. By the time of Sahure (c. 2488–2475 B.C.), there are reports of an Egyptian fleet reaching the 'Land of Punt',[27] a contact which was reaffirmed in other inscriptions, such as that telling of the famous expedition of Queen Hatshepsut in 1496 B.C. It is interesting to speculate on how many contacts by unchronicled voyagers were made before and between these great undertakings. The drawings of Queen Hatshepsut's ships in Punt, laden with goods of that country, suggest that trade was not unusual to the people of Punt. Nor has the importance of the little-known 'Nubian Corridor' or the Sennar in Ethiopia-Egypt contacts yet been determined. Already in Middle Kingdom times (c. 2040–1700 B.C.), Kerma, just south of the third cataract, served as an Egyptian trading post and a break in transport for the river and caravan traffic from the south. The facts that the Egyptians fortified the post and had permanent settlers there,[27] suggest that their trade with the south at this time was a regular affair. Though the southern limits of Egyptian control have fluctuated through history, it is known that Tuthmosis I (1525–c. 1512 B.C.) left a boundary inscription beyond the fourth cataract at Kurgus, fifty miles south of Abu Hamed,[28] within reasonable distance, along well-watered valleys, for trade with highland Ethiopia. Moreover, the 'country lists' of Tuthmosis III (1504–1450 B.C.) show, if Ernest Zyhlarz's reconstruction[29] is correct, Egyptian knowledge—presumably by overland routes—of northern highland Ethiopia, and of coastal Eritrea and beyond as far south as the Gulf of Tadjoura. Though the likelihood remains that Egyptians made direct early contact with Ethiopia, at various times intermediaries must also have been involved. Among likely early candidates are the C-Group people (described by Arkell),[30] who settled in Lower Nubia about 2181–2040 B.C., a pottery-making pastoral people (presumably with subsidiary agriculture) whose

[24] George Peter Murdock, *Africa: its peoples and their culture history* (New York, 1959), 183.
[25] Helbaeck, op. cit. 367, 370.
[26] James Henry Breasted, *A history of Egypt* (New York, 1912), 115.
[27] Ibid. 127; John A. Wilson, *The Burden of Egypt* (Chicago, 1951), 138.
[28] A. J. Arkell, *A history of the Sudan* (London, 1955), 84.
[29] Ernest Zyhlarz, 'The countries of the Ethiopian empire of Kash (Kush) and Egyptian Old Ethiopia in the New Kingdom', *Kush*, VI (1958), 7–38.
[30] Arkell, op. cit. 46–54.

remains are also found from Agordat in Eritrea to the Wadi Howar in Darfur. The possibility of a C-Group introduction of wheat and barley to Ethiopia is supported by J. Desmond Clark.[31]

Whether wheat and barley arrived by land or by sea, it is likely that the Cushites of Ethiopia had knowledge of these cereals long before 1000 B.C. It seems unreasonable that the Agow-speaking Cushites, viewed by Murdock as 'one of the culturally most creative peoples' in all of Africa,[32] would have failed to take over these cereals. In this regard, it is interesting to consider the careful study of Ethiopian wheats done by Raffaele Ciferri and Guido Renzo Giglioli. This study shows that the greatest abundance of the 42-chromosome soft wheat varieties (including bread wheat and club wheat) is found in Eritrea, the goal of the largest Semitic invasions. It shows further that in Ethiopia itself soft wheat cultivation is concentrated round the centres of Semitic influence, Axum, Harar, and Addis Ababa.[33] This information may suggest to some that the soft wheats, which account for only 10 per cent of Ethiopia's wheat production, were introduced by the Semites, but it still allows the possibility that certain of the 28-chromosome hard wheats, which account for 90 per cent of Ethiopia's production, especially emmer, were cultivated in pre-Semitic times.

The case of the plough is equally intriguing. Field study in North-West Ethiopia reveals that the plough—always of the same basic type[34]—is not associated specifically with the Semites, but instead is used wherever plough animals are found. Where there are animals suitable for ploughing, both Cushites and Semites use the plough; but where, as along the Sudan border, these animals are excluded by disease, even Semites turn to the hoe or digging stick for preparing their fields. There is also the case of the Semitic Gurage of Central Ethiopia who, though they use the plough for certain things, employ a curious double-pronged digging stick which is more suitable for ensete cultivation and other digging.[35] There is no doubt, however, that the plough is an admirable implement in preparing fields for cereals, and that it would have been equally so to the ancient Cushites for cultivating sorghum, finger millet, and *t'eff* (leaving wheat and barley out of it). Linguistic evidence collected by Marcel Cohen, furthermore, suggests that the word for plough, and thus the implement, was present among the Cushites before the Semitic conquest, and that the Cushitic word was taken over by the Ge'ez-speaking Semites.[36] Consideration of

[31] J. Desmond Clark, 'The spread of food production in sub-Saharan Africa', *Jour. Afr. Hist.*, III, 2 (1962), 213, 219.

[32] Murdock, op. cit. 182.

[33] Raffaele Ciferri and Guido Renzo Giglioli, 'La cerealicoltura in Africa Orientale. III. I frumenti volgari e compatti', *L'Italia agricola*, 76 (1939), 767–8.

[34] See Frederick Simoons, 'The agricultural implements and cutting tools of Begemder and Semyen, Ethiopia', *Southwestern Journal of Anthropology*, 14 (1958), 388.

[35] Frederick Simoons, 'The forked digging stick of the Gurage', *Zeitschrift für Ethnologie*, Band 84, Heft 2 (1959), 302–3.

[36] André G. Haudricourt and M. J.-B. Delamarre, *L'Homme et la charrue à travers le monde* (Paris, 1955), 301–2.

the form of the peculiarly constructed Ethiopian plough, however, permits no satisfactory conclusion. Present-day South Arabian and Egyptian ploughs are mostly of common Mediterranean types, and quite distinct from those of highland Ethiopia. It is true that a plough depicted on a South Arabian rock-carving of Sabaean date[37] has been claimed to be of Ethiopian type, but the rock is chipped in such a way as to make the determination uncertain. Present-day Ethiopian ploughs show greatest affinities for types found in present-day Palestine and the western part of the Fertile Crescent, and thus can be related to the Sumerian plough.[38] The mystery is compounded by consideration of the variety of ploughs within Ethiopia itself. Apart from minor variations in form and materials, ploughs of the north seem to be of the one basic type. In the south, however, there are also two strange ploughs, one of which has been likened by G. W. B. Huntingford[39] to a plough of New Kingdom Egypt. Whatever the validity of this claim, it is remarkable that such variation should occur in the south—where the plough is assumed to be recent and where it is less important—rather than in the north.

A consideration of Ethiopian hoes is equally suggestive, if also inconclusive in establishing an early contact between Egypt and Ethiopia. The tied hoe, found in Ethiopia only in the south, bears, for example, an undeniable resemblance to certain tied hoes of ancient Egypt.

Acknowledging the scantiness of the data, I am suggesting that the Agow or other northern Cushites had the plough—derived from the north end of the Red Sea—and practised cereal cultivation involving *t'eff*, and perhaps finger millet, sorghum, wheat, and barley, in pre-Semitic times. If this suggestion is correct, the struggle between plough-cereal agriculture and ensete monoculture may go further back in time than is now assumed. It would thus be an internal distinction which arose among the Cushites themselves, and for historical or environmental reasons that have not yet even been considered.

SUMMARY

This paper considers several questions in the economic prehistory of Ethiopia. Who domesticated the banana-like ensete, the food plant which in parts of southern Ethiopia forms a monoculture? Was the ensete cultivated in ancient Egypt? Was it once cultivated extensively in northern Ethiopia as a food plant? Did the Semites, who invaded Ethiopia from South Arabia, starting about 1000 B.C., introduce the plough to Ethiopia and first develop cereal-plough agriculture there?

The Sidama peoples of southern Ethiopia are viewed as likely candidates in

[37] J. and H. Derenbourg, 'Études sur l'épigraphie du Yémen, v', *Journal Asiatique*, 8e Série, II (1883), Plate 3.

[38] Haudricourt and Delamarre, op. cit. 287, 301.

[39] G. W. B. Huntingford, *The Galla of Ethiopia. The Kingdoms of Kafa and Janjero*, Ethnographic Survey of Africa; North-eastern Africa, pt. II (London, 1955), 109.

ensete domestication. The evidence for ensete cultivation in ancient Egypt is weighed and judged inconclusive. The cultivation of ensete for food in northern Ethiopia is viewed as recent. The suggestion is made that cereal-plough agriculture pre-dated the Semitic invasions. The ancient Cushitic inhabitants of northern Ethiopia are seen as having been in an excellent position for contacts with countries at the north end of the Red Sea, particularly Egypt, whence wheat and barley and the plough could have been introduced.

8. SOME DEVELOPMENTS IN THE PREHISTORY OF THE BANTU LANGUAGES

By MALCOLM GUTHRIE

IN a field like Africa it is reasonable to hope for some assistance from
linguistic data for the general study of prehistory. In fact there is a real
temptation to use material of this kind in such a way that the results cannot
be verified, or, to put it more baldly, to make guesses that are no better than
other guesses. Clearly the serious investigation of the prehistory of Africa
demands something more than speculative hypotheses, and for this reason
it is essential that any conclusions drawn from linguistic information shall
be based on a firm basis of codified data.

There are areas in Africa where it still proves to be impracticable to find
linguistic data that are coherent enough for prehistorical purposes. In the
case of the Bantu languages, however, the situation is different, and this has
been recognized for a hundred years since Bleek first put forward in 1862 a
theory of common origin based on the material that was available to him.
The relationship between the members of the Bantu family has never
subsequently been called into question, and further investigations have
merely served to make it even clearer. As more and more of the Bantu
languages have been studied by means of increasingly accurate techniques,
the volume of data available for comparative purposes has become very
great indeed. Nevertheless, the techniques of comparative study used in the
treatment of the material provided in this way have remained almost
unchanged since the last century, when Meinhof first propounded his reconstruction of Ur-Bantu. The main characteristic of this type of study is
that it introduces speculative hypotheses into the handling of the data, so
that few of its conclusions can really be substantiated. The persistent use of
this approach to Bantu prehistory has led to a crop of unverifiable theories
which have gained general acceptance, the latest of these being the
Niger–Congo group introduced into Greenberg's classification of African
languages, which in turn has been accepted by Murdock as having a factual
value.

In order to meet the fundamental condition that hypotheses should be
built only on facts that are demonstrably true, I began some fifteen years
ago to adopt a quite different method of comparative study. The aim of
the investigation was to produce results in prehistory that would be based
on verifiable observations. To do this involved a great deal of sifting and
codifying of the evidence before even a beginning could be made in the
direction of discovering the probable origins of the Bantu family. A detailed
statement about the technical details of the method I developed has been

Greenberg

131

presented elsewhere,[1] and so all that is necessary here is a bare outline of the procedure adopted.

I. COLLECTING AND ARRANGING THE DATA

The raw material for any comparative study of languages is the existence of groups of cognates from language to language, characterized by what are known as sound-shifts. The difficulty is that the recognition of cognates may call for a degree of precision and skill that can be commanded only by a specialist. Frequently there are instances of a specious relationship that can easily mislead the inexperienced investigator, who may equally find it difficult to believe that some true cognates are related at all. Thus for example Kikuyu –rut– 'teach' is very similar in shape to Sotho –rut'– 'teach', but this can be shown to be a purely fortuitous resemblance, whereas Hai (Chaga) *ifwo* 'bone' and Mbundu *ekepa* 'bone' really are cognates in spite of their dissimilarity. Although the working out of the rules governing the relationships between cognates is sometimes a complicated operation, it does prove to be possible to formulate rules that can be strictly applied in the construction of numbers of sets of cognates. In this way a coherent corpus of organized data is obtained that can provide an adequate foundation on which theories about prehistory can be built. In practice over 2300 such sets of cognates have been constructed with items from some 200 of the Bantu languages.

Once a corpus of this kind has been formed, it is possible to infer that all the items in a given set are due to some item in some ancestor language, which is then termed a 'root', while the items contained in any set of cognates are known as 'reflexes' of the root to which they are attributed. In other words there are as many roots involved as there are sets of cognates, but it would be a quite unjustified assumption at this stage to speak of all these 2300 roots as though they belonged to the same ancestor language. Indeed, certain features of these roots make it highly unlikely that they could all be attributed to one language, as for example the fact that there are seven roots meaning 'yesterday', five meaning 'egg', and four meaning 'six'. It is clearly improbable that any language would have such a wealth of words for meanings of this kind.

One of the first things to be attempted is to produce some classification of the roots into various types, and this does not prove to be very difficult. If it is possible to discover all or most of the reflexes of a given root, the area covered by the languages in which the reflexes are found can be considered to be the geographical spread of the root itself. Although there are many languages where the available evidence is inadequate, those which have been examined cover a sufficiently large proportion of most parts of the Bantu field to provide a reasonably clear picture of the spread of each of the

[1] 'A two-stage method of comparative Bantu studies', *African Language Studies.* III (London, School of Oriental and African Studies, 1962).

2300 roots. As is inevitable, the patterns of geographical spread are of many different kinds, and a certain amount of experimenting was necessary to discover how to assort these patterns so as to produce the greatest possible simplification of their variety. One type of root, however, presented no difficulty in this respect, since its reflexes cover the whole or the greater part of the Bantu area. The total collection of these roots, which are known as 'general', forms a very important body of information, which we may term the 'general group' of Bantu roots.

The other patterns of geographical spread which are less than general can be assorted into two main groups according as they are confined mainly or exclusively to (a) the western part, or (b) the eastern part of the Bantu area. These two distinct subdivisions of the Bantu field are termed 'regions', and the two groups of roots just referred to are known as 'western' and 'eastern' respectively. The miscellaneous group of roots that cannot be classified as either general, western or eastern contains less than 14 per cent of the total. In order to increase the usefulness of the information contained in the 86 per cent of classified roots, it proved necessary to choose a certain number of 'test languages', and to make a note of every reflex of the roots found in them. In all, twenty-eight test languages were selected, and the noting of all the reflexes they each contained increased the total collection of cognates to about 22,000. It is then this body of codified data which provides the basis for the investigation of Bantu prehistory.

Even when the roots with their reflexes have been classified, a considerable amount of work has to be done to bring out facts that have a bearing on the probable origins of the family. For one thing some analysis of the actual structure of the different roots is necessary, and in particular the way these structural features are distributed in the three main groups of roots. In addition, a number of statistical operations are possible, ranging from the simple adding up of the totals of reflexes from each of the test languages to computations based on special formulae to obtain a measure of the relationship between any two languages. There is also a need to codify the features that distinguish some pairs of roots which have everything else in common. Thus for example there are a number of cases where two roots with the same meaning differ in that one of them has *U where the other has *O, as for example between *-NUN- 'get fat' and *-NON- 'get fat'.[2] The geographical spread of each of such pairs then has to be determined, as well as any correlation between the difference in the vowel of the root and the difference in the spread of the reflexes.

From such an investigation it is possible to obtain a reasonably clear picture of the whole situation as reflected in the body of data contained in the sets of cognates, and this is set out briefly in the next section.

[2] Roots are regularly spelt with upper case characters preceded by an asterisk. In more precise representations distinctions of tone are shown by accents, but these are omitted here for the sake of typographical simplicity.

2. THE OVERALL COMPARATIVE BANTU PICTURE

At this point it is not proposed to introduce any hypotheses about Bantu origins, but simply to outline the state of affairs that will require some explanation in terms of prehistory in the concluding section of this paper. Some facts will be given first of all about the meanings expressed by the general roots, and then about the relative totals of reflexes found in the test languages. A certain amount of statistical information obtained from computations will also be presented but in a very general form. Finally it will be possible to set out a few typical facts only about the way pairs of apparently related roots differ in their geographical spread.

In all there is a list of over 500 general Bantu roots which show a relatively uniform spread of meanings. Thus the list contains some thirty names of animals, birds, and insects, which include most of those found throughout the Bantu area, such as 'dog', 'goat', 'cattle', 'pig', 'elephant', 'hippopotamus', 'buffalo', 'ant-eater', 'squirrel', 'puff-adder', 'guinea-fowl', 'hawk', 'pigeon', 'tick', 'spider', 'bee', 'mosquito'. There are a number of omissions from the list, and the more interesting of these are the following. There are several roots for both 'domestic fowl' and 'hyena', and while the total spread of all the reflexes covers most of the field, no individual root has a wide geographical spread. The case of the roots meaning 'crocodile', 'lion', and 'bat' is somewhat similar except that here there is a sharp division between the western and eastern regions. The reflexes of the roots for 'scorpion' and 'parrot' are confined to the western region, and those for 'frog' and 'louse' to the eastern, no satisfactory set of cognates having been made from the other region in these cases; while no set whatever has so far been constructed from words for a few animals and insects, as for example for 'jigger'.

The list of general roots also contains about thirty names of parts of the body, but these call for no special comment. Among the remainder of the general roots there are terms for various kinds of cultural activity, and a few of these may be noted, such as words for 'pot', 'to mould pottery'; 'basket', 'to plait'; 'to fish with line', 'fish-hook'; 'trap', 'to set trap', 'birdlime'; 'iron ore', 'iron', 'to forge metal', 'to blow bellows', 'hammer', 'knife'; 'cloth', 'to sew'; 'canoe', 'paddle', 'to paddle'; 'journey', 'to carry on the head', 'headpad'. The actual geographical spread of the general roots with these meanings varies slightly, but in a brief outline of this kind cannot be described in detail, and one or two examples only must suffice. The root meaning 'to paddle' has no known reflexes in the central part of the eastern region, while that meaning 'paddle' has none in the southern part of the same region. The root meaning 'to forge iron' covers the whole area except certain parts on or near the coast in the centre of the eastern region, where two quite distinct sets of cognates occur, one being reflexes of a peculiar root, and the other apparently related to a root meaning 'to pound'.

In respect to trees and items of food the number of general roots is limited, containing mainly those meaning 'fig-tree', 'palm-tree', 'banana', 'bean', 'honey', and 'mushroom'. The roots for words referring to other foods have mainly a regional distribution. Thus there are distinct western and eastern roots for 'sugar-cane' and 'salt', while there are western sets of cognates only for 'palm-nut', 'palm-oil', 'kola nut', 'yam', 'maize', and 'pepper', but eastern sets only for 'pumpkin', 'ground-nut', and 'millet'.

There are many other categories of meaning represented among the general roots, among which the presence of the following may be noted, 'chief', 'polygamy', 'war', 'bow', 'courtyard', 'fireplace', 'platform', 'bedstead', 'pestle', 'ladle', 'year', 'cold wind'.

A simple procedure by which the total number of reflexes of the general roots in each test language is reckoned up provides a series of figures that can be plotted on a map as percentages of the total number of general roots. The state of affairs revealed by the map includes a belt of high figures, termed the nucleus, stretching right across the Bantu area on both sides of the boundary between the regions. Thus there are on the western side Kongo 44, Lwena 46, Luba-Kasai 47, Luba-Katanga 50, and on the eastern Bemba 54, Ila 43, Rundi 44, Swahili 44. From the nucleus the figures decrease both to the north and to the south, but the diminution, which is fairly uniform to the south in the west, and on both sides in the east, is more abrupt to the north in the west. Thus from Kongo 44 and Lwena 46 in the west, going southwards there are Mbundu (Umbundu) 38 and Herero 33; and in the east southwards from Bemba 54, Swahili 44, and Ila 43 there are Nyanja and Yao both 35, Zezuru (Shona) 37, Venda 30, Sotho 28, Zulu 29, and Xhosa 26, and northwards from Bemba 54, Rundi 44, and Swahili 44 there are Sukuma 41, Ganda, Nyoro, and Nyankore all 37, Kikuyu 32 and Kamba 30. To the north of Kongo 44 and Luba-Kasai 47 on the other hand are Bali (Teke) 28, Tetela 26, Bobangi 24, Bulu 20, and Duala 14.

A similar operation performed on the two groups of regional roots gives a very similar pattern of distribution in that the highest figures of all are obtained for languages in the nucleus. The principal difference in these figures from those obtained for the general roots is that apart from Kongo, which has the high value of 53, there is an even diminution in both regions from around 38 in the centre (in the western region Bali 38, Bobangi 38 and in the eastern Bemba 38, Swahili 39), to about 20 or just under at the extremities (N.W.: Duala 17; S.W.: Herero 17; N.E.: Kamba 21; S.E.: Xhosa 16).

A more complicated statistical procedure exists on the basis of which a taxonomic classification can be produced by taking into account the joint occurrences of reflexes of individual roots in each pair of languages. This is feasible only with the aid of an electronic computer, but its results show a nuclear area that is similar to that revealed in the distribution of the percentages of the general roots.

One further aspect of the statistical characteristics of the roots and their reflexes, has been investigated by means of a special formula designed to express numerically the degree of relationship between any two pairs of test languages. This has been applied to the reflexes of the total range of roots as well as to the general and the two regional groups taken separately. By this means many very detailed indications have been obtained that supplement the taxonomic picture just referred to. To attempt to present even part of this here is scarcely practicable, but the following diagrammatic representation expresses in a very concise form the situation revealed by the computations. The siting of the names in the diagram roughly corresponds to the relative geographical location of the languages, the linking lines being based on the information shown up in the whole range of statistical operations, including the taxonomic classification just referred to. The double connecting line links the languages of the nucleus, while the single lines give an approximate indication of the order of relationship of the remaining languages.

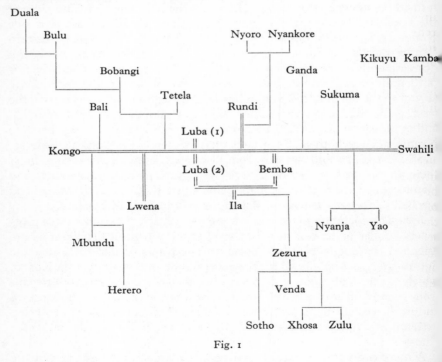

Fig. 1

This diagram inevitably grossly over-simplifies the picture presented by the statistical analysis that has been carried out, but it must suffice as a illustration of the situation revealed in a large number of such diagrams tha have had to be constructed.

From the investigation of sets of cognates that have to be attributed t roots which differ in one respect only, a great deal of information has bee obtained. The following typical example must suffice to show the kind of facts that are involved. There are a number of pairs of roots where one begins with *B and the other with *P, such as *–BEGA 'shoulder', *–PEGA 'shoulder', but in no case is either root in the general group, nor are there any clear cases where the reflexes of the one root are in one region and those of the other are in the other. On the other hand, in pairs where one root as *G and the other *K, as for example *–GOMB– 'scrape', *–KOMB– 'scrape', there are two or three where the root with *K is general, and at least one where the one with *K is eastern and the other western. It is therefore clear that any distinction between *K and *G has a different status from one between *P and *B. A number of differences of this kind have been established and these provide a means of classifying some of the roots.

3. PROVISIONAL HYPOTHESES ABOUT BANTU PREHISTORY

The very brief outline given in the previous section of the picture built up from features present in the corpus of Bantu roots and their sets of reflexes has disclosed a situation that calls for some hypotheses to account for it. These hypotheses fall roughly into two types according to what object is in view. This may be (a) the probable nature of the ancestry of the Bantu family or (b) the more difficult question of the provenance of any hypothetical ancestor or ancestors. As the first of these involve mainly inferences and the second much more speculation it is convenient to consider them separately.

(a) *The Family Ancestry*

Not only can a large number of direct inferences be made which do not involve recourse to speculation, but in practice a relatively detailed network of such inferences has been constructed. As is inevitable in any procedure of this kind, however, it can never be asserted that no other hypothesis fits the facts. The only claim made therefore for the suggestions in this sub-section is that no more satisfactory explanation of the situation has yet been found. In a paper of this kind it is possible to give no more than the barest outline of such tentative conclusions as have been drawn, but the following are the more important of them.

(i) As there is a well-defined group of general Bantu roots, it may be inferred that these occurred in a single ancestor language to be called 'Proto-Bantu'. Assuming then that such an ancestor existed, the fact that every Bantu language contains reflexes of the general roots must mean that all the Bantu languages are descended from this one original stock.

(ii) Since Proto-Bantu was presumably a language of the same general type as the present-day languages, it probably had at least 2000 unrelated items in its vocabulary. The fact therefore that there are no more than just over 500 general roots means that a large amount of the Proto-Bantu material has disappeared. It is conceivable that some of the lost Proto-Bantu roots are preserved in the regional groups of the sets of cognates, but since they could not be identified even if present, inferences about the original stock can be drawn only from those sets of cognates that are indisputably general.

(iii) The pattern of geographical distribution of the reflexes of the general roots seems to indicate that Proto-Bantu was spoken somewhere near the centre of the nucleus, i.e. in the bush country to the south of the equatorial forest midway between the two coasts.

(iv) The meanings expressed by the general roots suggest that the speakers of Proto-Bantu were presumably a people with a developed culture that included a knowledge of such things as iron-working and river craft.

(v) The occurrence of two well-defined groups of regional roots with exactly the same sound-shifts can only mean that dialectal variants developed within Proto-Bantu. The statistical features displayed by these regional groups seem to show that the western dialect separated from the original stock well before the eastern dialect came into being.

(vi) As the figures obtained to express the degree of relationship between the test languages display well-defined patterns of distribution, it is probable that there was a certain amount of cross-contamination between the original stock and its dialects while the ancestor languages were still in the nucleus area. The information revealed in a study of roots that differ in one feature only confirms this inference and even throws some light on the details of the contaminations.

(vii) The fact that the figures for the distribution of the reflexes of roots in each of the three groups show a progressive diminution from the nucleus presumably means that the ancestors of the present-day languages dispersed northwards and southwards from the nucleus. As the sharp drop in the percentages in the reflexes of the general roots to the north in the west coincides with the boundary of the equatorial forest area, it is probably due to a greater rate of decay under forest conditions. The fact that there is no comparable drop in the figures for the reflexes of the western roots could be due to the development of a large number of fresh items in some intermediate ancestor of the north-western languages.

(viii) Since there is regularity in the sound-shifts in the reflexes of all the roots, it is probable that the development of the present-day languages from Proto-Bantu and its dialects proceeded uniformly without noticeable contamination. This means that it could in theory be possible to construct a genealogical table with the proto-language and its dialects at the source, and the diagram of relationships in fig. 1 may well provide a framework for this.

(b) *The Origin of Proto-Bantu*

The general outline of the probable ancestry of the Bantu languages just presented is clearly incompatible with either of the two previous theories of Bantu origins. Johnston located the ancestor language in the Lake Victoria region,[3] while more recently Greenberg has speculated that the point of origin was near the Cameroons–Nigeria border.[4] Since the Greenberg theory has gained a wide currency, it is worth noting that it apparently ignores such things as terrain and vegetation, but treats Africa as though people could have migrated equally easily in any direction.[5] Any coherent hypothesis however must take account of the possibilities of movement as well as of the linguistic data.

There is a certain amount of evidence found scattered here and there throughout West Africa that may shed some light on the probable origin of Proto-Bantu. The significant fact is that features reminiscent of Bantu languages occur irregularly in a number of apparently unrelated West African languages. If we assume that these are vestiges of some earlier language, fragments of which were absorbed into various languages at some time in the prehistorical period in West Africa, then such a language, which we will term 'Pre-Bantu' might also have been the source of Proto-Bantu. If that were so, then we have to imagine the speakers of Pre-Bantu moving in two directions, some to the Proto-Bantu area, and others to West Africa. One hypothesis which could fit this requirement is to suppose that Pre-Bantu was spoken somewhere in the Lake Chad region by people who had some skill in the use of canoes, and that one group of these used the water-ways of the Congo basin to traverse the otherwise impenetrable forest.

An elaboration of this basic speculation could envisage that the original Proto-Bantu speakers had no knowledge of iron-working, but that this arrived subsequently by the same route, being brought by descendants either of their own ancestors who had remained in the Chad area, or of collaterals. This would mean that when the skill of iron-working reached them, the Proto-Bantu speakers may well have become fairly numerous, since there could have been a considerable lapse of time between the coming of the first group and the subsequent arrival of the smiths.[6] The acquisition of iron tools and weapons could then have been a major factor in the ultimate dispersion of the speakers of the Proto-Bantu dialects.

The westward movement of still other groups of speakers of Pre-Bantu,

---

[3] The principal vestige of this almost forgotten idea is in the practice of some writers of referring to the languages of this area as 'old' Bantu.

[4] There seems no way of reconciling the Greenberg hypothesis with the distribution of the percentages of the reflexes, which is in exactly the opposite order to what would have been expected.

[5] Having made the land journey by two different routes between Duala and the bush country beyond the equatorial forest to the south and south-east, I find it inconceivable that the progenitors of the speakers of the Bantu languages should have traversed such impenetrable forest.

[6] The presence of a quite unrelated root meaning 'to forge' in the south-eastern coastal belt could be due to the introduction of iron-working from another source.

which could account for the fragmentary occurrence of Bantu features in West African languages, may have taken place at any time. It is however conceivable that it was provoked by the same events, whatever they were, which impelled the smiths to make their journey southward.

As is inevitable in a hypothesis involving so much speculation, Pre-Bantu has a much smaller degree of certainty than Proto-Bantu, the picture of which is constructed largely from direct inferences.

9. THE PROBLEM OF THE BANTU EXPANSION

By ROLAND OLIVER

THE British Institute of History and Archaeology in East Africa, with the help of the Astor Foundation, has recently launched a major research project concerning the origins of the Bantu-speaking peoples, who today number some seventy millions and occupy most of Africa south of the Equator.[1] At first sight it may seem surprising that this project is being launched under the direction of a group of archaeologists, and from an East African base which is clearly far from the centre of the Bantu world. How, one may ask, can any archaeologist possibly know what kind of language was spoken by the subjects of his investigation? Is it not one of the first principles of archaeology that it is about cultures and not about peoples, and that an archaeologist should never assume an ethnic identity for the makers of any particular culture unless he can demonstrate a really convincing continuity between that culture and some historically identifiable human society? The purpose of this article is to fill in some of the background thinking which has led to the definition of the Bantu Origins project in its present form. Granting from the start that the Institute, even if it has all the luck in the world, is not going to solve the problem of Bantu origins, granting that at best it is going to attack one tiny corner of a vast subject, why is it that a mid-twentieth-century approach to the Bantu problem can be taking this particular form?

Our primary source of evidence about the origins and early history of the Bantu is, of course, the linguistic one. And first and foremost it consists in this one fact, that the Bantu languages, though they are spoken over so vast an area, are so very closely related to each other. Whereas to the north of the Bantu line any two neighbouring languages of the Western Sudanic or the Eastern Sudanic language families are likely to be far more distantly related to each other than the most distantly related members of the Indo-European family, the Bantu languages, all three hundred of them, are in most ways as closely related to each other as English and German. On this all linguists are agreed. And they are also agreed on the implication, which is that, whereas the Western Sudanic and the Eastern Sudanic families must be regarded as comparatively *old* families, whose members have been diverging from each other for a long time, the Bantu family must be regarded as a distinctly *new* family, the speakers of which must have expanded very rapidly indeed in order to have achieved such a wide geographical dispersion along with such a small degree of linguistic divergence.

[1] This article is based on a paper read at the Royal Society of Arts on 5 May 1966 and printed in that Society's *Journal*, CXIV (1966), 852–69. It is reprinted here with the agreement of the R.S.A.

There is nothing new about this fact. It has been recognized and discussed by linguists for the best part of a hundred years. But it is still the great and undoubted fact with which archaeologists and historians of Africa have to wrestle. They have to try and explain it, and not only in terms of where the first few hundred Bantu speakers ultimately came from, but also in terms of the whole dynamic process of expansion through the centuries—a process which must have involved the substantial repopulation of half a continent.

If one looks at the older theories about the Bantu expansion, one finds that most of them have been conceived essentially in terms of migration and conquest. For example, Sir Harry Johnston, who was by far the greatest Africanist of his day, in a famous paper read to the Royal Anthropological Institute in 1913, pictured hordes of Bantu invaders fanning out over the southern half of the continent like so many hordes of nineteenth-century Zulu raiders. 'All Bantu Africa of today,' he said, 'except the heart of the Congo forest and the regions south of the Zambezi, must have been more or less thickly populated before the Bantu impressed with extraordinary rapidity and completeness their own type of language on the tribes they conquered.'[2] Even as recently as 1960 one very perceptive scholar, Dr C. C. Wrigley, after carefully weighing the alternatives, has come down un-equivocally on the side of migration and conquest. 'I see these people', he says, 'not as agriculturalists spreading over a virtually empty land, but as a dominant minority, specialized to hunting with the spear, constantly attracting new adherents by their fabulous prestige as suppliers of meat, constantly throwing off new bands of migratory adventurers, until the whole southern sub-continent was iron-using and Bantu-speaking.'[3]

The only alternative to a conquest theory is, it seems to me, a theory of population growth which can show how the speakers of the Bantu languages grew in numbers much more rapidly than their rivals. Such a theory would not, of course, exclude the element of conquest altogether, for that would imply that there were no earlier populations than the Bantu in Africa south of the Equator. But it would mean, for example, that a closer analogy is to be found in the European settlement of Australia or North America than in the Teutonic invasions of western Europe in the Dark Ages. Of course the European migrants of modern times were better armed than the Australian aborigines or the North American Indians, but that was not the main reason for their successful occupation of these two continents. The *main* reason for their success was that they brought with them from Europe a way of life which was capable in frontier conditions of pro-ducing population explosions which provided the main dynamic of their settlement. The vital point was that they were increasing their numbers

    [2] H. H. Johnston, 'A survey of the ethnography of Africa: and the former racial and tribal migrations of that continent', *Journal of the Royal Anthropological Institute*, XLII (1913), 391–2.
    [3] C. C. Wrigley, 'Speculations on the economic prehistory of Africa', *Journal of African History*, I (1960), 201.

so rapidly that the aboriginal inhabitants were soon left behind as unimportant minorities.

If this is the sort of analogy which we have to seek in investigating the Bantu expansion, then the mind obviously travels first to the supersession of hunting and gathering cultures by food-producing cultures in Africa south of the Equator. If we consider what we know about the coming of food production to Africa, we find that in fact it falls into three well-marked phases, in which Bantu Africa figures mainly in the last. The first phase began with the introduction of the earliest grain crops, wheat and barley, which were first domesticated in western Asia, into Egypt during the second half of the fifth millennium B.C.[4] Up till that time the Upper Palaeolithic hunting population of the Nile Valley can hardly have numbered more than about 20,000 people. Yet within about 2,000 years of the introduction of agriculture Egypt was on the edge of the Dynastic Period, with towns and large villages every few miles, and was soon to have a labour force which has been reckoned at 100,000 people engaged on pyramid building alone. This was the first big population build-up made possible by food production, and from Egypt it spread, though much more slowly, over the rest of Africa north of the Sahara. The populations which benefited most from this phase were of course the 'Caucasoid', Hamito-Semitic-speaking populations of the north and east.

The second phase of the food-producing revolution was that which took place in the Sudanic belt to the south of the Sahara, all the way from the Atlantic in the west to the Ethiopian highlands in the east. The underlying ideas probably came south from Egypt,[5] but their implementation depended upon the domestication of suitable drought-resistant cereals native to the sub-Saharan savannah, such as the sorghums and the millets and, in the western Sudan, the dry rice called *Oryza glaberrima*. There is on the whole a consensus of opinion among botanists and archaeologists that this development should be placed at least as far back as the second millennium B.C. and perhaps as far back as the third.[6] At all events, starting somewhere within this time bracket, we have the second big population build-up in Africa, among the ancestors of the mainly Negro populations of the western and eastern Sudan. So far as one can see, this build-up was a long, slow one—very different from the population explosion which happened in Egypt and from the Bantu explosion which I shall come to presently. Linguistically, the Sudanic build-up was reflected in comparatively small language units, in which even closely neighbouring languages are only very distantly related to each other, suggesting that communities expanded side by side, and at much the same pace, over a very long period indeed.

Just as the first phase of the food-producing revolution encountered a

[4] C. B. M. McBurney, *The Stone Age of Northern Africa* (1960), 234.
[5] Ibid. 244.
[6] Roland Portères, 'Berceaux agricoles primaires sur le continent africain', *Journal of African History*, III (1962), 195–210; J. Desmond Clark, 'The spread of food production in sub-Saharan Africa', ibid. 211–28.

natural barrier in the Sahara, so the second phase encountered a natural barrier in the equatorial forests and the Nile swamps. In so far as the cereals of the second phase did find their way into any part of what is now Bantu Africa, it was probably through the Ethiopian highlands into the drier parts of eastern Africa, and the populations most affected were probably the outliers of the Kushitic subgroup of the Hamito-Semitic-speaking peoples of Ethiopia and the Horn. The people who practised the Stone Bowl culture of Kenya in the first millennium B.C. very likely belonged to this group, and there are some archaeological indications that peoples practising a similar, mainly pastoral but partly agricultural way of life with neolithic equipment penetrated in widely dispersed pockets scattered here and there among the mainly Wilton cultures of Bushman hunters as far south as the eastern highlands of Zambia and as far west as southern Angola and northern South-West Africa.[7] It would seem that these scattered groups may indeed have performed the inestimable service of introducing into the future Bantu Africa the Ethiopian varieties of eleusine millets and sorghums, which the Bantu later adopted.[8]

However, none of these developments touched the humid regions of the Guinea coast and the Congo basin, the Great Lakes and the Zambezi valley, where, according to all the evidence we have at present, hunting and gathering cultures, fortified by a little, possibly ancient, but certainly tenuous, tropical vegeculture, prevailed until approximately the beginning of the Christian era. Just *how* tenuous this ancient vegeculture must have been in terms of the population it was capable of supporting was demonstrated by an American anthropologist, Professor G. P. Murdock, in a work of seminal importance published in 1959.[9] Africa, said Murdock, had been left by Nature peculiarly deficient in food plants suited to the humid tropics. There was the oil-palm. There was the kaffir potato. There were a few indigenous, but not very promising, species of yams. But it was not, he suggested, until the arrival in Africa of the South-East Asian food plants —particularly the bananas, the Asian yams and the cocoa-yams or *taros*— that the food-producing revolution had been able to get going on any serious scale in the humid regions of tropical Africa. The South-East Asian food plants could not have reached Africa until the beginnings of Indian Ocean navigation, and therefore they could not have arrived much before the beginning of the Christian era. Hence the gap of two thousand years or more between the start of the food-producing revolution in the sub-Saharan savannah and its spread to the humid regions.

Thus far Murdock had made a significant contribution. Unfortunately, he went much further by asserting roundly that the introduction of the South-East Asian food plants provided the whole answer to the expansion of the Bantu-speaking peoples, thus seriously reconfusing a problem which

    [7] Brian Fagan, *Southern Africa* (1965), 46.
    [8] Cf. G. P. Murdock, *Africa: Its Peoples and their Culture History* (New York, 1959), 290–1.   [9] Ibid.

he had done much to clarify. The temptation which led Murdock on was the linguistic work of another American scholar, Joseph Greenberg. Working from a lexical comparison of the equivalents for about fifty common words in a large number of Western Sudanic and Bantu languages, Greenberg had reached the conclusion that Bantu belonged to the Western Sudanic language family. He concluded further that the Bantu languages, for all their vast extension, did not even form a single distinct subgroup within this family, but that, taken all together, they merely formed part of a subgroup which included also most of the languages spoken in the central Cameroons and East-Central Nigeria. Greenberg was in no doubt about the historical inference to be drawn from his work. It was, quite simply, that, at the period when the speakers of the Western Sudanic languages had moved southwards from the savannah to occupy the forest belt as well, those of them who started from the eastern Nigerian end of the line, and who were not therefore brought to a halt by the Atlantic coast, simply moved straight on southwards and eastwards into the Congo basin, and from there fanned out to occupy the whole of what is now Bantu Africa. 'The assumption of Bantu movement made here', he says, 'agrees well with the analyses of [the ethnographers] Herskovits, Ankermann and Frobenius, which make the Guinea Coast area and the Congo Basin part of the same culture area.'[10]

To Greenberg's conclusion Murdock simply added the rider that what enabled the Western Sudanic peoples to expand southwards into the forest was their reception of the South-East Asian food plants, which, on his hypothesis, entered Africa through the Ethiopian lowlands and travelled along what he calls 'the yam belt'—that is to say, across the extreme south of the Sudan, along the Nile-Congo watershed, and so on westwards, following the northern margin of the forest to the Upper Guinea coast.[11] About all this there are, it seems to me, insuperable difficulties. Is it not a little strange, one might ask, that the South-East Asian food plants should have reached Bantu Africa via West Africa? Even assuming that the Ethiopian lowlands were the entry point, is it not rather an odd proposition that the Eastern Sudanic speakers living in the eastern part of the yam belt, immediately to the north of what was to become Bantu Africa, did nothing to penetrate southwards themselves, but merely speeded the new plants westwards until they reached the apparently more enterprising speakers of the Western Sudanic languages? Finally, one might ask whether it is not much more likely that the South-East Asian food plants reached Bantu Africa directly from the east coast. After all, we know that Madagascar was first colonized by sea-borne Indonesian migrants during the first few centuries A.D., and it is surely most unlikely that some of these migrants did not end up on the adjacent East African mainland. If that mainland had then been unoccupied, or occupied only lightly by hunter-gatherers, the Indonesian colonists would presumably have multiplied and taken over the

[10] J. H. Greenberg, *Studies in African Linguistic Classification* (New Haven, 1955), 40.
[11] Murdock, op. cit. 222–3.

land, and we should have had an Indonesian-speaking population in South-
East Africa today, just as we have in Madagascar. From all this I should
think it nearly certain that by the time of the Indonesian colonization of
Madagascar the adjacent mainland of East Africa was already occupied
by cultivators numerous enough to absorb the colonists and able to take
over their food plants and develop them for themselves. And, from the
evidence which follows, I should further conclude that these people were
already the ancestors of the Bantu.

The next piece of evidence is again linguistic, and it is not in my view
fundamentally contradictory of Greenberg, though it modifies Greenberg's
very simple hypothesis in a very important way. This is the evidence which
comes from Professor Malcolm Guthrie's work on the classification of the
Bantu languages themselves. I have said that Greenberg's work was based
on a comparison of about fifty common meanings over the languages of
Africa as a whole. Guthrie's work is of an altogether different order of
detail. It is based on a comparison of about 22,000 related words in some
200 Bantu languages. And, very roughly, his conclusions go like this. In
these languages there turn out to be some 2,300 common word roots, which
have a wide regional distribution. Something over 500 of these roots are
distributed throughout the Bantu area as a whole. These 500 he calls the
'general roots'. And if you count the number of these 'general roots'
that occur in each individual language and turn it into a percentage, and
then plot the percentages on a map, you get a very significant result. You
find that the percentages vary from about 15 % up to about 55 %. And you
find that the highest percentages form a cluster on the map, in the shape of
a long, flat ellipse, with its main axis running east and west, roughly from
the mouth of the Congo to the mouth of the Rovuma, with its centre in the
Luba country of northern Katanga. The Luba and Bemba languages at the
centre of the ellipse have the highest percentages of the 'general roots',
with 50 % and 54 % respectively. And the percentages fall away steadily
as you move east and west from here, with Kongo and Swahili each showing about 44 %. As you move outside the elliptical area, however, whether
to the north or to the south, the percentages fall away further still, as I shall
describe in a moment. About the historical inference to be drawn from his
work, Guthrie is as certain as Greenberg is about his. It is that, wherever the
first few hundred Bantu speakers may have come from, the region in which
their descendants multiplied, and from which they progressively dispersed
over the rest of Bantu Africa, lies within the elliptical area and, above all,
towards its centre, in the woodland region of the Katanga.[12]

Now what is significant here is that Guthrie's elliptical area is *not* predominantly a forested area. It is predominantly a light woodland area,
intersected by many rivers, with a rainfall of about 20–30 inches a year,
neither very dry, therefore, nor very humid. It is a region that corresponds

[12] Malcolm Guthrie, 'Some developments in the pre-history of the Bantu languages',
Journal of African History, III (1962), 273–82.

ecologically with the country of the Nigerian 'middle belt' and the central Cameroons and the Ubangi–Shari watershed, to the north of the equatorial forest. It is sorghum and millet country, with first-class hunting and fishing. At its centre it is unusually well endowed with minerals, especially with iron and copper. If this is indeed the centre of the Bantu world, then we should think of its founders not as forest people, but as people of the northern woodlands, who burst through the forest barrier into the southern woodlands and established there a way of life comparable to that which they had known in the north. And, if we consider what might have been the new development which enabled them to do this, then I think we should look, not in the direction of the South-East Asian food plants, but much more likely towards the coming of the Iron Age, with its attendant improvements in woodwork, boats, tools and weapons—above all weapons for hunting and fishing. There can be no certainty on this point until we have more dates; but at least those which we have so far are possible ones. We now know that the practitioners of the Nok culture in the light woodland just north of the middle Benue were smelting iron by about 250 B.C.,[13] while the earliest Iron Age date so far obtained from any site in Africa south of the Equator is that from the Machili Forest Station in eastern Barotseland, which has been placed at the end of the first century A.D.[14]

As I said, one does not have to think of Greenberg's conclusions and Guthrie's conclusions as contradictory. It is a perfectly sound interpretation to think of them as referring to successive stages in time. Stage 1 may very well have consisted, as Guthrie himself has conjectured, in a very rapid migration, following the Congo waterways, of a few dozens or hundreds of what he calls 'pre-Bantu speakers' from the central Cameroons or Ubangi–Shari woodlands to the woodlands south of the Congo forest.[15] Stage 2 would then have consisted in the consolidation and settlement of these first migrants and their gradual expansion through the southern woodland belt from coast to coast. What Guthrie's evidence does imply is that it was here, in the southern woodland belt, that they achieved their first, main population increase. It was here that they established a bridgehead comparable to the bridgehead established by the European settlers on the Atlantic coast of North America. It was here that the parent Bantu language developed its final character. It was here, if we may use the word just once and for purposes of illustration only, that the Bantu came nearest to being a *race*. Their obvious success over against any earlier hunting, gathering and tenuously vegecultural peoples whom they found in this region would be more than adequately explained by their possession of a rudimentary iron technology and a knowledge of cereal agriculture which enabled them to

[13] From Mr Bernard Fagg's 'layer 3' at Taruga, containing iron slag and Nok figurines. Accompanying charcoal carbon-dated to 266 B.C. ± 120. Personal communication from Mr Fagg.

[14] Unless otherwise stated, all carbon dates are taken from the summaries published in the *Journal of African History*, II (1961), 137–9, and IV (1963), 127–8.

[15] Malcolm Guthrie, loc. cit. 281.

148 ROLAND OLIVER

take over and develop with Iron Age equipment the East African varieties of sorghums and millets introduced by the neolithic Kushites. Such accomplishments would also have put them in a position to control and benefit from sea-borne contacts reaching their eastern territories on the Indian Ocean coast. As is well-known, the first-century sailor's guide to the Red Sea and the Indian Ocean, called the Periplus of the Erythrean Sea, though its author probably knew the East African coast as far south as the Rufiji, contains no reference to black men inhabiting the coast. However the Geography of Ptolemy, which, in the texts known to us, is probably to be regarded as a fourth-century compilation, speaks of 'man-eating Ethiopians' who lived still farther to the south, perhaps around Cape Delgado.[16] This may well be the first documentary record of the Bantu.

Some time during the first five centuries A.D. Madagascar, and therefore doubtless also the East African coast, were colonized by sea-borne migrants from Indonesia,[17] and this, as I have already hinted, is therefore the stage at which we need to reconsider the influence of the South-East Asian food plants, for which Murdock has made such overriding claims. Given the previous settlement of the southern light-woodland belt by some hundreds of thousands of iron-working and cultivating Bantu speakers, who were the only large-scale food producers in Africa south of the Equator, it would be wholly logical to suppose that the coming of the South-East Asian food plants would have enabled them to expand rapidly into the more humid, more perennially watered regions to the north and the south. Given the banana and the coco-nut, and incidentally the Indonesian outrigger canoe, the eastern Bantu could occupy in force the humid coastal belt, and we know from the Arab geographers that by the tenth century at least they had done so as far north as the Juba.[18] And for the interior we have an important indication of a parallel northward movement in Guthrie's linguistic classification, because, when you move outside his basic elliptical nucleus and look for the languages with the next highest incidence of 'general roots', you find them forming a long bulge to the north, which coincides on the map with the region of the great lakes, from Lake Tanganyika right up to Lake Albert. Rundi shows 44%, Sukuma 41%, Ganda, Nyoro, Nyankore all 37%. The only comparable figure to the south of the basic ellipse is Shona, also with 37%. In other words, when we move on from stage 2 to stage 3 of the Bantu expansion, we find that the original light woodland belt has been extended to include areas of higher rainfall, in which we know that the South-East Asian food plants, and especially the banana, have played a vital role. Where rainfall is distributed throughout the year, the banana can become not merely a seasonal luxury but a staple food. It can support a relatively dense population and requires practically no

[16] Gervase Mathew, 'The East African coast until the coming of the Portuguese', in R. Oliver and G. Mathew, *History of East Africa*, 1 (Oxford, 1963), 96.

[17] This was an Iron Age colonization; therefore it cannot have been earlier in time than the spread of the Iron Age in Indonesia around the first century A.D.

[18] G. S. P. Freeman-Grenville, *The East African Coast* (1962), 15, etc.

labour. The lake region provides the ideal conditions for its culture, and it would be entirely logical to suppose that a population explosion in the lake region occurred as a result of its introduction. Stage 3, I would tentatively suggest, was enacted mainly during the second half of the first millennium A.D.

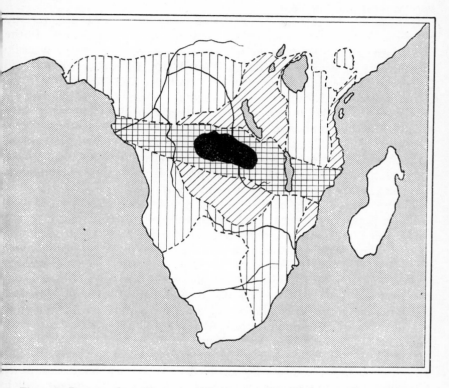

Fig. 1. ■, Bantu nucleus; ⊞, stage 2 of Bantu expansion; ▨, stage 3, of expansion; ⊪, stage 4 of expansion; □, non-Bantu. Scale: 1 : 34,000,000.

Stage 4, which I believe belongs mainly to our present millennium, would then have consisted of the colonization of the remainder of the present Bantu Africa by the surplus populations generated within the area occupied at stage 3. Certainly, as you move farther away from Guthrie's extended nucleus, whether to the north-east or to the south or to the north-west, the incidence of 'general' Bantu roots drops steadily. Kikuyu has 32% and Kamba 30%. To the south, we have Venda at 30%, Zulu at 29%, Xhosa at 26%. To the north-west, the fall is even sharper: Teke 28%, Bobangi 24%, Duala 14%.[19] In geographical terms what we are thinking of here is a much more gradual colonization, by the agricultural Bantu peoples of the intermediate zone of the woodlands and the forest

[19] Malcolm Guthrie, loc. cit. 277.

margins, of the areas less favourable to agriculture—on the one hand the
drier regions, the dry middle of East Africa, the dry middle of Central and
South Africa, the dry middle of Angola and South-West Africa; and on the
other hand the *very humid* region of the equatorial forest, through which
the original Bantu ancestors must have penetrated, but which was certainly
not the focal point of their expansion.

It is noteworthy that these very dry and very humid areas are precisely
the areas of Bantu Africa which still contain remnant populations. In the
rain forest are the Pygmies, now linguistically absorbed, but physically
identifiable. In Angola and South-West Africa, as also in Central and
South Africa, there are the remnants of Bushmen and Hottentots. In the
dry centre of East Africa there are a whole miscellany of remnant peoples.
There are the Hadza Bushmen; there are the Sandawi Hottentots; there
are Kushitic remnants like the Iraqw and the Gorowa; there are Nilo-
Kushitic remnants like the Tatog and the Dorobo. Classified in economic
terms, these remnants include not only hunter-gatherers like the Pygmies,
the Bushmen and the Dorobo, but also pastoralists like the Hottentots and
the Tatog, and even cultivators like the Iraqw.

There is ample evidence that even in comparatively recent times these
remnant populations were much more widespread than they now are.
When the Dutch reached South Africa, the Hottentots extended over
most of South-West Africa and much of the Cape Province. Bushmen were
intermingled with Hottentots at the Cape and with Bantu over large
stretches of the interior. Bushman remains occur over most of the country
occupied by the South-Eastern Bantu, and both Bush and Hottentot
clicks survive in the Sotho and Nguni languages as evidence of their comparatively recent absorption. In East Africa tradition shows clearly that the
Bantu are comparatively recent colonists in the dry middle belt. North-
east of Lake Victoria, the Luyia have incorporated a whole variety of Nilo-
Kushitic peoples who originally occupied their country. South-east of the
Lake, the Tatog provide an example of a Nilo-Kushitic people still in
course of Bantuization by Sukuma and other Bantu cultivators expanding
from west to east. The eastern Nyamwezi are all relatively recent colonists
of a formerly non-Bantu area. The traditions of the Gogo tell plainly of the
arrival, only ten generations or so ago, of the first Bantu cultivators in a
country then occupied partly by a small hunting people and partly by tall,
fair-skinned pastoralists. And there is a similar tale of recent inland penetration by the coastal Bantu. The Kikuyu, the Kamba, the Chagga all have
traditions of migrations from the coast following the disastrous encounters
of the coastal Bantu with the Galla and Somali invaders of Jubaland.[20]
Thus the recent picture which we see nearly everywhere in eastern and
southern Africa is that of the penetration of the more marginally cultivable
areas by the surplus populations generated in the more favourable, more

[20] R. Oliver, 'Discernible developments in the interior, *c.* 1500–1840', in R. Oliver
and G. Mathew, *History of East Africa*, I (1963), 194–204.

humid areas, and in every case it is the cultivating Bantu who move in and absorb the representatives of older and less successful cultures. It is no wonder that the Bantu, especially on the eastern side of Africa, exhibit such a wide variety of physical types and social customs. Without doubt, these are attributable to the variety of earlier peoples they have absorbed.

These, then, are the four stages of the Bantu dispersion, so far as we can reconstruct them from the linguistic, cultural and traditional evidence available in 1966. What, now, can archaeology add to this picture? The answer, briefly, is *dates*. By dates, I mean radiocarbon dates for the first 1,500 years of the Iron Age in Bantu Africa, which is roughly the same as the first 1,500 years of the Christian era. A year ago, in April 1965, we had precisely 52 such carbon dates from the whole of Bantu Africa. More telling, however, is the distribution. Of the 52 dates we had last year, 4 came from East Africa—2 from Kenya, 1 from Uganda, 1 from Tanzania. Two more came from the Congo, 2 from Angola and 1 from Madagascar. No less than 38 of the 52 dates came from Zambia and Rhodesia, and the remaining 5 from South Africa. During the past year nearly 40 new dates have been added, but the pattern of their distribution remains similar. As things stand, therefore, more than four-fifths of our chronological evidence for these 1,500 years comes from the region immediately to the south of the Bantu nucleus. Within the nuclear area only two Iron Age sites have so far been dated. North of the nucleus we have today a total of six dated Iron Age sites.[21]

Thanks to the wholly exceptional state of archaeological work in Rhodesia and Zambia, the Iron Age sequence to the south of the centre of the Bantu nucleus is now, in outline, clear. The earliest Iron Age site is the Machili site, just to the north of the upper Zambezi, carbon-dated to the late first century A.D. By the fourth century Iron Age sites begin to appear in Rhodesia; and by the seventh and eighth centuries there is evidence of a fairly wide spread of Iron Age culture, extending at least over the southern province of Zambia, through the western and central parts of Rhodesia and into the northern Transvaal. The people who practised this culture were mixed farmers, who sowed a little millet and kept some cattle and, of course, added considerably to their diet by hunting. Their iron tools were few and simple. Nevertheless, they mined not only iron ore, but also gold and copper, where these were present. And they had some kind of tenuous trade relations with the east coast, for glass beads have been found in many sites. At least one site belonging to the early part of this period has yielded really rich finds of gold and copper jewellery, welded iron gongs, cloth, beads and copper crosses evidently used as currency. This is the site at Ingombe Ilede on the north bank of the Zambezi, some thirty miles below Kariba, which must have been a trading settlement of some importance, with links running north to the Copper Belt and south into Rhodesia, as well as east to the coast. The carbon dates run from the seventh to the tenth centuries with the richest finds in the eighth and ninth.[22]

By the eleventh century we have the beginnings of stone building at Zimbabwe—first at what seems to have been a ritual centre rather than a fortress on the Acropolis Hill, and then, perhaps a century or two later, the larger royal village in the valley below. The early buildings were technologically the least impressive. The primary significance of these sites is that they were permanent. Their existence in an area of stock-raising and shifting cultivation implies the existence of a well-established political system capable of drawing supplies and wealth from a wide surrounding region. Permanence apart, these sites are culturally significant not only for the first rudimentary building techniques but also for the technically superior pottery and ironwork known to archaeologists as Iron Age B, which seems to have been strictly an aristocratic or court culture confined at this stage to Zimbabwe itself.[23] By the fourteenth century we have evidence of another permanent centre of the same kind in the Limpopo valley at Mapungubwe. By the time the Portuguese arrived in the area at the beginning of the sixteenth century a third main centre of power had emerged, with its base on the northern edge of the Rhodesian plateau, to the north of modern Salisbury, where a powerful monarch bearing the dynastic title of Mwenemutapa ruled over a nuclear state and a whole series of tributary kingdoms extending right down the southern side of the Zambezi valley from Zumbo to the coast and round through the eastern highlands of Rhodesia and the lowlands of southern Moçambique. The Zimbabwe capital site was, as we know from archaeological evidence, still being occupied and added to throughout the sixteenth, seventeenth and eighteenth centuries; but, because its rulers were independent of and hostile to the Mwenemutapa, the Portuguese never penetrated this kingdom. Portuguese descriptions of the Mwenemutapa's dominions are, however, clear and detailed, and they leave no doubt that here, south of the Zambezi among the Shona and the Thonga, was a typical cluster of Bantu states, similar in their political institutions and their kingship rituals to the state clusters which grew up in other comparatively densely populated parts of the Bantu world, such as the Luba–Lunda region of the Katanga and the Kasai, the Kongo–Teke region along the Lower Congo, and the interlacustrine region of southern Uganda, Rwanda and north-west Tanzania.[24]

Thus, from archaeological evidence, from Portuguese documents and increasingly, from the Shona traditions now at last being collected by M Donald Abraham of the University College, Salisbury, we are beginning to have a fairly convincing outline picture of Iron Age society to the south of the Bantu nucleus, from its first humble stages around the beginning of th

---

[22] Brian Fagan, *Southern Africa*, 94–9.
[23] Ibid. 100–10, with the primary authorities cited on p. 176.
[24] G. M. Theal, *Records of South-East Africa* (Capetown, 1898–1903), vols. III and VI

Christian era to a stage at which hundreds of thousands of people were grouped under powerful chiefs with large courts and elaborate rituals, supporting themselves by agriculture and stock-raising, conducting large-scale mining operations, and exporting considerable quantities of gold and ivory to the Indian Ocean markets against imports of Indian cloth and beads, and even of Chinese porcelains for the royal tables. Only two fundamental questions about this process remain unanswered. The first is whether Iron Age development can be equated with *Bantu* development. The second question, which is very close to the first, is how far this development, especially on the political side, was affected by later waves of conquest and migration from the north.

Regarding the first of these problems, there certainly seems to be some evidence that the expanding wave of Iron Age material culture rolled southwards somewhat in advance of the expanding wave of negroid physical features. Skeletal evidence from early mining sites in Rhodesia, from the eleventh-century site at Bambandyanalo near Mapungubwe, and even from the fourteenth-century burials at Mapungubwe itself, indicates the widespread survival into Iron Age times of a physical type which is probably most sensibly described as Hottentot or Khoisan. Nevertheless, the Kalomo culture of southern Zambia, which was in all essentials the same as the Iron Age 'A' cultures of Rhodesia, was certainly practised from the first by negroid people, and the Iron Age 'A' culture remained the basic material culture of the Rhodesian plateau until the Zulu invasions of the nineteenth century. The Iron Age 'B' cultures of Rhodesia are associated strictly with the stone-built capital sites. They are the specialized products of a 'court culture'. They could be identified with an immigrant aristocracy, but hardly, as some have suggested, with the first speakers of the Shona language.[25] Therefore, I think the logical deduction is that the Iron Age 'A' culture was in origin a Bantu culture, but that it spread, as I have suggested, rather faster than the expansion of Bantu people themselves, especially in the pastoral areas of the central plateau, where Hottentot peoples seem to have been quite capable of assimilating it. The second question is a more complex one, which will be more easily answered as more traditional evidence is added to that of archaeology. Almost certainly, however, we should think of the southward expansion of the Bantu as a cumulative process, in which the surplus population generated in the favourable conditions at the heart of the Bantu world was constantly pushed out towards the perimeter in an unending sequence of migration, conquest and absorption. On present evidence the explosive nucleus at the heart of the whole system would seem to have been, again and again, the Luba-speaking peoples of the Katanga.

If I have dwelt at some length on the developing situation to the south of the Bantu nucleus, it is in order to point the contrast in our present knowledge between the Zambian–Rhodesian area and almost all other parts

[25] For example, Brian Fagan, *Southern Africa*, 110.

of Bantu Africa. From Portuguese documentary evidence as well as from recovered tradition, we can detect the outlines of a situation analogous to the Rhodesian situation to the north and south of the Congo estuary, but the documentary evidence dates only from the late fifteenth century.[26] From traditional evidence we can reconstruct the history of another state-cluster in the interlacustrine region of East Africa from about the same period.[27] For the Luba–Lunda region our traditional knowledge extends backwards only to the sixteenth century.[28] For the earlier Iron Age history of these regions or of any others, we have only a few random shafts of light cast by a handful of pioneer archaeologists working without plan or system.

We have, as I said, only two sites of real importance from within the Bantu nucleus itself. The first is the lakeside cemetery of Sanga on Lac Kisale in the heart of the Luba country of north Katanga, which was excavated by Hiernaux and Nenquin in 1957 and 1958. This is a site dated to the eighth and ninth centuries A.D., and revealing in the grave-goods an astonishing level of wealth and technical skill. The cemetery, which was recognized by its surface deposits of unfamiliar pottery sherds, stretches for ten miles along the shore of the lake, and it must contain tens, if not hundreds, of thousands of graves. Sixty of these graves were excavated, more or less at random. There is no suggestion that they were anything but those of ordinary commoners. Yet the skeletons were accompanied by rich collections of beautiful and skilfully worked pottery, and in many instances by elaborate copper jewellery, copper crosses, and imported beads.[29] Owing to the post-independence troubles of the Congo Republic, work on this marvellous site has had to be abandoned; but at least we know that here, in the very centre of the Bantu world, there must have flourished a dense and highly skilled population, which was already mining and working the copper of the Katanga and trading regularly with the east coast. Here, as at the settlement of Ingombe Ilede on the Zambezi, is evidence of most of the skills employed in the Iron Age 'B' cultures of Rhodesia, and three centuries earlier than it appeared at Zimbabwe. If Iron Age 'B' is indeed the culture of an immigrant minority, this is where it could have come from.

The second early Iron Age site from within the Bantu nucleus is that at Kalambo Falls, at the south end of Lake Tanganyika. The interest of this site for the expansion of the Bantu is a very special one, for it is one of a series of sites, running from Rhodesia in the south to Lake Victoria in the north, which are linked by an identically decorated pottery, known by some archaeological perversity as 'Channelled Ware' in the south and 'Dimple-

[26] A. Ihle, *Das alte Königreich Kongo* (Leipzig, 1929).

[27] Oliver and Mathew, op. cit. 180–91. The rough chronology established on genealogical evidence has recently been confirmed by radiocarbon dates from Bigo, the earliest site identifiable in the dynastic tradition of the region.

[28] E. Verhulpen, *Baluba et Balubaisés* (Antwerp, 1939).

[29] J. Nenquin, 'Notes on some early pottery cultures in North Katanga', *Journal of African History*, IV (1963), 19–32.

based' in the north. 'Dimple-based' is in fact nothing but dimple-based 'Channelled Ware', and the site at Kalambo Falls contains 'Channelled Ware' with, and without, dimpled bases. Ignoring the presence or absence of dimples, channel-decorated pottery has so far been found at nine sites widely scattered through Zambia. It has also been found at Tshikapa on the upper Kasai, at Kalambo Falls, in Rwanda and Kivu Province, on the west and north-east shores of Lake Victoria, and at one site in north-central Tanzania. Clear derivatives of the Channelled Ware tradition occur in the early Iron Age sites of Rhodesia. Everywhere it occurs, Channelled Ware has been found in the earliest Iron Age stratum, and its very wide distribution suggests that its makers expanded very rapidly. The suggestion has been made by many people that here may be the hall-mark of the expanding Bantu. Owing to the prevalence of a north–south conception of the Bantu expansion, however, there has so far been a marked reluctance to accept the clear message of the existing carbon dates, which are as follows: Zambezi valley, first century A.D.; Rhodesian derivatives, fourth to ninth centuries A.D.; Kalambo Falls, sixth to sixteenth centuries A.D.; Uganda eleventh century A.D. Three leading archaeologists—Professor Desmond Clark, Dr Merrick Posnansky and Dr Brian Fagan—have somehow managed to persuade themselves that these figures indicate a migration from north to south.[30] To me they seem to indicate a movement spreading north and south from the Zambezi. They suggest to me that the nuclear Bantu learnt the typical designs of Channel decoration from some intrusive, possibly Indonesian, group in South-East Africa, and carried it north in the later phase of their expansion, when they occupied the northern sector of the lake region. The clear implication would seem to be that it was the Bantu who brought the Iron Age to Rwanda and Uganda and western Kenya, and that they brought it from the south. I would be the first to agree that many more Iron Age dates are needed from the area north of the Bantu nucleus before such a hypothesis could be firmly established, but this is the hypothesis which best fits the present facts.

The reason why the interlacustrine region is a specially important one is that it stands at the northern frontier of the Bantu world, and on the part of that frontier most exposed to outside influences from the north. During the last five or six hundred years, for which we have a considerable amount of traditional evidence, the history of this region has clearly been very much dominated by the pressure of Nilotic and perhaps also of Kushitic invaders from the north and the north-east. As I have attempted to show elsewhere, it seems to have been the impact of these northern invaders which was mainly responsible for the emergence of the large states which grew up in this area.[31] In other words, even though the Bantu population

[30] J. Desmond Clark, 'The spread of food production in sub-Saharan Africa', *Journal of African History*, III (1962), 222; B. Fagan, *Southern Africa*, 48–51.
[31] R. Oliver, 'Discernible developments in the interior, c. 1500–1840', in R. Oliver and G. Mathew, *History of East Africa*, I (1963), 180–91.

of the interlacustrine region may have built up from the south, it still looks
as though the political institutions owed much to comparatively late non-
Bantu influences diffused through conquering minorities from Ethiopia
and the Sudan. So far as the interlacustrine region itself is concerned, there
is no problem if the Bantu population established itself during the second
half of the *first* millennium, and if the northern influences then percolated
through to them during the first half of the *second* millennium. The
problem which I merely pose, and do not seek to answer, arises in connexion
with the percolation of the same influences further to the south, and
apparently at a considerably earlier date.

SUMMARY

This paper outlines four stages of the Bantu expansion: first, the initial push
through the equatorial forest from the northern to the southern woodlands;
second, the occupation of the southern woodland belt from coast to coast;
third, the colonization of the Tanzania, Kenya and southern Somali coastline
and of the northern sector of the lake region; fourth, the colonization southwards, north-westwards and north-eastwards from this extended nucleus. The
evidence for the first stage is largely linguistic and is likely to remain so. The
outlines of the fourth stage can be established very largely from traditional
evidence. It is for chronological data concerning the second and third stages that
we can now turn hopefully to archaeology. In both these stages the Bantu
expansion seems to have coincided fairly closely with the spread of the Iron Age;
and, if the spread of the Iron Age through the area north of the southern woodlands can now be traced in something like the detail which we already have for
Zambia and Rhodesia, the mystery of the Bantu expansion will have been largely
unravelled.

10. THE RHODESIAN IRON AGE
(*an approximation to the history of the last 2000 years*)[1]

By ROGER SUMMERS

THE name 'Iron Age' has been given to a series of post-Stone Age industries in Rhodesia. The industries themselves vary very considerably, but all are characterized by the use of iron for tools and weapons. Unlike the sequence in Europe and the Near East, that of south-central Africa shows no copper or bronze-using stage between the stone and iron-using phases and even the Neolithic seems to be missing from this part of the world.

The sudden appearance of iron in the archaeological record has therefore been attributed to the arrival of metal-working people from the north and, indeed, the whole period of the Iron Age has, somewhat loosely, been termed 'the Bantu Migrations'. The word 'Bantu' is itself a cause of confusion, since it is now applied indiscriminately to a group of languages, a complex of cultures, and a racial group. A century ago Bleek invented the word to classify the languages spoken south of 5°N. and, since we do not know what language was spoken by the iron-using migrants, it is incorrect to use this word in reference to culture or race: for that reason 'Iron Age' was introduced in 1950 when the first overall survey of the period was made.

It has long been realized that the Rhodesian Iron Age is the archaeological expression of several different cultural elements, and ever since 1950 the various complexes have been separately classified. Recent work has however suggested that there are fundamental connections despite

[1] This paper first appeared in the *Journal of African History* in 1961, having been used in draft at the 1960 S.O.A.S. Seminar on African History. Since then a great deal more light has been thrown on the subject by current research, while the Burg Wartenstein proposals for a more precise terminology for African pre- and proto-history have rendered the 1961 version terminologically obsolete. The paper has therefore been rewritten in 1967.

The Wartenstein proposals are discussed in full in Bishop and Clark, *Background to African evolution*, Chicago Univ. Press, 1967. It is sufficient to say here that the term *industry* has been substituted for 'culture' in an archaeological context, that industries are subdivided into named (not numbered) *phases*, and that the alphabetical classification of *complexes* given in the 1961 version has now been dropped. This matter has been discussed at great length by archaeologists, and the writer is convinced that the new proposals are greatly to be preferred over the former practice: the new terms have been tested by Rhodesian archaeologists and have been found acceptable.

New names of industries and phases are enclosed in quotation marks since they are still informal, but to provide for continuity and to assist non-archaeological readers familiar with the older practice, the old terms are given in brackets after the new ones wherever there is any difference between new and old.

superficial differences, and the separate classification has been abandoned pending deeper analysis. In this paper, however, attention will be drawn to the apparent grouping of certain industries, but no attempt will be made to force the data into a formal classification.

Radiocarbon dates, most of which are mutually supporting, are used as the basis for chronology before 1500. Thereafter ethnohistory and new archaeological studies of imported wares provide a more secure basis for a chronological framework.

A PROBLEMATIC INDUSTRY
(*formerly Iron Age A1*)

The first traces of cultural advance beyond Stone Age hunting appear in rock shelters in the Matopo Hills, where pottery of a sophisticated type has been found mixed with stone implements of the Later Stone Age (the Southern African cultural equivalent of the European Mesolithic). Although this pottery, like all Rhodesian Iron Age ceramics, is hand-made and unglazed, it is clearly the product of a long ceramic tradition. This early pottery has been called by the name 'Bambata', after the cave site where it was first found in 1917.

'Bambata Ware' is a very distinctive pottery and as it was first described as long ago as 1940, it is remarkable that it should have been found only in very limited areas in Rhodesia and not at all south of the Limpopo. One must conclude, therefore, that the bearers of this early industry were few in number and did not penetrate beyond the Limpopo (fig. 1).

Radiocarbon dates are pre-300 A.D. for the most easterly site, and eighth century for the southerly one.

The close association between sherds of Bambata pottery and Later Stone Age (Wilton) artefacts, has led to suggestions that pottery was part of the material culture of the Wilton people, i.e. of Bushmen. This is now regarded as unlikely owing to the advanced type of the pottery, which has nothing experimental or tentative about it. The consensus of opinion now is that the pottery is an intrusive element, and it is regarded as a sign of 'trade' between Bushmen hunters and pottery makers.

Trade implies peaceful intercourse without any rivalry between the groups concerned. Latterly this was not the case, for Bush groups were pushed into marginal and unfertile country until, in the nineteenth century, they were hunted as vermin by Hottentot, Bantu and Afrikaner alike. The reason for this oppression is that Bush hunting lands had been restricted and they were preying on herded cattle. At the beginning of the Iron Age, conditions were apparently different; either there were no immigrant cattle, or else they were too few to cause concern to the Bushmen. There is evidence that the earliest immigrants of whom Bantu tradition speaks were without cattle.

In a recent paper, C. K. Cooke has suggested that this pottery may indicate the presence of nomadic sheep herding groups, with a culture

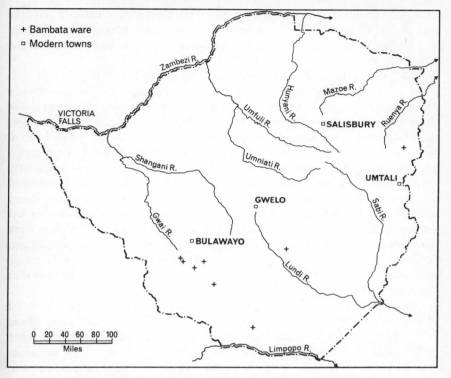

+ Bambata ware
□ Modern towns

Fig. 1. Rhodesia, showing distribution of Iron Age sites (A1)

somewhat akin to that of the Hottentots known to early travellers in South Africa. Since Cooke's paper appeared, a certain amount of place-name study has been done, and his hypothesis has received a measure of confirmation.

If this proves to be the case, the cultural level of the nomads would scarcely be that represented by our later industries, and may not even belong strictly to the *iron* age.

The problem has attracted attention at intervals for many years, but so far it is still unsolved.

EARLY CATTLE KEEPERS AND MINERS
(*formerly Iron Age A2*)

Far better known than the enigmatic 'Bambata Ware' is a very widespread ceramic tradition which has as decorative features shallow channels and impressions of square toothed stamps. There is considerable variety in decoration, but pot forms are fairly constant throughout; cattle were kept; hut forms were primitive and little advanced from Bushman wind breaks; contracted burials were universal; metal work in gold, copper and iron was practised and, as a corollary, metallic ores were mined; imports (usually small bluish cane glass beads) were uniform enough to indicate a single source of supply; above all, 23 dates with two anomalies, form a consistent pattern (see Appendix).

In Rhodesia, this industry is known generally as 'Gokomere'.

In some phases, clay human figurines also appear. Some are readily identifiable, but others are stylized and it is often so difficult to recognize them that at one time they were called 'phalli'. More recently, however, they have been critically studied, and most of the so-called 'phalli' prove to be female figures, although others have now been found to be the tips of horns in clay figurines of cattle. The human figurines are very frequently broken, and they occur very widely, often in domestic refuse, sometimes in other domestic contexts, and in at least one case in a grave. They appear only in association with this stamped and sometimes channelled pottery. Their function is unknown: it has been suggested that they were connected with initiation, but it is also thought that they may have been religious or fertility symbols. Clay models of sheep and oxen were made and also small models of pots; one can scarcely escape the suggestion that these were playthings.

Associated with the 'Ziwa' phase of Gokomere and with all phases of 'Leopard's Kopje' was the practice of mining gold and copper ores. These mines (or 'ancient workings' as they are known locally) were primitive affairs, mainly open stopes which followed the ore body down as far as possible, but which were open to the sky at the top. The minimum amount of surrounding rock was cut, so the actual working was often very narrow indeed.

The 'miners' had no knowledge of explosives, nor had they any hard steel tools, and, as the ore body consisted in most cases of quartz, it was necessary to split the rock by alternately heating and cooling it before using soft iron picks. Despite their very limited equipment, the Rhodesian miners reached very considerable depths—sometimes over 100 feet— being stopped only by water or by insufficient ventilation. From the frequent occurrence of skeletons of young females in the fillings of old workings, it appears that much of the underground work was done by girls.

Most of the mines were concerned with the mining of gold, and any ore over one ounce to the ton seems to have been regarded as payable; poorer ore, if brought to the surface, was left in rubble dumps untreated. 'Payable' ore was, however, carried to the nearest stream, crushed and concentrated in running water.

There is scarcely a modern gold mine in Rhodesia which is not on the site of an 'ancient working', so it is clear that the 'miners' had a good knowledge of prospecting. It has been deduced that originally the zone from the surface down to about 20 feet was exceptionally rich in gold, and it seems very probable that immense quantities of gold were exported.

India was the probable market, and Indian brassware has recently been found in some of these old mines.

Besides gold, copper was also mined, the oxide or carbonate ores being smelted with charcoal in simple furnaces. Tin was also mined in the country, and bronze alloy was made; the tin content was, however, variable. On technological grounds, it is thought that Rhodesian mining methods were learned from southern India (Mysore), since techniques are identical in closely similar geological contexts.

The only date so far established for an 'Ancient Working' is early thirteenth century, but as this is in a 'Leopard's Kopje' area it is very probable that gold mining and the gold trade is far earlier. Ingombe Ilede, just north of the Zambezi, was a gold trading post, and its seventh to tenth century dates help to confirm this view. As the production of gold in India is believed to have fallen off, due to the exhaustion of mines, in the fourth century A.D. it seems quite reasonable to suggest that Indian miners, looking for fresh supplies, should have found them in Rhodesia and commenced exploitation, with local labour, sometime between the fourth and seventh centuries. Contacts between India and the East Coast are well known, and the fact that Indian Ocean shells are found in 'Gokomere' and 'Ziwa' contexts indicates a trading connection between the east coast and Rhodesia.

Figure 2 gives a general idea of the distribution, some sites being omitted to ensure clarity. Ignoring Leopard's Kopje for the moment, reference to the Appendix will show that the Zambian and Zambezi sites fall into the same chronological bracket (first ten centuries A.D.) as those in eastern Rhodesia. For geological reasons, none of the Zambezi sites is connected with 'ancient workings', nor are those in the south-eastern 'Mabveni/Gokomere' phases. The 'Ziwa' phase sites, however, are in the midst of gold bearing rocks, and many of the rivers in this area carry alluvial gold; consequently we find 'Ziwa' material in some ancient workings.

'Leopard's Kopje' sites occur in rich gold areas, and this is the archaeological industry most closely connected with mining: It will be seen too that this industry is later than the others (eighth to fifteenth centuries). Typologically, it is an offshoot of the 'Mabveni/Gokomere' and 'Ziwa' phases, but it appears to owe very little to the Zambezi valley phases.

Gardner's report on Mapungubwe has appeared since the 1961 paper was written, and it is now clear that the site K2 is a Leopard's Kopje mound, similar to others known in Rhodesia; it falls chronologically and culturally into the 'Mambo Hill' phase (Leopard's Kopje 2).

Although the rich site on the top of Mapungubwe Hill (Transvaal) has often been compared to Zimbabwe, an examination of a number of lesser sites in Rhodesia containing equivalent cultural material shows that these are nearer to the 'Woolandale' phase of 'Leopard's Kopje' (Leopard's Kopje 3). These sites (previously Northern Transvaal culture) are there-

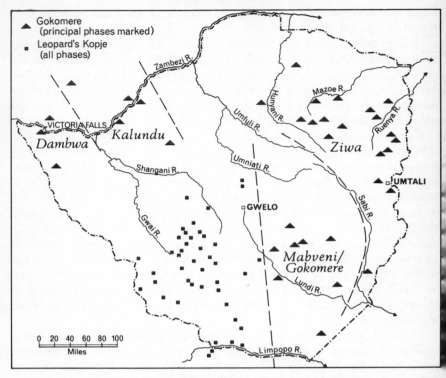

Fig. 2.   Rhodesia, showing distribution of Iron Age (A2) sites
and ancient mines

fore included as a *facies* of 'Woolandale', which itself is related to
Zimbabwe.

Expressing the position in its simplest terms, we may write:

'Mambo Hill' (LK 2) + 'Middle Zimbabwe' (Zimbabwe Period 3)
= 'Woolandale' (LK 3)

'Woolandale' + x = Mapungubwe Hill *facies*.

Unfortunately Gardner's work on Mapungubwe Hill was far less thorough
than at K2, and so we do not yet know what x is. Gardner has, however,
shown that x is not Zimbabwe; it is quite possible that it is not any
particular archaeological element, since it appears on this site only. Indeed
it may merely be the expression of wealth, social stability and increased
time to spend on decorating pottery. Gardner has also shown that the fine
shallow bowls, which form such a spectacular part of the earlier accounts,
have no part in the Mapungubwe Hill facies, but are quite a separate
element occurring very late in the sequence—so this is not x either.

Finally, two sites in the southern Transvaal contain cultural material
which appears to be related to 'Leopard's Kopje' and K2. This is the
'Uitkomst' industry, with dates of the eleventh and seventeenth centuries

We may now interpret the purely archaeological evidence as pointing to the whole group having had a common origin somewhere to the north-east—in Southern Malawi, northern Moçambique or Tanzania—moving up the Zambezi and splitting into two near the present Tete, the southern party giving rise to all the early iron age industries of Rhodesia. Connection between the Zambezi valley and the Rhodesian groups was difficult or impossible because of a variable but persistent tsetse fly belt along the southern Zambezi escarpment in Rhodesia; consequently Zambian and Rhodesian iron ages developed on different lines.

The Rhodesian development was much helped by the rich gold trade possible as a result of local mineral wealth. 'Leopard's Kopje' now proves to have been a fairly wealthy industry; both 'Mambo Hill' and 'Woolandale' (Leopard's Kopje 2 and 3) were gold producers, and the Mapungubwe *facies* of 'Woolandale' was a gold-user on a large scale.

THE FIRST ZIMBABWE BUILDERS
(*formerly Iron Age B1*)

It was the existence of 'ancient ruins' that first attracted attention to the remains of the Rhodesian Iron Age, and very unwelcome attention it was, since the first investigators were mere treasure-hunters who ransacked Zimbabwe and many other ruined stone buildings for the sake of a little gold. At one time Rhodesian 'ruins' were treated as if they were mere old mines (for some years there was an item in the Mining Commissioner's report headed 'Ancient Ruins'), and by the time this iniquitous practice was stopped, the archaeological potential of many ruins had been greatly impaired, if not entirely destroyed. Despite this we still possess a great deal of useful information and it is being rapidly added to.

New discoveries, and a reconsideration of earlier ones in the light of fresh radiocarbon dates, have led us to look more closely at the relationship between the various archaeological levels on Zimbabwe Hill. Apart from a 'Gokomere' level sealed under hillwash at the bottom of the sequence, there were three closely related industries: the uppermost was already quite well known; the middle one was distinguishable from it, and contained the earliest of the Zimbabwe walls; but the lowest level contained something new—material belonging to ancestors of the Zimbabwe builders who did not themselves build.

It was the discovery of this industry, coupled with the apparent lack of connection with other stone building traditions, especially those of the east coast Arabs, that led to the suggestion that Zimbabwe building might be an independent invention. However, more objective dates and more excavation on 'Leopard's Kopje' sites has led to a less exciting interpretation.

There are only five sites, including Zimbabwe, where this type of *Zimbabwe Class 2 ware* is found, and most of these lie twenty miles or so to the west. Two hundred miles northward, however, around Salisbury, there are a number of slightly later burial sites (no settlements have yet been found) which contain pottery and other cultural material rather like this new Zimbabwe industry. The parallel is not an exact one, and both groups of sites are very tight ones, no more than thirty miles across.

Far closer to Zimbabwe than the group around Salisbury, are the 'Leopard's Kopje' sites which, as we now know, contain a considerable amount of simple stone walling used to retain material for platforms: the earliest Zimbabwe walls were of this same type.

Thus in the walls of the 'Mambo Hill' phase of 'Leopard's Kopje' (Leopard's Kopje 2) we see the origin of Zimbabwe building. Building techniques at Zimbabwe developed far in advance of the 'Leopard's Kopje' ones, possibly due to better building material.

Nevertheless the builders seem to have been culturally quite distinct from the Gokomere group; they used different (and much plainer) pottery, they eschewed figurines, and they had a different taste in bead-work. Moreover, their pottery appears only on ruin sites, and accordingly it has been suggested that they were few in number.

Their first appearance in the south-east, and the fact that they possessed different material culture from the Gokomere group, suggests an entirely different origin from the previous people.

Naturally we do not know what language the first builders spoke, but oral evidence connects the buildings with Shona-speaking peoples, and accordingly one feels inclined to equate the earliest buildings with the arrival of the first Shona.

Despite incomplete exploration, we now know of over 500 'Gokomere' and 'Leopard's Kopje' sites, and their numbers are constantly growing despite the fact that all are buried; in addition 1100 'ancient workings' have been traced. Against this, we have a bare 330 sites connected with stone building or allied industries, and few new ones, except burials, have appeared during the past six years. Most of these sites advertise themselves by their spectacular surface remains.

This has been interpreted as meaning that the Gokomere/Leopard's Kopje group established themselves and formed the mass of the local population, while the builders of Zimbabwe and similar places formed a ruling minority. There was a long overlap between Gokomere and Leopard's Kopje on the one hand and Zimbabwe on the other. The upper limit of Leopard's Kopje has yet to be determined.

If I am right in suggesting that the first builders were Shona immigrants then one is left with the problem, who were the Gokomere group and what language did *they* speak?

Here little more can be done than to state the problem, as it is insoluble by archaeological means, and so far it has not been tackled by other disciplines.

The Gokomere/Leopard's Kopje group, which is now taken to include Mapungubwe, are said by physical anthropologists (A. Galloway, P. V. Tobias *et al.*) to belong to the 'Boskopoid' racial group and to have no 'Negro' admixture. The latter point is understandable if one equates 'Negro' with West Africa, for, as we shall shortly see, West African influences only appear in Rhodesia with the next part of the Iron Age. But what of 'Boskopoid'? The use of the term to determine a 'race' has been severely criticized by R. Singer, while L. H. Wells has suggested that both 'Boskop' and 'Bush' are variants of the basic African type of *Homo sapiens*. The 'Boskopness' of a number of South African Stone Age fossils has also been called into question. Thus both terminology and classification are in the melting-pot, and it is necessary for the archaeologist and the historian to tread most warily until the physical anthropologists have reached some conclusion on the question.

On the question of language, little research has yet been undertaken. As a matter of observation, however, it may be said that a number of place-names appear to be of Bantu origin, but are not intelligible when interpreted by any of the existing local languages—there are also some non-Bantu place-names which can probably be traced to one of the Khoisan languages spoken by the 'Bush' people. Thus there are grounds for thinking that there may once have been a Bantu-type language spoken in Rhodesia of which scarcely any trace remains. Much work, however, requires to be done before any valid conclusions can be drawn.

When stone walls were first built at Zimbabwe, about A.D. 1100, they were constructed of plain split blocks, untrimmed, varying in thickness and built without mortar. Whenever possible they were laid on a rocky foundation, and in consequence they have stood for nine centuries, their 'elastic' construction enabling them to withstand slight movements and occasional earthquakes far more easily than a rigid, mortared construction.

The building of walls and the slight change in pottery style represented more than some fresh cultural stimulus, for at the same time one finds a great increase in quantity of glass beads and a much wider variety of their colours. Later, there is a small but steady flow of Celadon glazed ware from China, possibly brought in as gifts for chiefs.

The cultural position of Mapungubwe Hill has already been mentioned, but it may here be noted that this site is contemporary with the end of this industry of 'Middle Zimbabwe' (Zimbabwe Period 3), while anyone handling pottery from Zimbabwe (Class 3), Mapungubwe Hill (Schofield's M¹—excluding shallow bowls), Woolandale or its many associate sites, cannot fail to be struck with a basic continuity. There are, however, sufficient significant differences to prevent us lumping them all together in one industry.

One interpretation is that Mapungubwe represents an outpost of

Zimbabwe whose cultural influence was thinly spread over some local culture.[2]

NEW CONTACTS WITH THE NORTH

In the last few years, the work of Robinson, Garlake and others has added a fresh industry to the tale of the Rhodesian Iron Age.

A very distinctive pottery type, quite different from anything else in Rhodesia, appears at a few sites in the extreme north, near the edge of the Zambezi escarpment. Few non-ceramic elements are so far known, but the industry has been given a provisional name of 'Musingezi' from the river near which it was first found. There are thirteenth century dates, and trans-Zambezi connections seem probable.

It will be noticed that this industry is contemporary with the 'Harare' phase, and in view of the strong concentration of the latter in the Salisbury area, one visualizes the possibility of its withstanding an influx from the north; certainly we know of no 'Musingezi' sites south of 17°S.

'Musingezi' does not fit into the old alphabetical classification, and provides the most convincing reason for abandoning it.

LATER BUILDINGS
(formerly Iron Age B2)

During the fifteenth century a change in building style occurred at Zimbabwe, and the earlier, rougher style was replaced by one which is not only more mannered, but is also technically of a good deal better quality than the earlier work. The new style shows signs of a steady improvement for some while, but later the quality of workmanship began to fall off.

The change in architectural style was but one facet of a new culture: pottery was sometimes profusely decorated, there was a greater variety of beads used, copper and bronze ornaments appeared in quantity, and gold, too, began to be used as an adornment both of persons and also of objects (which were covered with gold plate). Oriental imports occur in the more important sites, and altogether the culture appears to have been a very rich one.

Once again, the number of people enjoying this high culture seems to have been comparatively small, and these builders are now considered to have been an aristocracy.

There are two distinct types of buildings at this time: structures with free-standing walls, as at Zimbabwe; and those, as at Khami, where the principal stonework is concentrated in the building of platforms. The 'Zimbabwe' type seems to have derived a good deal of its inspiration from the earlier Zimbabwe builders, although other features were added to the earlier technique; while the 'Khami' type appears to have been developed from the retaining walls of 'Leopard's Kopje'.

[2] This word is used in a cultural anthropological sense, not an archaeological one.

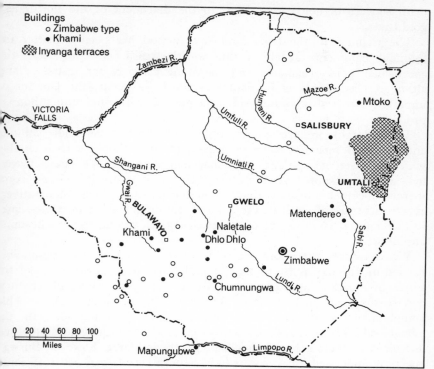

Fig. 3. Rhodesia, showing later buildings

There are oral traditions which connect 'Khami'-type buildings with the later Rozwi chiefs of the Changamire dynasty, and it may well be that the 'Zimbabwe' type betokens the earlier Mwene Mutapa (Monomotapa) dynasty which was at one time paramount over the whole area, and was later confined to the north-east. The splendours of Monomotapa's court have been recorded by Portuguese writers, and many of its features, especially those relating to divine kingship, have been considered critically by cultural anthropologists such as Schebesta and, later, Wieschhoff. The West African connections of the Building Cultures then become even clearer. Certainly the distribution map shows that 'Zimbabwe'-type buildings tend to be all over the ruin area, whereas 'Khami' buildings are densest in the south-west (fig. 3). This distribution reflects the division of our area into the two units called by the Portuguese 'Monomotapa' and 'Butwa'[3] respectively, and, when read with the distribution of gold mines, also shows why it was that Butwa maintained a control over the

[3] Their local names were probably *Bukaranga* and *Guruwuswa*. The first name appears very occasionally in Portuguese sources, the second has traditional warrant and has been established by D. P. Abraham.

main sources of gold production, to the detriment of the Portuguese gold trade.

The richness of the later Zimbabwe period has been a matter for frequent comment. Much of this wealth was locally produced—the spectacular gold ornaments and soapstone carvings for instance; and although glass beads and oriental ceramics do occur, the amount of imported material is infinitesimal compared with the autochthonous products.

These durable imports are naturally only a part of the whole volume, and we cannot form any estimate of the quantity of those—such as cloth—which have left no mark in the archaeological record. We can, however, look at the question from the other end, for there are Portuguese commercial documents to show that 'Monomotapa' was taking comparatively small quantities of cloth in 1508–9 and, although the quantity rose later in the century, cloth seems always to have been second to glass beads as an import.

We know less still about the trade of Butwa, which was presumably carried on through ports under Arab administration to the north of the Portuguese area. These ports were in decline by the sixteenth century, and so the overseas trade from Butwa via the east coast was probably comparatively small, However, there was inter-African trade with the Congo and West Coast, as is shown by Congo-type iron gongs at Zimbabwe, and what art there is has Congo leanings. By and large, however, Butwa's economy under the Rozwi seems to have been very largely self-sufficient.

By the time the sixteenth century is reached, we pass into the realm of ethnohistory, in which oral traditions and written records become increasingly important and provide a personal and political picture which archaeology cannot attempt. Nevertheless, archaeology is important in providing information about the background, and about people rather than persons. Where archaeologist and ethnohistorian disagree over some point where both are involved, it behoves them both to re-examine their position, preferably in collaboration, for neither has all the cards in his hand.

TERRACES IN THE EAST
(formerly Iron Age B2—eastern)

As an example of archaeology's place in drawing the historical picture the 'Inyanga' industry may be cited.

Contemporary with the aristocratic cultures is a very different building complex in the Inyanga mountains on the eastern border of this country. Here are hundreds upon hundreds of miles of stone-faced agricultural terracing with which are associated many hundreds of stone-walled enclosures, stock pits and a certain number of strongholds, the remains covering about 3000 square miles.

Unlike Zimbabwe, Mapungubwe, and other sites farther westward

Inyanga displays an extremely impoverished material culture—inadequately fired pottery, very few beads, hardly any iron and but a tiny scatter of copper ornaments; indeed one phase of this culture was so poor that there was no trace of large pots, interpreted by the excavators as indicating that the Inyangans were too poor to brew beer. Anybody familiar with Bantu life will appreciate what depths of poverty this implies.

The terraces have made a great impact on the landscape of the eastern mountains of Rhodesia, where hundreds of square miles of mountain forests have been felled or burned out, and where the hillsides have been covered from foot to summit with terraces, and accordingly they have been given a great place in the archaeological record. Later one finds modified Inyanga-type buildings spreading westwards, but terracing as such is confined to the eastern mountains, and the typical Inyanga cultures are no more than a provincial manifestation which had little effect on the history of the country as a whole.

The interesting thing about Inyanga is that here we can see, fossilized as it were, the life of the ordinary people, whereas at Zimbabwe or Khami we see the relics of the life of the nobility and gentry of the realm.

The Inyanga Culture merged imperceptibly into modern tribal cultures in that area, so that local Africans working as labourers on the Inyanga excavations were able to identify every find made, often giving the name to pots of which but a few sherds remained.

There is one radiocarbon date of late seventeenth century for this industry. This is near the limit of C-14 reliability, and so it must be taken with reserve; the date does however fit with other considerations. Unfortunately, there do not seem to be any ethnohistorical sources for this aspect of Rhodesian history.

Although Inyanga lives on in the Manyika, Wesa and other tribal groups today, the aristocratic Zimbabwe Culture has utterly disappeared. It rested on the political power of the Rozwi, who were defeated by the Ngoni under Chief Zwangendaba in a battle about fifty miles north-east of Bulawayo in 1834; shortly after this, their king was killed at Thaba za ka Mambo (Mount Mambo), where the ruins of his palace still stand. Thereafter the remnant of the Rozwi was scattered, and they are being rapidly absorbed into the various groups with whom they made their homes.

THE NINETEENTH CENTURY

For events from about 1830 onwards we have ample oral evidence, now being supplemented by archaeology.

The Ngoni and other Nguni-speaking groups from what is now Natal were expelled by the Zulu king, Shaka, and some came northward. They laid waste the prosperous Rozwi kingdom, burning and smashing the stone buildings as is shown by 'destruction levels' in all ruins. After taking slaves and cattle, they moved on across the Zambezi in 1835 to Malawi and other parts of East Africa.

Following the Ngoni came the Ndebele under Mzilikazi, who settled in the country around and just north of Bulawayo and kept most of the Rhodesian peoples in subjection, the remainder being harried by another Nguni group, the Shangaan from the east. During the half-century or so of Ndebele and Shangaan domination, the earlier inhabitants were apparently so mixed that the material culture, as recovered by archaeology shows a mingling of traits descended from 'Leopard's Kopje', 'Khami', 'Upper Zimbabwe', 'Inyanga' and a certain amount of so-called Venda (but more probably Sotho) material from the south.

APPENDIX:

Industry	Phase	Former name
'Gokomere'	'Machili'	(Situmpa)
'Gokomere'	'Kalundu'	
'Gokomere'	'Dambwa'	
'Gokomere'	'Mabveni'	(Gokomere)
'Gokomere'	'Gokomere'	(Gokomere)
'Gokomere'	'Malapati'	(Gokomere)
'Gokomere'	'Ziwa'	(Ziwa'
'Leopard's Kopje'	'Mambo Hill'	(Leopard's Kopje
'Leopard's Kopje'	'Zhiso Hill'	(LK 1)
'Lower Zimbabwe'	'Gumanye'	(Zimbabwe 2)
'Lower Zimbabwe'	'Harare'	(Mashonaland)
'Musingezi'		
'Leopard's Kopje'	'Woolandale'	(LK 3)
'Middle Zimbabwe'	'Acropolis'	(Zimbabwe 3)
'Upper Zimbabwe'	'Great Enclosure'	(Zimbabwe 4)
'Upper Zimbabwe'	'Khami'	(Khami Ruins)
'Inyanga'	'Niekerk'	(Inyanga Lowla

Certain other archaeological techniques, especially air photographic interpretation, are valuable for this period, since areas cleared round Ndebele kraals have not had time to recover and can be found even on small scale air photos.

The arrival of the railway in Rhodesia in 1897 may be taken as the end of the local Iron Age, as it marked the introduction of heavy machinery and the commencement of the 'industrial revolution' among local African peoples.

RADIOCARBON DATES

Date and reference (A.D. except where noted)	Site R—Rhodesia T—Transvaal Z—Zambia
20±100 (SR–24)	Situmpa forest (Z)
100±200 (C–829)	
240±100 (SR–40)	
300± 90 (SR–65)	Kalundu mound,
790± 90 (SR–41)	Kalomo (Z)
900±100 (SR–66)	
1080±100 (SR–74)	
?20 B.C.±80 (UCLA–929)	Calder's cave, Gokwe (R)
620±110 (SR–62)	Livingstone (Z)
810± 90 (SR–73)	Kapula, Wankie (R)
180±120 (SR–43)	Mabveni, Chibi (R)
320±150 (M–913)	Zimbabwe Acropolis (R)
530±120 (SR–26)	Gokomere (R)
850±100 (SR–33)	Malapati (R)
300±100 (SR–17)	Ziwa farm
850±100 (SR–32)	Inyanga (R)
1010±110 (B–223)	
700±110 (SR–55)	Leopard's Kopje, Khami (R)
830± 90 (SR–69)	Tshangula cave (R)
870±100 (SR–68)	Thaba zika Mambo (R)
1050± 65 (Y–135–17)	Mapungubwe K2 (T)
1040±130 (Tx∫228)	Zhiso hill, Matopos (R)
before 1070±150 (M–914)	Zimbabwe Acropolis (R)
1270± 60 (GrN–2341) } 1280±100 (Y–722)	Granitside, Salisbury (R)
1270± 95 (SR–100) } 1285± 95 (SR–101)	Mbagazewa Umvukwes (R)
1310± 90 (SR–44)	Woolandale, Bulawayo (R)
1380± 50 (Y–135–14) } 1420±60 (Y–135–9)	Mapungubwe Hill (T)
1070±150 (M–914)	Zimbabwe Acropolis (R)
1380± 90 (SR–47)	Zimbabwe Great Encl. (R)
1440±150 (M–915)	Zimbabwe Acropolis (R)
1300±120 (SR–25) } 1340± 90 (SR–70) } 1510± 90 (SR–70)	Harleigh farm No. 1 Ruspape (R)
after ?1440±150 (M–915)	Zimbabwe Acropolis (R)
1450± 95 (SR–94)	Khami Ruins (R)
1670± 90 (SR–35)	Harleigh farm No. 2 Rusape (R)

LITERATURE

The archaeology of the Rhodesian Iron Age is still not too well covered by published sources. There is a rapidly increasing number of papers dealing with specific sites in the *Occasional Papers of the National Museums of Rhodesia*, in *Arnoldia* (another National Museums publication), in the *South African Archaeological Bulletin* and elsewhere. Books dealing with individual sites are Fouché, *Mapungubwe* (1937); Summers, *Inyanga* (1958); Robinson, *Khami Ruins* (1959) and Gardner *Mapungubwe* Volume II (1963).

Caton-Thompson *Zimbabwe Culture* (1931) and *Mediaeval Rhodesia* by Randall-MacIver (1906) are basic reading despite their age, indeed Caton-Thompson needs to be studied before reading the most recent Zimbabwe excavation report (*Occasional Papers* No. 23A—1962).

Syntheses are very few. I summarized the position in 1950 in *South African Journal of Science*, 47, 95–107 and the first version of this paper gave the 1961 position. However, the subject is one of current research and interpretation is constantly changing in the light of fresh evidence. My *Zimbabwe: a Rhodesian mystery* (1963) was intended for the general reader, but may be useful as a brief review for the busy scholar.

Oral tradition still remains, for the most part, unrecorded although the University College of Rhodesia is accumulating tapes and D. P. Abraham has a vast amount of unpublished tradition in addition to published work in various journals. H. von Sicard, who collected widely among the Karanga and Venda groups in the 1930s and 40s, has published his collections in book form in *Ngoma Lungundu* (1952) and *Ngano dze CiKaranga* (1965) (*Studia Ethnographica Upsaliensia* 5 and 23, both in German). Shorter studies, but perhaps more useful to the historian, are Sicard's notes in *NADA*, a local Rhodesian journal wherein officers of the old Native Administration Department recorded a great many brief notes on oral histories as well as on customs, social structure and so forth.

11. THE GREEFSWALD SEQUENCE:
BAMBANDYANALO AND MAPUNGUBWE

By BRIAN M. FAGAN

THE Iron Age sites known as Mapungubwe and Bambandyanalo on the farm Greefswald, 55 miles west of Messina in the northern Transvaal, South Africa, have aroused world-wide speculation ever since their discovery in the early 1930s. This international interest has been considerably stimulated by the publication of the second volume of the Mapungubwe report in late 1963.[1] Much unnecessary confusion as to the significance of the Mapungubwe and Bambandyanalo sites has been caused by the long delay in the publication of this second volume, and this has made a critical review of the Iron Age sequence in this desolate corner of the Middle Limpopo valley a matter of some urgency. The Greefswald sequence is of vital importance to South African history, for the sites have been held to show that the earliest Iron Age population of South Africa was non-Negro. In addition, they have been used to provide a fairly accurate indication of the date at which Bantu-speaking peoples first crossed the middle reaches of the Limpopo.

It was in 1933 that a farmer and prospector named van Graan persuaded an African to show him the Mapungubwe Hill and its secret ascent. Finds of gold and other objects made by the party eventually reached the possession of Professor L. Fouché, and the site was officially investigated by an Archaeological Committee set up by the University of Pretoria. After preliminary work in 1933, the Hill was excavated in 1934 by the late Dr Neville Jones and the late Mr J. F. Schofield. The results of their work were promptly and carefully published in *Mapungubwe*, Volume I, in 1937.[2] In addition to studying the cultures of the Hill, they discovered various other sites in the Messina region and made extensive surface collections of pottery. The most important of these new localities was the settlement known as Bambandyanalo or K2.

The Archaeological Committee, determined to continue its operations, appointed Captain G. A. Gardner as director of excavations on Greefswald. He worked on the ranch for six long seasons between 1935 and 1940, concentrating initially on K2, and later excavating a large trench at the western end of Mapungubwe Hill. Twenty-three years, however, elapsed before the second volume on the Limpopo excavations appeared in 1963. This inordinately long delay was caused by the war and other factors, and

[1] G. A. Gardner, *Mapungubwe, Vol. II* (Pretoria, 1963).
[2] L. Fouché, *Mapungubwe* (Cambridge, 1937).

173

Captain Gardner most unfortunately died before his book was published. The long delay between excavation and publication led to unnecessary confusion in archaeological circles about the significance of the finds, for the K2 site was publicly ascribed to the Hottentots without detailed supporting evidence.[3] Now that the findings of the excavations are published in their entirety, we can review the problem in the light of the latest Iron Age research from north of the Limpopo. It is unfortunate that many of Gardner's conclusions are supported by what is, by modern standards, inadequate evidence. The techniques of excavation are those of twenty-five years ago, and it is more than probable that some aspects of the archaeological evidence were missed in the field, whereas today we might have obtained a more complete picture. In discussing the Greefswald sequence we are hampered by inadequate documentation and a lack of up-to-date fieldwork. The picture of the Greefswald peoples presented in this paper can only be regarded as tentative, for it is based on slender and inadequate evidence; but it will, I hope, help in providing a basis for future work in the region.

In the Greefswald area, the Limpopo river flows through a shallow, flat-bottomed valley broken up by steep-sided sandstone hills intersected by flat plains covered with scrub vegetation. The hill known as Mapungubwe ('the hill of the Jackals') stands out conspicuously amongst those that surround it, both because of its precipitous cliffs, over 200 feet high in places, and because of the wide valley around the Hill. It has a flat top, covered with an estimated 20,000 tons of soil,[4] most of which has every appearance of having been carried to the top of the Hill by the inhabitants. With the passage of time, great masses of the material have been washed from the summit and deposited as a talus around the sides of the Hill. On the southern side of Mapungubwe is a well-defined terrace of occupation debris, which lies far enough away from the cliffs to be clear of the talus slopes. This was presumably occupied at much the same time as the Hill, but so far is almost untouched by excavators.

Immediately to the south of Mapungubwe is Bambandyanalo Hill, to the south-west of which lies the settlement named Bambandyanalo or K2.[5] It consists of a large, circular mound of occupation debris, some 200 yards in diameter and up to 20 feet deep at its highest point. Stratigraphical profiles have revealed that the occupants settled in the Bambandyanalo valley, and, by successive or continuous occupations, accumulated the mound of habitation debris which survives today. The centre of the village was used as a cattle kraal, around which the houses were built.[6]

K2 is the earlier of the two sites, for K2 pottery is found underlying

---

[3] G. A. Gardner, 'Mapungubwe, 1935–1940', *S. Afr. Arch. Bull.*, x (1955), 73–7.
[4] L. Fouché (1937), op. cit. 5.
[5] The earlier of the two Greefswald sites is known either as Bambandyanalo or K2. Following Captain Gardner, I have used K2 throughout this paper, as Bambandyanalo can be taken to refer to the Hill as well as the site.
[6] G. A. Gardner (1963), op. cit. 3.

Plate 1. Mapungubwe Hill from the south, showing the burial area and the site of Gardner's excavations.

Plate 2. K2, showing, in the foreground, the area in which the Beast Burials were found. The central figure is standing by the end of .... and trench wall

the main Hill sequence. The midden has been radiocarbon-dated to
A.D. 1050 ± 65 (Y—135.17)[7] at a depth of 66 inches, and the settlement
appears to have no particularly formal pattern. The material culture was
of the simplest, and metal objects are rare or non-existent. Captain
Gardner's excavations revealed a total of seventy-four skeletons, most of
them deposited on the southern side of the village. The bodies were
normally lying on their sides in a flexed position, surrounded by pots. The
remains of at least forty individuals were studied by Dr Alexander
Galloway in 1937, but his report was not published until 1959.[8] He had
previously studied the Mapungubwe skeletons, and found marked
similarities between the K2 and Hill populations. In the case of the former
remains, he showed that the bones differed in practically every case from
those of the Negro, but that they corresponded to what was known of the
Bush and Boskop bones. He concluded his report: 'I state deliberately and
with a full comprehension of its significance that there is not a single
specifically Negro feature in any skull hitherto recovered at Bambandyanalo.'
The skeletal material was thus considered to be pre-Negro. From his
study of the material culture and economy of K2, Captain Gardner
assigned the main occupation to Hottentot peoples. Undoubtedly, in
reaching this conclusion he was greatly influenced by the conclusions of the
physical anthropologists.

The sequence of human occupation at Mapungubwe is more complicated,
and, in spite of Jones's and Gardner's work, needs further fieldwork before
it is fully clarified. The first occupants of the Hill were the people who
occupied K2 in its latest stages. Their occupation is sealed from the later
levels by a layer of black ash.[9] According to Gardner there is a complete
break in the pottery sequence at this stage; spindle whorls and abundant
iron tools make their appearance, and traces of a more elaborate occupation
are found. Complicated daga[10] structures were now built, including
houses with courtyards or verandahs, and there is evidence of repeated
rebuilding of houses. Gold and copper ornaments both occur in the
deposits and are associated with burials, and finer pottery was made. Two
radiocarbon dates for the Hill have been published, dating the middle levels
to the late fourteenth and early fifteenth centuries A.D.[11] Both of the
archaeologists who dug on the Hill in 1934 considered that all the
inhabitants of Mapungubwe were Bantu in culture, and that they had
connexions with the Zimbabwe culture. It came as a surprise when Dr
Galloway submitted his report on the skeletons, which he concluded with
the words:

The human remains from Mapungubwe, although few in number, show such
similarity in their important diagnostic features that they constitute a much
purer physical type than would be expected from such a site. It represents a

---

[7] Ibid. 82. All radiocarbon dates in this paper have been calculated to 1950.
[8] A. Galloway, *The Skeletal remains of Bambandyanalo* (Johannesburg, 1959).
[9] G. A. Gardner (1963), op. cit. 88.   [10] Ibid. 20.   [11] Ibid. 88.

homogeneous people, which had stabilised over many centuries, since the racial features are so constant. It is a Bush-Boskop people showing sporadically a few Negro features.[12]

According to Captain Gardner, however, there is a short phase of Hottentot occupation at the very end of the Hill sequence.[13] The evidence for this, as well as the earliest occupation by late K2 people, came from his later work on the Hill. K2 pottery becomes more common again, and Gardner uses this and the skeletal evidence to postulate a new Hottentot tenure of Mapungubwe at the end of its long history.

*   *   *

We have mentioned that K2 consists of a mound of midden deposit some 200 yards across and some 20 feet deep, and that the site antedates Mapungubwe. The radiocarbon date in the eleventh century for the middle phases of the site would suggest that the origins of K2 go back some centuries earlier. It is thus contemporary with the Leopard's Kopje culture of Southern Rhodesia and its relative, the Kalomo culture from north of the Zambezi, both of which are thought to be the work of Bantu-speaking peoples.

Although Captain Gardner ascribed most of the K2 sequence to the Hottentots, he indicated that the site was occupied at a late stage in its history by Bantu-speaking peoples of Nguni stock who intermarried with them. These Nguni brought with them their 'primitive hoe culture, the use of iron, and the practice of hut-building'.[14] Unfortunately, however, he does not illustrate the cultural material associated with the upper horizons, and we are unable, in the absence of the collections, to confirm his statement. On the surface of the site today can be found both typical K2 sherds and finer pottery, which is probably to be connected with Schofield's M1 ware. Schofield himself states that all the exotic pottery from K2 can be matched with M1 ware from Mapungubwe,[15] but Gardner does not comment on this point. In the absence of more precise stratigraphical information on the vertical distribution of both pottery types and other cultural traits, we cannot confirm or deny Gardner's evidence for new immigrants at K2. But it seems probable that the occupation of the mound shows no major discontinuity, although there are some changes in material culture connected with the arrival of a new and as yet unidentified group in the Greefswald region later than the eleventh century. These were probably a small group of the people who, with the K2 people, were the first occupants of Mapungubwe.

Gardner's reasons for attributing the lower levels of K2 to the Hottentots are complex, but based on careful observation and wide reading. At the time when he studied the K2 material, almost nothing was known of the

[12] A. Galloway, 'The skeletal remains of Mapungubwe', in L. Fouché (1937), op. cit. 127–74.   [13] G. A. Gardner (1963), op. cit. 90.
[14] Ibid. 81.   [15] J. F. Schofield, *Primitive Pottery* (Capetown, 1948), 137.

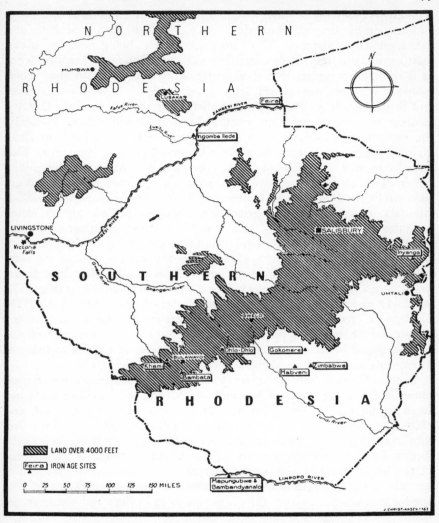

Fig. 1. Map showing Iron Age sites in southern Africa.

contemporary cultures of the Rhodesias. Also, the techniques of economic reconstruction from archaeological data, developed after the Second World War by Clark[16] and others, were in their infancy. This trend towards economic reconstruction and an increased volume of research has meant that we have far more background data on the Iron Age at our disposal than had Captain Gardner, and can carefully re-examine the grounds upon which he attributes the K2 mound to Hottentots rather than to a Bantu-speaking Iron Age group. The Hottentots are pastoral people, whose

[16] J. G. D. Clark, *Prehistoric Europe: the economic basis* (Cambridge, 1950).

economy is based on their herds of long-horned cattle and fat-tailed sheep,
and also on hunting and gathering. They do not practise agriculture and
live a nomadic existence. Their huts are simple, being made of sticks,
matting, or skins, and can be carried on the back of an ox.[17] Such evidence
as is available suggests that their settlements were small in size. Their
weapons were wooden spears, later tipped with iron, bows and arrows,
and throwing sticks. There are no satisfactory records to show that the
Hottentots used stone implements within historical times; certainly,
the more northerly Hottentots have worked iron and copper in small
quantities ever since they have been observed by the European. This
knowledge was probably obtained from contact with Bantu-speaking
tribes. The earliest Bantu-speakers were on a higher level of culture
than either the Bushmen or Hottentots. They were primarily pastoralists
who also practised simple agriculture, living in settled villages, often
in quite large communities. Later groups, many of them of Congo
Basin origin, were primarily agriculturalists, practising a simple form of
hoe agriculture. Iron weapons and tools and copper ornaments were
worked by all Bantu-speaking groups of importance, their houses are
permanent affairs of sticks and mud, and their settlements often large. The
whole level of technological achievement was higher than that of the
Hottentots. Archaeological finds present an incomplete picture of any
people, but it should be possible, by a full use of the evidence from K2,
to distinguish between two such contrasting forms of culture as those of
Hottentots and Bantu-speakers.

Captain Gardner was immediately struck by the absence of baked mud
floors in the lower levels of K2, and concluded that the inhabitants had
lived in much more impermanent structures made of grass, wood, and
skins, a characteristic of Hottentot pastoralists. Daga structures are,
however, fragmentary and rare in many Early Iron Age sites, such as the
Leopard's Kopje settlements and Kalomo culture mounds. Their absence
in the lower levels of K2 cannot be regarded as conclusive evidence of
entirely different dwelling habits, especially as most of our knowledge of
the basal strata comes from the south side of the village and not from the
centre, where, logically, one could expect to find the earliest houses.[18]
Structures which leave little trace in the archaeological record are
characteristic of many modern African peoples, especially in areas of great
heat and in regions where special ecological conditions make temporary
shelters desirable.

The K2 peoples' flimsy dwellings were connected in Gardner's mind
with an emphasis on pastoralism. He noted the absence of carbonized
seeds and declared that agriculture was not practised. The preponderance
of cattle bones suggested to him a predominantly pastoral economy, and

[17] I. Schapera, *The Khoisan peoples of South Africa* (London, 1930).
[18] The dung levels at K2 are shown in Gardner's sections to occur in the middle levels.
Structures might well have been erected in the centre of the village in its earliest stages.

hence Hottentots. Evidence for agriculture is, by the nature of the finds, normally indirect or even invisible; whereas pastoralism can be deduced from an abundance of cattle bones, which are commonly preserved on sites of this period. Often in cases where agriculture is known to have been practised, the abundant domestic animal remains make it easy to overstress the importance of stockbreeding, even to the exclusion of agriculture. At K2, surface finds of hoe butts and grindstones strongly suggest agriculture, at any rate in the later stages of the settlement, but until further excavations are undertaken, we cannot say whether such finds come from the earlier levels as well. Undeniably, agriculture, if it was practised, was less intense than in the heyday of Mapungubwe, for here carbonized seeds are abundant. It is obvious from the domestic animal bones that pastoral activities played an important part in the economy of K2, but it should be remembered that many of the earliest Iron Age groups in southern Africa were probably ultimately of East African origin, and, as such, were probably more concerned with stockbreeding than agriculture, which, with few iron tools of any strength, could not involve the clearance of large tracts of woodland. It has been suggested that early farmers north of the Zambezi[19] were practising bush-clump and ant-hill agriculture on the edges of grassy clearings in woodland regions. Stockbreeding was probably important in these circumstances. Although, in the absence of more fieldwork, we cannot deny Captain Gardner's conclusion, I am inclined to feel that agriculture, albeit on a small scale, was practised, and that the economy of this large settlement was based on mixed farming and food-gathering rather than on pastoralism alone. The exponents of the latter would tend to live in smaller and less permanent settlements than that represented by the mound at K2.

Long-horned cattle were kept by the early Hottentots,[20] and Gardner considers that the K2 beasts belonged to this breed. Dr A. S. Brink studied the cattle bones from K2,[21] but stated that he could not draw any conclusions as to the species of cattle found there from the fragmentary material available to him. At Mapungubwe, Curson[22] identified both 'Sanga and Afrikander types'. There appears in fact to be no osteological evidence to support Gardner's opinion. Both long- and short-horned Sanga cattle are known from Leopard's Kopje sites in Southern Rhodesia,[23] and Curson's report makes it likely that there was similar variation in size in the Limpopo herds. It is certainly impossible to infer, as Gardner does, that long-horned cattle can only be assigned to Hottentots in this region.

The material culture from K2 also shows some features which were attributed by the excavator to the Hottentots. In his report he compared

[19] J. D. Clark and B. M. Fagan, 'Charcoals, Sands, and channel-decorated pottery from Northern Rhodesia', *American Anthropologist* (1964). (In the Press.)
[20] I. Schapera (1930), op. cit. 229.
[21] G. A. Gardner (1963), op. cit. 28.
[22] Ibid. 29.
[23] I am grateful to Mr Keith Robinson for allowing me to study Leopard's Kopje horn cores from sites which he has investigated.

the pottery to Cape Hottentot wares, quoting[24] descriptions by Ter Rhyne and Schapera. As Mason[25] has quite rightly shown, neither of these passages is a sufficient basis for relating K2 ware to Hottentot pottery. Even a cursory study of Schofield's remarks on Hottentot potting[26] reveals drastic differences between the two types of ware. Pointed bases, oval shapes, horizontally pierced lugs, and other features of Hottentot vessels are not significant features of K2 pottery. Since Gardner wrote his report, Robinson[27] has published a series of descriptions of the Matabeleland pottery known as Leopard's Kopje ware. This culture is widespread over the western and central parts of Southern Rhodesia, and extends into the Limpopo valley. Unfortunately, many of the more important excavated sites are still unpublished, but Robinson[28] has remarked on the similarities between K2 pottery and that from Leopard's Kopje sites. The straight-sided beaker, characteristic of K2, is especially common on Leopard's Kopje sites in Southern Matabeleland, and is also found in Bechuanaland.[29] K2 pottery is thus in no way unique, and evidently belongs to the widespread, Iron Age, Leopard's Kopje ware tradition, which had evidently spread beyond the Limpopo at this period. Schofield compared it to ancient Sotho wares, on the basis of Mangwato parallels, but this is probably premature.

The rarity of metalworking and the relatively abundant rough bone points were taken to be further indications of Hottentot occupation. The iron objects at K2 are concentrated in the upper levels, and are stated by the excavator to belong to the post-Hottentot occupation. In a number of contemporary Iron Age sites further north, iron tools have a similar stratigraphical distribution to that at K2,[30] but their absence or rarity in the lower horizons is attributed to the poor preservation qualities of the mound deposits. Unfortunately this late period at K2 is badly documented, and the densities of iron slag are not recorded. It may, therefore, transpire from future excavations that metalworking was practised, albeit very sporadically, in the earlier stages of the occupation. The distribution of iron slag at Rhodesian sites shows that metal was worked, even if iron tools are themselves rare or absent. Careful re-examination of this problem in the field may show that K2 was occupied by a community who had a knowledge of ironworking acquired from their Leopard's Kopje culture contemporaries, and that for some reason they did not practise the craft very regularly, nor did their tools survive the heavy corrosive effects of the

[24] G. A. Gardner (1963), op. cit. 60.

[25] R. J. Mason, *The Prehistory of the Transvaal* (Johannesburg, 1963), 382.

[26] J. F. Schofield (1948), op. cit. 56–70.

[27] K. R. Robinson, 'Four Rhodesian Iron Age sites, an account of stratigraphy and finds', *Occ. Pap. Nat. Mus. S. Rhod.* II (1953), 22A (see also *Khami Ruins* (Cambridge 1959).)

[28] K. R. Robinson (1953), op. cit. 88.

[29] K. R. Robinson, 'Further excavations in the Iron Age deposits at the Tunnel site, Gokomere Hill, Southern Rhodesia', *S. Afr. Archaeol. Bull.* XVIII (1963), 72, 160.

[30] B. M. Fagan, *Iron Age cultures in Northern Rhodesia*. In preparation.

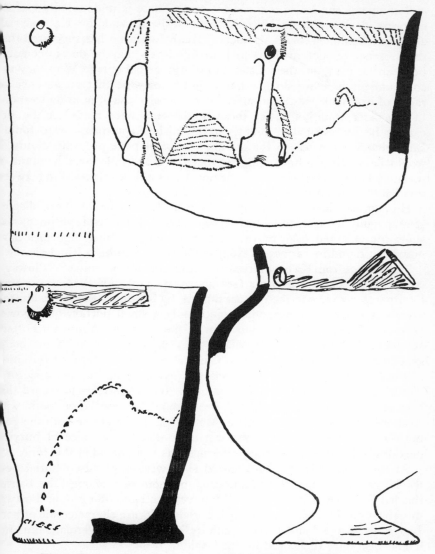

Fig. 2. Pottery from K2, known as 'M2'. After Schofield, 1937.

2 soil. Bone arrowheads and link shafts, which are known from Iron
ge levels at Zimbabwe and elsewhere,[31] are abundant at K2, and their
undance may be correlated with the scarcity of iron. Captain Gardner
notes descriptions of Hottentot arrows by Sparrman[32] and Le Vaillant,[33]

[31] K. R. Robinson, 'Excavations on the Acropolis', in K. R. Robinson, Roger Summers,
d A. Whitty, *Zimbabwe Excavations, 1958* (Bulawayo, 1961).
[32] Andrew Sparrman, *A voyage to the Cape of Good Hope* (London 1785), 199.
[33] Le Vaillant, *Travels in the Interior of Africa* (London, 1790), II, 66–7.

and compares the K2 specimens to them. There is undoubtedly a clos
correspondence between Hottentot missile heads and the K2 materia
and some Bushmen forms also occur. Keith Robinson has suggested th;
the presence of such artifacts in Iron Age levels may be due to contac
between farmers and their Later Stone Age neighbours.[34] Why they a:
so abundant here we do not know, but it may be that an absence o
rarity of iron tools led to the survival or extensive use of hunting weapor
in the older tradition. That these implements were made on the si·
cannot be in reasonable doubt, for unfinished specimens were foun·
But, whatever the reason for the abundance of bone projectile heads,
would be surely wrong to suggest that the K2 people were ignorant o
metalworking when their pottery demonstrates a close relationship betwee
them and contemporary Leopard's Kopje ironworkers.

Human figurines of clay were made at K2. Some of these displa
steatopygous features, and it has been suggested that several specimens als
show the enlarged *labia* of the Hottentot female. Such figurines ha·
now been found in Leopard's Kopje contexts in Southern Rhodesia.

The burials from K2 have already become famous as a result of Galloway
study of the skeletal remains (see above, p. 339). Of the seventy-fo¹
interments, six were termed 'Beast Burials' by Gardner. But, as he himse
says,[35] the term is a misnomer, since only a small portion of a bovi
normally the mandible, was buried with the skeleton. Abundant potte
surrounded these burials, especially the richest, No. 6. With the bac
ground of his Egyptian experience, Gardner considered that the associatio
of bovid bones with these skeletons was evidence for the presence of
'bovid cult of possible Hamitic tradition'. It is of interest to record th
fragmentary bovid remains have been found in association both wi
Leopard's Kopje culture burials in Matabeleland,[36] and also with the go
burials at Ingombe Ilede.[37] We can infer that the practice of buryi:
portions of bovines as funerary offerings was widespread at this time.

At the time when the Greefswald sites were dug, flexed burial ne
dwellings was thought to be an unusual phenomenon amongst the Bant
this led Gardner to attribute the K2 graves to a Hottentot group. Postw
investigations have shown that such burial habits are characteristic of bo
Leopard's Kopje[38] and Kalomo culture[39] peoples; the Venda, Zulu, a:
Tonga also bury their dead in this fashion.

Culturally, therefore, it would seem that the main occupation levels
K2 have some affinities with contemporary Iron Age settlements north
the Limpopo. The pottery and figurines are related to Leopard's Kop
ware; the burial habits are paralleled in the Southern Rhodesian Iron A
sites of the time, and the bovid funerary cult is also known in the Rhodesi:

[34] K. R. Robinson (1961), op. cit. 215.   [35] G. A. Gardner (1963), op. cit. 54.
[36] K. R. Robinson: personal communication.
[37] B. M. Fagan, op. cit. in preparation.   [38] K. R. Robinson (1959), op. cit. pl. VI.
[39] B. M. Fagan, 'The Iron Age sequence in the Southern Province of Northe
Rhodesia', *Journal of African History*, IV, 2 (1963), 166.

There is still doubt as to whether the main K2 occupation was the work of ironworkers, although their contemporaries in Matabeleland certainly made iron tools. The abundance of bone arrowheads suggests that metals were scarce, even if they were used. With the exception of the bone points, and perhaps certain aspects of the economy, there is nothing at K2 which must be ascribed to Hottentots rather than Iron Age peoples.

The problem now arises that if we accept the K2 site as belonging to the Iron Age, at what date did Iron Age people first cross the Limpopo? We have no stratigraphical evidence to suggest that there was an earlier Iron Age occupation of the northern Transvaal than that at K2, but surface finds from elsewhere in the province throw some light on the problem. The earliest Iron Age peoples in Southern Rhodesia were the makers of Gokomere ware, which has been dated to between about the fourth and the ninth centuries A.D. At Malapati on the Nuanetsi river, a tributary of the Limpopo, Robinson[40] has found a late form of Gokomere pottery, now dated to 850 ± 100 A.D. (SR—33).[41] Sherds with features in common with Malapati are known from Matokoma,[42] 13 miles west of Louis Trichardt, to the south of the Zoutspansberg Mountains in the northern Transvaal. Similar pottery is known from Bechuanaland,[43] and it can confidently be expected that further sites of this type will come to light on South African soil. The Rhodesian makers of this pottery are known to have practised ironworking, to have been in the possession of domestic animals, and to have cultivated cereal crops,[44] and it is quite reasonable to suppose that their South African neighbours did the same.

It would appear, therefore, that Iron Age peoples in the Gokomere tradition entered South Africa during the middle or late first millennium.[44a] Gokomere ware can be linked with the Channel-decorated pottery makers of Northern Rhodesia, who are thought to have entered southern Africa from the Dimple-Based ware provinces of East Africa.

But if we regard the K2 site as being an Iron Age settlement, which implies that it was occupied by Bantu-speaking Negroids, there is a marked anomaly between the cultural and skeletal evidence. Professor Galloway classifies the large K2 population as non-Negro, and this immediately implies that they are pre-Bantu, which the archaeological

[40] K. R. Robinson, *Schoolboys Exploration Society expedition to Buffalo Bend, 1961* (Bulawayo, 1961).

[41] K. R. Robinson (1963), loc. cit. 160.

[42] I am grateful to Dr J. B. de Vaal of Pretoria for allowing me to examine this important collection, which he discovered many years ago. Mr K. R. Robinson kindly advised me on the typology of the sherds.

[43] J. F. Schofield (1948), op. cit. 128.

[44] K. R. Robinson, 'An early Iron Age site from the Chibi District, Southern Rhodesia', *S. Afr. Archaeol. Bull.*, XVI (1961), 75–102.

[44a] Ironsmelting was being practised at Melville Koppies in the Southern Transvaal by the end of the first millennium A.D. A smelting furnace there has been dated to 1060 ± 50 A.D. (Y—1338), and assigned to the Uitkomst culture. R. J. Mason and N. J. van der Merwe, 'Radiocarbon dating of Iron Age sites in the Southern Transvaal: Melville Koppies and Uitkomst cave', *S. Afr. Journ. Sci.*, LX (1964), 142.

evidence does not. Galloway goes so far as to call the K2 skeletons '
homogeneous Boskop-Bush population physically akin to the first Bosko
inhabitants of the coastal caves'.[45] The male skeletons from K2 are thos
in which the Boskopoid elements are best preserved; they have massiv
proportions and heavy skeletons, with a tendency to a pentagonoid sku
profile and a wedge-shaped occiput. On the other hand, the femal
skeletons have a more delicate build, and the characteristics of the Bus
type. It might be argued that the differences between the Bush an
Boskopoid types simply represent sex differences, but a similar phenomeno
has been observed amongst the /? Auni – ≠ Khomani and Naron Bush
men.[46] Tobias has been led to suggest that the concept of two physic
types in the one population is valid.[47]

There is considerable argument amongst physical anthropologists abou
the validity of both the Boskop and Bush-Boskopoid concepts. The Bosko
'race' concept dates back to 1913, when part of a massive calvarium wa
unearthed on a farm near Boskop in the Transvaal. The archaeologic
context of the skull has never been completely satisfactorily establishe
Professor Van Riet Lowe studied a single flake found with the skull, an
assigned it and the human remains to the Middle Stone Age.[48] Dart
compared the skull to the Later Stone Age Zitzikama remains of Bush
Hottentot type in 1923, and suggested that the fossilized Boskop type wa
representative of the physical type which had been widely distributed i
southern Africa before the Bushman occupation. The Boskop physic
type was taken up by Dart's students and expanded into the Boskop 'rac
by Gear,[50] Galloway[51] and others. Galloway defined his use of the Bosko
physical type in the context of the K2 population as follows:

although Boskop Man as a living race and pure physical type belongs to th
Middle Stone Age, yet by hybridisation with later types, his physical characteristi
were handed on through these later types long after the living race of Bosko
Man had died out. Our use of the term 'Boskopoid' as applied to the persistenc
of this Middle Stone Age physical type in living African races is analogous t
Boule's use of the term 'Cro-Magnon' as applied to present-day types living i
the south of France.[52]

[45] A. Galloway (1959), op. cit. 125.
[46] R. A. Dart, 'The physical character of the /? Auni – ≠ Khomani Bushmen', Ban
Studies, XI (1937), 176–246.
[47] P. V. Tobias, 'Some developments in South African physical anthropology, 1938
1958', in A. Galloway (1959), op. cit. 129–51.
[48] C. Van Riet Lowe, 'An artefact recovered with the Boskop calvaria', S. Afr. Archaeo
Bull., IX (1954), 135–7.
[49] R. A. Dart, 'Boskop remains from the South-East African Coast', Nature, CXII (1923
623–5.
[50] H. S. Gear, 'A further report on the Boskopoid remains from Zitzikama', S. Af
Journ. Sci., XXXIII (1926), 923–34.
[51] A. Galloway, 'The Characteristics of the skull of the Boskop physical type', Am.
Phys. Anth., XXIII (1937), 31–46.
[52] A. Galloway, 'Man in Africa as a result of recent discoveries', S. Afr. Journ. Sci
XXXIV (1937), 89–120.

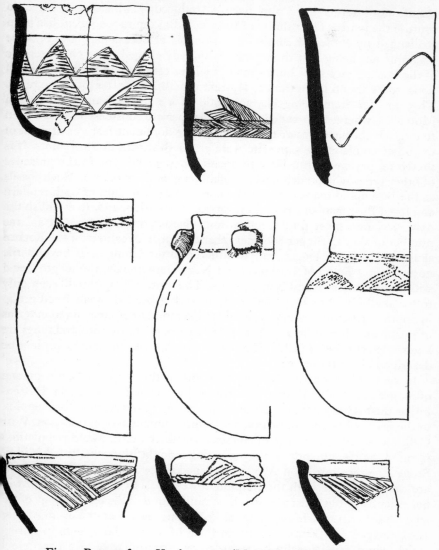

Fig. 3. Pottery from K2, known as 'M2'. After Schofield, 1937.

The specimens upon which the Boskop race concept is based come from
bout ten sites,[53] and the features of the physical type are alleged to be a
arge skull and massively constructed bones. Pedomorphic features such
s strong cranial bossing and a low vault are also present. Tobias has
ecently subdivided Middle Stone Age skulls into two subdivisions: the
Boskopoid for large or giganto-pedomorphic types, and the Rhodesioid for
he extreme gerontomorphic types such as Broken Hill Man. Other

[53] R. Singer, 'The Boskop race problem', Man (1958), 232.

classificatory terms have also been introduced,[54] which only serve to
confuse the issues. The validity of the whole Boskop race concept has been
challenged by Professor Singer on a number of occasions,[55] the basis of
his argument being that the features originally alleged to be characteristic
of the Boskop race have been shown, by later research on modern populations, to be found in Bushman, Hottentot or Bush-Hottentot admixtures.
They are far from being characteristic of a new African racial group.
Moreover, wherever so-called Boskopoid types are considered to have been
found, whether in caves or rock-shelters, the dominant features of most of
the other crania in the same site were either Bushman or Hottentot. It is
therefore, perhaps, unrealistic to create a new racial type in the presence
of other types which adequately explain its genetic make-up. Such fossils
as the Boskopoid materials must be appraised in the light of both modern
and fossil Bushman and Hottentot ranges of variation, and, to establish the
new race, one must find identical and characteristic features in a large
number of skulls. Singer considers that the specific features of the Boskop
skull are its great length and width, the latter falling well beyond the
normal outer limits of Bushman and Negro individuals, the length being
within the Hottentot and Negro ranges. The term Boskop should refer only
to the skull found in 1913, and if there is a big-headed, small-faced group
in South African prehistory, it should at the moment be considered in terms
of Bushman, Hottentot, and Negro, for no other definite ancestral types are
known, except the so-called Rhodesioid skulls, which cannot at present be
described along these lines.

In view of the controversy which surrounds the Boskopoid concept, and
of Singer's claim that Boskop features can be detected in Bushman, Hottentot, or Bush-Hottentot populations, the validity of referring to 'Boskopoids'
in the first and second millennia A.D. comes immediately in question. With
Galloway's use of the term in connexion with the Greefswald population
in mind, one is unhappy about projecting a doubtfully constituted Middle
Stone Age race into Iron Age times, especially when Bush characteristic
are well marked in both the Mapungubwe and K2 collections. Brothwell
has recently published a plea for the simplification of the terminology of the
later South African fossil material.[56] He suggests that the East African
Kanjera type represents the earliest form of man so far known in Africa
which could provisionally be regarded as representative of a basal stock
from which a large Bush type might have originated. During the movements of the latter southwards, various proto-Khoisan varieties became
differentiated, such as the pygmy Bushman form, which has not been found
in an early context. There may have been some interbreeding of ancestral
Rhodesioids with the new peoples, resulting in a more robust, partly Bush

[54] D. R. Brothwell, 'Evidence of Early Population Change in Central and Southern
Africa', *Man* (1963), 132.
[55] R. Singer (1958), op. cit.
[56] D. R. Brothwell (1963), op. cit.

form. To these new stocks Brothwell has assigned the definition 'large Khoisan', a deliberately loose term, which, with Rhodesioid, Khoisan, and Negro covers the very limited material more satisfactorily than the proliferation of terms used in the older literature. It seems to be a suitable compromise term, which will serve until such time as more material is available, or a detailed reassessment of the South African fossil material is made with the aid of the latest techniques of physical anthropology. Our K2 population can be classified with this 'large Khoisan' group, which simplifies our problem considerably, and shows that the inhabitants of the mound were of the indigenous, pre-Negro stock.

The non-Negro K2 population is the largest Iron Age skeletal group to have been studied, and we know little of the contemporary physical type in the Rhodesias. Very few skeletons from Iron Age sites in Southern Rhodesia are available. Tobias[57] reviewed the evidence from Southern Rhodesia in the Inyanga monograph. He suggested that the skeletal remains associated with mining activities are predominantly Bush-Boskopoid in character; some, however, show traces of hybridization with Negroes. Other skeletons, mostly recent, not associated with mining, are almost all Negro. Unfortunately no large population of Gokomere or Leopard's Kopje skeletons has been studied, but Shee[58] has suggested that a skeleton of a child of between 12 and 18 years from Gokomere shelter is of 'non-Bantu' type. This site dates to the middle of the sixth century A.D. In the absence of more skeletal material, we are obliged to conclude that a non-Negro 'large Khoisan' population was probably gradually hybridized with a Negro stock. North of the Zambezi, several groups of Iron Age skeletons have been excavated in the last five years. These range in date from the early first millennium A.D. to the nineteenth century; in addition, important series of Later Stone Age skeletons have been recovered from Gwisho Hot Springs, Lochinvar.[59] The Iron Age material is still under study, but there are said to be Negro elements in many of the skulls.[60] Gabel has shown that the Gwisho skeletons, of the third millennium B.C., are of Bush type. A number of tribes in Northern Rhodesia, amongst them the Tonga[61] and the Twa, are said to retain Khoisan traits even today, as do the Sandawe of Tanganyika. The Nebarara Iron Age skull from the same country[62] also shows Khoisan features. Although the evidence is extremely tenuous, it seems probable that Khoisan traits were well represented in the early Iron Age populations of the Rhodesias. The probability is, indeed, that in Southern Rhodesia the contemporaries of the

[57] P. V. Tobias, 'Skeletal remains from Inyanga', in Roger Summers, *Inyanga* (1958), 159–72.
[58] J. Shee, 'Skeletal remains from Gokomere', in K. R. Robinson (1963), op. cit. 170.
[59] C. Gabel, 'Further human remains from the Central African Later Stone Age', *Man* (1963), 44. (In addition, twenty-one skeletons have been found in recent excavations by F. Van Noten and B. M. Fagan at neighbouring Wilton sites.)
[60] Mr Adrian Martin, in discussion.
[61] P. V. Tobias, 'Tonga resettlement and the Kariba Dam', *Man* (1958), 88.
[62] A. Galloway, 'The Nebarara Skull', *S. Afr. Journ. Sci.*, xxx (1933), 585–96.

K2 people were also of predominantly non-Negro physical type, and that similar 'large Khoisan' groups, practising a somewhat similar type of economy and material culture, were spread over a wide tract of East and southern Africa at the end of the first millennium A.D.

But if they were basically of 'large Khoisan' stock, the K2 people's economy and material culture, and that of their Rhodesian contemporaries, is not that of Khoisan people. Of the Khoisan peoples, the Bushmen cannot have been the occupants of K2. Domestic animals were kept, and surviving Bushmen are purely hunter/gatherers. Hottentots practise an economy based on pastoralism, food gathering, and hunting. I know of no record of Hottentot cultivators under prehistoric or historical conditions, and the evidence for agriculture may well have been overlooked at K2. We have drawn attention to the similarities between K2 pottery and the Leopard's Kopje wares of Southern Rhodesia. The latter are associated with definite evidence of a mixed farming economy, ironworking, and mud-hut building. All these economic and technological features are characteristic of the Iron Age, to which I feel K2 belongs. There is an undeniable contrast between the material culture and economy of Khoisan peoples, and also of Hamitic pastoralists on the one hand, and those of the southern African Iron Age peoples on the other. It is and always will be impossible from archaeological evidence alone to say whether the K2 people, or any other Iron Age people for that matter, were Bantu- or click-speakers. But they were not Negroids, if Galloway is to be believed, and we are left with the contradiction between the archaeological and anthropological evidence to which we have already referred.

But this is not as unexpected as has been made out. Recent research has established that ironworking, probably introduced into southern Africa by Negro peoples, dates to the first century A.D. in Northern Rhodesia[63] and to as early as the fourth century in Southern Rhodesia. In the Transvaal itself pottery of a type associated with the earliest ironworkers north of the Limpopo may date to at least two centuries before the heyday of K2. Tobias's observations from Southern Rhodesian crania have shown that hybridization between large Khoisan and Negro occurred during the Iron Age, and there is evidence of this from the Mapungubwe population. Thus it is not inconceivable that 'large Khoisan' people took over the material culture and perhaps the language of the earliest Negro groups, who, arriving in small numbers, were assimilated without trace in the indigenous 'large Khoisan' population. This situation may have arisen throughout south-central Africa and even in East Africa. With the increasing migrations of Negroid peoples into the southern parts of Africa, the process of hybridization probably increased in momentum, helped by the introduction of non-African physical traits from the coastal trade routes.

*   *   *

[63] J. D. Clark and B. M. Fagan (1964), op. cit.

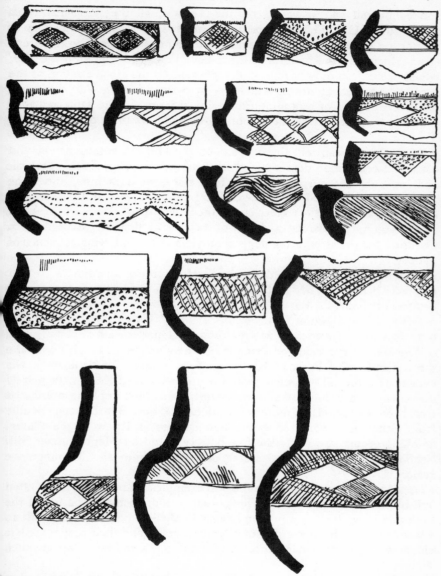

Fig. 4. Pottery from Mapungubwe Hill, known as 'M1'. After Schofield, 1937.

All those who have worked at Mapungubwe agree that it was occupied later in the Iron Age than K2. As we have already mentioned, the site may be divided into two distinct entities: the Hill itself, the summit of which is mantled with occupation debris and imported earth, and the occupied Terrace on the southern side of the kopje. Although isolated cuttings have been put into the talus slopes, and the University of Pretoria some years ago conducted an excavation on the Terrace, all the published work relates to the Hill. This is unfortunate, for it is obvious that only a small proportion of the population could have lived on the summit, and there is clear evidence for occupation of the valley. The stratigraphy on the Hill, whilst useful, can only have been complicated by the erosive action of the occasional torrential storms which occur in the summer. Very little undisturbed deposit of stratigraphical value remains on the Hill, and it is probable that future work at Mapungubwe will have to be confined to the Terrace.

As far as one can tell, the deposits on the Hill are homogeneous, and consist of occupation debris mixed with subsoil. Lenses of ash, charcoal, and hut rubble occur, as do numerous traces of daga huts, and some retaining walls. The best stratigraphical record comes from Gardner's trench dug at the north-western end of the Hill in 1939. There, a depression in the summit preserved a depth of 11 feet of deposit. According to Gardner, the deposits in the depression yielded the following sequence of pottery:[64]

Present surface–2 feet: 'K2 derivatives'; Hottentot occupation
2–4 feet: Schofield's M1 and M2
4–7 feet: Schofield's M1
7–9 feet: K2 and Nguni
9–11 feet: sterile sand with Middle Stone Age underneath.

The excavator considered that the first inhabitants of the Hill were the same people who lived at K2 in its final stages. Unfortunately, the evidence for the cultural changes in the upper levels of K2 is inadequately documented in Volume II, and must remain uncertain until the collections have been re-studied and more fieldwork carried out. But it seems possible from Schofield's work[65] that the new settlers at K2 were the Bantu-speaking group who made the fine pottery found on Mapungubwe Hill. Schofield recognized three classes of pottery from the Mapungubwe region:[66]

Class M1 : 'a fine ware of which the best examples are beautifully decorated and burnished a deep black'. This pottery is more common on top of the Hill, and is typified by a preponderance of shallow bowls. In contrast to Class M2, there are fewer different types of vessel and their shapes are less elaborate. Scratched decoration is rare and the standard of finish much higher.

Class M2 : 'a coarse ware usually finished with a brindled burnish, and of which the most common decoration was a line of diagonally patched loops. In many cases we found the lines of the decoration were engraved on the burnt pot. This class also shows a much greater variation of shape. . . .' M2 pottery is the characteristic K2 pottery and is also found on the Hill

[64] G. A. Gardner (1963), op. cit. pl. LXI.
[65] J. F. Schofield (1948), op. cit. 137.
[66] J. F. Schofield, 'The work done in 1934: pottery', in L. Fouché (1937), op. cit. 32–102.

Class M3: 'all pottery of which there is reason to believe that it was imported from neighbouring tribes using a different pottery tradition'. Pottery found on the Hill which is considered to be imported, including polychrome sherds, comes under this heading.

According to Gardner's published section, K2 pottery underlies the main sequence where M1 and M2 are mingled. But he also states that there are Nguni elements in the industry and that it is similar to the late K2 pottery. Schofield said little about the stratigraphy of the Hill wares in 1937, but returned to the subject in 1948:

> throughout the excavations on Mapungubwe Hill, M1 pottery was found in conjunction with a very different type of ware that occurred in increasing quantities with the depth of the excavation. Thus, for the first foot of the excavation, 91·5% of the pottery found belonged to Class M1, 4·8% belonged to this second type (provisionally called Class M2), and 3·7% was indefinite; but in the seventh foot the proportions were respectively 33·7%, 51·7% and 14·6%.[67]

Unfortunately, we cannot tell whether Schofield is referring to Gardner's cutting, which extends down to 9 feet, but there is certainly a strong indication that the proportions of M1 pottery increase throughout the sequence, this class of pottery being present from the beginning. Gardner lays considerable stress on two ash layers in his trench at 8 feet and 5 feet, which he considers to represent breaks in the occupational sequence and, by inference, periods of unrest. But his stratigraphical profiles do not prove that these breaks are of more than local significance, and the earlier investigators make no mention of them. It was common practice for settlements to be burnt and rebuilt during Iron Age times, and it may be that this explanation will fit the facts more readily than the invasion theory. There is no indication from Schofield's pottery sequence that there was a major break in culture during the occupation of the Hill, but merely a gradual refinement of the pottery. Undoubtedly, however, there was considerable enrichment of the Mapungubwe culture in the later stages of the occupation, for spindle whorls, elaborate houses, and trade objects become common. The probability is, therefore, that the Hill was occupied by a single community, whose culture was gradually diversified and improved as the imprint of the M1 people upon the region became stronger.

Two radiocarbon samples from Gardner's cutting on Mapungubwe were dated at Yale as follows:

Y—135-9, 3 feet below surface: A.D. 1420 ± 60.
Y—135-14, 5 feet below surface: A.D. 1380 ± 60.

Four feet of deposit underlay Y—135-14, so these dates come from the middle phases of the occupation. If the heyday of the Hill was in the late fourteenth and early fifteenth centuries, then we can expect the first occupation of Mapungubwe to have taken place as early as the thirteenth century. As yet we have no dates for the upper horizons of K2, but on the

[67] J. F. Schofield (1948), op. cit. 107.

basis of the stratigraphical evidence they may date to the twelfth century or later. The new immigrants responsible for the development of Mapungubwe as an important ritual and commercial centre probably arrived at Greefswald about 750 to 900 years ago.

In their heyday, the Mapungubwe people had a rich and varied culture. In the absence of work on the Terrace, our knowledge of it is probably one-sided, for there is every reason to believe that the Hill was only occupied by a few important people, whilst the bulk of the population lived in the valley below.

Traces of elaborate daga structures were found by all investigators. These included houses with courtyards, huts with verandahs, and more simple structures. In several cases there was evidence of repeated rebuilding of houses. Mapungubwe technology was elaborate. Gold beads, tacks, and foil were in use, but the metal was not worked locally. Copper was used for ornaments and bangle-making. Iron tools include flat-bladed arrowheads, spearheads, hoes, and ornaments. Such implements were more profuse than at K2. No gongs or other ceremonial objects were found. Bone points, some split to receive barbs, and linked shafts are common in the upper levels of the Hill. These were made of ostrich bone or ivory, and are finer than the K2 specimens. Clay figurines of animals were made, but human figures are rare and display no steatopygia.

The economy was based on mixed farming. Sorghum and cow peas were cultivated, and wild produce gathered. The bones of both cattle and small stock were common and outnumbered those of game animals, suggesting a less important role for hunting at this period. This agricultural economy is a typical Iron Age subsistence pattern of the period. In addition, the Mapungubwe people took advantage of the natural resources of the Limpopo valley to engage in extensive trading. The valley is rich in ivory, and the copper mines of the Messina region were certainly worked at this time and their output was perhaps controlled from Mapungubwe. The results of this trading activity can be seen in the Hill deposits. Glass beads and other imported objects occur, the former in abundance; fragments of ivory and abundant copper ornaments are found. Cloth was probably imported as well as being woven on the site. The richness of the Mapungubwe people can best be visualized from their burials. Twenty-four skeletons were recovered from the upper levels of Mapungubwe in 1933 and 1934.[68] The skeletons were buried with a rich array of gold and copper objects, and were associated with M1 pottery. Eleven of the burials were studied by Galloway in 1937, and his conclusions have already been quoted (see above, pp. 339–40). Fouché and his collaborators were in no doubt that these remarkable burials were to be associated with the makers of M1 pottery.[69] But Captain Gardner reached other conclusions from his later excavations to the west of the burial area. In the uppermost 2 feet of his cutting, he

[68] Neville Jones, 'The 1934 expedition', in L. Fouché (1937), op. cit. 25.
[69] L. Fouché (1937), op. cit. 26.

was struck by the reappearance of considerable quantities of M2 pottery. Furthermore, he observed that daga huts were not built and that agricultural implements were absent from the upper horizons of the trench. On the basis of these observations and Professor Galloway's conclusions on the skeletal material, he argued for a brief Hottentot reoccupation of Mapungubwe at the end of its history.[70] A Khoisan clan is alleged to have driven off the Bantu occupants, but to have retained some of the splendours of the culture of its predecessors, and their burial customs, accounting for the gold burials and the shallow bowls of M1 type found with the bodies. Undoubtedly, Gardner in producing this extraordinary theory was strongly influenced by Galloway's conclusions on the skeletal remains. Since the predominantly non-Negro burials were confined to the latest levels of the Hill and were deposited according to K2 custom, he felt justified in postulating a dramatic new occupation of the site by a people at a far lower level of culture. But the burials are associated with M1 pottery, and with other objects characteristic of the main occupation. Furthermore, we have already shown that, even if the skeletons are non-Negro, the K2 and Mapungubwe method of burial is typical of contemporary Iron Age communities. M2 (K2) pottery occurs throughout the Mapungubwe sequence in association with M1, and to imply that M1 vessels were not made in the upper levels when they are associated with contemporary burials is manifestly absurd. We have no means of telling whether agricultural implements or huts were made in the upper levels in other parts of the Hill, whatever discoveries were made in Gardner's cutting. But even if we accept Gardner's conclusion, it is hard to believe that a group of Hottentot pastoralists would be capable of adapting themselves to such a radically different economy and material culture as that of the Bantu occupants of Mapungubwe. There is every indication that the Hill was settled throughout its history by Iron Age peoples, who were probably speaking a Bantu language.

The archaeology has shown that two distinct pottery traditions were practised throughout the occupation of Mapungubwe. Mr Schofield assigned his M2 pottery to an ancient Sotho strain, and we know that Sotho peoples were occupying eastern Bechuanaland during the period of expansion of the Shona empire.[71] He also drew attention to the strong Shona influences in M1 pottery. Both wares can be connected with southern Rhodesian Iron Age peoples. The pottery from K2 belongs to the Leopard's Kopje group of industries from Matabeleland, which both antedate and are contemporary with the Ruin cultures. There are also strong Shona influences in Class 3 pottery at Zimbabwe, which resembles M1 ware. This pottery belongs to the third phase of Zimbabwe's history, when Shona peoples built the first stone structures on the Acropolis. At

[70] G. A. Gardner (1963), op. cit. 89–90.
[71] D. P. Abraham, 'The early political history of the kingdom of Mwene Mutapa 50–1589)', *Historians in Tropical Africa* (1962), 62.

both Mapungubwe and Zimbabwe the older pottery traditions surviv
alongside the new. The Shona dominated the indigenous Iron Age minin
peoples of Southern Rhodesia, whom they found in occupation of th
country upon their arrival.[72] Comparatively small groups of the newcomer
were able to dominate the indigenous population by virtue of their superic
organizational and ritual powers. The Acropolis at Zimbabwe became a
important centre for the monotheistic *Mwari* cult and the headquarters c
the chieftainship.[73] The Shona took over control of the trade with th
Arab traders from the east coast, and with Arab support expanded the
commercial empire over a vast area of south-central Africa. It is known th
their influence extended to the Limpopo valley, rich in ivory and coppe
and the strong Shona traits in M1 pottery suggest that Mapungubwe wa
one of their centres on the Limpopo. The radiocarbon dates for Period I
at Zimbabwe show that it lasted from the eleventh to fifteenth centurie
Mapungubwe is contemporary with the later part of this period. The gla
beads at Mapungubwe are very similar to those from Period III deposits c
the Acropolis,[74] and serve to emphasize a close connexion between the tw
sites. At both sites a prominent hill dominates the settlement and probab
had important ritual attraction to roving adherents of the *Mwari* cult seel
ing a permanent settlement. It is likely that the Hill was first occupied c
account of its ritual importance. A small group of Shona may have reache
the Bambandyanalo settlement as early as the twelfth or thirteenth cer
turies and settled amongst the K2 people. With them they brought th
Mwari cult, which they established on the summit of Mapungubwe. Init
ally, the Shona were in a minority, and their characteristic material cultu
was submerged in the indigenous traditions. But as time passed and th
Mapungubwe settlement prospered, the influence of Shona culture becam
much stronger, although the indigenous pottery tradition survived until th
abandonment of the Hill. This seems the most logical way to explain th
mingling of two well-established pottery traditions on the same site.

Period IV, the phase of Rozwi dominance, began at Zimbabwe in abo
1450, and the Shona empire fell under Rozwi control. It is not knov
exactly when the Venda, who are of Rozwi origin, crossed the Limpo
and settled in the Greefswald region. But it is likely that they did so with
a few centuries of the Rozwi occupation of Zimbabwe. No evidence
Venda culture has been found on Mapungubwe.[75]

We must now retrace our steps and attempt to reconcile the archaeologist
contention that the occupants of Mapungubwe were Bantu-speaking peop
with Professor Galloway's judgement that the fifteenth-century burials c

---

[72] D. P. Abraham (1962), op. cit. 61.

[73] Roger Summers, *Zimbabwe: a Rhodesian Mystery* (Johannesburg, 1963).

[74] K. R. Robinson, 'Zimbabwe beads', in R. Summers, K. R. Robinson, and A. Whit
(1961), op. cit. 213.

[75] Gardner considers that Nguni, Sotho, and Venda peoples were the princip
inhabitants of the Hill. His interpretation is not supported by impressive evidence, at
in the interests of clarity I have disregarded it in this paper.

the Hill are of 'Bush-Boskopoid' people with sporadic Negro features. The archaeologists ascribe M1 and M2 pottery to the Shona and Sotho, both of whom are Bantu-speaking tribes, and all Bantu we know of are to a considerable extent Negroid. 'Sporadic Negro features' can hardly be taken to mean the same thing, especially as there must have been considerable Negro influence at some stage to bring about a change from click tongues to Bantu languages. Abraham's ethno-historical studies in Southern Rhodesia have suggested that the pre-Ruin population was one of pale-skinned and tall people,[76] and there is every indication that the Negroid Shona new-comers were comparatively few in number. The effect of a small influx of Negro elements into the Iron Age population must have been small, with a correspondingly slow rate of hybridization, especially if intermarriage with the indigenous population was discouraged. Undoubtedly, the process of hybridization must have accelerated sharply during the second millennium, when there were greater population movements and a higher density of farmers. But the truth is that we know almost nothing about the physical anthropology of the Iron Age, and until more large samples both of pre-historic and living populations are available it is impossible to explain this anomaly. Clearly, however, Iron Age technology and economic practices spread into southern Africa far faster than either the language or physical type associated with them in the first place. Negroid Bantu-speakers in small numbers may have introduced ironworking and agriculture into south-central Africa, but their characteristic physical type was submerged by their large Khoisan neighbours, who adopted Iron Age culture with some rapidity. Although future research may show that Galloway's assessment of the Mapungubwe population is incorrect, I do not think that the anomaly between the physical anthropology and archaeology is as serious as has been made out. It is well within the bounds of possibility that most of the Iron Age population of Greefswald was predominantly of 'large Khoisan' type until well into the second millennium.

I end this tentative summary of the Greefswald sequence with a plea for more research work. There is a need for further field and laboratory work in two directions. Firstly, the physical anthropology needs reassessment in the light of the latest scientific techniques and the larger samples of Iron Age and modern populations now available to us. In particular, we need to know whether the term Bush-Boskopoid can be justified in the second millennium A.D., or whether, indeed, it is justified at all. Much more evidence is now available on modern Negro populations. Are there really only 'sporadic Negro features' in the Mapungubwe skeletons? Secondly, much more archaeological work is needed. The excavations were adequately published by pre-war standards, but leave many questions unanswered. It is essential that the stratigraphy of the pottery sequences on both sites be studied in great detail. We know almost nothing of the economies of either settlement. In particular, the relationship between the latest occupants of

[76] D. P. Abraham (1962), op. cit. 61.

K2 and the earliest settlers on the Hill must be clarified. A great deal of information could be obtained from a large dig on the Mapungubwe Terrace.

The Greefswald sequence is of vital importance to students of South African history. But until more excavations and laboratory work are carried out, our knowledge of this fascinating region must remain tragically incomplete.

GENERAL CONCLUSIONS

We can suggest a tentative chronology for the Iron Age sequence of the Middle Limpopo valley as follows:

Middle to Late First Millennium A.D.: Peoples making pottery belonging to the Gokomere tradition occupy parts of the northern Transvaal. Their racial type is unknown, but they were Iron Age peoples.

About 1000 or earlier: K2 is occupied by peoples whose pottery in some respects recalls Leopard's Kopje ware. These are Iron Age people, but still of Large Khoisan racial type.

After 1100, but before 1400: Domination of Mapungubwe by Shona peoples. Development of trading as a result of the extension of Monomotapa's empire. Large Khoisans still predominant, but some Negroid features.

1500 or later: Abandonment of Mapungubwe and arrival of the Venda.

1830s—Ndebele invasion.

1898—European settlement began.

ACKNOWLEDGEMENTS

I am grateful to the Editors of the *Journal* for their invitation to write this paper and to Professor Roland Oliver, Mr K. R. Robinson, and Mr S. G. H. Daniel for their invaluable comments on the manuscript in draft. Mr D. R. Brothwell kindly checked my archaeological remarks on the physical anthropology. Thanks are also due to Mr J. F. Eloff, not only for reading the manuscript, but also for accompanying me on a stimulating visit to the sites; the University of Pretoria kindly gave me permission to visit Greefswald. Fig. 1 is the work of Mr John Christiansen, the other text figures were traced by Miss Marion Goddard from Mr Schofield's drawings; I am indebted to both of them for their skill.

SUMMARY

This paper reviews the results of the excavations conducted on the farm Greefswald in the middle Limpopo valley, South Africa between 1934 and 1940. The evidence from the excavations is re-examined in the light of the latest Iron Age discoveries north and south of the Limpopo. It is established that Iron Age peoples had crossed the Limpopo during the first millennium A.D., and that the earliest South African farmers were related to the makers of Gokomere pottery in Mashonaland. Gardner's conclusion that the occupants of K2 were Hottentots is now regarded as invalid, since the pottery and other objects from the site considered by the excavator as being of Hottentot origin have now been found in Rhodesian Iron Age sites. Mapungubwe Hill was occupied later than K2, but the identity of the earliest occupants is unknown. They were probably of Shona stock. Mapungubwe was at the height of its prosperity in the fifteenth century, and the Hill was finally abandoned about 1500. Throughout most of the Iron Age, the Greefswald population was predominantly Khoisan rather than Negroid, showing that there was a disassociation between racial hybridization and the diffusion of Iron Age culture.

Good Summary

12. THE IRON AGE SEQUENCE IN THE SOUTHERN PROVINCE OF ZAMBIA

By BRIAN M. FAGAN

THE Iron Age cultures of Zambia have until fairly recently remained largely unknown, while work in Rhodesia and parts of South Africa has revealed a long cultural sequence in both those territories. Mr R. R. Inskeep undertook some excavations in 1958,[1] and since 1959 Iron Age research has expanded considerably. Work has been concentrated in the Southern Province of the country, but is now being extended over other regions of the Zambian plateau. This paper gives an outline of our general conclusions as they appeared at the middle of 1967.[2]

The Southern Province of Zambia lies for the most part at an altitude of c. 4000 feet above sea level. The vegetational cover consists of *Brachystegia/Julbernardia* woodland which merges into watershed grasslands on the highest points of the Batoka plateau, or into swampy depressions known as *dambos*. To the west, the borders of Barotseland lie in the Kalahari Sand country, which extends into the Province with its typical *Baikiaea* woodland country. To the south-east, the plateau is dissected by the Middle Zambezi valley, the floor of which is about 1200 feet above sea-level. The flat flood-plain of the Zambezi is bounded on both sides by steep 2000-foot escarpments which must have formed a formidable obstacle to human migration onto the Rhodesian plateau. As far as our limited knowledge extends, we can suggest that there was some degree of cultural continuity between the Batoka plateau and the Middle Zambezi valley during the Iron Age. Today, much of the Province is occupied by the Ila and Tonga tribes, who are thought to have a common origin.

THE LATE STONE AGE

Before the first Iron Age people arrived in the Province, the country was occupied by Late Stone Age Wilton hunter-gatherers who lived near rivers and streams as well as by the banks of the Zambezi and Kafue.

[1] R. R. Inskeep, 'Some Iron Age sites in Northern Rhodesia', *S. Afr. Archaeol. Bull.* 1962), XVII, 67, 136–80.

[2] This paper in its original form, as printed in the *Jour. Afr. Hist.*, IV, 2 (1963), 157–77, was presented to an African history seminar at the Institute of Commonwealth Studies in October 1962. I am grateful to Professor Roland Oliver for the opportunity for doing this. Much of the research described in this paper was supported by the Nuffield Foundation.

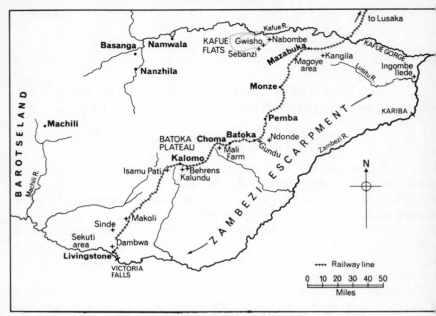

Fig. 1.   Map of the Southern Province, Northern Rhodesia,
showing Iron Age sites.

Clark[3] has described the salient features of their industries and econom
which was probably based to a great extent on fishing and plant-gathering
Much of their material culture was in wood or bone, and our knowledg
of these people is based on large scale excavations at Lochinvar Ranch o
the edge of the Central Kafue Basin.[4]

The sites at the Gwisho hot-springs on Lochinvar have yielded vit
economic data from their waterlogged lower levels, where woode
implements, seeds, grass, and traces of structures were found.[5] A larg
series of Khoisan burials was recovered from the sites, and their physic
characteristics have been provisionally described by Gabel.[6] The Wilto
occupation of the Gwisho sites has been radiocarbon dated to betwee
the third and second centuries B.C.

Stone and wooden tipped arrows were used in the chase, while tube
were dug up with digging sticks made from hardwood, and sometim
weighted with stone weights.[7] The people lived in temporary wind-break
of grass and sticks, and hunted animals ranging in size from the hippo an

[3] J. D. Clark, *The Stone Age cultures of Northern Rhodesia* (1950), S. Afr. Archaeologic
Soc., Capetown.
[4] Creighton Gabel, *Stone Age hunters of the Kafue*, (Boston, 1965).
[5] B. M. Fagan and F. Van Noten, 'Wooden implements from Late Stone Age sites
Gwisho Hot-springs, Lochinvar, Zambia, *Proc. Prehist. Soc.*, n.s., (1966) XXXII, 246–6
[6] Creighton Gabel (1965), op. cit.
[7] B. M. Fagan and F. Van Noten (1966), loc. cit., Fig.

rhinoceros down to small rodents. Barbel and bream were an important source of protein in the diet.

The exceptionally detailed information available from the Gwisho settlements can probably be taken to apply in general terms to many Wilton communities living in the Province. Presumably there were regional variations of culture which resulted from a different economic balance in various areas.

Apart from the Lochinvar samples, there are few radiocarbon dates for the Wilton of southern Zambia. A Wilton hearth with a scatter of implements near Lusu rapids, Mambova, yielded a date of 186±150 B.C. (C–829). This is an average reading,[8] and may not be entirely reliable. A few Iron Age sherds immediately overlie the Wilton hearth.

Occasional sherds of Iron Age pottery have been found on Wilton sites on the Zambezi sand scarp near Livingstone and in the Gwembe valley. Such finds are an indication that there was some overlap between remnant Late Stone Age groups and farming peoples.

THE EARLIEST FARMERS

The earliest stage of the Iron Age in southern Zambia is still inadequately known. Fortunately, however, the identification of its villages is facilitated by their association with a characteristic pottery type with grooved decoration. Phillipson has recently prepared a detailed survey of the available archaeological evidence for the Early Iron Age settlement of Zambia.[9] It can be postulated that the earliest Zambian farmers may have settled in the country as a result of the expansion of Bantu-speaking peoples from their nuclear dispersal area in the Congo. However, the grounds for attributing the earliest Iron Age to Bantu-speakers are speculative and require confirmation by future research.

In 1952 Professor J. Desmond Clark investigated a series of forestry pits in the Kalahari sands at the Machili Forest Station on the eastern borders of Barotseland.[10] A scatter of sherds including a grooved vessel with thick walls and a rolled-over rim were found on a buried land surface some 4 feet below modern ground surface. Associated charcoal yielded a series of dates, the fragments from the pottery level giving a reading of A.D. 96±212 (C–829). This date has been widely quoted as dating the arrival of Iron Age peoples in southern Zambia.[11] Recent research is beginning to imply that this particular date may be a little early. But the standard error lies within the limits of other dates from

[8] Brian M. Fagan, 'Radiocarbon dates from Sub-Saharan Africa—I', *Journ. Afr. Hist.* I, 1 (1961), 137.
[9] D. W. Phillipson, 'The early Iron Age in Zambia: regional variants and some tentative conclusions', *Journ. Afr. Hist.*, IX, 2 (1968), 191–212.
[10] J. D. Clark and B. M. Fagan, 'Charcoals, sands, and channel-decorated pottery from Northern Rhodesia', *Amer. Anth.*, (1965), 67, 2, 354–71.
[11] See among others: B. M. Fagan, *Southern Africa*, (London, 1966).

early levels both at Kalundu mound[12] and elsewhere in the country.[13]
Now that our knowledge of the earliest Iron Age is more complete, the
Machili pottery is too small a collection to be used as a type series.

Beyond some doubtful evidence for bog iron at Machili, no evidence
for ironworking has been recovered from the earliest Iron Age levels in
the Province. Isolated lumps of iron slag have been recovered from the
lowest levels of Gundu mound near Batoka,[14] and when radiocarbon
dated, these will probably provide evidence for very early ironworking in
this area.

Early Iron Age occupation levels have been recovered from the lowest
levels of a number of mound sites in the Kalomo and Batoka areas. At
Kalundu mound, near the Kalomo township, Inskeep[15] and, later, the
present writer recovered considerable numbers of grooved potsherds,
which have some distant relationship to the channelled or grooved
potsherds found at the Dambwa site near Livingstone and possibly at
Machili itself. Until recently it was considered that this was merely an
early phase of the Kalomo culture, described below.[16] Recent research in
central Zambia, especially at the Kapwirimbwe site near Lusaka, has
isolated a well-established Early Iron Age pottery tradition with grooved
decoration as a prominent feature of the industry.[17] Some of the vessels
found at the Central Province sites have features in common with the
basal mound industries. Kapwirimbwe is dated to the fifth century A.D.;
at the present time the only sample from a basal mound level in the south
is from Kalundu, where there is a reading of A.D. 300±90 (SR–65). This
has been considered to be an early and aberrant date,[18] a conclusion which
may prove erroneous when more dates are obtained. The lowest levels of
the Kalundu site are much disturbed by storage pits and animals, resulting
in some doubt as to the stratigraphical reliability of the published sample.
There is a sharp distinction between the grooved wares from the basal
levels of the Kalundu site and the pottery defined as typical of the Kalomo
culture found in the overlying levels. This fact, highlighted by the latest
excavations at the Gundu and Ndonde sites in the Batoka area,[19] has led
to a gradual recognition that the lowest levels of many of the Iron Age
mounds of the Batoka plateau are probably the result of the earliest Iron
Age settlement of the Province. Their abandoned settlements were
probably reoccupied at a later date by the Kalomo culture people. The
earliest date for the latter is A.D. 650±90 (SR–19).

[12] B. M. Fagan, *Iron Age cultures in Zambia—I*, (London, 1967), 41.
[13] D. W. Phillipson, loc. cit.
[14] B. M. Fagan and T. N. Huffman, 'Excavations at Gundu and Ndonde, Zambia, 1967'. Mimeographed circular for publication in *Archaeologia Zambiana*, 1967.
[15] R. R. Inskeep, (1962), loc. cit., 173.
[16] B. M. Fagan, (1967), op. cit., 156
[17] D. W. Phillipson, loc. cit.
[18] B. M. Fagan and D. W. Phillipson, 'Iron Age chronology in Southern Zambia', *South Afr. Archaeol. Bull.*, 21, 2.
[19] B. M. Fagan and T. N. Huffman (1967), op. cit., 1.

At the Gundu and Ndonde sites, the lowest horizons reach a greater thickness than those at Kalundu. Some 36 ins. of Early Iron Age occupation are overlain by a thick deposit of Kalomo ware. In the lowest levels of Gundu, grooved pottery is common, but it is gradually replaced by horizons where comb-stamped vessels are dominant. At Ndonde, the sequence begins with comb-stamped pottery, the grooved tradition being absent. Kalomo ware once again overlies the comb-stamped vessels. It is unfortunate that the critical levels in mound sites where these early pot forms are found have been disturbed by later occupation, agriculture, and burrowing animals. This leads to the blurring of dateable stratigraphical interfaces in the trenches, and to less accurate dating of population changes. Single level sites which would allow accurate dating and definition of the Early Iron Age pottery traditions of the Province have not yet been discovered, with the exception of the Dambwa site, near Livingstone, excavated by Daniels and Phillipson in recent years.[20]

Dambwa lies at the edge of a grassy clearing in sand country. A discoloured occupation zone extends some 42 ins. below the surface. This has yielded large quantities of pottery, traces of daga structures, and much iron slag. A series of radiocarbon dates have assigned this important site to the seventh century A.D.[21] The pottery has important connections with Gokomere ware from Rhodesia,[22] as well as some possible links with the grooved ware from basal Kalundu and, perhaps, with Machili pottery.

Phillipson has provisionally distinguished at least two regional variants in the Early Iron Age of our area. The first, found at Kalundu, and also at the Gundu mound, is related in some respects to the Kapwirimbwe wares near Lusaka. Dambwa and some unimportant sites in the Zambezi area have closer links with the south, although there are some ties between the two Zambian groups. This picture is likely to be modified considerably by future research; early sites are now being found and excavated by Vogel in Chief Sekuti's area, some 35 miles west of Livingstone.[23]

Economic data for the earliest Iron Age is still scanty, but there is evidence from Gundu to suggest that the Early Iron Age inhabitants were keeping cattle and possibly goats. Cereal crops were undoubtedly cultivated, and it has been argued that they were using an agricultural system based on *dambo*-side gardens and careful soil selection.[24]

In earlier publications we have argued that the earliest Iron Age pottery of Zambia may be related to the so-called Dimple-based wares of

[20] S. G. H. Daniels and D. W. Phillipson, 'The Early Iron Age at Dambwa near Livingstone', in B. M. Fagan, D. W. Phillipson, and S. G. H. Daniels, *Iron Age cultures in Zambia—II*. London. In the press.
[21] B. M. Fagan, 'Radiocarbon dates from Sub-Saharan Africa—V', *Journ. Afr. Hist.* (1967), VIII, 3, 513–28.
[22] K. R. Robinson, 'Further excavations in the Iron Age deposits at the Tunnel Site, Gokomere Hill, Southern Rhodesia', *S. Afr. Archaeol. Bull.* (1963) XVIII, 160.
[23] Mr J. O. Vogel: personal communication.
[24] J. D. Clark and B. M. Fagan (1965), op. cit.

East Africa.[25] Increasing evidence is coming forward to support the notion that Early Iron Age peoples over an enormous area of eastern and southern Africa were making pottery according to a somewhat similar generalized tradition. Within this broad continuum there are many regional variations which are the result of a wide variety of economic and cultural factors. It is premature to suggest the direction of population movements during the Early Iron Age until many more sites have been excavated and radiocarbon dated.

THE KALOMO CULTURE

The Kalomo culture was first discovered in 1957,[26] and has become one of the better known Iron Age cultures in Southern Africa. It is known from large scale excavations at Isamu Pati and Kalundu mounds, and by exploratory soundings at Gundu and Ndonde. A detailed description of the excavations at Isamu Pati and Kalundu was recently published,[27] but this has been considerably modified by later fieldwork by Vogel and the present writer.

Kalomo culture sites are more common than Early Iron Age settlements, and most of them form part of mound villages occupied by both earlier and later peoples. The centre of the Kalomo culture territory appears to be the Batoka highlands, where over twenty-five mound sites have been found near the watershed grasslands between Kalomo and Choma.[28] The most northerly sites are Gundu and Ndonde in the Batoka-Pemba region, while scattered villages were found in the Gwembe valley before it was flooded.[29] The distribution of the culture extends south to the Victoria Falls area, and westwards to the borders of Barotseland. It seems that the distribution of population was somewhat similar to that today, with the Gwembe populated by Kalomo peoples who presumably shared many common traits with their plateau relatives. Fishing may have been an important activity in the Gwembe, for fish bones were common at least at one site in the Zambezi valley.

A large number of radiocarbon dates have been released for Isamu Pati and Kalundu, and their significance is discussed in *Iron Age cultures in Zambia—II*[30] by Daniels. The earliest date associated with pottery which belongs in the re-defined Kalomo culture is SR–19, A.D. 650±90. The upper and middle levels of both Isamu Pati and Kalundu date to the end of the first millennium A.D., while the mounds appear to have been abandoned for the last time as late as the thirteenth century.

The deposits at Isamu Pati have a total depth of 10 feet of accumulated

[25] B. M. Fagan (1966), op. cit., 52.
[26] R. R. Inskeep (1962), loc. cit., 138–53.
[27] B. M. Fagan (1967), op. cit.
[28] B. M. Fagan (1967), op. cit., Fig. 6.
[29] R. R. Inskeep, (1962), loc. cit., 138–53.
[30] S. G. H. Daniels, 'Time Scales', in B. M. Fagan (1967), op. cit., 192–4.

midden debris and sub-soil. Cornwall[31] has shown that the deposits of the Kalomo mounds were piled up in part by the inhabitants while they were living on their traditional village sites. Chemical tests by Sampson[32] indicate that the mounds were abandoned at intervals over the four hundred years or more of Kalomo culture occupation. The inhabitants were probably occupying a number of traditional village sites on some form of rotation pattern, cultivating abandoned sites and returning to each one after an interval. The watershed grasslands of the plateau are badly drained and waterlogged during the rains, and the farmers settled on the better drained ridges, comparatively near to semi-permanent water supplies.

The economy of the Kalomo culture was based on a balance of hoe and digging-stick cultivation, pastoralism, hunting and gathering.[33] Sorghum was grown, and probably other cereal crops as well, although no carbonized remains of them have been found. Iron hoes and wooden digging sticks were used for agriculture,[34] but wild seeds and vegetables provided an important part of the diet. Carbonized remains of fig and other fruit trees are commonly found. Cattle and small stock were kept by the villagers, becoming much more common in the upper levels of the mounds. To judge from clay cattle figurines, the oxen were small, short-horned Sangas, some with humps. Many of them were slaughtered in their prime. The goats were generally small, and are never as common as cattle.

Dog bone fragments were found at all levels, including one almost complete body. Degerbøl, who studied the bones,[35] was able to show that they were slender, long muzzled beasts.

Numbers of iron arrowheads and spear fragments confirm that hunting was an important part of the economy, particularly in the earliest stages of the culture. The species hunted included buffalo, zebra, eland, kudu, waterbuck, impala, and a large number of smaller antelope, especially the duiker. The importance attached to hunting is also shown by the discovery of two caches of antelope skulls under the floors of huts at Isamu Pati.

Small rodents were eaten, especially the cane rat (*Thrynomys swinderianus*), which is regarded as a delicacy even today. The pouched mouse (*Saccostomus campestris*) was probably also eaten. Several crania of *Rattus rattus* were discovered; this is an imported species which has not been recorded in a modern context south of Lusaka and the Copperbelt.[36]

[31] I. W. Cornwall, 'Two soil samples from Kalundu mound, Zambia', in B. M. Fagan (1967), op. cit., 190–1.
[32] C. G. Sampson, 'Phosphate analysis of the Isamu Pati deposits', in B. M. Fagan (1967), op. cit., 176–91.
[33] Full description in B. M. Fagan (1967), op. cit., 59.
[34] B. M. Fagan, 'Bored Stones from the Kalomo culture', *S. Afr. Archaeol. Bull.* (1962), XVII, 67, 197.
[35] Magnus Degerbøl, 'Dogs from the Iron Age in Zambia . . .' in B. M. Fagan (1967), op. cit., 198–207.
[36] D. H. S. Davis and B. M. Fagan, 'Subfossil house rats (*Rattus rattus*) from Iron Age sites in Northern Rhodesia'. *Bull. Zool. Soc. S. Afr.*, June 1962.

Presumably this creature came from the east coast of Africa, whence it was introduced by trading contacts. Fish were not eaten at Isamu Pati, and only rarely at Kalundu, to judge from the absence of fish-bones, although these are notorious for their poor preservation properties.

It is likely that the economy of the Kalomo people was basically similar to that of many Early Iron Age peoples in Southern Africa. Unfortunately there is very little comparative information of value available from other areas. The Leopard's Kopje sites from south of the Zambezi which have been excavated by Robinson and others[37] have yielded a number of domestic and wild animal bones, but there are insufficient samples for a detailed analysis of economic patterns. The Mapungubwe excavations also produced important series of animal bones, but they were inadequately published in the primary monographs on the sites at Greefswald.[38]

The evidence for huts and village layout from Isamu Pati has been published in detail in the definitive monograph on the site.[39] The Kalomo people appear to have lived in circular pole and mud huts, with walls of closely packed stakes plastered with anthill clay. In one case the hearth was at the back of the hut. No evidence for verandahs has yet been found, and the average diameter of huts appears to have been between 10 and 12 feet. Substantial daga floors are comparatively uncommon on Kalomo culture sites, and we may presume that much of the population lived in more flimsy structures which have not survived in the archaeological record. Several suggestive concentrations of grindstones and other rocks may be evidence for grain-bin foundations. At one spot on Isamu Pati, grindstones had been piled on one spot for several hundreds of years, for a great pile of them was found extending through 5 feet of vertical section.[40]

Small pits were dug into the body of the mound and, by the earliest occupants, into the granitic sand bedrock. At Kalundu, however, Inskeep discovered a deep pit, almost 9 feet deep.[41] More recent excavations there revealed traces of two medium-sized holes, each about 3 feet deep. Some wild seeds and rodent bones were found in the Isamu Pati pits.

Extensive grading over the surface of Isamu Pati mound down to the level of the most recent occupation has shown that the huts were clustered on the top of the hill in two groups, with a few scattered on the sides of the central area.[42] The central area itself was bare of hut floors, and occupation debris was also rare, suggesting some form of central open

---

[37] K. R. Robinson, 'The Leopard's Kopje culture, its position in the Iron Age of Southern Rhodesia', *S. Afr. Archaeol. Bull.* (1966), XXI, 1, 81, 5–51.

[38] L. Fouché, *Mapungubwe* (Cambridge, 1937); G. A. Gardner, *Mapungubwe, vol. II* (Pretoria, 1963); B. M. Fagan, 'The Greefswald Sequence; Mapungubwe and Bambandyanalo', *Journ. Afr. Hist.* (1964), V, 3, 337–62.

[39] B. M. Fagan (1967), op. cit., 45–57.

[40] B. M. Fagan (1967) op. cit., Fig. 15.

[41] R. R. Inskeep (1962), loc. cit., 141–2.

[42] B. M. Fagan (1967), op, cit., Fig. 16.

space during the final occupation of the village site. This open space was probably a cattle kraal; human skeletons were certainly buried in the middle of it. Earlier in the mound's history, when the settlement was smaller, huts were built in the centre of the village.

A long trench from the centre of the site to the western boundary showed no trace of a substantial stockade of stakes, nor of a ditch, but it is possible that the village was surrounded by a thorn fence to protect both stock and inhabitants from the predators which still abounded in this area as late as 1910.

Twelve burials were recovered during the mound excavations. Ten of them came from Isamu Pati, most of them belonging to the later stages of the Kalomo culture. Nine of the Isamu skeletons were found in the central area of the site. The tenth, more elaborately decorated than the others, was about 30 feet away from a hut floor, with which it was probably associated. Several variations in body position were observed, although seven of the Isamu Pati skeletons were buried in a crouched position, lying on their sides. One was buried in a semi-seated position, while another was seated, and a third deposited on its back with the knees drawn up to the chin. Most of the skeletons were of people in their twenties.

Grave goods were confined in three cases to a broken pot, in another to a copper bracelet, and in yet another to a string of glass beads. Most of the bodies wore one or more iron bangles on their legs. In contrast to such poverty, however, one skeleton at Isamu Pati was buried with much richer adornment. Two *conus* sea-shells, a few glass beads, and thousands of shell beads adorned her breast and pelvis. Two metal rings with fibre cores lay around her neck and waist, and an ivory bracelet was worn on her right wrist. Since the body could be related on stratigraphical observation to one of the most substantial floors, it is probable that this burial was that of an important female member of the leading family groups on the site.

During the centuries of Kalomo culture occupation, there were fairly radical changes in pottery styles. There are some elements of continuity reflected in the persistent appearance of certain decorative motifs. In the earliest stages of the Kalomo culture, coarse comb-stamped vessels and spherical bowls, which may be part of a separate pottery tradition, give way to the main Kalomo-type pottery. Simple pots with rounded bases and a fine finish are decorated with a single narrow band of comb-stamping. This was normally applied immediately below a simple rim band which was sometimes burnished to enhance the decorative effect. Undecorated pots are common, but incision and grooving are almost unknown.[43]

In the uppermost levels of the Kalomo mounds, the pottery changes radically, with a preponderance of globular, liquid-carrying vessels

[43] A catalogue description of Kalomo pottery can be found in *Inventaria Archaeologia Africana* (1967), 3.

decorated with a narrow band of incision immediately beneath the sharply everted rim. At Isamu Pati, where this stage is well represented, the pots were made from a special micaceous clay found a short distance from the site. In the Kalomo culture monograph, this phase, which is also characterized by a sharp rise in the proportion of cattle bones, is regarded as an integral part of the Kalomo culture. But recent research by Vogel in Sekuti's area[44] and by Huffman and the present writer at Gundu and Ndonde has indicated a possibility that the final occupation of the Kalomo mounds may be separate from the lower levels. Future research at Kalomo should provide the confirmatory evidence lacking at this stage.

Recent research has revealed that the Kalomo culture is somewhat more diverse than had previously been suspected. At Gundu and Ndonde, while the vessel forms are similar to the Kalomo sites, decorative motifs differ, with fingernail motifs common, a rare feature of the more southerly sites. The Kalomo levels in the Sekuti sites are associated with more elaborate decorative motifs, although some of the decoration is clearly in the Kalomo tradition. These levels are overlain by horizons which contain a quite different type of pottery whose exact status is still not established.[45]

The research work projected in the next few years is likely to alter our conception of the Kalomo culture very considerably. There is an urgent need to discover single level sites which will allow a more precise definition of the various pottery types involved.

We are unable, in our present state of knowledge, to suggest an origin for the Kalomo people. There are indications both from the provisional distribution of the culture and from the natural geographical barriers to migration in the north and west, that we must look to the west for Kalomo origins. Botswana to the south was inhabited by a considerable population of Stone Age hunters until very recently. The picture to the west is still unknown, but White[46] records oral traditions from the Balovale district of north-western Zambia of early Bantu-speaking peoples. They entered the country from the north and north-west during the closing centuries of the first millennium. Such people had only a rudimentary social organization and depended on food gathering for much of their diet. The evidence from the Kalomo mounds suggests that the people were relying on hunting for much of their diet, as well as food-gathering. There are no indications from the archaeological record of any degree of complexity in the social organization.

INGOMBE ILEDE AND EARLY TRADE

The Early Iron Age sites described above have yielded only a few

[44] Mr J. O. Vogel: personal communication. B. M. Fagan and T. N. Huffman (1967), loc. cit.
[45] Mr J. O. Vogel: personal communication.
[46] C. M. N. White, 'The Balovale peoples and their historical background', *Hum. Prob. Centr. Afr.* (1949), 3, 30.

traces of imported objects. A cowrie shell was found in the basal levels at the Kalundu site, while two more were unearthed in the still undated lowest horizons at Gundu. Glass beads are always uncommon on Batoka plateau sites; only a few were found at Isamu Pati and Kalundu. These belong to the general continuum of Early Iron Age bead types found at many sites in southern Africa.[47]

Such sporadic traces of imports can be taken to indicate some form of very infrequent bartering in trade objects passed far into the interior from the east coast. The earliest such finds appear to date to the early centuries of the first millennium A.D. Imports were obviously passed from village to village along the complicated barter networks which were a source of many domestic commodities such as salt, skins, hut poles, and some metals. Evidence for more concentrated trade with the east coast comes from the Middle Zambezi valley, where the Ingombe Ilede site was discovered by accident in 1960.

The ash topped ridge called Ingombe Ilede lies on the north bank of the Zambezi river some 32 miles downstream of the Kariba Dam, just below the confluence of the Lusitu river. In 1960, the then Northern Rhodesia Government began digging the foundations for a 23,000 gallon water tank on the top of the ridge. This was part of a programme to supply water to Tonga tribesmen who had been resettled in the area from upstream of the dam wall. The workmen unearthed a human skeleton with rich ornaments. Fortunately for science the discovery was reported to the late Mr J. H. Chaplin, at that time Inspector of Monuments for the territory. He went to the site immediately, and recovered the remains of eleven richly decorated burials from the foundation area.[48]

In 1961 a season of highly selective excavations was carried out to obtain as much economic and cultural information as possible about the former inhabitants of the hill. In January 1962, a final visit was paid to the site to remove a series of human skeletons found in an area on the southern side of the site, which in 1961 had been regarded as being outside the perimeter of the settlement. The account of Ingombe Ilede which follows is based on these three seasons of work, and the final monograph on the site has recently been published.[49]

The people buried in the centre of Ingombe Ilede were buried in an extended position, with their arms by their sides and the feet together, although there were exceptions to this rule. Round the necks and waists of several skeletons were beads of gold and glass, some copper, iron, and freshwater shell specimens also being worn. The arms and legs were

[47] A. P. du Toit, 'The glass beads of Isamu Pati and Kalundu', in B. M. Fagan (1967), op. cit., 212–7.

[48] J. H. Chaplin, 'A preliminary account of Iron Age burials with gold in the Gwembe valley, Northern Rhodesia', Proceedings, *First Federal Science Congress (1960)*, (1962), 397–406.

[49] B. M. Fagan, 'Excavations at Ingombe Ilede', in B. M. Fagan, D. W. Phillipson, and S. G. H. Daniels, op. cit.

encased in copper and iron bracelets, with one skeleton wearing a series of gold wire bangles at its elbows. The copper salts derived from the bracelets had preserved several layers of cloth on some bodies, wrapped around the arms. Several varieties of cloth have been identified by Bushnell[50]; at least one of these may be an imported variety. Spindle whorls made from potsherds are commonly found in the site, as if much cloth were woven locally. All the fabric is cotton, a crop still grown in the Lower Zambezi today.

The principal individual, a man of about 28 years, wore no less than eight *conus* shells at his neck, one with a finely hammered backing plate of gold. At his wrist he wore a copper razor and another *conus*, associated with two amulets which may have Islamic connections.[51]

Copper crosses were found at the head or feet of four individuals, together with rectangular cross-sectioned copper trade wire and several sets of wire-drawing tools, including hammerheads, spikes, tongs, and drawing plates. Bobbins of copper wire were also recovered; the principal inhabitants made their own bangles on the site from trade wire. *Raphia* palm cores were used for the bracelets. Ceremonial iron tools were also found with the burials, including flange-welded single gongs, ceremonial iron hoes, and a number of smaller objects. Iron ore is very rare in this area, and such artifacts were probably traded from the plateau.

Compared with the richly decorated skeletons of the central tank area, those of the other sectors of the site were very poorly adorned. A few of the thirty-five burials involved had strings of glass or shell beads, but most were buried without any decoration at all. It is probable that they passed naked in life as well as in death, a feature noted of the Gwembe Tonga by Livingstone when he passed through the area in 1860. Most of the burials came from the upper levels of the site; the three from the lowest levels were also undecorated.

The dating of Ingombe Ilede has been a matter for considerable discussion. In the original version of this paper, a date of A.D. 1464±87 (R-908) was quoted for the lower levels of the settlement. This sample was subsequently recounted, giving a result of A.D. 680±87, the difference being due to a laboratory error. A series of dates for the occupation levels range between A.D. 850 and 950, while the burials are placed in the fourteenth or fifteenth centuries. Their significance is discussed in a forthcoming paper.[52]

The deepest deposits at Ingombe Ilede reach a depth of 8 feet, within which there are significant changes of pottery styles. The earliest pottery is rather coarse, with a high preponderance of incised decoration,

---

[50] G. H. S. Bushnell. 'Woven textiles and cords from Ingombe Ilede', in B. M. Fagan, D. W. Phillipson, and S. G. H. Daniels, op. cit.

[51] Dr. B. Martin: personal communication.

[52] D. W. Phillipson and B. M. Fagan, 'The date of the Ingombe Ilede burials', *Journ. Afr. Hist.* x, 2 (1969), 199–204.

and bowls of a type common on the Batoka Plateau. In some earlier literature, there has been a tendency to ascribe such resemblances to Kangila pottery makers who were settled in the Gwembe valley. Increased knowledge of the pottery types of the Province has led to abandonment of this provisional interpretation. As the occupation developed, the vessel forms became finer, with a gradual introduction of many shallow, thin-walled bowls and beakers with beautifully executed comb-stamped decoration. Incised decoration declined, and graphite burnishing was used for decorative purposes. In the closing stages of the settlement, deep bowls became fashionable, with a decline in the numbers of fine bowls. The burials are associated with the finest pottery from Ingombe Ilede.

Although the pottery as a whole represents a gradual evolution of the basal, Early Iron Age material, there is a strong probability that external influences were exercised on the later pottery. This would be a logical development in a village where there was more than average interaction with other communities. The pottery from the burial levels is known from another site near Karoi in the copper mining areas of northern Mashonaland, some seventy miles south-east of Ingombe Ilede,[53] and the possibility of Shona influence on the potting styles cannot be ruled out.

The village had a subsistence economy based on the cultivation of sorghum, and used iron hoes of various sizes to break up the soil. The meat of domestic animals and game supplemented their diet. Cattle, goats, chickens and dogs were kept. The oxen were small beasts, apparently with short horns, but it has proved impossible to make a detailed study of the remains, as they are too fragmentary. The area is in a tsetse belt today (although it is now sprayed), but must have been a favourable, fly-free pocket for cattle in an area rich in agricultural soils and grazing grass, with abundant water supplies.

A wide variety of game was hunted with iron-headed spears and arrowheads. As well as the economically valuable elephant, the people were not afraid to tackle hippo, rhinoceros, crocodile, and buffalo, as well as a wide range of antelope, principally of small sizes, with a definite preponderance of duiker. The butchery patterns for the fauna found at Ingombe Ilede show that a considerable proportion of the game was dispatched when mature, implying advanced hunting methods, and perhaps the use of poisons. The faunal remains are extremely fragmentary, for the carcasses were chopped to pieces with heavy iron axes.

Small rodents were again trapped and eaten, particularly the cane rat. Monitor lizards were also consumed, as were several other small creatures, including the tortoise. Fish bones are rare, but this may be a reflection of poor preservation rather than of dietary preference.

It appears that the Ingombe Ilede people were practising a mixed farming economy, making use of a wide variety of garden plots. Game

[53] I am grateful to Mr P. L. Garlake for showing me the pottery from this interesting ite.

animals and evidence for collecting emphasize that the natural resources of the environment were an important factor in famine years, which are common in the Middle Zambezi valley with its uncertain rainfall pattern.

Inhabitants of Ingombe Ilede probably spent most of their lives in the open air. Their mode of life must have been similar in many respects to that of the Gwembe Tonga today, to whom huts are comparatively unimportant owing to the great heat and small diurnal temperature range during much of the year.[54] Beyond some daga rubble lines, no traces of huts were found in the excavations, which makes it possible that most of the villagers lived either in wood or grass shelters or in stilt huts. There were traces of a large baked mud floor over the burials in the central tank area, but this was destroyed by the Government workmen before scientific investigations began.[55]

The concentration of imported objects with the central burials is especially significant because the site is located in an area where there are no mineral deposits except for extensive salt pans. These were exploited in the nineteenth century, and the salt distributed widely as a vital trade commodity.[56] Unfortunately the sources of the minerals that have been found cannot be identified with any degree of reliability at this stage in research. The closest gold and copper outcrops to Ingombe Ilede are in the Urungwe region of Rhodesia; sites yielding Ingombe Ilede-type pottery have been provisionally identified near Karoi. When excavated these may provide evidence for a southern origin for the Ingombe Ilede metals.

While the copper was traded in ingot and wire form for reshaping on the site, there are no signs of goldworking at Ingombe Ilede. The bead and wire ornaments were studied by Frey, who concluded that they were made by a lost wax technique similar to that used at Mapungubwe.[57] They were probably traded in finished form, gold being handled as beads or in dust filled quills.

The glass beads at Ingombe Ilede are predominantly reds, blues, yellows, and greens with little variation in the types. They have a wide chronological range, as do the three species of sea-shell found at the site. These imports, together with some cloth, probably made up the main commodities of the import trade. Ivory is widely accepted as having been the staple of Africa's export trade, together with slaves, for which there is of course no archaeological evidence at Ingombe Ilede. Ivory fragments are common, especially in the lowermost levels of the site. Some minerals were probably also traded, but much gold and copper was probably

[54] E. Colson, *The Social Organization of the Gwembe Tonga* (Manchester, 1960).
[55] The floor was observed in section by Mrs J. B. W. Anderson, and is recorded in the forthcoming monograph.
[56] C. and D. Livingstone, *Narrative of an Expedition to the Zambesi and its tributaries* (London, 1865), 225.
[57] E. Frey, 'Methods of gold-working at Ingombe Ilede', *in* B. M. Fagan, D. W. Phillipson, and S. G. H. Daniels, op. cit.

handled by the Ingombe Ilede people for local consumption. The proximity of the site to extensive salt deposits must have been an important factor in its inhabitants' barter trade with the plateaux on both sides of the river. Ingombe Ilede occupied a geographically important position relative to the highlands, on the one hand, and to the Zambezi trade routes on the other. There is every reason to believe that the inhabitants made use of it.

There are a number of possible interpretations of the Ingombe Ilede site. It could be regarded as a village devoted to trading activities alone, the villagers relying on barter for much of their food supplies. The quantity of trade goods relative to the depth of deposit is small, making this an unlikely explanation for the richness of the finds. The Zambezi trade was probably conducted by a series of complicated barter networks, which were activated whenever the need arose. Sporadic trading of imported objects, such as beads and shells, in exchange for ivory and other raw materials would cause an occasional flurry of commercial activity among the principal inhabitants. The life of the village, even if it were a widely known and important centre, must have been solidly based on subsistence farming. The trade at Ingombe Ilede cannot have been anything but irregular, and dependent on the whims of neighbouring peoples whose commercial activities were not regularized to the degree apparent in the Empire of Monomotapa.[58]

The earliest possible record of trade in the Middle Zambezi comes from the well-known report of Antonio Fernandes's travels in Rhodesia. He records a silent trade between the Moors and men with ox-skins who lived on the far side of a great river in the north. This has been interpreted as being the Zambezi near the Kafue confluence.[59]

In the seventeenth century, the Middle Zambezi was famous to Portuguese settlers for its ivory; this reputation can only have sprung from some trading activity in the region. Not later than the 1720s, the Portuguese established a trading station and mission at Feira, by the Luangwa confluence.[60] The inhabitants appear to have had little contact with the Gwembe valley, for the Tonga living there told Livingstone that he was the first white man they had ever met.[61]

Ingombe Ilede is one of the most important Iron Age sites so far discovered in southern Africa, but its exact significance is still a matter for speculation rather than excavated fact.

[58] D. P. Abraham, 'Maramuca; a combined exercise in the use of Portuguese records and oral tradition', *Journ. Afr. Hist.* II, 2 (1961), 211–26.
[59] Hugh Tracey, *Antonio Fernandes descrobridor de Monomotapa* (1514–15), (Lourenço Marques, 1940). W. A. Godlonton, 'The journeys of Antonio Fernandes', *Proc. Rhod. Sci. Assoc.*, 40, 71 103.
[60] Eric Axelson, *The Portuguese in South East Africa 1600–1700* (Johannesburg, 1960).
[61] C. and D. Livingstone (1865), op. cit., 224.

SEBANZI, KANGILA AND THE TONGA

The Plateau and Valley Tonga occupy most of the central, southern and eastern parts of the Southern Province today, while the Ila, whose linguistic and cultural relationship to the Tonga is close, live to the north-west of the most thoroughly studied archaeological sites. The Tonga have never possessed an elaborate social or political organization. They lack the strongly centralized chieftainship characteristic of many Zambian tribes. Their loosely-knit form of political cohesion has meant that they have suffered greatly at the hands of better organized and more warlike groups, such as the Ndebele and Lozi, who raided them unmercifully during the nineteenth century. The result is that there is little oral tradition relating to the early history of this large Zambian tribe. There are significant differences between the material culture of the Tonga and Ila and their northern and western neighbours, who have highly developed ironworking skills, and who possess elaborate ceremonial iron tools as well as different agricultural systems. Both the Ila and Tonga are cattle people, pastoralism playing an important part in their culture; their languages have some archaic features which are not found in other Zambian dialects. For some time it had been suspected that the Tonga were early settlers in Zambia, and there was considerable speculation in the literature as to their origin.[62] Archaeology has recently provided some valuable evidence which shows that the Tonga have been living in the northern parts of the Southern Province for at least 800 years.

The Sebanzi Hill overlooks the Kafue Flats, and is situated on the southern side of the Central Kafue Basin, on Lochinvar Ranch and close to the Gwisho hot-springs. The site was excavated in 1964,[63] and yielded a 5-foot sequence of Iron Age occupation, the base of which was dated to slightly before A.D. 1200. The inhabitants were farmers and cattle herders, who also hunted the game on the flats and made use of the excellent fishing to be found near by. A sequence of pottery from the trenches can be linked in the upper horizons with probable eighteenth- and nineteenth-century Tonga wares from Nabombe and other sites near Sebanzi. The upper horizons pass downwards into earlier levels, in which incised decoration is more common than the stamped triangles found at the end of the occupation. The earlier levels contain vessels bearing an alternating triangle motif, which is incised in bands on the shoulder of bowls. Such vessels, and simple incised pots, are characteristic of a group of sites found between Batoka and the Kafue on the plateau highlands to the east of Lochinvar. These sites, described below, are only single level occupations; Sebanzi provides evidence for the continuity of Tonga

[62] J. D. Clark, 'The Native tribes', in J. D. Clark, (ed.), *The Victoria Falls Handbook* (Livingstone, 1952).
[63] B. M. Fagan and D. W. Phillipson, 'Sebanzi: the Iron Age sequence at Lochinvar and the Tonga', *Journ. Roy. Anthrop. Inst.* (1965), 95, 2, 253-94.

pottery tradition, albeit with major changes, in the northern parts of the Province for over seven centuries.

The early date for the Tonga at Sebanzi is corroborated by recent discoveries at Gundu and Ndonde, where Kangila-type pottery with its incised bowls immediately overlies Kalomo culture levels, which are firmly radiocarbon dated to c. A.D. 1000 at Isamu Pati. Unfortunately these important sites are still undated, but samples are being tested at the present time, which should refine our dating for the arrival of the Tonga in the Southern Province.

The Kangila site, which has provided the type series of vessels for the definition of Kangila-type pottery, was found by Mrs J. B. W. Anderson in 1961. It lies some 15 miles east-south-east of Mazabuka. The site consists of a small midden, 42 ins. deep, which forms an ash capping on a conspicuous ridge on the highlands. Kangila is situated in excellent cattle country with a sparse tree cover. As a result, there was no charcoal in the deposits which could be used for dating the settlement. A fresh bone sample yielded a date of A.D. 1440±100 (SR–42). The finds consisted of pottery, some iron tools, and animal bone fragments.

Kangila pottery is typified by a straight-necked shallow bowl form which bears a band of incised decoration immediately below the neck and on the shoulder.[64] Incised decoration is also common on the simple, small pots which make up another part of the industry. Criss-cross and alternating triangle motifs are common, but there are many undecorated vessels. Graphite burnishing is rare. The Kangila pottery, which is found at a number of sites in the immediate vicinity and as far south as the Batoka area, is a simple type. Unfortunately the stratigraphical evidence from the shallow sites which predominate in this area is very incomplete, except for the sequence at Sebanzi, which lies to the west of most of the Kangila sites. Many sites await excavation, however, and it should be a comparatively easy matter to fill in the gaps in the sequence.

Ironworking was practised at Kangila and other sites. Only a few arrowheads and razors have been found. These have simple or ogee cross-section blades. Their shape is characteristic of the earlier Iron Age. No copper or trade beads have yet been found in the Mazabuka region, but some isolated beads were found at Sebanzi.

Cattle and goat bones were very common at Kangila, and form an important percentage of the fauna from other sites, such as Sebanzi. Dogs were kept, and small antelope hunted. Direct evidence for agriculture is lacking, but grindstones are common, and a hoe blade came from the Kangila levels at Gundu.

The settlement pattern of early Tonga villages remains to be established with any accuracy. At Sebanzi, the surface topography of the site suggested central cattle enclosure with the huts surrounding the kraal.[65] A similar

[64] B. M. Fagan (1967), op. cit., 146.
[65] B. M. Fagan and D. W. Phillipson (1965) op. cit., 1.

surface layout has been deduced at Gundu. Kangila yielded few traces of structures, as if most of the huts were flimsy, though in one case it was possible to make a plan of a hut foundation.

Early Tonga levels, represented by Kangila-type sherds, were found at Ndonde and Gundu overlying the Kalomo levels. In the southern parts of our area, Kangila ware is absent, but we have already mentioned that the uppermost levels of the Kalomo mounds may in fact reflect a different and later occupation of the sites. Vogel[66] has found considerable quantities of later pottery overlying Kalomo occupations in Sekuti's area even farther south. Except for these possible but highly tentative indications of later Iron Age occupation, the stratigraphical equivalents of Kangila-type pottery are as yet unidentified south of Batoka.

THE NINETEENTH-CENTURY TONGA

A major gap in the Iron Age sequence of the Southern Province occurs between c. A.D. 1450 and the eighteenth century. Late Tonga sites dating to the past 200 years are widespread on the plateau and in the Gwembe. They have been found near the Kafue Gorge, and in the Maz-abuka, Monze, and Magoye regions, as well as throughout the southern parts of the Province. Most of these sites consist of surface scatters of potsherds and daga, which sometimes form quite extensive deposits. The best preserved sites are in the Kalomo and Choma regions, where extensive Tonga middens have been known for many years. These sites are normally characterized by an undulating topography, the village site being dissected by a series of humps and hollows, the occupation apparently being clustered around the hollows. The hollows have no particular form, but tend to interconnect. Such topography cannot have been achieved by natural processes of formation. Our sections across the sides of hollows revealed no traces of spoil heaps thrown up during the excavation of the hollows by the inhabitants. Somewhat similar topography is found in Hima villages in Uganda, where cattle tend to excavate the ground in their enclosures, gradually forming a hollow. A probable explanation for the topography of the Kalomo and Choma sites may well lie in the large herds of cattle which the Tonga are known to have possessed in the early nineteenth century.[67]

The excavations carried out on these sites have been limited in size by financial considerations. The largest excavations were made at the Behrens site, south-east of Kalomo.[68] A single hump and hollow complex was examined. It was found that huts, associated with burials and rubbish heaps, as well as grain-bins, were built around the hollow. Piles of grind-

[66] Mr J. O. Vogel: personal communication.

[67] D. Livingstone, *Missionary Travels and Researches in South Africa*, (London, 1857) 553.

[68] B. M. Fagan, 'Early Tonga settlements in the Kalomo District', in B. M. Fagan, D. W. Phillipson, and S. G. H. Daniels, op. cit.

stones litter this and other sites of this type. Many of the stones are severely worn, as if they were piled together after rejection, or when the sites were abandoned. Livingstone[69] describes the early nineteenth-century Tonga as living in large 'towns', which survived in his day as areas of enormous concentrations of grindstones. Undoubtedly he was referring to sites such as Behrens, where hundreds of grindstones are concentrated within a small area.

The middens yielded a large vertebrate fauna, in which small, short-horned cattle are overwhelmingly dominant. Some goats, fowls, and dogs are also present, with game animals only minimally represented. The cattle are small in size, and probably belong to the diminutive, so-called Ila breed described by Livingstone, Selous, and others.[70] Butchery patterns show that the herd surplus of male beasts was slaughtered in its prime for meat; a substantial number of the bones come from old beasts, however.

The Behrens economic evidence is one-sided, for only indirect signs of agriculture were found. In the nineteenth century the Tonga were cultivating maize, millet, sorghum, and groundnuts.[71] There is no reason to believe that similar crops were not grown for a hundred years or so before Livingstone traversed the Batoka Plateau. Both Colson, in her many studies of the Tonga,[72] and Livingstone have emphasized the important role of cattle in Tonga life. This is confirmed by the archaeological evidence from Behrens, where the rubbish heaps were densely packed with broken cattle bones to the exclusion of those of almost every other animal. The presence of large numbers of cattle on the village sites would account for the topography, the houses, gradually rising above the level of the kraal floors, being clustered around the cattle enclosures.

A large site on Mali Farm, south of Choma, is the type locality for the pottery associated with the later Tonga. It has been named Mali ware, and is a flamboyant pottery industry which has basically the same form between the Zambezi and the middle portions of the Province, if not farther north. Carinated vessels are common, globular forms are also frequently used, both of them with moderately thick walls and a fairly coarse texture. Decoration is normally in triangles or zig-zags, the former being filled with stamping, grooved lines being used to delineate the triangles. The stamping is fairly coarse, and quite distinct from the finer comb-stamping found on Kalomo ware. A description of the Mali ware from Makoli cemetery and from a very late nineteenth-century site at Sinde Mission has been published by Inskeep.[73] It is sufficient here to

[69] D. Livingstone (1857), op. cit., 548.
[70] D. Livingstone (1857), op. cit., 192. F. C. Selous, *A hunter's wanderings in Africa*. London, 1881). A description of Sala cattle, which are obviously of the same breed.
[71] D. Livingstone (1857), op. cit., 541.
[72] The most relevant work to archaeology is E. Colson, *Life among the cattle owning Plateau Tonga* (Livingstone, 1949).
[73] R. R. Inskeep, (1962), op. cit., 161.

note that there is a major contrast between Mali ware and earlier pottery types found in the Province. The contrast can also be extended to economies as well, for the earlier Iron Age inhabitants of the Plateau depended to a greater degree on hunting for their meat supplies.

HISTORICAL RECORDS

The earliest historical record of the Tonga was made by Livingstone who visited the Batoka plateau twice during his African journeys. He has left us invaluable and penetrating accounts of the Tonga of his time. At the beginning of the nineteenth century, the Tonga were living through out the Province in large villages with a peaceful and undisturbed existence. Their herds were enormous, and it is clear from Livingstone' accounts of abandoned village sites, that these are the Tonga settlement represented by Behrens and other similar localities. A radiocarbon date for the Behrens site gave a reading of A.D. 1840 ± 90 (SR–57). This is, of course, meaningless in itself, but is at least confirmation for a modern date for the site.

About 1820, so Livingstone tells us, the inhabitants of the Batoka plateau suffered under a raid from a chief named Pingola who came from the north. His identity is lost. From then onwards, Tonga country was ravaged by Ndebele, Lozi, and other professional raiders such as the Chikunda, who reached the plateau in 1860.[74] The Tonga were soon reduced to poverty, and the population decimated. They moved their villages away from open country, making scattered settlements in the bush, where they hoped to be safe from marauders.

Raids continued until the closing years of the nineteenth century. The last raid, by the Ndebele, took place in 1893, when two impis were decimated by smallpox near Choma. In 1898 Major Harding and his British South Africa Police founded Fort Monze, from which time the history of the area has been fully documented.

CONCLUSION

The Iron Age sequence outlined in this article can only be regarded as highly tentative. This version of the paper, when compared to the original first published in the *Journal of African History*, will give some idea of the major changes which have taken place in this small research field within a period of four years. Equally dramatic progress can be expected in the next few years. Research in this region will continue; it is hoped to extend systematic investigations into Ila country, and to examine some of the important mound sites known to exist in the Basanga-Nansizhila area.

The research carried out since 1963 has confirmed one tentative conclusion already reached four years ago. The Iron Age sequence in southern Zambia, except perhaps in its earliest phases, shows important

[74] E. Colson, 'A note on Tonga and Ndebele', *Northern Rhodesia Journal*, II, (1950) 35–41.

differences to that set up for western Rhodesia. To some extent this must be due to the severe natural geographical barriers of the Zambezi escarpments, which probably formed a barrier to population movement across the Gwembe from the Batoka plateau and also northwards.

SUMMARY

The southern parts of Zambia were settled by iron-using peoples during the early first millennium AD, and a number of regional variations of Early Iron Age culture soon developed. Grooved pottery is characteristic of the earliest sites, and belongs within the broad pattern of Early Iron Age pottery typology throughout eastern and southern Africa. Mound villages were occupied intensively during the late first millennium, and the Kalomo culture flourished in the watershed grassland areas of the Batoka plateau. The Kalomo people had a mixed farming economy which still relied on hunting and gathering for a substantial part of the diet. The inhabitants of the mounds lived in villages of pole and mud huts which were sometimes built around a central cattle enclosure. They had little contact with the outside world, in contrast to the peoples of Ingombe Ilede in the Middle Zambezi who were involved in long distance bartering by the fifteenth century. Archaeological excavations have shown that the present, Tonga, inhabitants of the Southern Province have been settled in their present homelands for at least seven centuries. For most of the Iron Age the peoples of southern Zambia lived in isolation, and share few cultural links with their contemporaries to the south of the Zambezi. The investigations in this region have given us a clear picture of subsistence farming in South Central Africa a thousand years ago.

13. NOTES ON SOME EARLY POTTERY CULTURES IN NORTHERN KATANGA[1]

By JACQUES NENQUIN

THE original draft of this article started with a quotation from O. G. S. Crawford: '. . . Irrelevant theorizing has been the besetting sin of the local archaeologist from the earliest times, and it is time it stopped . . .'[2] and continued by giving a rather detailed description of some pottery and metal objects found during the 1957 excavations of the Iron Age cemetery discovered at Sanga on the northern shore of Lake Kisale (northern Katanga). Especially for an area like the (ex-Belgian) Congo, where very little work indeed has ever been done on the protohistoric pottery cultures, we thought it essential first of all to give objectively as close a description as possible of the material remains of these prehistoric communities. Dr R. Oliver pointed out, however, that there is a great difference between 'irrelevant theorizing' and presenting new material against the background of known fact. Since the publication of the excavation report is expected shortly, we therefore have tried to give here a more general picture of the three different cultural groups distinguished at Sanga, keeping in mind all the time, however, that it is only later, after much more field-work and research in museums, that it may be possible to try and propose a general scheme of the cultural sequence for the region under discussion.[3]

Although a considerable number of publications have been devoted to the different aspects of the population groups of Katanga, not very many have touched upon the difficult question of their origins. Perhaps the most important work is the still useful one written by E. Verhulpen,[4] in which numerous oral traditions are collected, and which tries to give a coherent picture of the successive Luba empires which were centred around lakes Kisale and Upemba. It does not seem possible, however, by these means to go back any further than the sixteenth century, which in view of the radiocarbon dates obtained from the Sanga necropolis, is not sufficient to

---

[1] This article is based on the text of the excavation report, *Excavations at Sanga, 1957, The Protohistoric Necropolis*, published by the Musée Royal de l'Afrique Centrale at Tervuren, Annales Série in-8°, Sciences humaines No. 45, 1963.

[2] *Antiquity*, VII, 25 (1933), 3.

[3] A short account of the excavations was published in *The Illustrated London News*, CXXXIII, 6225 (27 September 1958), 516–18, and in the *Ber. V. Intern. Kongress für Vor- . Frühgeschichte, Hamburg, 1958* (Berlin, 1961), 601–3. A collection of Kisalian pottery from the Musée Royal de l'Afrique Centrale at Tervuren was described in the *Bull. de la Soc. royale belge d'Anthropol. et de Préhist.*, LXIX (1958), 151–210.

[4] *Baluba et Balubaïsés du Katanga* (Anvers, 1936). See also W. F. P. Burton, 'The Country of the Baluba in Central Katanga', *The Geographical Journal*, LXX, 4 (October 1927), 321–42, and id. *Luba Religion and Magic in Custom and Belief* (Tervuren, 1961).

correlate our Kisalian discovered there with one of the Luba empires.[5]
The same author[6] mentions the Bakalanga as being the original inhabitants
of Lubaland before the conquest by Kongolo, and says: '. . . le pays des
Baluba aurait été habité par des Bakalanga, résidant aux bords des rivières
et des lacs, excellents potiers, probablement très bons forgerons, utilisant
des ornements et des croisettes en cuivre . . .'. The questionable validity
of these sources, however, means that supreme importance attaches to
archaeological evidence, which alone enables one to substitute factual
history for legends.

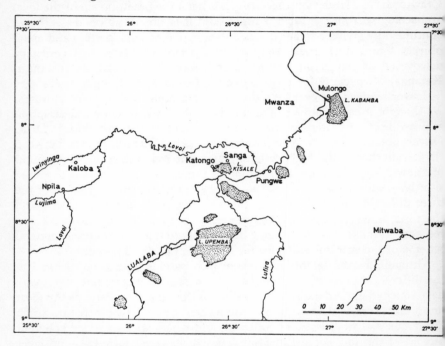

Fig. 1. Map of the Upemba-Kisale area, with sites mentioned in the text

The upper reaches of the River Lualaba in the region of the Kamolondo
depression with its innumerable small and larger lakes—Upemba, Kisale,
Kabwe, Kabile, etc.—do not seem to have changed much since Du Plessis
passed through there on his way south:[7] '. . . Lake Kisale . . . is so completely overgrown with tall papyrus, that the traveller only occasionally
catches a glimpse of stretches of open water . . .' (see Plate I). It is on the
northern shore of Lake Kisale, in the village of Sanga (fig. 1), that the

[5] See below.
[6] E. Verhulpen, op. cit., 70–1.
[7] J. Du Plessis, *Thrice through the Dark Continent* (London, 1917), 306; see also Havard
Duclos, 'Monographie de la Chefferie de Kikondja', *Terre-Air-Mer*, LIX (1933), 261–83
and 389–408.

Plate I. View of Lake Kisale, seen from the village of Sanga

Plate II. Kisalian pottery from Sanga

Plate III. Burial 53, partly uncovered, Sanga

Plate IV. Detail of copper and iron objects from Burial 53, Sanga

excavations, which led to the discovery of a very large cemetery, took place in 1957.

Many previous workers who have published on the Luba area (Burton, Verhulpen, etc.) or who have sent documents which are now in the archives of the Tervuren Museum (Hutsebaut, Schilz, Stoky, Maesen, Mortelmans) have noticed the abundance of protohistoric pottery along the shores of Lake Kisale. The Sanga excavations have proved that it is possible for the moment to distinguish three different groups of wares. One may perhaps venture to suggest that these three pottery traditions belong to three separate cultural groups, in each of which the pottery is the most typical guide-fossil. Until more is known about the physical characteristics of the bearers of these cultures, it would be rash indeed to attribute them to one particular ethnic group. These three groups are, in the proposed chronological sequence:[8] the Kisalian, the Mulongo ware group, and the Red Slip ware group. Since a preliminary excavation report has already been published elsewhere, it will not be necessary again to describe in detail the circumstances of discovery. Suffice it to say that in all about sixty graves were discovered, with quantities of pottery, iron and copper ornaments and weapons, some glass beads, cowrie shells, etc.

The Kisalian (see figs. 2 and 3, and Plates II, III, and IV) is represented in the Sanga necropolis by twenty-seven burials. Much Kisalian material was also found in Katongo (fig. 2), another village on the shores of Lake Kisale a few miles to the west of Sanga. It is interesting to note that identical pottery was found over a distance of more than ten miles along the lake, and that the whole area seems to be one huge burial-ground. In certain cases the graves were dug so close together that the older ones were observed to have been disturbed by more recent burials. It is perhaps no exaggeration to say that here alone several thousand graves await the spade (or the trowel!) of the archaeologist. The typical Kisalian pot has a rounded base, contracted shoulder, outwards-flaring neck, and inwards-turning rim. The shoulder is often decorated with an incised half-moon motif, the lip is either incised or comb-impressed, or shows a series of horizontal grooves. Other pots have a sharply carinated shoulder. The bowls—which have the same decoration on the lip as the larger pots—often have a triangular handle and a spout. Still other types are the trilobate cups and the vases with human face decoration.[9] It is not so easy to find specific Kisalian characteristics in the metal objects, as many of these (bracelets, knives, etc.) are of the same type in all three groups. Certain composite copper chain belts, however, seem to belong to this particular culture. Copper croisettes were found only in two out of twenty-nine Kisalian pottery groups. Of particular interest are certain elaborate copper necklaces which were discovered in a number of graves. As regards burial ritual, the Kisalian seem

[8] Names subject to approval by the Commission for Nomenclature of the Panafrican Congress on Prehistory.
[9] J. Nenquin, 'Quelques poteries protohistoriques à face humaine trouvées au Katanga (Congo)', Jnl. de la Soc. des Africanistes, xxx, 2 (1960), 145–50.

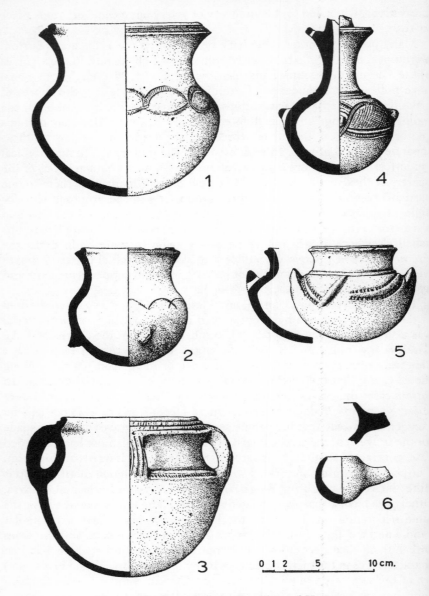

Fig. 2. Kisale ware from the village of Katongo

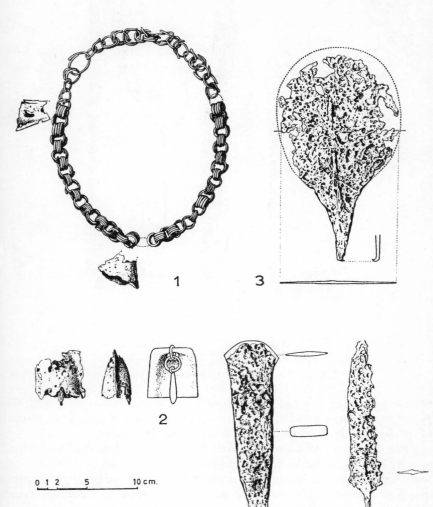

Fig. 3. Metal objects found in different graves of the Sanga necropolis

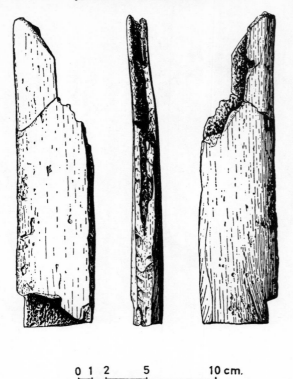

0 1 2   5   10 cm.

Fig. 4. Bone implement from Burial 3, Sanga

to have a certain preference for the north–south orientation; only with thi
group were some skulls found resting upon an upturned pot. The presenc
of perforated human teeth was noticed in three cases.

From study of museum material anterior to the excavations, it ha
already become apparent that a number of pots and sherds found in 195
—though not during systematic excavations—seemed to belong to anothe
group of pottery. This group we tentatively termed as 'Mulongo type
after the locality where the greater part of these pots were discovered
Mulongo ware was found in six graves at Sanga, concentrated in a fe
square metres at the northern end of the excavations. It is perhaps usefu
to emphasize this grouping, as—in our opinion—this circumstance give
additional weight to the contention that this pottery indeed forms
separate group. These pots (see figs. 5, 6, 7, and 8) have a somewh
flattened aspect, with wide body, constricted neck and everted rim
Several examples are decorated with a number of horizontal grooves aroun
the neck. Of particular interest are the trilobate bowls from Burials 11 an
12, a form unknown to us from any other region in Central Africa, at lea
in protohistoric times. Their use is problematical, but it is not impossibl

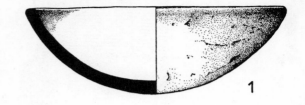

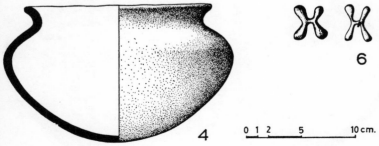

Fig. 5. Mulongo ware, Kisalian sherd and croisettes from Burial 1, Sanga

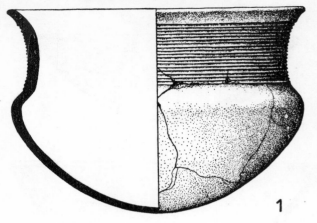

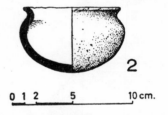

0 1 2   5   10 cm.

Fig. 6. Mulongo ware from Burial 4, Sanga

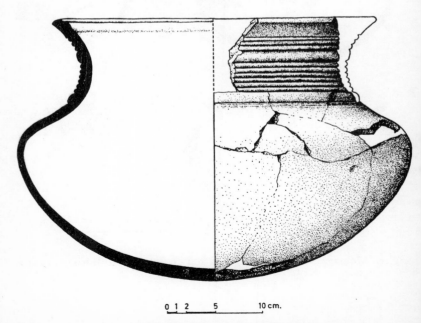

0 1 2   5   10 cm.

Fig. 7. Mulongo pot from Burial 9, Sanga

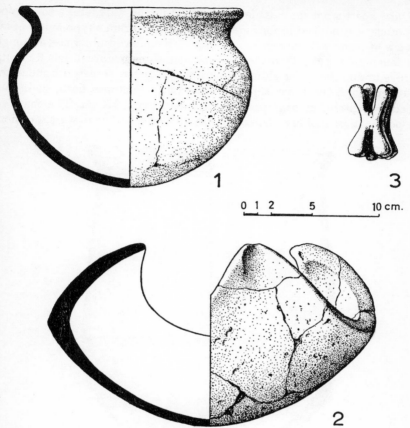

Fig. 8. Pottery and croisettes from Burial 12, Sanga

that they served as small stoves or charcoal-burners, as is still the case with certain tribes of North-western Congo.[10] As regards the metal objects discovered in association, in all Mulongo burials copper croisettes were found. From Burial 12 also came two anklets consisting respectively of sixteen and fourteen rings, made of spirally wound iron band. In several places the string, around which the iron was wound, is still visible.[11] The burial ritual seems to have been more fixed for the Mulongo groups than for either of the others. The orientation of the skeleton was south–north in five cases out of six, and in four cases the body was observed to be lying on its right side.

[10] i.e. the Ngombe, who use this sort of trilobate bowl in their dug-out canoes. A cultural analogy with the bowls discovered at Sanga is all the more possible, since fishing still forms an essential part of the economic life of the population groups living along the River Lualaba.

[11] J. Nenquin, 'Korte bijdrage tot de protohistorische metaaltechniek in Katanga', Africa-Tervuren, VII, 4 (1961), 97–101.

Quite apart from the Kisalian and the Mulongo ware, still a third type of pottery was noticed in four graves (see fig. 9). From a typological point of view, it seems to have certain affinities with modern Luba ware, although it is much more carefully made. The distinguishing feature of this Red Slip ware is undoubtedly the shiny red slip which covers sometimes the outer and sometimes the inner surface of the pot, sometimes both, giving an aspect not dissimilar from provincial Roman *terra sigillata*. The shape of the pots is more globular than is the case with the Mulongo ware, but here

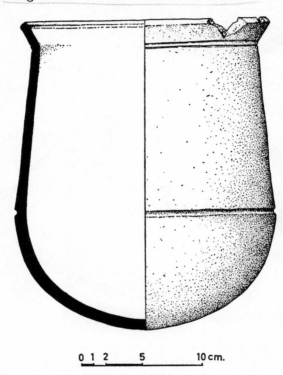

0 1 2   5   10 cm.

Fig. 9. Pot from Burial 45, Sanga

too they have a constricted neck and an everted rim. The ornamentation is very simple and consists of a few grooves or incisions on the neck. Perhaps typical for the Red Slip ware burials is the fact that in all four considerable numbers of copper croisettes (about three hundred and sixty) were found. Nothing distinguishes the metal objects from those found in Kisalian or Mulongo graves. Only four Red Slip ware burials having been discovered, it is not possible to say anything definite about the burial ritual.

So much for the three different pottery groups. The illustrations clearly show the different characteristics just mentioned. It is impossible to mistake Kisalian ware for any other sort of protohistoric pottery yet known from Central Africa. The general shape, the ornamentation, and the sophisticated form of some of the vessels are all extremely characteristic. The distinction between Mulongo and Red Slip ware would be more difficult to make, were it not for the shiny red varnished appearance of the last group.

It is not easy at this moment to prepare a good distribution map of the sites where these three groups have been found, since the information is still very sketchy and the documents (letters of the occasional traveller, diaries, etc.) are unfortunately very vague as to the precise localization of

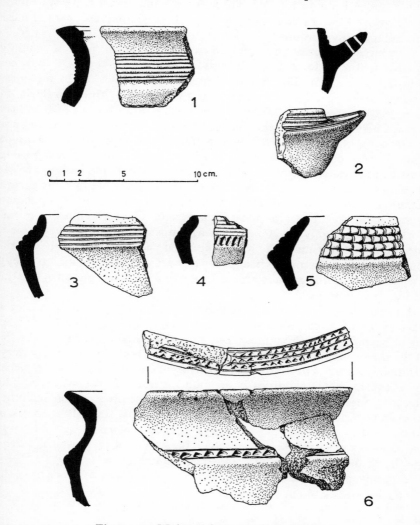

0 1 2   5   10 cm.

Fig. 10. 1: Mulongo fragment from Kaloba
2–6: Kisalian sherds from the Mpila cave

the finds. However, a few other sites where Kisalian and/or Mulongo pottery have been found are known, Katongo and Mwanza (see fig. 1) being two of the more important ones. One sherd from the village of Kaloba (fig. 10, 1) was seen to resemble very closely the Mulongo ware. From the Npila cave a number of Kisalian sherds are known (fig. 10, 2–6), and several pots of a degenerate Kisalian (?) were found at Mitwaba. Kisalian ware therefore is known over a distance of about a hundred and twenty miles between the Npila cave and Mitwaba. Mulongo ware has been found in several sites between Kaloba and Mulongo itself, which means a distance a little under a hundred miles. There is no doubt that a more systematic examination of the area under discussion will reveal even more sites of these interesting pottery groups.

As regards trade relations with other areas in Kisalian times, it can only be said that the perforated cowrie shell found in Burial 54 probably comes from the East Coast. The results from the examination of the few glass beads were disappointing, in that the ones found in the Mulongo Burial 12 were of a type unknown to the specialist who studied them. More may perhaps be expected from the material found in 1958,[12] when more glass was discovered than in the year before. The copper croisettes are of a type found in very many places along the River Lualaba, and if a relationship must be established between that area and Zimbabwe, one hesitates to see in this fact a sure sign of trade. It seems more probable that the manufacturing of croisettes formed part of the material culture of the population groups living in that region ten centuries ago. The techniques of metal-working being highly developed at Sanga in the eighth century A.D., it is not impossible that they may have influenced peoples living farther to the south, the other alternative being that this art was taken along on one of the numerous southward migrations during this formative period of Central African protohistory.[13]

The excavations at Sanga have given some information relative to the ways of life of these protohistoric inhabitants of the Kisale shores.[14] As might be expected, fishing must have played an important part in the life of the three communities which are represented by their different pottery. Fishbones were discovered in a number of graves; indeed, in some places quite considerable quantities were found during the excavations. The presence of possible iron fish-spears has been noted. Skeletons of other animals were found in the graves (*capra* and birds), as well as traces of liquid food in certain burials. Perhaps equally important were the large fragment of a quartzite quern from the Kisalian Burial 53, as well as several iron hoes; these undoubtedly point to agriculture.

Certainly, among the most important results of the excavations were the

[12] Renewed excavations by Dr J. Hiernaux.
[13] See A. H. Quiggin, 'Trade routes, trade, and currency in East Africa', *Occ. Pap. Rhodes-Livingstone Mus. no. 5* (1949).
[14] J. Desmond Clark, 'The spread of food production in sub-Saharan Africa', *Journal of African History*, III, 2 (1962), 211–28, see pp. 225–6.

absolute dates which were obtained by analysis of the bone material from two burials.[15] They gave the following results (dates from 1960):

Burial 10 (B-264) 1070 ± 200 (= A.D. 890 ± 200).
Burial 18 (B-263) 1240 ± 120 (= A.D. 720 ± 120).

A date in the eighth or ninth century may therefore perhaps be proposed for this culture. No absolute date for either the Mulongo group or the Red Slip ware group could be obtained. Some information regarding the relative age of Kisalian and Red Slip ware is available, thanks to the fact that Burial 29 (Kisalian) was cut into and partly destroyed when digging the grave-pit for Burial 45 (Red Slip ware), which therefore must be later. Even a relative age is difficult to give for the Mulongo ware, as these graves were found at the same depth as the ones with the Kisalian material, and the metal objects found in both are identical. As has been said, from a stylistic point of view, the third group with red polished surface seems much later, and appears to have been influenced by the shape of certain Mulongo pots and bowls. The cultural sequence therefore seems to be as follows:

Kisalian   seventh to ninth century A.D.;
Mulongo ware   no date available, but with certain forms reminiscent
                  of Kisalian;
Red Slip ware   no date available, but in three cases cutting into
                  earlier burials (one certainly Kisalian); many forms
                  similar to Mulongo ware, and at least one type very
                  like modern Luba pottery.

Despite the increasing number of radiocarbon dates published during the last couple of years, it is perhaps still too early to try and look for influences and parallelisms with other protohistoric cultures in Central Africa. The dates for the Kisalian, however, might be read in conjunction with:[16]

A.D. 1020 (± 110) from Ziwa Farm, and
A.D. 1055 (± 65) from Bambandyanalo for Summers's A2 complex, and
A.D. 1085 (± 150) from the Zimbabwe Acropolis for the beginning of his B1, as well as[17]
A.D. 1080 (± 80) from a Channelled ware horizon at Kalambo Falls.

It might, on the other hand, also be useful here to point to certain possible typological affinities of the Kisalian pottery with Summers's Ziwa ware.[18]

[15] Radiocarbon analysis made by Dr Oeschger of the Bern Laboratory; see J. Nenquin, 'Two radiocarbon dates for the Kisalian', *Antiquity*, XXV, 140 (December 1961), 312.
[16] R. Summers, 'The Southern Rhodesian Iron Age', *Journal of African History*, II, 1 (1961), 1–13.
[17] B. Fagan, 'Pre-European Ironworking in Central Africa with special reference to Northern Rhodesia', *Journal of African History*, II, 2 (1961), 199–210; see also J. D. Clark, 'Carbon 14 chronology in Africa South of the Sahara', *Actes du IVe Congrès Panafricain de Préhistoire et de l'Etude du Quaternaire*, II (Tervuren, 1962), 303–13.
[18] R. Summers, *Inyanga* (Cambridge, 1958), especially pp. 134–9, and id. 'The Southern Rhodesian Iron Age', *Proc. First Federal Science Congress* (1962), 431–9; id. 'The Southern Rhodesian Iron Age', *Journal of African History*, II, 1 (1961), 1–13.

Indeed, his description of the material culture '. . . clay human figurines, fragment of iron, copper wire, shell beads, worked bone beads, awls and some decorated bone-work, and a few imports such as cowrie shells and glass beads . . .'[19] might almost be taken as an enumeration of the objects found in the Kisalian burials, if one were to replace 'clay human figurines' by 'clay vases decorated with a human face in relief'. The date of A.D. 1020 ($\pm$ 110) for a late phase in the Ziwa ware would seem to correspond very well indeed with the dates obtained from the Sanga necropolis, if one were to suppose a southward movement in the ninth and tenth centuries. The origin of the Kisalian, however, remains obscure. It is therefore with the greatest interest that one awaits the results of further work both north-westwards in the Congo and also in Northern Rhodesia, which may throw much light upon this still obscure period of Central African protohistory.

[19] R. Summers, 'The Southern Rhodesian Iron Age', *Proc. First Federal Science Congress* (1962), 432–3.

14. KILWA AND THE ARAB SETTLEMENT OF THE EAST AFRICAN COAST

By Neville Chittick

THE aim of the inquisitorial studies is often described as extending the frontiers of our knowledge; but the study of the remoter past of Black Africa is rather the discovery of islands in the ocean of our ignorance, or the sighting from afar of mountains protruding through the mists which obscure knowledge of what rivers and ridges lie between. Soon a rift in the clouds will make plain the valleys of which we had guessed—or reveal instead an unimagined landscape. So it is that any appreciation of African history is likely very soon to require revision; it is tempting to defer making such an appraisal in the knowledge that it will shortly be possible to improve it.

Nevertheless, it seems timely now to attempt to set out, so far as can be deduced, some new evidence bearing on the earlier history of the eastern littoral of Africa derived from recent archaeological work, in particular that carried out at Kilwa;[1] this essay will not, however, include any detailed account of the material culture of the peoples concerned.

The historical sources available to us in this study are few, and in general unsatisfactory.[2] The first in time and importance is the *Periplus Maris Erythraei*, written in the first century A.D. The contents of this mariners' guide, which may be considered along with the *Geographia* of Ptolemy, will be familiar to most readers. The sections dealing with the East African coast in both works are very difficult to interpret, and must be inaccurate to some extent. Archaeology sheds little light on the texts, since no remains which show any Roman, or pre-Islamic South Arabian, influence have been found. It cannot conclusively be shown that any of the reputed finds of Hellenistic or Roman coins were made *in situ* in Africa; the excavations by J. S. Kirkman at Ras Mkumbuu (Ndagoni) on Pemba Island,[3] the only reputed find-spot investigated archaeologically, make it almost certain that the coins supposed to have come from that place did not in fact do so.[4]

[1] By 'Kilwa' in this paper is intended the site of the ancient town round the village now known as Kilwa Kisiwani ('Kilwa on the island') some 160 miles south of Dar es Salaam.
[2] These sources have been frequently reviewed, e.g. by J. Schacht, 'An Unknown Type of Minbar and its Historical Significance', *Ars Orientalis*, II, 165–70. Additional to those there cited is 'Kitāb al-Zanūj' in Cerulli, *Somalia*, I, 233–92. The earlier of two (Arabic) manuscripts of this dates from the end of the nineteenth century. The text, which was evidently compiled on the southern Somali coast, seems to be based on more than one document, one of which deals with early Arab settlements on the East African coast. See also G. S. P. Freeman-Grenville in *Discovering Africa's Past*, Uganda Museum Occasional Paper 4, 8–10. [3] *Tanganyika Notes and Records*, 53 (Oct. 1959), 161–75.
[4] The supposed finds of pre-Muslim coins are examined by Dr G. S. P. Freeman-Grenville, 'East Africa Coin Finds', *Journal of African History*, I (1960), 32–4.

239

Not only are no settlement sites of Classical age known, but none whatever of any period have been found which do not show evidence, in the form of imported glazed pottery, of contact with the Islamic world. On the other hand significant finds of stone artifacts, mostly of Middle Stone Age aspect, have been made on the coast, as on Kilwa Island,[5] at Lindi,[6] and Kilwa Kivinje; these may be compared to material collected long ago from the region north-west of Lindi.[7] Others are of Late Stone Age type, as at Kisiju and Kilwa Masoko,[8] and odd flakes, no doubt derived, occasionally turn up in debris of 'mediaeval' date; one such at Kaole is of obsidian which must have been brought at least three hundred miles, the distance to the nearest source of that material. Hand-axes, as well as other stone implements, are reported to have been found on Mombasa Island.[9]

Faced with these facts, the writer is inclined to believe, on admittedly inadequate evidence, that the first permanent settlements, other than those which we can deduce grew up at Rhapta and perhaps elsewhere under the stimulus of trade from Arabia, were contemporary with, or only a little anterior to, the beginning of trade with the Islamic countries.

Now it appears from the description of the inhabitants of Zinj in the *Periplus* that they were not negroid; and as we are told they imported iron implements they may have been ignorant of how to smelt the metal. As we might expect a Bantu people to possess pottery and iron, the evidence yielded by surface exploration does not disagree with this deduction. On the other hand the Later Stone Age peoples are taken to be in general of Bushman type, which accords even worse with the *Periplus* description of the inhabitants. Perhaps they were of Hottentot stock—could one compare the situation with that of van Riebeeck and his Dutchmen at the Cape sixteen hundred years later? Much to be hoped for is some evidence from skeletal remains; to date we have no such from the coast of any period before the arrival of Islam.

Let us now turn to the Muslim geographers. The evidence that they provide which is relevant to what follows is:

1. That the island of Qanbalu[10] was Muslim but 'Zang' speaking in the time of al-Mas'ūdī (died A.D. 950) and ruled by Muslim kings. It is said to have been occupied by the Muslims at the beginning of the Abbasid dynasty (A.D. 750). Part of the population was infidel.

2. Yāqūt (died A.D. 1229) states that the people of Langujah (Unguja, Zanzibar) have moved to Tumbatu (an island just off Zanzibar), the inhabitants of which are Muslim.

[5] *Annual Report*, Department of Antiquities, Tanganyika (1960), 11, Plate II.
[6] Ibid., 12.
[7] G. Smolla, *Actes du IVe Congrès Panafricain de Préhistoire et de L'Etude du Quaternaire*, Section III, 243–7.
[8] J. R. Harding, 'Late Stone Age Sites on the Tanganyika Coast', *Man* (1961), 221.
[9] Dr L. S. B. Leakey, verbal information.
[10] Variously equated with Madagascar, Zanzibar and Pemba. Zanzibar is perhaps the most probable.

3. Ibn Baṭṭūta, who visited the coast in A.D. 1331, tells us that the inhabitants of both Mombasa and Kilwa are of the Shafi'i persuasion, and
that the mosques at Mombasa and the buildings at Kilwa were of wood.

Of the historical chronicles, the most important is that of Kilwa, which
can be shown to be an accurate account of events as known in about
A.D. 1530; coins and Ibn Baṭṭūta corroborate certain details as far back as
about A.D. 1300. The chronicle begins with an account, evidently mythical
in certain details, of an emigration from Shiraz, in Fars, to Kilwa and other
places, apparently in the second half of the tenth century A.D., but makes it
evident that there were already Muslims living on the island.

De Barros, writing also in the first half of the fifteenth century, gives an
account derived from the Kilwa chronicle; but also states there was an
earlier immigration to the East African coast from Lasah (al-Ahsa on the
western side of the Persian Gulf). Schacht has suggested that this is merely
a variant of the Shiraz account.[11] In addition, de Barros mentions what
appears to be an immigration at a still earlier date of (Shi'a) Zaidis.

Other sources cannot be traced back earlier than the nineteenth (or, in
one case, eighteenth) century. An Omani source gives an account of an
emigration led by members of the Julanda family at the end of the seventh
century A.D.; descendants of this family are mentioned as resident in
Mombasa by the *Kitāb al-Zanūj*. The latter, after giving an account of the
settlement of Arabs in East Africa before Islam and their conversion in
A.H. 41, writes of an Amir who brought troops of the Umayyad Caliph
'Abd al-Malik ibn Marwān (A.D. 685–705) to Mogadishu and Kilwa, at
which place he built a fort.[12] Expeditions were, we are told, subsequently
sent to the East African coast by the Abbasid Caliphs al-Mansūr, Hārūn
al-Rashīd and al-Ma'mūn in the second half of the eighth century A.D. and
beginning of the ninth to quell revolts. The governors established in East
Africa by Hārūn were Persians. Both the chronicles of Pate and Lamu have
similar traditions of immigration under 'Abd al-Malik and (Pate only)
Hārūn.

With the exception of the account given by the Kilwa chronicle, all these
traditions of early immigration into East Africa have rightly been considered
as highly suspect, particularly since the numerous stone-built remains have
almost all been dated to the fourteenth century or later, and excavation has
yielded only some rather scanty pottery assigned to a date earlier than
A.D. 1250. As Kirkman wrote in 1956,[13] 'the earliest historical fact on the
east coast of tropical Africa is still the inscription on the *mihrab* of the Jamia
of Kizimkazi on Zanzibar Island, with its date A.H. 500 (A.D. 1107)'.
Recent surveys and excavations, however, are beginning to shed more light
on the period preceding A.D. 1300, and to suggest that there may be more
substance in the traditions of immigration from the Arab homelands in the
first centuries of Islam than has hitherto been thought to be the case.

[11] Op. cit., 167.   [12] Cerulli, op. cit., I, 238, 266.   [13] *Antiquaries' Journal*, XXXVII, 23.

Work at Kizimkazi[14] has shown that, while the mosque there was rebuilt
in the eighteenth century (though incorporating the inscription and other
elements from an earlier building), both beneath the mosque and in lower
levels elsewhere on the surrounding site, are deposits which appear to be
contemporary with the inscription. The only datable pottery is of (imported)
Islamic *sgraffiato* type, mostly of the variety predominantly brown in colour.
Associated with this deposit are walls of coral rubble with mud mortar, but
the area in which these deep strata were excavated is too restricted for it to
be possible to say anything of the plan of the building. Above this zone,
over most of the area examined there is a long gap in occupation, marked by
the accumulation of a sand dune, on which buildings were erected in the
eighteenth century. We may recall Yāqūt's statement that in his day the
Zanzibaris had removed to Tumbatu, where indeed there are ruins of a
mosque and much destroyed remains of other buildings; these have not yet
been satisfactorily dated archaeologically, but a fourteenth century rather
than a thirteenth century date for them would seem more probable.
Freeman-Grenville[15] has made out a convincing case that rulers were
minting their own coins in Zanzibar in the fifteenth century; three are
named, and one coin of a fourth (Muḥammad ibn 'Alī or 'Alī ibn
Muḥammad) was found at Kizimkazi, and is probably also of that century
since it has the peculiarity shared only with al-Ḥusain ibn Aḥmad, that the
name is arranged in triangular form. That there was a dynasty (or dynasties)
of sultans in Zanzibar is also implied by the Kilwa chronicle.

Of greater importance, however, are recent discoveries on the island of
Kilwa. The site of the town there extends along the western end of the
northern shore of the island for a space of about one kilometre, and for
perhaps three hundred metres inland. It is not proposed here to give a
general account[16] of these remains, the earliest of which date from c. 1300
or a little before (Plate 1).

Some eight hundred metres west of the apparent limit of the town are
two large buildings, excavation of which has been begun, first by the
Tanganyika Department of Antiquities and, in 1961, on a bigger scale,
by the British Institute of History and Archaeology in East Africa in
collaboration with the Department.

The two structures are built facing north overlooking the sea on a cliff;
they are separated by a gully of steep gradient (Plate 2). The larger and
more westerly of the buildings is now called Husuni Kubwa ('the Great
Fort'), and the other Husuni Ndogo ('the Small Fort'). The only tradition
concerning the origin of these two buildings that the writer has heard from
the natives of the place is that Husuni Ndogo is 'where the Portuguese
kept their pigs'; in fact it was maintained by Dorman[17] to be the fort which

[14] *Annual Report* (1960), Department of Antiquities, Tanganyika, Appendix II.
[15] 'Coinage in East Africa before Portuguese times', *Numismatic Chronicle*, Sixth series,
XVII, 170.
[16] For which see the author's 'Notes on Kilwa', *Tanganyika Notes and Records*, 53,
179–203.   [17] 'The Kilwa Civilization', *Tanganyika Notes and Records*, 6 (1938), 67.

the Portuguese are known to have erected, but which is almost certainly to be identified with the castle on the shore of the town site.

The shape of Husuni Kubwa is governed by the configuration of the high ground on which it is built, the northern two-thirds of the complex being triangular and the southern third square. The northern part has now been completely cleared, and partial excavation of the southern section has been sufficient to ensure that the plan[18] (Figure 1) is virtually complete; there is, however, some doubt about minor points in connexion with rooms on the north-western part of the building and at the extreme northern end, in which areas the sandstone cliff is precipitous, and sections of the structure have collapsed down to the cliff below. The whole complex is some 150 metres in length by a maximum of 75 metres in width and covers about two acres. It is built in coral rag set in lime mortar throughout; cut stone is in general only used for decorative pieces, door jambs, and vaults. Sandstone slabs, many of which have been robbed evidently after the building was abandoned, are employed for the treads of the many steps and seats. The rooms were high (usually rather over three metres), and should have been pleasantly cool, though many must have been very dark. Except as noted below, the roofs were of rectangular cut coral blocks laid on narrowly spaced cut timbers; in some rooms of lesser importance round mangrove poles were employed. The floors were of white plaster, in many cases laid directly on the subsoil; the courtyards, however, were unpaved. No important alterations appear to have been carried out to the buildings as originally built.

The nucleus of the building is conceived on an axial plan, consisting essentially of two courtyards, 'A' and 'D', with ranges of buildings between them and at their northern and southern ends respectively. Other rooms run along the eastern and western sides. To the west are structures ('B' and 'C' on the plan) of a different character, and to the south a large courtyard ('E'), most of the rooms surrounding which are of a simpler character than the rest of the structure.

The main entrance is from the shore. This leads to a wide staircase of twenty-eight steps in two flights with a landing between (Plate 3) which takes a visitor to the top of the cliff. Thence one can pass into the courtyard 'A' and so into the group of what were evidently reception rooms at its northern end. These were roofed with barrel vaults, and some of them ornamented with decorative stone-work (Plate 4). Three inscriptions, once evidently incorporated in the two more southerly of these rooms, were found in the debris.

The long narrow courtyard 'A' is flanked on its east and west sides by plain terrace walls; steps at either side lead down to the floor which is one metre below its surroundings. South and south-east of the court are ranges of rooms on which it is unnecessary to comment at length in the present context. All are of one storey with flat roofs and walls finished in smooth

[18] Surveyed and drawn by Mr P. S. Garlake.

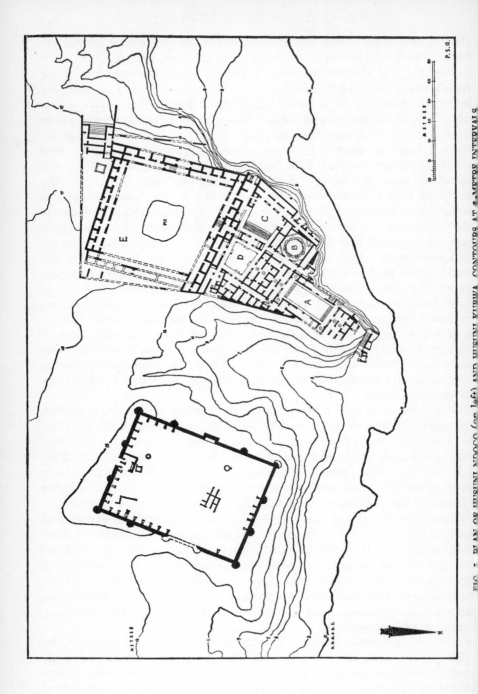

FIG. 1. PLAN OF HUSEINI NEBOGO (on left) AND HUSEINI KRIFWA. CONTOURS AT 4-METRE INTERVALS

plaster; several are provided with recesses in the wall which served as cupboards. In others, twin rows of holes running along the wall about two metres from the floor seem to be the relics of pegs, perhaps for supporting wall hangings. Many of the rooms, as also some of those to the north, have in the centre of their floors what seems to be a form of drain, consisting of a roughly-built pit of corbelled construction beneath the floor narrowing from bottom to top, into which gives a small round hole through the floor.

West of these ranges of rooms is a remarkable structure ('B' on plan) which, it seems, can only be a bathing pool.[19] In shape it is a regular octagon, and in each of its sides is constructed a small apse fitted with steps (Plate 6). The angles of the corners are cut in blocks of stone, and not by butting blocks together, clearly to keep the tank water-tight. A drain leads off from its western side and under the floor of the adjacent room, which is partly cut out of the cliff side; but there is no trace of any arrangements for filling the pool; water was presumably carried by hand. Surrounding the pool is a sort of ambulatory, with a seat-like kerb. The whole was open to the sky.

North of the courtyard is another remarkable feature (Plate 7, 'C' on plan). It consists of an open space flanked by high terrace walls to north and south; between them, across the eastern end, is an imposing bank of nine (including the topmost) seats, or steps, fourteen metres wide; there is a small footbath at one end of the lowest seat. The western end, which is wider, is backed by two long chambers each with three wide entrances. The terrace walls are pierced by triple rows of square recesses about the size of pigeon holes (22 × 19 cm.) contrived out of cut coral stone. These have no obvious purpose, and it is assumed they are purely decorative. The general impression given by the courtyard is as of a theatre (though it is not suggested that this was its function). It was certainly a place of assembly.

East of this court 'C', and separated from it by a long airy room provided with big windows giving a fine view towards the west and the site of the town, is another, but very shallow, sunken courtyard. Running along the southern side of this and of Court C is a triple range of rooms. The eastern end of this consists of plain chambers on one storey, but the western half, together with the southern part of the range of rooms on the western side of court E, are much more complex. These last were of two storeys; the lower of these is very simple in finish throughout, the walls for example being left unplastered. Into them have collapsed the upper floors, which to judge by the sophistication of their design, incorporated the main reception rooms. These were mostly roofed with vaults or domes; one of the latter has fallen virtually intact (Plate 8).

The rooms ranged along the eastern and southern sides of the large courtyard ('E' on the plan) are very plain. Their roofs appear to have been of temporary materials and the floors of those examined on the southern

---

[19] It was certainly designed to hold water; and being shallow and unprotected from the sun is unlikely to have been a cistern.

side were of earth. They were lit by small holes pierced through the walls, which were unplastered. They would seem likely to have served as store-rooms.

Projecting from the south-west corner of the complex is a nearly square structure which was of two storeys. The upper, which is now wholly destroyed, was approached from the west by a wide staircase. In the angle between this structure and the south end of the main part of the building is a very large well, 3·60 metres square, which was formerly roofed; we may remark also a smaller well within the main complex east of courtyard 'D'.

The objects found in the course of the excavation of Husuni Kubwa are somewhat meagre. As to the pottery, the imported, glazed wares are almost exclusively Chinese celadon, with some Ying Ch'ing and stoneware sherds. A fine Yüan dynasty flask with light blue glaze and incised floral decoration beneath was the only substantially complete imported vessel to be recovered (Plate 10); the fragments of this were found spread over a wide area near the base of the fill, but not in an occupation deposit, at the northern end of courtyard 'A'. To this flask is ascribed a date of about A.D. 1300.[20] Islamic wares are lacking, for reasons that are not clear; though one large block of ornamental stonework seems to have been designed to receive the star-shaped tiles manufactured in Persia from the mid-tenth to the beginning of the sixteenth century. The locally made pottery is somewhat coarse; the most characteristic type is decorated with applied ridges, often ornamented with incisions.

Four coins found together in the fill of the smaller well, all of Sulaimān ibn al-Ḥasan (c. 1294–1308), suggest that it was out of use by the early fourteenth century. But coins ascribed to the last quarter of the fifteenth century have been found in certain parts of the buildings associated with local pottery of the characteristic Husuni type.

The three more important inscriptions are still being expertly examined. All are cut in coral stone of the finer sort, with texts in good Arabic and rounded script.[21] They may be briefly described as follows:

1. A single block measuring 55 × 23 centimetres inscribed with a text intricately interlaced with foliage. This has not yet been read, but Dr Fehérvári, who kindly consented to examine the photographs of the inscriptions, compares it to an inscription in Cairo of A.D. 1240.

2. Six blocks of varying lengths (the longest 57 centimetres, the shortest 30 centimetres) and 21 centimetres high, form an inscription with a rhyming text, also not yet fully read, which seems to have been set over a doorway.

3. Two blocks measuring 52 × 33 centimetres. The text invokes God's guidance for al-Malik al-Manṣūr al-Ḥasan bin Sulaimān who is described

[20] This is the opinion of Mr Basil Gray and Mr John Ayers, for whose advice the writer expresses his grateful thanks.
[21] Until the middle of the twelfth century the angular Kufic script was used for inscriptions, being subsequently replaced by the rounded nashki.

as 'helping the Commander of the believers' (Nāsir 'amīr al-Mu'minīn), by which phrase he evidently acknowledges the supremacy of the Caliph.

It is deduced from these finds that Husuni Kubwa was built before about A.D. 1300, probably in the thirteenth century.

Despite the present name given to the building,[22] it is very unlikely that it was built with defence as a primary consideration, and it is doubtful whether that object entered into the matter at all. There are no plainly defensive works, and the nature of the buildings, in particular the entrances, is very unmilitary. The very great scale and comparative sophistication of much of the structure point to it having been the residence of a very powerful personage, almost certainly the ruler of Kilwa. It may well have been constructed by the sultan mentioned in Inscription 3 above, which was evidently built originally into one of the walls. There are four rulers of the name al-Ḥasan ibn Sulaimān mentioned in the Kilwa Chronicle, but the name or soubriquet al-Mansūr occurs in neither this nor any other source. Of the four, the second, who ruled c. A.D. 1191–1215, is most likely to be in case.

It is remarkable that no mention of any building which can be identified with Husuni Kubwa occurs either in the Kilwa Chronicle or in the Portuguese accounts. Ibn Baṭṭūṭa's account reads as if the sultan's residence was in the town not far from the Friday Mosque at the time of his visit in 1331.[23] However, it is probably this 'fort' which Morice was offered as security for his treaty with the sultan in 1776, which he was told had been built 963 years earlier.[24]

Husuni Ndogo, which lies to the east across the other side of a gully, is a quite different sort of building. It consists of a very thick rectangular enclosure wall reinforced with solid towers, round at the base and solid above, disposed one at each corner, and the others at equal distances along the sides (Plate 9); at the centre of the west side, however, in place of a tower is a rectangular projection within which is a raised platform with plastered floor. The walls, built of coral rubble in lime mortar, with cut stone quoins, stand to a height of about two and a half metres; their

[22] The standard dictionary meaning of Husuni is 'fort', 'castle'. G. S. P. Freeman-Grenville, 'Husuni', *Tanganyika Notes and Records*, 58 and 59 (1962), 227–30, points out that the Arabic word *husn* (from which the Swahili *husuni* is derived) denotes in Southern Arabia a fortified residence. Other words are usually used for 'fort' in Swahili.

[23] *The Travels of Ibn Battuta*, edited Sir Hamilton Gibb (Hakluyt Society) II, 381. Ibn Baṭṭūṭa's statement that Kilwa was built entirely of wood is hardly credible. Ignoring the buildings under discussion, there is convincing evidence in the Kilwa Chronicle that the Great Mosque was built in stone at an earlier date, and trial excavations in the town have disclosed stone walls almost certainly datable to before the beginning of the fourteenth century. It would seem that Ibn Baṭṭūṭa's memory was at fault (as it on occasion was: Suakin is described, for example, as six miles from the coast, whereas it is very close to the mainland; on the other hand no mention is made of Kilwa being an island). Freeman-Grenville has suggested an alternative reading for the passage, which, however, Gibb (Ibid., 380, note 62) rejects.

[24] Sir John Gray, 'The French at Kilwa', *Tanganyika Notes and Records*, 44 (1956), 47.

foundations are very massive and extend to a depth of two metres. From
the inside of the walls project stub walls about 1·80 metres in length; few
of these are intact, but they seem to have existed all round the perimeter at
approximately equal intervals, except near the centre of the northern wall.
Two, destroyed to below ground level, are placed closer together. At this
point there are traces of what seems to be a shallow apse let into the inner
side of the wall, which has here for the most part collapsed down the hill.
The entrance to the building is at the southern end, and leads into a simple
sort of gatehouse, behind which is a well, with a small octagonal tank nearby;
these elements appear to have been added to the original building. No other
intelligible structures have been found within the walls except the rough
foundations of a poor building, evidently of later date than the remainder,
to the north of the centre.

The function of Husuni Ndogo is uncertain, though it gives the impression of having been built as a fort, or at least a defensible cantonment, the
possible apse in the north (*qibla*) wall noted above, could be the remains of
a *mihrab*. This and other details suggest that it may, at least for a period,
have served as a mosque.[25]

Let us now examine the architectural origins and relationships of the two
Husunis. Husuni Ndogo is entirely different in concept from any other
building known on the East African coast. It is, however, so far as the outer
walls are concerned, markedly similar to buildings constructed in Arab
lands under the Caliphs of the Umayyad (A.D. 661–750) and early Abbasid
dynasties. We may compare, for example, those of Mshatta in Jordan[26]
and of the Great Mosque at Raqqa in Iraq (late eighth century A.D.);[27]
though Husuni Ndogo is, of course, on a much humbler scale. It is
tempting to recall the fort which the *Kitāb-al-Zanūj* records as having been
built at Kilwa by the Amir Musa.[28] Such material as has been found in the
building, however, is similar to that from Husuni Kubwa. Though no
occupation deposit and no material incontrovertibly associated with the
enclosure wall has been found, it seems probable that Husuni Ndogo
constitutes rather a survival in East Africa of a style into a period later than
that in which it is found in the Arab lands; that it is related to Umayyad or
early Abbasid architecture appears certain.

[25] Sir John Gray, 'Fort Santiago at Kilwa', *Tanganyika Notes and Records*, 58 and 59
(1962), 178, suggests that this building is that referred to by Vespucci who writes of a
castle with four towers which was half built which the Portuguese saw in 1508. Considerations of date apart, this identification seems unlikely as, first, mention would surely have
been made of the distance from the town if Husuni Ndogo was in point, and, second, one
would expect the much more impressive Husuni Kubwa to be mentioned as well.

[26] K. A. C. Creswell, *Early Muslim Architecture*, Penguin Books (1958), 125, 142. He
dates Mshatta to the mid-eighth century A.D.

[27] Ibid., 188.

[28] See above, p. 181. This is the only building the Umayyads are recorded as having
erected; note also that the Arabic word employed, *husn*, used is the equivalent of the
Swahili *husuni* (see note 22). De Barros, however, in his version of the Kilwa Chronicle
mentions the building of a fortress at Kilwa by 'Soleiman Hacen' (Sulaimān bin al-Hasan
bin Daud, c. 1170–88).

Plate 1. The Great Mosque at Kilwa (fourteenth and fifteenth century) from the northern end

Plate 2. Husuni Kubwa: General view from the air, facing east. Husuni Ndogo in background

Plate 3. Husuni Kubwa: The staircase leading up from the shore

Plate 4. Husuni Kubwa: Decorative stonework fallen from rooms at the northern end

Plate 5. Inscription and decorated stonework fallen from rooms at the northern end

Plate 6. Husuni Kubwa: A section of the swimming pool

Plate 7. A general view of the excavated area facing north; Court C in foreground

Plate 8. Husuni Kubwa: The fallen dome

Plate 9. Husuni Ndogo: One of the corner towers

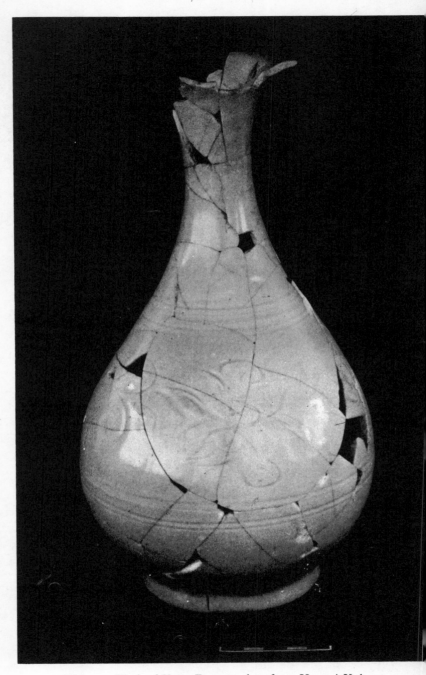

Plate 10. Flask of Yuän Dynasty date from Husuni Kubwa

While Husuni Kubwa is in certain respects not so foreign to the style of other medieval buildings in East Africa, it too has characteristics to which we have no parallels. The bathing-pool is of the Abbasid type; it appears that it closely resembles in plan the tank in the *sahn* of the Great Mosque at Harran, excavated by the late Dr D. S. Rice, but as yet unpublished. The ambulatory round the pool may be compared with a similar feature in Qubbat as-Sulaibiya dating from the ninth century A.D.[29] This, though a mausoleum, is of the same architectural family.

The dome illustrated (Plate 8) is very unusual in form; the ribs on the interior and rounded ridges on the exterior resemble those on the cupola of the (Umayyad) Great Mosque at Kairouan.[30] The conical shape and exterior ridges also show a curious resemblance to Yazidi shrines in northern Iraq.

There is thus evidence of an Umayyad-Abbasid tradition of architecture at Kilwa. As we have observed, the *Kitāb al-Zanūj* and other late sources refer to immigrants from Arab lands coming to East Africa in the time of these dynasties, during the first two Islamic centuries; these traditions are suspect, but al-Mas'ūdī also records that Qanbalu was overrun by Moslems in the eighth century A.D. Are we to associate this architectural tradition with these supposed early immigrants? Or do we suppose the style was brought by the immigrants who according to the Kilwa Chronicle came from Shiraz[31] and settled at Kilwa in about the tenth century A.D.? Against the latter theory is the fact that no buildings remotely resembling the Husunis or their style of architecture of a date consonant with the supposed emigration are known in the Persian Gulf,[32] though certain caravanserais in the Persian hinterland are of not dissimilar design. Indeed, the few 'medieval' buildings still standing on the Gulf, as the Sūq al-Khamīs mosque on the island of Bahrain, the ruined mosque at the site of Siraf, and the few (later) buildings still visible at Hormuz are all very different in style from the architecture of the East African coast of any period.[33]

We may, in conclusion, cast a glance at the later architectural developments at Kilwa and elsewhere. While Husuni Ndogo is unrelated to any subsequent buildings on the coast, many of the characteristics of Husuni Kubwa are found in the fourteenth and fifteenth centuries. The mode of

[29] Creswell, op. cit., 286–8.

[30] G. Marçais, *L'Architecture Musulman d'Occident* (Paris, 1954), 20–1.

[31] 'Shiraz' is, in view of the paucity of Persian elements in the culture of the east coast both in the past and at present, taken to include the Arab-influenced coast of the province of Fars; and, indeed, if the tradition of the emigration of the seven brothers of Lasa is another version of this story, the whole of the northern end of the Persian Gulf may be involved.

[32] Schacht, op. cit., 170 and *passim* maintains that a type of *minbar* common in mosques of the last two centuries is a survival from Umayyad times and is evidence of the spread of Islam to the coast as early as the eighth century A.D. But the apparent absence of this type of *mihrab* in the intervening centuries is unexplained.

[33] The archaeological examination of Islamic sites in the Gulf has hardly been begun, and we are even more ignorant of Oman. Investigations in these areas might well alter the present picture.

setting rooms in rows one in front of the other continues, and indeed survives into modern times, as also does the method of building flat stone roofs. Sunken courtyards are also found in these later periods as in a large house at Kilwa[34] and in the fifteenth century palace at Gedi in Kenya.[35] Vaults and domes are hardly known outside the Kilwa region. Plain barrel vaults with thin stone voussoirs, similar to the simpler vaults found at Husuni Kubwa, are incorporated in parts of the Great Mosque at Kilwa ascribed to c. A.D. 1300, or rather before. A dome of the early fourteenth century is rounded, with stone voussoirs, whereas in the fifteenth both domes and vaults are built of lime concrete, and are set on pillars. No octagonal buildings are known, nor are there any parallels to the shape and mode of construction of the conical domes. The decorative motifs employed on the stonework at Husuni Kubwa are lacking except for architectural mouldings; their place seems largely to be taken by glazed bowls set in walls and roofs which come into use at Kilwa in the fifteenth century.

These later developments seem to have taken place independently of foreign influences, and reflect the evolution of a civilization on the east African coast with a distinct flavour of its own. It continued of course to rely for its wealth on the sea-borne trade, and when the Portuguese occupied Sofala and gained control of the Indian Ocean trade decline was very rapid.

NOTE

This article was written when the excavations at Kilwa were still in progress. Subsequent work has shed more light on questions raised herein; notably it is now believed that Husuni Kubwa was built in the early fourteenth century. The paper should therefore be read in conjunction with later articles by the author, 'The "Shirazi" Colonization of East Africa', which is the next chapter in this volume, and, more recently, 'Kilwa: A Preliminary Report', *Azania* I, 1966. Husuni is admirably described in greater detail in 'The Early Islamic Architecture of the East African Coast' by P. S. Garlake.

[34] *Annual Report*, Department of Antiquities, Tanganyika (1960), 6.
[35] Kirkman, op. cit., 20 and Plate 10c.

15. THE 'SHIRAZI' COLONIZATION OF EAST AFRICA

By NEVILLE CHITTICK

IN this paper I set out some new views on aspects of the history and chronology of the East African coast before the fourteenth century, views which hinge on the date of the immigration of the 'Shirazi' mentioned in the traditional chronicles of the coast. These views are based on evidence from recent excavations, chiefly at the site of Kilwa (Kilwa Kisiwani), and on a re-appraisal of the historical sources. The excavations are still continuing and these interpretations are necessarily somewhat tentative, but it seems well to set them out at the present juncture with a view to inviting public discussion.[1]

For information about the period before the arrival of the 'Shirazi' we have to rely on the meagre information provided by the Arab geographers, supplemented only by recent traditions of poor reliability from the Lamu region and the Banadir coast to the north. These sources have been analysed by numerous writers, the earliest[2] being the most exhaustive and the latest,[3] though selective, perhaps the most perceptive. It is not necessary here to set out these sources, but only to summarize in a few words some generally accepted facts which we learn from them.

At least as early as the first centuries A.D. there was trade between the East African coast and the lands at the northern end of the Indian Ocean; people from south-western Arabia settled at least one place, Rhapta, and intermarried with the native inhabitants. Commerce and probably sporadic immigration continued in the first three centuries of the Islamic era. By the early tenth century A.D. (al-Mas'udi), there were Muslims in Qanbalu (Pemba?) and there were already Bantu settled in this zone. By the mid-twelfth century (al-Idrisi), most of the inhabitants of Zanzibar were Muslim; there were numbers of towns on the mainland, most of which appear to have been pagan, though Merka and probably also Mogadiscio (Maqdishu) were Muslim. The latter was the most important place on the coast in the early thirteenth century according to Yaqut, who regards it as on the frontier between Barbar and Zanj. Yaqut also tells us something of Zanzibar (the Muslim inhabitants of which had by this time moved to Tumbatu), and of Pemba. He is also the first person to mention Kilwa, simply as a town in the land of Zanj. None of our external, contemporary sources make any mention of the 'Shirazi'.

[1] I have already to thank Messrs G. S. P. Freeman-Grenville, J. S. Kirkman, J. S. Trimingham and J. Schacht, and Miss Helen Mitchell for valuable comments on the substance of this article.

[2] M. Guillain, *Documents sur l'histoire, la géographie et le commerce de l'Afrique orientale*, 3 vols., Paris, 1856.

[3] J. S. Trimingham, *Islam in East Africa*, O.U.P., 1964.

We have only two written sources of any antiquity which derive from
the eastern coast of Africa; these are versions of the Kilwa Chronicle, the
one in Arabic, and the other in Portuguese, the latter transmitted by the
historian de Barros, who was writing in the middle of the sixteenth century.
These have been set out at length in translation together with a commen-
tary, by G. S. P. Freeman-Grenville in his recently published *Medieval
History of the Coast of Tanganyika*.[4] In his interpretation of the different
versions of the Kilwa Chronicle, that author follows in general the received
opinion on the subject,[5] but analyses the details thereof much more ex-
haustively than has hitherto been attempted. I have therefore taken it
as the basis of the present discussion and have set out in Table I, page
279, a list of the rulers and their dates up to the middle of the fifteenth
century as computed by Freeman-Grenville from the regnal (Islamic)
years.

The currently accepted history of Kilwa can be summarized as follows:

In the latter part of the tenth century A.D. one 'Ali bin al-Hasan, or 'Ali
bin al-Husain, of the ruling family of Shiraz, came to Kilwa, established
himself there, and founded a dynasty of rulers. The two versions of the
Kilwa Chronicle differ considerably in the details of this event. We may
note that the Arabic version gives the names of five other places on the
coast, including Pemba and Mafia,[6] at which 'Ali's brothers settled, and
of a sixth, Hanzuan (Anzwani=Johanna in the Comoros), at which his
father the Sultan disembarked. The Arabic version states that there was
already a mosque, named Kibala, on Kilwa Island before his arrival, but
mentions only one Muslim family, the island being ruled by an infidel.
These accounts are thought to be in large part mythical, but it is generally
accepted that they represent the memory of a substantial immigration of
Arabs and/or Persians from the Persian Gulf. Related accounts are, or
were until recently, remembered in Tumbatu (Zanzibar), Kilwa Kivinje,
Kilwa Kisiwani, the Comoro islands and Moçambique.

'Ali bin al-Hasan/Husain eventually went to live in Mafia; subsequently
five of his sons and grandsons ruled at Kilwa (one of whom, like 'Ali,
moved to Mafia). Two other sons are also mentioned as rulers of Mafia,
just before and just after the death of 'Ali. A short time after this, Kilwa
was attacked and overrun by a people called the Matamandalin from a place
called شغ, probably to be transliterated Shanga (Xanga in the
Portuguese version). These people were eventually overcome, and the
dynasty restored.

Subsequently (*c.* A.D. 1131) the son of a ruler of dubious origin was

[4] O.U.P., 1962.
[5] J. Walker, 'History and Coinage of the Sultans of Kilwa', *Numismatic Chronicle*
Ser. V, XVI, 1936, reprinted *Tanganyika Notes and Records*, No. 45, pp. 33–58; the reprint
is referred to below. Also Sir J. M. Gray, 'A History of Kilwa': Part I, *T.N.R.*, No. 31
1951; Part II, *T.N.R.*, No. 32, 1952.
[6] Freeman-Grenville suggests this is an error for Mombasa, but this is not proven
Mafia is an island some eighty miles north of Kilwa.

summoned from Sofala, where he was Governor, and under him (no. 10 in the list), and his son Soleiman Hacen, Kilwa rapidly attained wealth, through her trade in gold, and power over her neighbours. There follows a period of nearly a century about which we know hardly anything, until about 1277 there ascended the throne one al-Hasan bin Talut (no. 18), described in the Portuguese version as related to the previous rulers, but in the Arabic as the founder of a new dynasty. His grandson, al-Hasan bin Sulaiman (no. 21), was visited by the traveller Ibn Battuta in about 1331, which date agrees with the computation from the regnal years that this last sultan was on the throne at the time. From this time onwards the accepted chronology must be in outline correct and, save for minor points, I do not wish to discuss this later period, which may be considered to end with the coming of the Portuguese at the beginning of the sixteenth century.

However, as a result of a re-examination of the two versions of the Chronicle and of evidence from excavations at the sites of Kilwa and Kisimani Mafia, I have come to the conclusion that the received chronology of the sultans ruling before the end of the thirteenth century is too long by about 200 years, and that the probable date of the arrival of the 'Shirazi' is the latter part of the twelfth century. My views on the dating of the main events on the coast, and of the early rulers of Kilwa, which will be argued below, are briefly set out in Table II, page 293.

Let us now compare the Arabic and Portuguese versions, with particular reference to the earlier period of the Kilwa sultanate, a comparison which, it will be maintained, indicates that while both are suspect in detail, the Arabic is both more intelligible and more reliable, and that grave inaccuracies may have arisen in the Portuguese version through an attempt to dovetail two different sources together.

First, let it be said that it is plain from internal evidence that de Barros could not read Arabic, and that he therefore worked either from translations or from matter verbally recounted to him. He is incapable of distinguishing between the names Hasan and Husain, and between 'Ali and Khalid, and many of the names are clearly corrupt.

The two versions corroborate each other very inadequately. Of the first nineteen rulers in the Portuguese version, only eight are listed in the Arabic, and the lengths of reign for these eight agree in only three cases. The pattern of the figures for the longer reigns is not such as to inspire confidence, particularly in the case of the Portuguese version, where there is a marked preponderance of reigns of fourteen, twenty-four and forty years.

Before citing in detail the main difference between the two versions of the Chronicle proper, we should note that de Barros,[7] in an introductory passage, tells us the story of the invasion from Arabia of the heretic Emozaydij, in connexion with which name he cites the authority of the Chronicle of

[7] Dec. 1, Book VIII, Chapter IV, set out in Freeman-Grenville, op. cit. 31.

the Kings of Kilwa. This is followed by the story of the immigration of
people (apparently orthodox Muslims) from Laçah (Al-Hasa near Bahrain)
and their foundation of Mogadiscio, the first town to trade with Sofala.
Later, he mentions Mogadiscio as having been founded some time before
Kilwa,[8] and in a further passage[9] he cites the Chronicle as his authority
for the story of the discovery of Sofala and the development of the gold
trade therewith by Mogadiscio. There is no parallel to these passages in
the Arabic version, but the story of the people of al-Hasa, with seven
brothers and three ships, is redolent of that of the emigration from Shiraz
in which, according to the Arabic version of the Chronicle, six brothers and
their father sailed in seven ships.

Apart from the above, the chief discrepancies between the two versions
are as follows:

1. The Portuguese version states that Ale, son of Hocen, Sultan of Shiraz,
came to Kilwa, bought the island for cloth, fortified and ruled it, installing
his son to rule Mafia and adjacent islands. After his death he was succeeded by his son Ale, who ruled forty years. The details about the former
closely correspond to what we are told about the sultan in the Arabic
version (1 in the list) who is equated with the second Ale. This is surely a
case of dittography. There was only one 'Ali; whether his father's name was
Hasan or Husain is arguable.

2. The Arabic version gives a much fuller account than the Portuguese of
the wars between Kilwa and the Matamandalin of Shanga, listing a usurper
installed by these people in the middle of the reign of al-Hasan bin Sulaiman,
no. 5. I agree with earlier commentators that the Arabic is to be preferred.

3. As successor to no. 5, the Portuguese version gives one 'Ali bin Daud,
who is mentioned in the Arabic only as having been appointed ruler by
his father Daud (no. 3) when the latter retired to Mafia. The Portuguese
version gives him a reign of sixty years, followed by a grandson of the same
name (no. 7) for six years. This looks like another case of dittography, and
the sixty years is improbable, particularly as, if the reign of 'Ali bin Daud
really falls at this point, he would seem to have been at least forty years old
when he succeeded. Lacking any better evidence, it is best to assume a
reign of six years for this man.

4. Much the most striking discrepancy is that the Portuguese version
lists a block of nine sultans (nos. 9 to 17) who do not figure at all in the
Arabic. We are told in effect nothing of six of these sultans except the
lengths of their reigns, and two of the names of these are plainly corrupt
and misunderstood (Hale Bonij and Bone Soleiman). Of the other three
the relationship of the first, Soleiman (no. 9), to his predecessors is not
stated, as is done in the case of other sultans. He is said to have been executed by his subjects, and succeeded by his son Daut, who was brought
from Sofala where he had grown rich in the gold trade. He in turn was

TABLE I

THE SULTANS OF KILWA DOWN TO THE MIDDLE OF THE FIFTEENTH CENTURY FOLLOWING THE RECEIVED CHRONOLOGY

Adapted from Freeman-Grenville, *Medieval History*, pp. 66–70

Portuguese version	Arabic version	Date (A.D.)
Sultan Hocen, King of Shiraz	al-Hasan bin 'Ali, Sultan of Shiraz	ante 957
Ale, his son, bought Kilwa Island; first king thereof. Son ruled Mafia		
1. Ale Bumale [= 'Ali bin 'Ali?]	1. 'Ali bin al-Husain bin 'Ali. Bought Kilwa Island and ruled 40 years	957–996
2. Ale Busoloquete, son of a brother in Mafia, ruled Kilwa 4½ years	2. 'Ali bin Bashat, ruled Kilwa 4½ years	996–999
3. Daut, son of Ale Busoloquete	3. Daud bin 'Ali, ruled 2 years. Preferring Mafia, appointed son 'Ali as ruler	999–1003
4. Ale Bonebaquer, usurper, 2 years	4. Khalid bin Bakr, usurper from Shanga. 2½ years; deposed	1003–1005
5. Hocein Soleiman, nephew of Daut. 16 years	5. al-Hasan bin Sulaiman bin 'Ali, ruled 12 years. Fled to Zanzibar.	1005–1017
	Muhammad bin al-Husain al-Mandhir, usurper, ruled 12 years, deposed.	1017–1029
	al-Hasan bin Sulaiman bin 'Ali, ruled a further 14 years	1029–1042
6. Ale ben Daut reigned 60 years [son of No. 3]		1042–1100
7. Ale ben Daut, 6 years		1100–1106
8. Hacen ben Daut, his brother, 24 years. Placed on the throne in the stead of one Soleiman, who was killed	8. al-Hasan bin Daud bin 'Ali, founder of Kilwa. Reigned 70 years (and 70 years old at accession)	1106–1129
9. Soleiman. 2 years. Executed	9. —	1129–1131
10. Daut, his son. 40 years	10. —	1131–1170
11. Soleiman Hacen, his son. 18 years	11. —	1170–1188
12. Daut, his son. 2 years	12. —	1188–1190
13. Taluf, his brother. 1 year	13. —	1190–1191
14. Hacen, his brother. 25 years	14. —	1191–1215
15. Hale Bonij, his brother. 10 years	15. —	1215–1225
16. Bone Soleiman, his nephew	16. —	1225–1263
17. Ale Daut. 14 years	17. —	1263–1277
18. Hacen, his grandson. 18 years	18. al-Hasan bin Talut. 18 years. First of house of Abu'l Mawahib	1277–1294
19. Soleiman, his son. 14 years	19. [mentioned only as father of no. 21]	1294–1308
20. Daut, his son. Regent for 2 years	20. Daud bin Sulaiman. Regent for 2 years	1308–1310
21. Hacen, his brother. 24 years	21. al-Hasan bin Sulaiman al-Mat'un bin al-Hasan bin Talut. Reigned 4 years, and ascended throne at age 14	1310–1333
22. Daut, his brother. 24 years	22. Daud bin Sulaiman. 24 days	1333–1356
23. Soleiman. 20 days	23. —	1356
24. Hacen, his uncle. 6½ years	24. al-Husain bin Sulaiman. 6½ years	1356–1362
25. Talut, his nephew. 1 year	25. Talut bin al-Husain. 2 years, 4 months and 10 days	1362–1364
26. Soleiman, brother of Soleiman and Talut. 2 years and 4 months	26. —	1364–1366
27. Soleiman, uncle of no. 26. 24 years, 4 months and 20 days	27. —	1366–1389
28. Hacen, his son. 24 years	28. al-Husain bin Sulaiman, son of no. 25. 23 years	1389–1412
29. Mahamed Ladil, his brother, 9 years	29. Muhammad bin Sulaiman bin al-Husain, surnamed al-Malik al-Adil. 22 years	1412–1421
30. Soleiman, his son. 22 years	30. Sulaiman bin Muhammad al-Malik al-Adil	1421–1442

succeeded by a man described as his son, but named Soleiman Hacen. This name *prima facie* indicates that his father's name was Hasan or Husain,[10] but presumably because this reading would make nonsense of the genealogy, 'Soleiman Hacen' has apparently been interpreted as a 'double name'.[11] No 'double names' of this sort occur anywhere else in the Chronicles. I think it much more likely that an error has been made.

The historicity of these nine sultans has not hitherto been seriously questioned, and a lacuna in the Arabic version has been assumed. It has been asserted that the existence of two of the rulers is proved by the existence of coins minted by them,[12] but this is not so. In fact the Arabic version reads perfectly well as it stands; two generations of rulers, sons and grandsons of 'Ali bin al-Hasan/Husain (the length of reign of the last grandson greatly exaggerated), followed in a new chapter by the first of a new dynasty, that of the house of Abu'l Mawahib, named al-Hasan bin Talut, who seized the kingdom by force. In the Portuguese version on the other hand, the passage corresponding to the supposed lacuna begins with one Soleiman, described vaguely 'of royal blood', and ends with (another) Ale Daut, followed by Hacen (presumably=al-Hasan bin Talut), described as his grandson but with no mention of his father.

If we compare the names of the rulers named only by de Barros with those that precede and succeed them, we find notable similarities. This is particularly so in the case of the first four of those mentioned only by de Barros (nos. 9 to 12) and the later rulers numbered 19 to 22. In view of the unsatisfactory nature of the information concerning nos. 13 to 18, one is led to question whether any of these nine really had any independent existence at all, and whether this is not another case of duplication.

Two of these nine sultans, however, Daut (no. 10) and Soleiman Hacen (no. 11), are presented as the authors of Kilwa's pre-eminence, gaining control of the trade with Sofala and of Pemba, Mafia and Zanzibar; the second of the two is stated to have built a fortress and houses of stone at Kilwa, the town before that time having been built almost entirely of wood. These deeds were certainly not imagined by de Barros; they might be attributed to sultans ruling either before or after the change of dynasty which, as we shall see, is the central feature of the Arabic version. The correspondence of names suggests that a date after this event is more likely; but if the al-Hasan bin Sulaiman, who was visited by Ibn Battuta, is indeed to be identified with Soleiman Hacen, famous for building in stone, Ibn Battuta's statement that all the buildings at Kilwa were built of wood is only intelligible if his visit took place near the beginning of the reign.[13]

---

[10] Cf. the fifth sultan, Hocein Soleiman=al-Hasan bin Sulaiman.

[11] Freeman-Grenville, op. cit. 91–2.

[12] Freeman-Grenville, op. cit. 51; the supposed lacuna is from the ninth to the seventeenth (not sixteenth) sultan. The coins mentioned in the note, loc. cit., will be referred to below.

[13] Cf. H. A. R. Gibb, *The Travels of Ibn Battuta*, II, C.U.P., 1962, 380–2.

It is concluded from the foregoing that the sixth reign of de Barros' version, and the ninth to seventeenth, with the possible exception of the tenth and eleventh,[14] are spurious, and that there has been duplication in regard to the first reign also. It is suggested that this confusion probably arose through de Barros using two sources, and that he set various of the sultans in series rather than in parallel. If this is correct, the second source would seem to be that which contains the account of the immigration from al-Hasa, the founding of Mogadiscio, and the discovery of Sofala, none of which figure in the Arabic version, and one is tempted to conclude that the two successive colonizations are but facets of a single myth. The corollary to this is that the Arabic version is the more reliable in its account of the Kilwa sultanate, and in fact this document reads more intelligibly as a whole, the only patent inaccuracy being the figures given in connexion with the eighth sultan, al-Hasan bin Daud.

I have indicated that we have little reason to accept as accurate the lengths of the reigns given in either versions, but it is nevertheless worthwhile to attempt to calculate dates on the basis of the Arabic version, preferring the Portuguese figure only in regard to the above mentioned eighth reign. Our most convenient point of departure is the reign of al-Hasan bin Sulaiman Abu'l Mawahib (no. 21) who was visited by Ibn Battuta in A.D. 1331. Calculating from known dates at the end of the fifteenth century, Freeman-Grenville has concluded that his visit occurred almost at the end of his reign. Let us, for the purposes of this discussion, accept this, and the twenty-four years ascribed to the reign of Ibn Battuta's host by the Portuguese version (as opposed to the fourteen of the Arabic). Let us accept also the reign of his father Sulaiman (no. 19), also fourteen years, who is not recorded as a sultan in the Arabic version (though coins have been ascribed to him[15]), and the longer span of the reigns of the Al-Hasan bin Sulaiman (no. 5), who was deposed by the people of Shanga, as given in the Arabic version. Calculating on this basis, we arrive at a date for the beginning of the reign of 'Ali bin al-Hasan/Husain of c. A.D. 1161. If we add the reigns of nos. 9 and 10 in the list the figure is c. A.D. 1105. If we ignore these two sultans, accept the lower figure, given in the Arabic version, for the length of the reign of no. 21 and place Ibn Battuta's visit near the beginning of his rule, we arrive at c. 1180. To take the interpretation giving the shortest chronology (viz. accepting only sultans mentioned in both versions, and the shorter reign where the lengths differ in the two versions) brings the figure down by about thirty-four Islamic years to c. A.D. 1214, which I suspect may be near the truth; though I do not suggest that an examination of the Kilwa Chronicle alone would point to this figure.

In view of the doubtful value of the regnal years for this period as given in the Chronicle, it is also worthwhile to calculate, following the Arabic

version, the date of 'Ali bin al-Hasan/Husain on a basis of generations.
There are two generations of his direct descendants, followed by the
usurper, al-Hasan bin Talut (no. 18). We do not (rejecting the Portuguese
version) know the latter's ancestry, so we can hardly fit him into the
scheme of generations. Al-Hasan bin Sulaiman (no. 21), visited by Ibn
Battuta, is his grandson. So that down to c. A.D. 1310 (or A.D. 1320), the
suggested date of his accession, when he is recorded as being only fourteen
years of age, there are only three generations, plus the reigns of 'Ali bin al-
Hasan/Husain and al-Hasan bin Talut, back to the arrival of the 'Shirazi'.
Even if we accept these last two[16] as full generations, the total is still only
five. Taking a generation at twenty-seven years, we arrive at the figure of
A.D. 1175 (or A.D. 1185) for the beginning of the rule of 'Ali bin al-Hasan/
Husain. Sixteen to seventeen years is a fair average for the reigns of rulers
of Islamic dynasties elsewhere; application of this figure here gives a date
of c. A.D. 1200 for this accession.

These analyses, then, suggest a date late in the twelfth Christian century
for the date of the arrival of the 'Shirazi'. This date agrees well with such
evidence as we have, for, as we have observed, Kilwa had become sufficiently well known to be mentioned by the Arab geographers early in the
thirteenth century.

It will be objected, however, that this date is incompatible with what we
are specifically told by the two chroniclers about the date of the 'founding'
of Kilwa. De Barros informs us that the father of the 'founder'
of Kilwa was ruling in Shiraz about A.H. 400 (=A.D. 1009), and about
seventy years after Mogadiscio and Barawa were built. The Arabic
version tells us that the reign of 'Ali-bin al-Hasan/Husain fell in the
middle of the third Islamic century (i.e. mid-ninth century A.D.[17]). The
chroniclers thus differ between themselves over this date, and the Arabic
differs drastically from the date computable as the sum of the regnal years
which it subsequently sets out. In view of these discrepancies, of the lack
of any mention of Kilwa by the earlier Arab geographers, and of the tendency of chroniclers, ancient and modern, to exaggerate the ages and
antiquity of their forebears, I do not think much weight need be allowed to
these statements. Excepted, however, is the remark of de Barros about
Kilwa having been founded later than Mogadiscio, which agrees with the
evidence from other sources.

*   *   *

[16] In passing, these are two of the three reigns before about A.D. 1300 concerning the
lengths of which the two Chronicles agree—forty and eighteen Islamic years respectively.
But I am suspicious of the former figure, which recurs, together with fourteen; though
the evidence of coins, which is summarized below, suggests that he did have a long reign.
On the other hand, the extreme rarity of the coins of al-Hasan bin Talut would, on the
same analogy, suggest his reign was very short.
[17] Freeman-Grenville (op. cit. 61) takes 'third century' as meaning that which followed
A.H. 300, but I do not think that without other evidence this interpretation is acceptable.

Let us now attempt to draw the archaeological picture of the East African coast in this period. In doing so I attempt, in the first instance, to consider this material evidence independently of the history with which it must in the event be reconciled. I hope in this way to avoid, so far as possible, the dangers of seeing the archaeological evidence through eyes already conditioned by the historical sources as to what they should see.

The picture will largely be drawn within the frame of Kilwa, which is the town-site I know best, and which I believe to be for our purpose the most important yet examined. It will be built up for the most part in terms of pottery, chiefly that imported from the Middle East and from China, which can be dated more accurately from evidence outside East Africa than any other aspect of the material culture of the past. In interpreting the pottery, I rely much on the important work of J. S. Kirkman in Kenya and Pemba, but in general my dates for the imported wares for this period are from fifty to a hundred years earlier than his, and in this respect are, I think, more in accord with the opinion of persons working elsewhere. The architecture and coins have an important part in the whole, but again are only depicted in the first place in their stratigraphic context, as it were. The very few dated inscriptions are in a category of their own.

No remains of settlements (as opposed to stone-age relics) on this coast dating from pre-Islamic times have yet been discovered; none of the few coins and stray objects alleged to have been found here are satisfactorily documented.[18] The earliest convincing firmly datable find is a gold dinar dated 182 A.H. (=A.D. 798–9) of Saif Ullah Ja'far ibn Yahya of the great Barmakid family and Vizier of Harun ar-Rashid.[19] This is almost certainly one of a group of gold coins evidently found at Unguja Ukuu in Zanzibar a century ago, and pottery of Sassanian-Islamic type which I have collected at this site is consistent with such a date. Similar pottery occurs at Manda near Lamu. The earliest antiquities yet discovered under controlled conditions are, it seems, in the lowest levels (at a depth of about six metres) at Kilwa. Here have been found the debris left by fish-eating folk, who probably either camped or built temporary huts on the low sandspit which was the aspect of the site at the time, just as transitory fishermen do on the coast to this day. The typical pots are bag-shaped vessels with indentations on the rim, and shallow red-burnished bowls with inturning rim, decorated with narrow lines of graphite—types of pottery which survive with little change until as late as the early thirteenth century. No permanent dwellings have been found at this earliest level, but this may well be due to

[18] The best authenticated find was made near Tanga in 1896 and has rested in the Museum für Völkerkunde ever since. This group of six coins, which it is hoped to publish shortly, includes one each of the Roman Emperors Carus and Constans, but as it comprises also a coin which is probably Fatimid, the hoard can hardly date before the eleventh century.

[19] The coin is described in a letter published in the *Journal* of the Bombay Branch of the Royal Asiatic Society, VIII, lxxxiii, for which reference I am greatly indebted to Sir John Gray.

the very restricted area which it has been possible to examine at this great
depth.

Soon, however, mud dwellings were erected on the sand. The material
of which these houses was built was the red sub-soil obtained farther to the
east on Kilwa Island, and this, plastered on a framework of vertical poles
and horizontal rods, continued to be almost the sole building material for
several centuries, resulting in the accumulation of some three metres of
red soil, which contrasts very markedly with the dark grey soil of the
upper levels. The extent of the settlement at this stage has not been fully
determined, but it certainly covered a large part of the area of the later
town.

Tin-glazed Islamic pottery, probably imported from Mesopotamia, has
been found at rather under a metre from the base of this red deposit. This
ware is ascribed in Middle-Eastern evidence to the ninth, or possibly tenth
century. This suggests that the earliest camps at Kilwa go back to the
eighth century, though they have not themselves yielded any remains
datable by comparative methods. A Carbon-14 date (GXO398) from charcoal in the stratum below that in which the tin-glazed ware was found has
given a date of A.D. 125 ± 110, but this appears impossibly early for deposits
80 cm. above the basal sand.

In strata contemporary with the tin-glazed ware is found also Islamic
pottery of 'sgraffiato' type. This ware had a long life (from the ninth until
at least the early thirteenth century) and it has not yet been possible satisfactorily to analyse minor variations in style in terms of their date. These
wares occur throughout the red earth strata at Kilwa, and at many other
sites on the coast, and this may be termed the 'sgraffiato' period. There
are a few imports of Chinese porcelain; Islamic glass flasks and vessels of
unknown origin in a type of soapstone, turned on the lathe, are also comparatively common.

Towards the end of this period at Kilwa, about one third of the depth
from the top of the red strata, stone buildings are fairly common. These
buildings, at sites on the centre part of the Tanzanian coast, are constructed
of roughly squared and coursed coral stone, sometimes with chips built in
between the courses further to level them. At Kilwa, the few walls of this
type exposed below ground are initially built with mud mortar; later, floors
of lime plaster appear, and soon after lime mortar is used in the walls. The
earliest part of the Great Mosque is built in this fashion. At Sanje ya
Kati,[20] six miles south of Kilwa, and Kisimani Mafia, some eighty miles to
the north, all the walls observed have lime mortar. The buildings include
mosques, all of one type, having flat roofs, supported by wooden pillars
and doors in each side equal in number to that of the rows of pillars, plu

[20] I believe this is the site of Shanga, the inhabitants of which conquered Kilwa shortl
after the beginning of the 'Shirazi' dynasty: see *Ann. Rept. Brit. Inst. Hist. Arch. E. Afr.*
1963–4, pp. 5–6. The only plausible alternative is the Shanga on Pate Island, which seem
altogether too distant. The sites on Songo (Songo Mnara) Island are too late in date to b
eligible.

a door at the south end. The lower levels at Kizimkazi Dimbani on Zanzibar Island belong to this period, and the famous inscription, built into a later mosque and dated to the equivalent of A.D. 1107, is probably contemporary with it.

During this period of roughly-coursed stone building, coins make their appearance for the first time at Kilwa. These were evidently locally struck in large numbers, and are all in the name of one 'Ali bin al-Hasan. The earliest type is that with the name, and the rhyming phrase on the obverse, each written in one line;[21] subsequent types had the name written in two lines. The script of the single-line type is somewhat angular, has very elongated verticals and the letters often end in flourishes; it is somewhat redolent of floriated Kufic script. The most cogent evidence that this is the earliest type of the first ruler to strike coins on this coast is the finding of 570 coins, all of this type and, beneath the corrosion, in fresh condition, during excavations at Kisimani Mafia in 1964. These coins were buried in a pot against the wall of a mosque of the type described above, in sand which had accumulated against the wall. This is also evidence that building in coursed masonry was undertaken before coins were struck. Even apart from this hoard, the coins of this ruler are the most plentiful of all at Mafia, and even commoner than at Kilwa. This period is thought to end in the thirteenth century, perhaps about the middle thereof.

At this point we must remark the only other early dated inscriptions, all at Mogadiscio. The earliest is the gravestone of a man with the surname al-Khurasani (and hence of Persian origin), dated A.H. 614 (=A.D. 1217); another nearby is dated 660. The third gives the date of the beginning of the building of the minaret[22] of the Great Mosque as the equivalent of A.D. 1269, which is perhaps the date of construction of this building. The fifth, dated to the same year, is in the mosque of Arba' Rukun and mentions one Khusrau bin Muhammad al-Shirazi. This is the only epigraphic mention of the Shirazi known to me.

The next event to recall is the appearance at Kilwa, in the palace known as Husuni Kubwa and the adjacent Husuni Ndogo, of new traditions of architecture, some showing affinities with Abbasid and Seljuk building. I have given some account of these buildings elsewhere in this *Journal*[23] and they have been examined in detail by P. S. Garlake.[24] They not only represent a break with the past, but also demonstrate by their enormous scale a marked increase in the wealth of Kilwa. The Great Mosque of Kilwa was greatly extended in this period, which it is convenient to refer to as that of the Husunis.

---

[21] Walker, op. cit. Type XII.

[22] Such minarets are not found south of the Banadir coast. The inscriptions are published in E. Cerulli, *Somalia*, 1, Roma, 1957, 2–10.

[23] *J.A.H.*, IV, 2 (1963), 182–4. Some of the conclusions there drawn are, in the light of recent discoveries, now somewhat modified, as will be seen.

[24] *Early Islamic Architecture of the East African Coast*, O.U.P. for B.I.H.A.E.A., London, 1965.

C.1300

By the beginning of this period the importation of 'sgraffiato' wares had ceased, or nearly so. In its place we find celadon, mostly of the Yüan dynasty, as the typical luxury ware, with a little of the poor 'black-on-yellow' glazed pottery whose origin may well have been Aden, and which was more commonly imported on the Kenya coast. By at least the end of this period a little of the earliest blue-and-white porcelain, in the form of large jars, was being imported. The local pottery is to a large extent different from that found in the 'sgraffiato' period, the characteristic ware having slug-like mouldings worked up on its surface. Imports of glass decline and those of soapstone vessels probably cease completely.

Husuni Kubwa has yielded the only inscriptions of this period.[25] One of these has been dated on stylistic grounds to c. A.D. 1250; another mentions (after titles) a ruler named al-Malik al-Mansur ('the victorious king') al-Hasan ibn Sulaiman.

This period is dated to within the span of the thirteenth and fourteenth centuries; on the evidence of imported pottery c. A.D. 1250 to A.D. 1350 or c. A.D. 1300 to A.D. 1400 could equally be maintained.[26]

Early in this period appear the coins of other rulers. These comprise, in order of numbers, al-Hasan bin Sulaiman, Sulaiman bin al-Hasan, Daud bin Sulaiman and al-Hasan bin Talut. These coins are all somewhat similar in style and weight; this is particularly so in the case of the two commonest types of Hasan bin Sulaiman and Sulaiman bin al-Hasan. A preliminary analysis of these coins shows no evidence that different varieties of coins showing the same name are not all due to one sultan. There is some slight evidence that al-Hasan bin Sulaiman is earlier than Sulaiman bin al-Hasan. Coins of al-Hasan bin Talut form less than one per cent of the whole; the only one usefully stratified would suggest that he might be earlier than other rulers in this group.

We are not here primarily concerned with the fifteenth century, but to fill in the picture we should add that at Kilwa no new types of coin appear to occur after the second quarter of the fourteenth century, save:

(a) coins of 'Ali bin Yusuf (rare, 1 per cent of a random sample). This man is probably a sultan of Mogadiscio, where these coins are commonly found. The coins are smaller and lighter in weight than those we have been dealing with, and the title 'sultan'—never found on Kilwa coins—is used.

[25] Chittick, *J.A.H.*, IV, 2 (1963), 186–7.

[26] Some confusion arises from the fact that some authorities date the Islamic wares half-century or more earlier than the Chinese wares with which they are found.

[27] Indeed this can lead to confusion: re-examination after further cleaning of the four coins found in the small well in Husuni Kubwa (Chittick, loc. cit. 132–4) has shown that while three are of Sulaiman bin al-Hasan, one is of al-Hasan bin Sulaiman. The French man, Morice, was informed that a building apparently to be identified with Husuni Kubwa was built 963 years before his visit in 1777 (see J. Gray, 'The French at Kilwa' *T.N.R.*, No. 44, 1956, p. 29), but such a date is virtually impossible to reconcile with the evidence of pottery and inscriptions found since 1961.

(b) coins of al-Adil Muhammad, also rare (about 2 per cent of sample). These are similar in style and weight to those of 'Ali bin Yusuf, and as they are also found at Mogadiscio I think they are more probably to be ascribed to a ruler of that place than to the Muhammad al-Malik al-Adil who ruled c. A.D. 1412–21 at Kilwa.

(c) coins bearing the name al-Nāsir Nāsir al-Dunia w'al-Din Muhammad.[28] These occur in fill-strata ascribed to the sixteenth century, and the ruler is probably a post-Portuguese sultan otherwise unknown. The coins are the commonest of all in the upper strata, and indeed comprise 27 per cent of all coins found in the excavations to date.[29]

There are also very rare (0·5 per cent) coins of one Daud bin al-Hasan, none of which have yet been found usefully stratified, all yet discovered occurring in upper, fill, levels. They are, however, two or three times as common among coins from the beach, which is presumably a random sample from all levels, so that it is likely that they are comparatively early. These coins closely resemble in style and wording the later coins of 'Ali bin al-Hasan, having the name in two lines.

It should be added that coins of early sultans occur in profusion through the late fourteenth and fifteenth century, and indeed still later, levels, so they (or the dies used in their manufacture) must have remained in use for a long time. It is thus only the first appearance of a new type of coin which is of real importance in the stratigraphic succession.

Not a single example of the coins of Sulaiman ibn al-Husain[30] is included among those, numbering about 2500, excavated at Kilwa and Kisimani Mafia. Only one specimen, acquired at Kilwa, has been identified among the further 2000 coins (casual finds from these and other sites[31] in the region), which I have collected. The provenances of the few hitherto recorded from Tanzania are all more or less uncertain, with the exception of one in an alleged hoard from Kilwa Masoko, which may be wrongly listed.[32] It seems unlikely that the author of these coins is a sultan of Kilwa;[33] it is noteworthy that specimens occur in three collections in Zanzibar.[34]

[28] I am indebted for this reading to Miss Helen Mitchell, who points out that the coins are modelled on those of the Mamluk sultan al-Nāsir Nāsir al-Din Muhammad, who ruled (with interruptions) A.D. 1293–1340. The coins are referred to by Walker, op. cit. 58.
[29] Except at the Husunis, where these coins are lacking in the fill, and finds of any sort are few, most of the volume of material excavated has been from these upper levels.
[30] Walker, op. cit. 50–1.
[31] Including Kua, Songo Songo, Songo Mnara and Mtandura, the last a new site, on the mainland about nine miles south of Kilwa.
[32] Freeman-Grenville, 'Coinage in East Africa before Medieval Times', Num. Chron., Sixth Series, XVII, 176, Table I, reprinted in Medieval History, Table I. However, the original publication in Num. Chron., 1954, reprinted T.N.R., No. 45, 1956, p. 2, lists what is apparently this coin as of Sulaiman ibn al-Hasan.
[33] Though there would certainly seem to have been a ruler of this name—no. 26 in the Portuguese version, of which no. 27 is probably a duplication, or vice versa; the Arabic version only makes sense on the basis that a Sultan, named Sulaiman, has been omitted here. In passing, the regnal years of nos. 25 to 27 as given in the two versions further exemplify confusions that have arisen.   [34] Freeman-Grenville, Medieval History, Table III.

No specimens have been found of the coins of Ismail bin al-Husain and Ibrahim bin ? which the Liwali of Dar es Salaam informed Freeman-Grenville[35] he had seen sixteen years before; these coins cannot be accepted until further authenticated.

*   *   *

Let us now attempt to relate this archaeological evidence to the historical. The Kizimkazi inscription, dated to A.D. 1107, may be compared with the prominent position indicated for the islands of the Zanzibar group by al-Idrisi (c. A.D. 1154), and the three Mogadiscio inscriptions with the pre-eminence given to that place by Ibn Sa'id about a century later. The early importance of Mogadiscio and Barawa is also indicated by the story of their foundation before that of Kilwa by the seven brothers of al-Hasa and their people.

In the Kilwa region, our first task is to attempt to relate the coins to the historical sources. Those of 'Ali bin al-Hasan have hitherto been ascribed to a sultan who ruled for a year and a half around A.D. 1481. The shortness of the reign of this sultan, on the period of which both chroniclers agree (and he reigned sufficiently near the time of the original composition of the Chronicle for us to agree that the figure is likely to be more or less correct), has always accorded unhappily with the great number of coins of this name.[36] Now, in view of the archaeological evidence that these are the earliest coins of all, dating probably from the late twelfth or early thirteenth century, and are apparently earlier by a considerable span than the main group, this ascription must be rejected.

If the author of these coins is to be identified with anyone named in the Chronicles, it can only be with 'Ali bin al-Hasan/Husain, the supposed founder of Kilwa. It is, of course, possible that they are of another, un-recorded, sultan of Kilwa of later date, but in fact the former assumption fits in very satisfactorily. On the evidence of coins of 'Ali bin al-Hasan found beneath the upper and middle floors in the Great Mosque it is pro-bable that the first stage of that mosque is earlier than this sultan. It is just possibly contemporary, but very unlikely indeed to be later. Now, by what seems to be a unique survival of tradition this mosque is known to elders of the present Kilwa Kisiwani as the Kibara Mosque;[37] this name appears to equate with the Kibala mosque which the Arabic chronicler tells us, 'Ali bin al-Hasan/Husain found on arrival.

Basing ourselves on the hitherto accepted chronology, it would be ob-jected that if, as would follow, these coins should be assigned to the second

---

[35] Ibid. p. 177.

[36] In addition, the name of the late fifteenth-century sultan was properly 'Ali bin al-Khatib al-Hasan. The 'title' al-Khatib [= preacher] does not appear on the coins, though this is only slight evidence against the ascription, for it might well be omitted.

[37] See H. N. Chittick, 'Notes on Kilwa', T.N.R., No. 53, 1959, p. 93 n. Since then, this name has been independently and without prompting confirmed by another of the elders of the island.

half of the tenth century A.D., we would expect the superscription to be in Kufic script, for the cursive Naskhi script was not employed for such purposes until after about A.D. 1150. But if the short chronology put forward in the first part of this paper is accepted, we find no objection to assigning these coins to the period indicated, say between A.D. 1150 and A.D. 1225; indeed the flourishes and somewhat rectangular style of the earlier, single line, type of these coins would seem to agree particularly well with such a date. In view of the resemblance of the coins of Daud bin al-Hasan to the later types of 'Ali bin al-Hasan, it is very possible that he succeeded him, in which case, in view of the paucity of his coins we might presume a short reign. It may be guessed that he was a brother of 'Ali; but he does not figure in either the Arabic or Portuguese Chronicles. It is possible that his name, which would have been Daud bin al-Hasan bin 'Ali, has been corrupted in the recorded tradition by the omission of his father's name, and that he is to be identified with Daud bin 'Ali (no. 3) and with the fathers of nos. 6–7, 'Ali bin Daud and also of no. 8, al-Hasan bin Daud.

It is arguable that 'Ali, and his supposed brother, ruled from Mafia. The coins of both of them are proportionately commoner at Kisimani[38] than at Kilwa; the material culture up to about the middle of the thirteenth century is richer at that site and the trade seems to have been more extensive. Foreign coins occur there, including one of gold,[39] while they are quite lacking at Kilwa. 'Ali is of course presented in the Chronicle as ruling at Kilwa, but we are told that both he and one of his sons retired to Mafia. And we must remember that we have no Mafia Chronicle to put Mafia's point of view; at the time the Kilwa Chronicle was written, the town at Kisimani, as the archaeological record shows, was of little account, and had been in decline for some two centuries.

It is certain, however, that both (Kisimani) Mafia and Kilwa were substantial settlements long before the time of 'Ali bin al-Hasan—probably for at least three centuries—and that during the latter part of this period there were considerable numbers of Muslims at these two places, and probably also at Sanje ya Kati. It is presumed, however, from the reputable written sources that most, or all, of the towns of the coast were pagan before about A.D. 1100. However, the contrary evidence of some late traditions[40] should not be ignored, and the lack of any evidence of mosques before the twelfth century could equally well be explained on the grounds that they would have been built of impermanent materials, like all the other buildings. It would be most instructive if we could examine a burial of this period, but none has yet been found, and excavation would in any case be a delicate matter in a Muslim community.

The common present-day tradition of the Tanzania coast that people

[38] An account of the site and earlier excavations there is given in H. N. Chittick, *Kisimani Mafia*, Occ. Paper I, Antiquities Div., Tanganyika Govt., 1961.
[39] *Ann. Rept. Brit. Inst. Hist. Arch., E. Afr.*, 1963–4.
[40] Summarized in R. Oliver and G. Mathew, *History of East Africa*, pp. 102–4, and bibliography.

called the Debuli came to these shores and settled there before the arrival of the Shirazi is probably to be related to this period. Sir John Gray[41] has set out the recorded traditions and concluded that part at least of these traditions refers to the fifteenth century. But all except one present the Debuli as the earliest immigrants remembered by the informants, and the three persons that have recounted traditions to me personally on this subject have been emphatic that they were earlier than the Shirazi. Ch. Sacleux, in his *Dictionnaire Swahili-Français*, s.v. 'mDibuli', also presents these people as the earliest colonists on the coast, and quotes a Swahili remark to the effect that they were white in colour. The only tradition inconsistent with this is one derived from the Hadimu of Zanzibar, which includes the statement that the Debuli had cannon.[42] I do not think that this isolated[43] remark is sufficient to override the other evidence that they came before the Shirazi. If this is accepted, the name Debuli most probably refers to Debal, known to the Arabs, who conquered it in A.D. 711–12, as Daybul. This port, situated near the mouth of the Indus, was not only the greatest in Sindh up to the thirteenth century, but also a notable centre of learning. It is identified by the excavators of the great mound known as Banbhore (Bhambor), some forty miles east of Karachi, with that site.[44] This had a long history from Scytho-Parthian times to the thirteenth century A.D. It is perhaps not without significance that the imported pottery in the last period before the abandonment of the town is to a large extent similar to that found at Kilwa at the end of the 'sgraffiato' period, and includes at least one rare provincial Islamic ware with carved, deeply recessed decoration which occurs also at Kilwa.[45]

Let us now turn to the period after 'Ali bin al-Hasan. We have noted a break in the archaeological record in the thirteenth (or possibly early fourteenth) century—a break which, in so far as the architecture is concerned, is so great that, were it not for the epigraphic evidence, one would guess that this marked the irruption of an immigrant people which one would identify with the 'Shirazi'. And indeed the isolated position of the Husunis, as well as their distinctive character, with half the huge area of Husuni Kubwa set aside evidently for commercial purposes, led us initially to interpret the buildings as a sort of 'factory' (in the eighteenth century sense) of a colonizing community.

Since, however, the 'Ali bin al-Hasan of the coins clearly lived at an earlier date than this, we have to look for another solution if we accept him as identical with the founder of the Shirazi dynasty.

[41] 'The Wadebuli and the Wadiba', *T.N.R.*, No. 36, 1954, p. 22.
[42] Archdeacon G. Dale, *The Peoples of Zanzibar—their Customs and Religious Beliefs*, U.M.C.A., Westminster, 1920, quoted by Gray, loc. cit.
[43] Though the first ruler set on the throne by the Portuguese was named Muhammad ibn Rukn ad-Din ad-Dabuli, this surname may well derive from very long before he lived —cf. families with the names ash-Shirazi and al-Barawi at the present day.
[44] F. A. Khan, *Banbhore; a preliminary report on the recent archaeological excavations at Banbhore*, Dept. of Arch. and Museums, Pakistan, 2nd ed., rev. 1963.
[45] Loc. cit. 35, fig. 7.

Let us first consider the coins which make their appearance in the Husuni period. It is very unlikely that the commonest of them, those of al-Hasan bin Sulaiman, are, as has hitherto been maintained, to be assigned to the sultan of that name who ruled c. A.D. 1479–85 with a short interregnum in the middle;[46] on stratigraphic grounds he must be at least as early as the first part of the fourteenth century. They are almost certainly near in date to the coins of Sulaiman bin al-Hasan, which they so closely resemble. It is tempting to ascribe these coins and those of al-Hasan bin Talut and Daud bin Sulaiman (see page 286), to al-Hasan bin Talut (no. 18) and his three successors of the early fourteenth century, and to equate the break in the tradition with the beginning of the dynasty of Abu'l Mawahib, and the al-Hasan bin Sulaiman of the coins with that of the inscription from Husuni Kubwa, who is likely to be the builder of that palace. But there are objections to this solution, for it is difficult to reconcile with what Ibn Battuta says about Kilwa[47] and with what the Arabic Chronicle says about the Great Mosque.[48] A case can equally be made out for identifying the author of the inscription with the earliest al-Hasan bin Sulaiman (no. 5), who was restored to the throne after the final expulsion of the Mataman-dalin; or if his independent historicity is accepted, with Soleiman Hacen (no. 11), assuming a reversal of the order of names. The objection to both these is the difficulty of assigning the coins, which we now know to be contemporary with the Husuni period, to the earlier sultans. Lack of space forbids the setting out of the evidence for and against these different theories; suffice it to say that up to the present it is inconclusive, and it may prove that the historical sources are so inaccurate that a satisfactory reconciliation is impossible.

* * *

Nevertheless we can now suggest with some confidence a new view on the outline, at least, of the history and cultural development of the coast. First, beginning at least as early as the ninth century A.D. we find settle-

[46] As first ascribed by Walker, loc. cit. 54. He argues that there cannot be coins of an earlier ruler of the same name owing to the occurrence on many of them of the phrase عتر نصره, 'may his victory be glorious', a phrase which, he states, occurs for the first time on a coin of the Egyptian Mamluk sultan al-Mansur in A.D. 1377. Miss Mitchell, however, observes that the phrase occurs on coins of Aleppo dated A.H. 717 (A.D. 1317), citing Balog (*Coinage of Mamluke Sultans*, American Numismatic Society, Numismatic Studies 12, 162). Walker also puts forward the argument that since coins of al-Hasan bin Sulaiman predominate in the two 'hoards' which he examines, they are likely to be the latest. This would be valid if they really were hoards, but this seems very doubtful in the case of the first, which was found lying about in the German post at Kilindoni in Mafia when it was captured by British troops in 1915; if the second really is a hoard, it would have been made in the time of 'Nsra al-Dunya', the commonest and latest type of coin included. The percentage of coins of al-Hasan bin Sulaiman in both collections is well within the range of a random sample.   [47] See above, p. 280.

[48] We are told that the mosque collapsed in the reign of Abu'l-Mawahib al-Hasan bin Sulaiman, with the exception of the dome in which he used to say his prayers. This dome, the remains of which survive, is certainly later than the first barrel vaults of the mosque, and on stylistic grounds is thought to be later than Husuni Kubwa.

ments, with buildings constructed of mud and wattle; the inhabitants we must presume on present evidence to have been pagan, despite assertions of late traditions to the contrary. They traded with the Islamic world, however, though nothing was imported from the Far East.

Towards the end of the eleventh century the first stone buildings were constructed, and early in the twelfth the first mosques were built in stone. Imports of porcelain from China assume significant proportions. This period, and perhaps the preceding, is that associated with the Debuli; during it the most important settlements would appear to have been on the islands of Zanzibar and Pemba.

The immigration of the Shirazi is, it seems, marked by the appearance of coins of 'Ali bin al-Hasan, probably in the second half of the twelfth century, perhaps rather later. At this time Mafia (Kisimani) and Kilwa assume great importance, though apparently secondary to Mogadiscio.

In the second half of the thirteenth century (possibly rather later) there took place a very great increase in the wealth of the sultans of Kilwa, probably related to a fresh influence of immigrants, and almost certainly founded on the expansion of the gold trade with Sofala.

From the middle of the fourteenth century Kilwa declined somewhat, though there appears to have been an increase in prosperity in the early fifteenth century, when several large buildings, some decorated with Islamic and porcelain bowls set in their roofs, were constructed. It is unlikely that any of the sultans of this period minted coins. This, it appears, is the time of the rise of Mombasa to a position of importance; at the date of the arrival of the Portuguese, with which this period may be said to end, it was a bigger town than Kilwa.[49]

In conclusion, it is recalled that J. S. Trimingham has suggested that the Shirazi civilization probably grew up on the Banadir coast, and that the Shirazi migration to places to the south, including Kilwa, came not direct from Persia or the Gulf, but consisted of a movement of Swahilized people from the Banadir. The male ancestors of these people would have settled on that part of the coast, calling themselves Shirazi in much the same way as Swahili people of Zanzibar do at the present day. This view may well be right; and the suggested equation of the 'Shirazi' myth with the 'al-Hasa' tradition supports it. Also relevant is the tradition that relates flags flown by the now extinct sewn boat (*mtepe*) of the lower region with a 'Persian' sultan 'Ali of Shungwaya, who is thought to be identical with the founder of the dynasty at Kilwa.[50] The testing of this theory of origin, however, must primarily wait on archaeological work at sites on the southern Somali coast.

[49] When Ibn Battuta visited Mombasa it was evidently a lesser place than Kilwa. But al-Idrisi, in the twelfth century, mentions it as the place where the King of Zanj resides, though its importance at this time remains unconfirmed by material remains. One wonders whether the word in the Idrisi's text might have been corrupted from Manfia, one of the ways of spelling the name of Mafia in the Arabic Chronicle.

[50] F. B. Pearce, *Zanzibar, the Island Metropolis of East Africa*, London, 1920, 26

TABLE II

SUMMARY OF SUGGESTED NEW CHRONOLOGY

Date A.D.	Events on the coast and accessions of Sultans of Kilwa	Comments
Second cent.	Trade with classical world. Dominance of south-west Arabia (of long standing?). Native population ? Hamitic	Ptolemy and Periplus only source. No sites of settlements found on coast. Coin finds of doubtful authenticity
Uncertain	Late Stone Age relics in Kilwa area	Not found usefully stratified, but apparently extinct at time of earliest settlement at Kilwa
Eighth–ninth century	First permanent settlements on coast of which remains found, notably Unguja Ukuu; all probably pagan	Imports from Muslim world, probably chiefly from Daybul and Siraf. Banadir coast not examined archaeologically
Tenth cent.	Most important settlements in Zanzibar, Pemba, and probably Banadir coast. Substantial Muslim populations at least in former	
c. 1100	Several Muslim towns on coast; first stone mosques	
Twelfth cent.	Rise of Mogadiscio	
End twelfth cent.	Movement of 'Shirazi' southward from Banadir Coast?	Close of period of 'Debuli'?
c. 1200	'Ali b. al-Hasan ruler of Kilwa. Mints first coins	Mafia of equal importance with Kilwa, and perhaps seat of rulers
	Succeeded by Daud, his brother (short reign), with possibly grandson 'Ali b. Bashat between	This Daud possibly confused with Daud b. 'Ali in Chronicles. Minted coins (Daud b. al-Hasan) but these very rare
c. 1240 (short reign)	'Ali b. Daud (stated to be grandson, but possibly nephew) of 'Ali b. al-Hasan	Possibly ruled after al-Hasan b. Sulaiman b. 'Ali as in Portuguese version
(short reign)	Khalid b. Bakr of Matamandalin (usurper)	Beginning of struggle with Shanga. Mafia lost by Kilwa?
c. 1250	al-Hasan b. Sulaiman I (grandson of 'Ali)	
c. 1260	Muhammad b. al-Hasan al-Mandhir (usurper)	
	al-Hasan b. Sulaiman (restored)	End of struggle with Shanga. Possible resumption of minting coins and building of Husuni Kubwa, etc., but see al-Hasan b. Sulaiman II below
	al-Hasan b. Daud	Stated to be grandson of 'Ali, but possibly nephew
c. 1300	End of dynasty	
c. 1300	al-Hasan b. Talut	First of Dynasty of Abu'l-Mawahib. Coins very rare, indicating short reign?
	Sulaiman b. al-Hasan, son of above	Omitted as sultan in Ar. version, but coins (fairly common) presumably of this man
	(Daud b. Sulaiman, regent 2 years)	
c. 1320	al-Hasan b. Sulaiman II	Visited by Ibn Battuta 1331. Probably builder of Husuni Kubwa, etc. Coins (if not of al-Hasan b. Sulaiman I above) very common. Mafia regained by Kilwa?
c 1340	Daud b. Sulaiman, brother of above	Last to mint coins in pre-Portuguese times, and these rather rare
c. 1400?	Nabhan Dynasty established at Pate	Revised date (vice 1204) suggested by application of assumed average generations and reign years to rulers listed in Pate Chronicle. Not confirmed by excavation, but surface finds consistent with suggested date
15th cent	Mombasa increasing in importance	
1498	Voyage of Vasco da Gama	

SUMMARY

The paper puts forward a new interpretation of aspects of the early history of the East African coast, and in particular maintains that the immigration of the 'Shirazi' took place some 200 years later than the date in the latter part of the tenth century which has hitherto been accepted.

After a brief summary of the Arabic sources bearing on the history of the coast, and of the received history of Kilwa before the beginning of the fourteenth century, the two versions of the Kilwa Chronicle are examined. The Arabic version is concluded to be more reliable than the Portuguese, though very little reliance should be placed on the regnal years of the sultans as given in either.

The archaeological evidence, based chiefly on recent excavations at Kilwa, is examined, with particular reference to the coins minted on the coast. Certain types of these coins are found to have been hitherto wrongly attributed, notably those of 'Ali bin al-Hasan, which are shown to be the earliest.

An outline of the history of the coast is presented, based on the combined historical and archaeological evidence. No satisfactorily attested relics of the period of trade with the Graeco-Roman world have yet been found. The earliest settlements discovered date from the eighth to ninth century A.D., most or all of which were probably pagan, but already trading with the Muslim world. By about 1100 there were several Muslim towns on the coast. This period is related to the Debuli of the traditions.

The arrival of the 'Shirazi' is related to the appearance of coins of 'Ali bin al-Hasan, who is identified with the first ruler of the 'Shirazi' dynasty at Kilwa (about A.D. 1200); Mafia was of equal importance at this time. A marked cultural break in the latter part of the thirteenth or early fourteenth century is thought to be related to a change in dynasty at Kilwa, a fresh settlement of immigrants, and the gaining of control of Sofala and the gold trade.

It is suggested that the Shirazi settlement consisted not of a migration of people from the Persian Gulf direct to Kilwa and other places, but rather a movement of settlers from the Banadir coast.

16. NEW LIGHT ON MEDIEVAL NUBIA

By P. L. AND M. SHINNIE

HISTORIANS of Africa have paid comparatively little attention to the Christian states which flourished in Nubia throughout much of medieval times. When these states have been mentioned they have usually been treated as unimportant backwaters on the fringe of the Islamic history of North Africa and the Near East. Such a view has always under-estimated the importance of Christian Nubia. There is sufficient evidence to show that at least the northern Nubian kingdom was well organized and culturally advanced, and played an important part in the politics of north-eastern Africa throughout a great part of the Middle Ages. The presence of a Christian enclave during a period of Muslim expansion in northern Africa was a factor of some significance, and it was certainly the presence along the Nile of a Christian power that made necessary the long and arduous pilgrimage route from West Africa across the Sahara and along the Mediterranean coast to Cairo—a route well known from the journey of Mansa Musa in 1324, but which must also have been used by many lesser men from the beginning of Islam in the west, until the final Muslim victory in the Nile valley made possible the shorter route south of Lake Chad and across to the Red Sea coast. Moreover, recent finds of Christian Nubian pottery far to the west of the Nile valley at Koro Toro and Tungur, both in Chad, are an indication of the extent of the influence of this Christian state, an aspect of its importance which had hitherto been unsuspected.[1] It is surprising that there seems to have been little or no contact with the neighbouring Christian state of Ethiopia. Nor on present evidence is there any suggestion that these two states were aware of each other.

Nubia was in every way the equivalent in power of the states of the western Sudan which, except for Ghana, it pre-dated; and our information about it is somewhat more abundant. It is time that a re-assessment of this important state of medieval Africa was made, and this article is an attempt to draw attention to some new features which may help in this.

Since a large number of the monuments and towns of the Christian period of Nubian history lie along that part of the Nile valley which will soon be flooded by the building of the Aswan Dam, many of them have been excavated in the last few years; and a considerable amount of new information, particularly with regard to artistic development and details of domestic life, has become available. It may therefore be useful to indicate in what way our picture of medieval Nubia has become more detailed, and in what way our ideas must be revised.

A full picture must wait on the final publication of recent excavations,

[1] *Kush*, XI, 315–19.

but until Old Dongola, which lies outside the flood area, has been excavated, it will still be incomplete.

There is no recent secondary work on the area in this period, but a historical survey was given by Monneret de Villard in 1938,[2] and, in the present state of knowledge, it needs little revision. The monuments, as then known, were listed and described by the same author at much the same date,[3] and there are several earlier books, mainly concerned with descriptions of churches.[4]

Until recently, these churches, visible in considerable numbers, were the only known monuments of the period, and the picture available to the historian had a heavy ecclesiastical bias. The culture appeared as that of a religious community with little activity other than prayer—in marked contrast to the impression of a warlike people given by Arab writers. The correctness of the Arab view is confirmed by the success of several Nubian invasions of Egypt—resulting, on one occasion, in A.D. 745, in the capture of Cairo, and the occupation for much of the tenth century of Upper Egypt at least as far north as Edfu, and also by Nubian resistance over many centuries to Arab attacks from A.D. 641 onwards. It is certain that Nubian warriors made an impression on the Arabs, and their skill as archers was particularly noted.[5]

Only the briefest historical summary need be given here. Suffice it to say that between the years A.D. 540–80 Christian missions were active in Nubia, the area of the old state of Meroe, which for more than two hundred years had been ruled, if not settled in large numbers, by the people known enigmatically to archaeologists as the X-group, perhaps to be identified with the Nobatae. The missionaries were of two opposed sects, Orthodox and Monophysite, and determination of the varying success of one or the other, and of the theological allegiance of the converted, has provided one of the major problems of Nubian history.

These missions were rapidly and remarkably successful in converting the pagan rulers along the Nile; and three states, with Christianity as their religion, can be seen to have existed by the beginning of the seventh century. Two of these, Nobatia (the most northerly) and Makuria (between the 3rd and 4th cataracts), joined together early in the eighth century, perhaps under king Merkurios, to form a single kingdom with its capital at Dongola;[6] whilst the southern one, with its capital at Soba, maintained an existence of its own until perhaps as late as the beginning of the sixteenth century.[7]

[2] Monneret de Villard, *Storia della Nubia Cristiana* (Rome, 1938).
[3] Monneret de Villard, *La Nubia Medioevale* (Cairo, 1935).
[4] Somers Clarke, *Christian Antiquities in the Nile Valley* (Oxford, 1912). Mileham, *Churches in Lower Nubia* (Philadelphia, 1910).
[5] Monneret de Villard, *Storia della Nubia Cristiana*, p. 72.
[6] Now known as *Dongola el aguz*, 'Old Dongola', to distinguish it from the modern town of Dongola, more properly known as el Urdi.
[7] But see Holt, *Journal of African History*, IV, 3 (1963), 39–55 for a reconsideration of the traditional date for the fall of Soba.

The conventional view has been that with the political end of the Dongola kingdom early in the fourteenth century (*c.* A.D. 1323), Nubia abandoned Christianity as rapidly as it had adopted it, though there have been suggestions[8] of Christian nuclei persisting until the latter part of the century. Recent discoveries at Qasr Ibrim make it necessary to reconsider this view, with its assumption of the immediate extinction of Christianity by Islam. Here, the excavation of the tomb of a bishop brought to light two scrolls, each 16 feet long, one in Coptic, the other its Arabic counterpart,[9] recording the consecration in Cairo in the year A.D. 1372 of a bishop of Ibrim and Faras, and authorizing his enthronement. This makes it quite clear that Christianity was still of significance in Nubia, even though political independence had ended.

The authorization by Cairo of this enthronement has no known precedent, and its necessity may only have arisen after political authority had shifted from Dongola to Cairo. The pluralist holding of two dioceses is also interesting. There is plenty of evidence for the separate bishopric at Faras, including the tombs and inscriptions of a number of bishops (see below), and perhaps the combining of the two under one bishop is a reflection of the dwindling of the number of Christians in the area.

Arab penetration of the Sudan, particularly in the Red Sea hills, from the tenth century onwards is well known from the existence of tombstones there;[10] but evidence of Arabs dwelling along the Nile amongst the Christian population has only just come to light. Until very recently, the earliest dated Arabic inscription from Sudanese Nubia was that in the church at Old Dongola, where, in A.D. 1317, Seif el Din Abdullahi claimed that he had 'opened a door of religion',[11] as a result of the military expedition sent by the Sultan of Egypt to place his nominee Abdullah, presumably an Islamized Nubian, on the throne. Now we have several Arabic tombstones of tenth- and eleventh-century date from the Wadi Halfa area,[12] some of these being found in a cemetery of predominantly Christian graves, whilst others, at Meinarti, had been re-used for building purposes at a date not much later than the burials which they were intended to mark. From this it can be deduced that Islam was already present in the area by the early tenth century, and it appears that Christians and Muslims must have been living in amity for some centuries.

Arabic religious inscriptions have also been found painted on the plastered walls of buildings at Debeira West, which otherwise contained predominantly Christian material, and are further evidence of the coexistence of the two communities.

From the date of the conversion of the Nubian states to Christianity until the fourteenth century, we know, mainly from Arab sources, of the

[8] Monneret de Villard, op. cit. 220–1.
[9] *Illustrated London News*, No. 6519, 11 July 1964, pp. 50–53.
[10] Glidden, *Kush*, II (1954), 63–5.
[11] This text, frequently referred to, has never been adequately published.
[12] *Kush*, XII (1964), 39 and 249–50.

course of events only in general outline. We have a chronological framework, and we know the names and approximate dates of a number of the rulers. The events related to us by the Arab writers are, in the main, military encounters between Nubians and Arabs, though a few general descriptions, such as that of Soba by Ibn Selim el Aswani, and the interesting information given by Abu Saleh begin to fill in the details.

The available information has, until very recently, been restricted to these Arab sources and to the rather superficial evidence as to material culture obtained by surface observation of sites and by the random collection of potsherds. During the last ten years more information has become available[13] which, though not making any radical change in the picture, has provided some detailed information as well as making possible more accurate dating of material remains. Much of this new information has been obtained during the excavations of the last four years, and, by normal academic convention, cannot be made known in advance of publication, but even at this stage some new aspects can be described.

The two most significant developments of the last few years have been the classification and chronological arrangement of the pottery, and the excavations of the Polish expedition at Faras.[14]

Dr Adams's classification[15] of the pottery, and the relative dating which his excavation of a number of stratified sites has made possible, have provided an invaluable tool for the chronological arrangement of sites over a period of some 700 years. The absolute dating he suggests may require some modification as work progresses, but it is unlikely that the main principles on which his work is based will be found to be wrong. A method for dating the pottery is of exceptional importance in Nubia, where the depredations of white ants have frequently left little else for the excavator to find, and where the pottery itself is abundant, and of great interest and beauty. Christian Nubian ceramic art, though it has been known ever since Crowfoot first described it[16] and made a very prescient guess as to its date, has been far too long ignored.

It is the richest indigenous pottery tradition in the African continent, and though no doubt it drew some of its inspiration from outside and some of the wares were certainly imported from Egypt,[17] it shows in the Nubian-made pottery a remarkable local talent for colour and design that is not

[13] From the excavation at Soba and Ghazali. See Shinnie, *Excavations at Soba* (Khartoum, 1955), and Shinnie and Chittick, *Ghazali—A Monastery in the Northern Sudan* (Khartoum, 1961).

[14] Michalowski, *Faras—Fouilles Polonaises* 1961 (Warsaw, 1962), and *Kush*, XI (1963), 235–56, *Kush*, XII (1964), 195–207.

[15] Adams, *Kush*, X (1962), 243–88. This classification has been much modified by a typescript 'Field Manual of Christian Nubian Pottery Wares' made available to expeditions in the field.

[16] *Journal of Egyptian Archaeology*, XIII (1927), 141–50.

[17] The tracing of such sources is a matter of some importance. Some seem to be Persian and some Fatimid Egyptian. But much is still unknown. Compare Shinnie and Chittick, op. cit. 30.

Fig. 1. Designs on Nubian pottery. All are painted except for the three
circular ones, which are stamped.

matched elsewhere at this period (some idea of the variety of design can be
seen in fig. 1).

Now that this pottery is better understood, and at least the main
historical periods associated with changes in the tradition defined, it
becomes possible to date sites and buildings and to study change and
development.

The pottery is seen to fall into three clearly defined periods[18] which can
be called Early, Middle, and Late, in accordance with the archaeologist's
normal practice. Adams uses the term Classic for the middle period, but
this, with its suggestion to traditional scholars of contact with Greece and
Rome, seems better avoided. The dating proposed here is: Early, *c.*
A.D. 550–750; Middle, *c.* 750–1100; and Late, *c.* 1100–1350. The only

[18] For the arguments on which this is based see Adams, op. cit. In the periods proposed
here Early is equivalent to Adams's periods 3–5, Middle is 6 and 7, and Late is 8. Adams
himself grouped these periods into three main ones similar to these suggested here in
Kush, XI, 32, 63 n.

change compared with the dating proposed by Adams is in pushing the
date for the beginning of the Middle period back by 100 years.

The significant element in the ceramic history which marks the break
between the Early and Middle periods is the cessation of the import of
pottery (mainly amphorae used to transport wine) from Egypt, and perhaps
some time later the development of the fine painted local wares. In seeking
for historical events to account for the break-down of trade with Egypt,
one guess is as good as another. Adams cogently argues that the fall of the
Omayyad dynasty in A.D. 750 and the disruption it caused in the Arab
world could well be the reason. Another possible cause is the backwash of
the Arab invasion of Egypt in A.D. 639. Although the *Baqt* of A.D. 641
implies that trading relations were maintained, the Arab raids, culminating
in the attack on Dongola in A.D. 651, must have been a considerable dis-
couragement to peaceful trade; nor is it probable that the Muslims would
have looked with favour on a trade in alcoholic drinks. But for the moment
the date of A.D. 750 can stand.

So far as the ceramic evidence goes, the early red pottery wares of
Nubia, according to Adams, continue until about A.D. 850, when their
place is taken by the fine painted 'classic' wares. These red wares are very
strongly reminiscent of late Roman pottery; in many cases they copy the
forms of Roman *terra sigillata*, and in other countries it is unlikely that they
would be dated later than the seventh century. Nubia certainly shows a
number of examples of the very late persistence of foreign traditions, but
it would be easier to accept a date a hundred years earlier. If this is done,
it is necessary to suggest that the painted 'classic' wares started earlier
than A.D. 850.

There seems no great difficulty in this. There is no certain evidence for
date, though at Soba, this ware (there called Dongola ware) is considered
to date from the ninth century.[19] But Soba is far from the area we are now
considering, and the ware may well have taken some time to get there.

Resemblances to some pottery of Omayyad date (A.D. 661–750) have
already been noted,[20] and the hints of Sassanian influence would also
suggest an earlier date. The stamped impressions with a crowned man's
head and the inscription (often blundered) *ΠΕΡϹΟϹ*[21] are clearly derived
from Sassanian coins of the seventh century, and even if not due to direct
influence at the time of the Sassanian invasion of Egypt in A.D. 616, are
unlikely to have taken over two hundred years before being used in
Nubia.

Such a date for the beginning of the fine painted ware would then bring
its introduction nearer to the date of the unification of Nobatia and
Makuria, an event from which certainly sprang the greater political power

---

[19] Shinnie, op. cit. 77.
[20] Shinnie and Chittick, loc. cit.
[21] Some were inadequately published, Shinnie, *Sudan Notes and Records*, XXXI, 297–9.
More have since been found and will shortly be published.

of Nubia and from which may also have come an important cultural advance.

At about the same time there was also a development of church building and of the fresco paintings with which these churches were decorated. The excavations at Faras have opened up a completely new vista of this other aspect of Nubian art. At Faras, the old capital of Nobatia, they have revealed, beneath an unpromising mound of sand already partly excavated many years ago, the cathedral which was the seat of the diocese of Faras[22] and the burial place of a number of the bishops. In this cathedral have been found an enormous number of frescoes of religious and historical scenes which, when they have been published, will provide a mass of information on iconography and religious practices. They will also provide criteria for dating the paintings, since in many cases the earlier ones are overlaid by later examples, and changes in artistic styles can be observed.

It is likely that some absolute dating can be given to these paintings since a number of dated funerary inscriptions of bishops have been found which can be associated with various periods of building in the cathedral.[23] Most of the dated inscriptions so far published[24] are of the eleventh century, and thus come towards the end of the middle period, which we have considered to be the period of greatest political and artistic development.

An interesting confirmation of the reliability of this chronology is found in the list of twenty-seven bishops written on the wall of the south-east chapel of the cathedral. This list gives the lengths of reign of the bishops but without dates. The dates can, however, be established from the fixed points given by the grave stones of Bishops Joannes (d. 1006) and Petros (d. 1062). Since these are the 22nd and 24th bishops in the list, it is certain that this series of bishops did not much outlast the end of the eleventh century, and suggests that the date of A.D. 1100, arrived at on archaeological grounds as marking a cultural change, may well be approximately right if there was also a break in the series of bishops at about that time.

Apart from the valuable chronological and artistic information now available, the most remarkable aspect of the Faras discoveries is the evidence it provides of an advanced culture in this part of the Nile valley. Here was no poor backwater, artistically and politically unimportant, but a state with a developed Church organization rich enough to build a cathedral, the superior of many of the buildings of medieval Africa and the Near East, and with a highly skilled artistic tradition in painting as well as in ceramic art. The painting, like the pottery, shows traces of eastern influence. This is particularly clear in the great painting of the 'Three Youths in the Furnace'[25] where, as the excavator has pointed out, the

[22] For a list of Nubian bishoprics see M. de Villard, op. cit. 162–5.
[23] The chronology is discussed by Michalowski, *Kush*, XII (1964), 195–207.
[24] *Kush*, XI (1963), 240 and 313–14.
[25] *Kush*, XI (1963), Pl. LXI.

youths are dressed in late Parthian clothes known from sculptures at Palmyra of the third century A.D. Though the style of dress may have persisted in Persia until later times and is perhaps another example of Sassanian influence, its use here shows the archaism of much Nubian art.

Amongst the mass of paintings of saints and religious scenes there is one of quite exceptional interest. This one, on the north wall of the cathedral, shows a queen mother of Nubia attended by a guard and protected by the Virgin, and is dated to the end of the tenth or beginning of the eleventh century.[26] The queen mother is shown with a dark face, unlike the figures of Christ, the Virgin, and the saints, who are always shown white. She is identified by a *graffito* in Greek, which reads *ΜΑΡΘΑ ΜΤΡ ΒΟΛ*—'Martha mother of the king'. This special prominence given to a queen mother is of importance, since it is the first confirmation from a Nubian source of the special role that such women played, though it is not infrequently hinted at by Arab writers, who also suggest that inheritance was through the female line. It seems likely that this is an old tradition, since there is some evidence that such queen mothers were of importance in Meroitic times also.

In addition to the new information on chronology and artistic development, far more detail of the nature of the material culture and of domestic life has been discovered. As already noted earlier, knowledge of medieval Nubia has shown a strong ecclesiastical bias because of the type of sites investigated. The site at Debeira West, excavated from 1961 to 1964 by the University of Ghana, is the first purely domestic site to be examined in the Sudan,[27] and has provided a mass of information on daily life and domestic architecture, as well as pointing to the organized nature of town life at the time. The site comprises a small town or large village, with associated churches and cemetery, as well as a number of other large isolated buildings spread along the river bank.

The main site consisted of a considerable and elaborate complex of buildings, which, probably starting in the seventh century as a single group of buildings of an official or religious nature, was abandoned during the ninth and tenth centuries, and then re-occupied at the beginning of the eleventh century for a period of about two hundred years. This second period of occupation was marked by the re-development of the original nucleus. This was brought back into use as a series of domestic dwellings by the blocking of connecting doors to make self-contained houses, and by considerable additions of other buildings, all apparently domestic in nature, and conforming, with minor variations, to a single plan.

From this small urban agglomeration, it is possible to draw a very good picture of Nubian domestic life and architecture. The buildings are all of sun-dried brick, a sensible and adequate material in which to build in that climate, and most are roofed with the Nubian vault, that interesting and

[26] *Kush*, XII (1964), Pl. XLIIb.
[27] *Kush*, XI (1963), 257–63, XII, 208–15.

specialized type of barrel vault which seems to be peculiar to Nubia.[28] In several cases the houses are two storeys high, and in many, even where they consist of only one storey, there is a stairway leading up to the roof. In all buildings considerable care was taken to exclude the winter north wind, which, apart from its coldness, causes drifts of sand to pile up if door or windows are open to it. Where openings were necessarily made to the north, protective walls were built, but in the main, openings were made to a different direction. Changes in architectural detail can be observed, and placed in chronological order, and the discovery of cellars cut into the rock under the floors of some of the earliest rooms is a new and interesting feature. A latrine and centralized drainage systems points to a measure of social organization, and the Debeira community must have consisted of several hundred people.

Life cannot have been very different from that in Nubia today, though the close-knit settlement is very different from the widely spaced houses of the modern villages. Agricultural methods must have been very similar, and there has certainly been little change in diet. The findings of a large number of the special pots used on the *saqia* (the local form of water wheel) indicates that the method of irrigation of crops was exactly the same as that practised today; and a circular brick built structure, with a central column, is so similar to oil presses seen elsewhere in the Sudan, that it seems likely that this must have been a press for sesame or some other local oil.

All the equipment for making *kisra*, the local unleavened bread, was found. Grinding stones, and the remains of pottery *dokas*, the flat dishes on which *kisra* is cooked, were found in quantity, as well as castor oil seeds, which are still used for greasing the dish before the mixture is poured for cooking.[29] These all testify to the importance of *kisra* in the diet, then as now, though we have no evidence as to whether it was made in the main of sorghum or, as is increasingly popular today, of wheat.

The large number of date stones found show that this fruit was extensively eaten, and the discovery of an amphora full of dried dates suggests that some form of drink was made, perhaps *dakai*, a date spirit still made in country districts today.

The remains of animal bones suggest that rather more meat was eaten than is usual now. The animals were the same as the present-day ones, goat, sheep, and cattle, with the significant addition of pig, which has disappeared since the coming of Islam, but which appears to have been common in medieval times. The comparative scarcity of fish bones implies that the same prejudice against eating fish existed then as obtains now, when a legend of armoured horsemen riding through the river allegedly deters people from fishing.

[28] The technique of building is described by Mileham, op. cit. 8–10.
[29] The castor oil seeds are cut in half and rubbed over the dish on to which is then poured a thin mixture of flour and water.

We must suppose that the majority of the inhabitants were employed in agriculture and we have little evidence for other activities. We know that certain handicrafts were practised, and pottery making was of great importance at some sites, for example at Faras. No kilns have been found at Debeira, however, and we must presume that Debeira got its pottery by way of trade with neighbouring settlements where kilns have been found. Fragments of cloth, together with spindle whorls and loom weights, show that cloth was woven, and objects of metal, wood, stone, bone, and ivory were made. A few fragments suggest that leather may have been a common material, but the white ants have left little trace of it. The glass objects found, mainly small bowls and flasks, were probably imported, though the discovery of a large lump of unshaped glass at one site in a bed of ash, may indicate that some manufacture of glass objects, probably beads, was carried on.

We know little or nothing of Nubian trade. It was presumably one of barter. The Nubians never entered a money economy; the only coins so far found in a medieval context are two Ommayad ones from Aksha.[30] We do not know what goods were offered by the Nubians in exchange for the quantities of pots, some of them filled with wine, which were imported from Egypt, but since the Arabs gave food and cloth in exchange for the slaves handed over under the terms of the *Baqt*, it is not likely that such goods were traded by the Nubians, and it is probable that the main product of the country, other than materials for local consumption, was, as in earlier times, gold.

Another aspect of medieval Nubia that is often overlooked is that it was a literate society, and that its language was one of the first African ones to be written, though it had been preceded by Meroitic. Nubian is one of the group of languages known as Eastern Sudanic in Greenberg's classification, and different branches of it are spoken today not only along the Nile, but also in the Nuba hills of Kordofan and in Jebel Meidob in Darfur. It was only River Nubian that was written, and the form we know under the name of 'Old Nubian' is closely related to the modern Mahas dialect spoken from Aniba to the Third Cataract. It was written with the Coptic form of the Greek alphabet, introducing a few extra letters for sounds which did not exist in Coptic. The number of known texts is very few and, with two exceptions, all are religious in nature. The exceptions are both leather rolls which appear to be legal documents.

The fewness of the documents and the limited range of subject-matter have been a barrier to further study of the Old Nubian language, but recent discoveries of further documents, particularly at Qasr Ibrim, where a rich haul was made, will provide much new material.

In addition to Nubian, Coptic and Greek were also in use and many gravestones have been found written in these languages. The persistence of Greek—the latest inscription in that language known to us is A.D. 1181—

after the breakdown in direct contacts with the Greek-speaking world after A.D. 639 is a remarkable phenomenon, even though later documents show some curious aberrations of spelling and grammar.[31]

This account has attempted to give only a brief review of some of the most important of the new discoveries that have been made in the last few years. Much of this material still awaits detailed study, but from what is already known we can see that the material culture of Nubia was of greater richness and complexity than has been apparent before. The significance of Nubia as an element in the medieval history of north-east Africa cannot yet perhaps be fully appreciated, but the possibilities which now exist for the close dating of material remains may have far reaching results. The hints of contacts northwards to Persia and Syria, and the finding of pottery far to the west of the Nile give an impression of a state more influential than had previously been suspected. Remaining an outpost of Christianity in a Muslim world, it was a state whose strength was acknowledged and respected, and whose ultimate defeat took five hundred years to achieve.

SUMMARY

The importance of the Christian states of Nubia in medieval times has hitherto been under-estimated by historians of Africa. There is now sufficient information to show that they played a significant part in the history of the Nile valley for some 800 years. Not only did the existence of Christian states impose a barrier to the expansion of Islam, but the Dongola kingdom at least was at times an important force in the politics of the area.

The recent campaign of excavations made necessary by the building of the Aswan dam has provided much new information about the material culture of the period, and shows a much higher artistic and social development than earlier emphasis on ecclesiastical monuments had suggested. Nubia is now seen to have had a highly developed civilization with considerable urban development. Detailed study of the pottery has made possible more precise dating of buildings and objects, as well as showing periods of increased and decreased trade with Egypt.

The discovery of important frescoes in the cathedral at Faras makes it possible to study the artistic development, and also adds new material for a study of the eastern, particularly Persian, influences already suspected in Nubian art. Information about domestic life is made available by the excavations at Debeira West, the first predominantly domestic site to have been excavated, whose material remains provide new evidence on diet, crafts and agriculture.

[31] Oates in *Journal of Egyptian Archaeology*, XXXXIX (1963), 161–71, has shown from a study of several gravestones how some of the aberrant spellings reflect contemporary Greek pronunciation, and argues that colloquial Greek must have been known in Nubia in the eleventh and twelfth centuries.

17. OLD KANURI CAPITALS

BY A. D. H. BIVAR AND P. L. SHINNIE

THE general lines of Kanuri history and its chronology have been known since Barth's visit to Bornu in 1851 and 1852. During his stay at Kukawa he collected both manuscripts and oral tradition and on his material most of our knowledge of the history of Bornu and Kanem is based.

Though the picture of the Kanuri nation forming in Kanem, to the east of Chad, in the early middle ages and its subsequent move west to Bornu is reasonably clear, the origins of the Kanuri remain obscure and much of the early history is a highly dubious myth. The collections of oral tradition contained in the works of Urvoy[1] and Palmer[2] are in the main unchecked and many statements made by both authors lack any known authority.

Much remains to be done to elucidate these problems, and archaeology should be able to make its contribution. Little or nothing has yet been done in Kanuri archaeology and, until a major site has been excavated, the information must remain sketchy and uncertain. The authors of this article, who visited a number of Kanuri sites in March 1959,[3] make no claim to have solved any problems nor to have made any detailed study of early Kanuri material culture, but their observations may be of some use in view of the complete lack of any previous descriptions.

The most conspicuous of the remains left by the Kanuri from earlier times are the ruins of red brick buildings. This type of building, rare until modern times in Africa and presumably of alien origin, is known from a number of sites stretching westwards from the Nile. The whole group, consisting of buildings of widely different type and date, need not detain us, but of these ruins four are firmly identified with the Kanuri, whilst a fifth, at one time suspected by us of belonging to the same group, is now shown not to be. So far as we know none of these sites has been fully described, though all except one are reasonably well known.

---

[1] Urvoy, *Histoire de L'Empire du Bornou=Mémoires de l'IFAN*, No. 7. This is an important and valuable contribution to Kanuri history but is difficult to use. Unfortunately the author died before publication and no revision or checking of references was carried out by the editor.

[2] *Bornu Sahara and Sudan* and *Sudanese Memoirs*, 3 vols. These curious works contain, if one can sort it out, a mass of information but are uncritical and full of inaccuracies.

[3] The expedition was a joint one of the Nigerian Federal Department of Antiquities and the University College of Ghana. In addition to the authors Mr D. S. Botting accompanied the party.

These sites are, in Nigeria, Birni N'gazargamo, Gambaru, and N'guru,[4] in the Republic of Niger, Garouméle,[5] and in the Republic of Chad, Tié.

Birni N'gazargamo[6] (fig. 1 and plates I and II) is the best known as it is the largest of the sites and its history—or at least the dates at which it

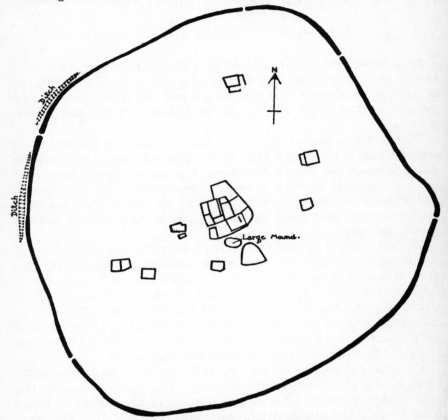

Fig. 1. Plan of Birni N'gazargamo. Scale 1:10,000

was first occupied and finally abandoned—are certain. It stands on the south bank of the river Yobé about 26 miles east of Geidam and about half-way between Geidam and Damasak. The village of Degeltera is 5 miles to the south-west.

The outline of the history of the site is reasonably clear. It is known to have been founded in about A.D. 1470 by Ali, son of Dunama, and re-

[4] Not visited by us but described by Fremantle in *Journal of the African Society*, XI, 62, 187.

[5] Called by Urvoy Widi, west of Garoumélé. He did not, it seems, visit the site himself.

[6] It was visited by Denham, Clapperton, and Oudney in 1823, *Narrative of Travels and Discoveries*, 154, and by Barth in 1851, *Travels*, II, 225. Neither of these accounts is helpful.

mained the capital of the kings of Bornu until its capture and destruction by the Fulani in 1812.

In its present state it is an impressive sight. It consists of an enormous earth rampart enclosing a rough circle. This rampart still stands about 7 metres high and the distance across the enclosure is about 2 kilometres. There are five entrances. Traces of ditch can be seen in a few places along the outside of the rampart and it is likely that originally it ran the whole way along but is now silted up. Inside this vast enclosure are a number of red brick ruins consisting of a large complex in the centre and a number of other smaller buildings scattered throughout the enclosed area.

In most places the walls stand only one course high, presumably having been destroyed in the first place by the Fulani invaders of 1811 and subsequently robbed for building material. There does not appear to be any great depth of deposit.

It can be safely assumed that the main complex was the palace of the Mais of Bornu, that the other red brick buildings were the residences of other leading persons, and that the majority of the inhabitants of the town lived in the flimsy grass huts typical of the neighbourhood, or in houses of sun-dried brick. These have left no surface indications. The plan gives as much information of the nature of the main central building as can be ascertained. Failing excavation, nothing useful can be said about the usage of the various rooms, nor as to details of internal layout or of any features not visible on the surface. The only additional information is that the small building to the south-east of the main complex is known to the local inhabitants as a mosque and, though there is nothing in the layout, as it can now be seen, to support such a view, they may be right. This mosque seems to be an afterthought and the bricks, though of the same size, look to be of different manufacture and perhaps made of clay from another source. Excavation may answer this question and we would like to urge that the careful and large-scale excavation of this site be regarded as a matter of priority in the archaeology of northern Nigeria. It is not likely that a great deal of occupation material will be found and there is no doubt that considerable erosion has taken place since the site was abandoned, but any further understanding of the nature of the buildings can be gained only by excavation.

Gambaru (plates III, IV), which is only 3 miles from Birni N'gazargamo and to its east, is clearly a site of a later period. Tradition, for what it is worth, collected by Palmer describes it as having been built by Queen Amsa, mother of Idris Aloma, in an attempt to separate him from the court and thus to protect his moral character. If this is so it must be a building of the sixteenth century and this date, rather later than that given for the founding of Birni N'gazargamo, corresponds well with what one can deduce from an inspection of the two structures. Gambaru is in a much better state of repair than the older site and there is some suspicion in our minds that the walls have been restored and repaired at some comparatively recent date. The most likely restorer is Palmer but we have been unable to find any record that he did in fact undertake work here and it may be that this is a mistaken view on our part. The walls stand as high as 3 metres in some places and are well constructed of good quality red brick held together by hard mortar. It is difficult to make out any accurate plan as so many of the walls have disappeared nor had we the opportunity to do so. The small number of potsherds to be seen on the ground and the apparent thinness of the occupation deposit indicate that there has been the same erosion here as at other sites, and it is again unlikely that excavation will produce much in the way of objects. It would, however, certainly produce a ground plan and it is this which is most urgently needed at this site.

The site of Garoumélé is in the Republic of Niger, immediately to the west of the road that runs from Niamey to N'guigmi at the north end of Chad. We joined this road at Mainé Soroa having come across trackless country from the Nigerian town of Geidam. From Mainé Soroa a good, though sandy, dry weather road runs east almost to the lake before turning north to N'guigmi and 28 kilometres before that place and close to Widi the ruins are to be seen. Plate v shows the distressing state in which this site now is, most of the red brick having been taken for the building of houses and offices in N'guigmi. Not only have all the surface bricks been taken, but the foundation trenches have been dug out to get the brick lying below the surface. This makes it possible still to see the original ground plan since the trenches remain open. This can be seen in the plate. The work of destruction is still going on and the piles of red brick put together by the contractor or the local administration were seen by us, as well as the tracks of the lorries that come from time to time to take them away.

Urvoy says that this site was the residence of the kings of Kanem before the foundation of Birni N'gazargamo. He recounts that after the flight from Kanem, Omar Said and Kade Alounou (1388–9) wandered on the south and west confines of Bornu; then their successors established themselves at Widi (Garoumélé).[7] If this is so, it makes the site considerably older than those of Bornu and geographical considerations make this highly likely. The story presumably comes from oral tradition and may well be right, but the archaeological evidence is at present too scanty to make a reasoned judgement. There are few Kanuri in the area today, though there are a number of Kanembu villages along the shore of the lake.

Garoumélé has already been published by Binet[8] who gives a sketch plan and comments that the site had already been badly damaged by the removal of bricks to N'guigmi and that some excavation had been carried out by a local doctor. We did not know of this reference at the time we visited the site so we were unable to make inquiries about the excavations or as to the fate of any objects found there.

The plan (fig. 2) is probably no improvement on that of Captain Binet;

[7] Op. cit. 55.   [8] Notes Africaines, LIII, 1 ff. (1953).

it was done by pacing and compass bearing, but it will give an idea of the general layout. The outer wall, which is built of egg-shaped bricks of sun dried mud (plates VI, VII), is very much destroyed and the alignment in

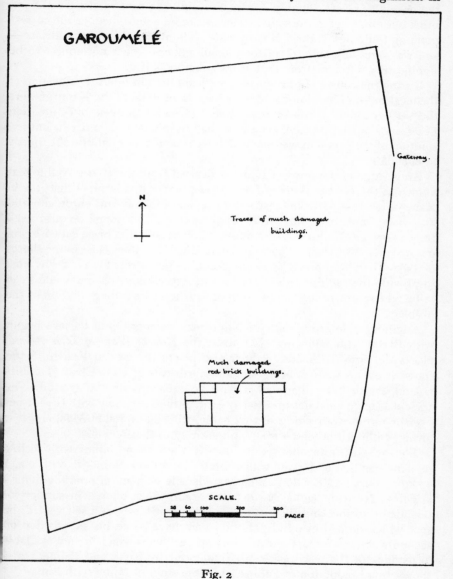

GAROUMÉLÉ

N

Traces of much damaged buildings.

Much damaged red brick buildings.

SCALE.

20   60   100   200   300
                                    PACES

Gateway.

Fig. 2

many places is most uncertain. It is about 2 metres thick. This feature of the use of egg-shaped bricks is still practised in the traditional architecture of Hausaland. In Hausa such bricks are known as *tubuli*.[9] They are a

[9] Bargery, *Hausa-English Dictionary* s.v. *tubuli*.

characteristic distinguishing Garoumélé very markedly from Birni N'gazargamo, where the great circular rampart is of earth, and from Gambaru, where there seems to be no surrounding wall. The layout of the enceinte is very roughly rectangular, and the central complex of red brick buildings much the same, so far as can be determined, as the corresponding buildings at Birni N'gazargamo. The material from the surface—and we were only able to collect a small amount—does not appear to be significantly different from that at the other sites.[10]

During the course of our journey, we had much in mind the question of the location of Njimi, known to have been the capital of the Kanuri before the settlement at Birni N'gazargamo. It had not been our intention necessarily to visit the site, even if we had been able to identify it, but the solution of the problem was one which we thought we might be able partly to elucidate.

Knowledge of the town of Njimi is derived from the Bornu Arabic text known as the *Kanem Wars of Idris Aloma*, where it is implied that it is in Kanem, i.e. east of Lake Chad: from several other Bornu chronicles and king-lists: and from the Arab geographers. The name is also well remembered in Kanuri oral tradition. There is indeed a place called Njimi marked on the Michelin Touring Map of Chad Territory close to the shores of Lake Fittri. On *prima facie* grounds this spot seems too far to the East to provide the requisite identification; nevertheless its claims would need to be taken into account in an attempt to reach a definitive solution of the problem.

Attempts to locate the site of Njimi may be considered to have begun with Barth, who following his source, the *Kanem Wars of Idris Aloma*, places the city in Kanem. Palmer also places the city in Kanem,[11] and shows it on his map as being situated north-east of Lake Chad. He does not appear to have identified it with any remains on the ground. The ancient Kanem need not necessarily be identified precisely with the former French administrative area of that name, with its capital at Mao, and it is unwise to limit the search for Njimi entirely to that region.

The only definite attempt to identify the city of Njimi with visible remains was that of Urvoy, who wrote[12] 'Njimi, ou Njimi-ye, ou Sima, à 55 km. environ à l'Est de l'actuel Mao dans le Kanem (et non N'guigmi à la pointe Nord du lac).' No detailed argument is offered in support of this identification, and there is no evidence that Urvoy himself visited the spot which he had in mind. He may well have based his supposition on accounts of local military and administrative officers which are not available to us and for the rest was deeply influenced by Barth and Palmer, as is shown by his adoption of Palmer's identification of Njimi with Sima.

Such inquiries as we were able to make indicate that present Kanuri

---

[10] Pottery found during this journey, all of it from surface collections, has been divided between the Nigerian Government Department of Antiquities and the Department of Archaeology at the University College of Ghana.

[11] *Sudanese Memoirs*, I, 1.   [12] Op. cit. 27, n. 2.

oral tradition is firmly against Urvoy's indentification, for in this tradition Njimi is unquestionably, if perhaps wrongly, placed at Garoumélé. We must, however, point out that neither of us is trained in the collection of oral tradition, a skilled and specialized technique, and that neither of us speaks Kanuri, so that we could only converse through the medium of our interpreter who himself knew no English. We were able to talk to him in Arabic which he translated into Kanuri.[13] There is, therefore, considerable doubt about the location of Njimi and linguistic misunderstandings no doubt abound in the information which we were able to collect. But the fact that the placing of Njimi at Garoumélé runs counter to the tradition reported by Palmer suggests that it may be a genuine one, since we found plenty of evidence to suggest that many traditions now retailed in Kanuri villages were derived from Palmer. This is not to suggest that Palmer deliberately falsified his material but it seems likely that when he had established one version to his satisfaction, he then passed this on to others telling them that this was their history. On more than one occasion, when talking to the Kanuri on historical matters and asking them where their information came from, we have been told 'It is so because Sir Richmond Palmer told us so.'

In an attempt to solve some of these problems, one of us (A.D.H.B.) went on from Fort Lamy to Mao whilst the others went down the Shari river. It was hoped that local information at Mao might provide information and that the name Njimi might be known in the area.

Inquiries at Mao[14] showed that the name Njimi was today unknown, at least as the name of any local landmark. Apart from the old town of Mao, known as Mao Kudu, and mentioned as being situated some three or four miles from the present settlement, a variety of remains in red brick were said to exist along an axis stretching from Ziguei at the north-east to Mussoro at the south-east. The only one of these readily accessible from Mao, and that seemed in any way to tally with Urvoy's description, was a site with red brick remains, mentioned by a member of the staff at the headquarters of the District, as existing at Tié, some 25 miles to the east. The actual distance to the ancient site was found to be almost exactly 30 miles.

Since the countryside is in many ways different from that of Bornu and is little visited, it is perhaps worth giving some description of it. This may help to explain some aspects of the development and early history of the Kanuri state.

The country falls into two areas; that of the dunes, often as much as 30 metres high and composed of fine sand, covered for the most part with

[13] We should like here to express our thanks to Bilal Omer who acted as our interpreter. In spite of his lack of English his excellent command of Arabic, Kanuri, and Hausa was of great value. '

[14] At Mao, A.D.H.B. had the benefit of discussions with the Chef du Cercle and the Sultan of Mao, and is also deeply indebted to Monsieur and Madame Laverdant for their hospitality and assistance.

long grass, tamarisk, or patches of acacia scrub; and the flats, which are
depressions of black cotton-soil, surrounded by girdles of palm trees, and
with water freely available from shallow wells. Settlements are generally
situated on the higher dunes to obtain the benefit of the evening breeze.
Water for the towns is carried up on camels from below. The flats are
humid and oppressive, but they have shade and with good cultivation can

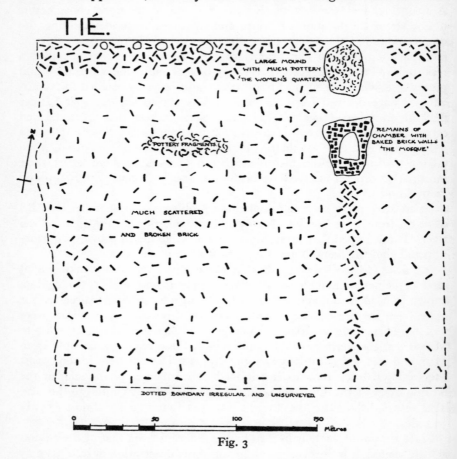

Fig. 3

produce a remarkable variety of vegetables. They have the appearance of
former lakes, and may still hold water in a generous rainy season. The
human inhabitants of the dunes are the Goraan, living in conical grass
huts and matting shelters, and possessing cattle, goats, and camels. By
contrast, along the flats the people are mainly cattle-raising Kanembu.

    The archaeological site at Tié, of which a sketch plan is given in fig. 3,
is chiefly characterized by its quantity of scattered brick. It is situated at
the crest of a large dune formation, and is nearly 2 miles from possible
sources of water. The total area is nearly square being some 243 metres by

Plate I. Great rampart at Birni N'gazargamo

Plate II. Birni N'gazargamo showing, on right, part of wall of central building

Plate III. Gambaru

Plate IV. Gambaru

Plate V. Garoumélé, showing foundation trenches dug out and a pile of red bricks waiting to be transported for modern building

Plate VI. Garoumélé. Outer wall of egg-shaped bricks

Plate VII. Garoumélé. Close up view of egg-shaped bricks

218 metres. There are no certain traces of a surrounding wall, but to the north and north-east the boundary is more sharply defined. Elsewhere it is vague and irregular. Apart from the two main buildings at the north-east of the site, and four small mounds along its northern edge, there are few signs of substantial buildings. The area to the west seems likely, however, to have been covered by a number of smallish huts. Only a small amount of pottery was to be seen on the surface. This pottery is fragmentary and featureless but one piece has the characteristic cream slip of the pottery from the Christian state of Dongola.[15] The most striking feature of the site was the bricks themselves; these were very irregular in size, being all flattish, mostly some 5 cm. thick, but of greatly varying length and width, and some extremely large. The larger bricks were longitudinally scored, evidently by drawing the fingers along the surface whilst the clay was still wet. This type of brick is also known from the Nile valley in Christian times. The local guide called one of the larger buildings the 'Mosque' and the other the 'Women's Quarters'. If these names have no factual basis, they at least provide convenient terms of reference for the features.

From this account it will be clear that although of some interest and probable antiquity, the site at Tié in no way fulfils the requirements of the capital of Njimi. By comparison with the other sites described it is insignificant in size and material remains. The dimensions indicate a small frontier outpost, or a distant monastery, not a busy metropolis. Certainly Idrisi described Njimi in unflattering terms[16] but he was writing long before its heyday and in later times it must have developed substantially, and would have left more than these relatively trifling remains. One fact appears clearly from an inspection of the site at Tié: whatever the structures originally built with the bricks, the whole complex has been systematically and effectively levelled. All the walls have been razed, and the bricks scattered far and wide. After this destruction the site has remained unoccupied, apart from a few camp fires of passing Goraan, and the occupation layer, such as it is, is very shallow.

Local opinion at Mao attributes this site, and indeed all the others which characteristically make use of baked brick, as of the Bulala period (c. A.D. 1300–1600). If this attribution were correct, it would be natural to connect the demolition of Tié with some episode in the Kanem wars of Mai Idris, and therefore probably attributable to the 1570's.[17] The appearance of a Dongola ware sherd together with reminiscences of the Nile in the bricks themselves suggests that some influence may have come from the East. This view is not so fantastic as it might once have seemed since we now have firmly attested examples of Dongola ware from Ain

[15] For a description of Dongola ware see Shinnie and Chittick, *Ghazali—A Monastery in the Northern Sudan*, Sudan Antiquities Service Occasional Papers v, 28–30.
[16] *Description de l'Afrique et de l'Espagne*, ed. Dozy and de Goeje (Leyden 1866), 15: 'Elle est très petite et a un petit nombre d'habitants, gens abjects et misérables.'
[17] Palmer, *Sudanese Memoirs*, I, 14.

Fara in Darfur, which is not so far from the region of Mao.[18] Although not suggesting that Tié was an outpost of Dongolese Christianity, the Bulala date allows for some overlap and it may well be that the peoples of the eastern side of Chad were in touch with the Nile valley. Such a suggestion opens up the possibility of the whole inspiration for red brick building having spread into West Africa from the Mediterranean via the Nile valley. Westward influences from the Nile have frequently been suggested as the origin of many culture traits in Africa, but archaeological evidence other than these buildings is scanty.

The usual view is that after the fall of Meroe in *c.* A.D. 300 there was a movement of defeated peoples to the west. This may have been so but archaeological evidence of such a movement at that date still remains to be found. On present knowledge it is easier to accept a westward migration towards the end of the Christian kingdom of Dongola in the mid-fourteenth century A.D., when under pressure of Muslim invasion there may have been movement to the west. The presence of red brick is consonant with either date.

Such a movement could account for the spread of a number of features which suggest influence from the east. In addition to the buildings and our solitary sherd, there are the alleged traces of Christian symbolism amongst the Tuareg, the development of the Zaghawa state, and even the Kisra legends may preserve some historical truth of the influences that came from Dongola and the Nile valley.

[18] Arkell, *KUSH*, VIII, 115–19.

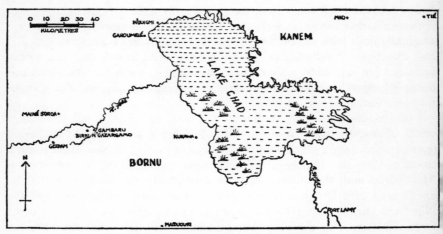

Fig. 4. Sketch map of Bornu and Kanem

18. IFE AND ITS ARCHAEOLOGY

By Frank Willett

No general account of the archaeology of Ife has ever been published, although the demand for such an account has been increasing with the growing interest in the art of Ife.[1] This paper attempts to fill the gap by providing a survey of the investigations which have been conducted there. The reader is also referred to a paper by William Fagg and the present author[2] which attempts to summarize the reliable factual knowledge about Ancient Ife, inferring from the archaeological finds evidence of the materials which have not survived. So far as possible repetition here of material contained in that paper is avoided. Moreover, since the archaeologist who works on ethnohistoric problems has other means of investigation than the pick and shovel, this paper will refer to ethnographic accounts as well as to excavations.[3]

According to Yoruba[4] tradition, Ife is the centre of the world. It was here that the children of the High God came down a chain from heaven with a five-toed chicken and a bowl of sand, which the chicken scattered across the primordial ocean to make the land. A little of the ocean was left to become the sacred pool illustrated by Frobenius,[5] but during the last five or six years the pool has silted up and has already been built over. The senior of these descendants from heaven was Oduduwa or Odua, who is regarded as the first ruler (with the title Oni) of Ife. In due course he presented his sixteen sons with beadwork crowns, and sent them out to found kingdoms of their own. Their descendants still wear beaded crowns and enjoy a special status among Yoruba kings (or *obas*), although in fact most *obas* now wear such crowns.

The pagan Yoruba accept such stories as historical fact, and there may well be a historical basis for some of them. The more sophisticated how-

---

[1] The fullest range of photographs of Ife art currently available is Willett (1967a), but additional photographs of the bronzes will be found in Leon Underwood's *Bronzes of West Africa*, (London, 1949).

[2] W. B. Fagg and F. Willett (1960).

[3] The most up-to-date summary of ethnography and oral traditions relevant to the archaeology of Ife is Willett (1967a).

[4] The Yoruba number about six million people, and are a group of related tribes organized into city states each with its own king. They occupy almost all of the Western State of Nigeria and a substantial area of the adjacent parts of the West Central State and of Dahomey where they are known as the Nago. Although they speak dialects of one language, and share many legends and gods, their culture is not uniform.

[5] (1913), Vol. I, facing p. 22; Hambly (1935) gives an account of the pool, p. 466.

ever, Christian, Muslim or Western style neo-pagan, have other ideas. Clapperton[6] has recorded Sultan Bello of Sokoto's account of the Arabian origin of the Yoruba, and this story is now current, particularly among Muslim Yoruba. Some of the Christian Yoruba would see themselves as a lost tribe of Israel, who followed the same route across the Sudan. And, of course, there is always Kisra to be invoked.[7]

The Yoruba are racially very mixed, ranging from typical Sudanic Negroes to what an earlier generation would have called 'pure Hamites', and it does seem likely that some of the people have come into the area from outside, very probably as a ruling group who eventually intermarried with the indigenes. In Ife indeed there are traditions of earlier occupants, known as the Igbo, who were driven away from Ife with the help of flaming brands. A re-enactment of this event is performed every year during the Edi festival,[8] which is one of the most important, perhaps because it is one of the most spectacular, festivals in the calendar.

Ife today is a prosperous town of about 150,000 inhabitants. Its wealth comes from cocoa grown as a cash crop to supplement subsistence agriculture. In spite of its wealth the town is squalid, and its population appears to be insensitive equally to appearances and to cleanliness. It is probably the least pleasing of all Nigerian towns, to Africans as much as to Europeans. In the old days no stranger would venture near Ife for fear of being sacrificed to the gods (though no Ife man could be sacrificed anywhere in Yorubaland) and Ifes, it seems, are still viewed with suspicion by other Yoruba. Ife is still however, as it has been from the time of Oduduwa, the centre of Yoruba paganism, and disputes of a religious nature are still supposed to be referred to Ife for arbitration. There are said to be 401 gods[9] in Ife, and most of them are still actively worshipped, since there is a festival of some sort celebrated almost every day. The major festivals, Edi, Itakpa (for Obatala, the white god who created mankind), Olojo (for Ogun, the god of iron) and Idio (for Oduduwa), have acquired something of the nature of public holidays, and are attended by many of the non-pagan élite of the town, rather in the way that English May Day ceremonies must have begun to become depaganized. Paganism, however, is

[6] In 'Journal of an Excursion', 165, appended to Major Denham, Captain Clapperton, and the late Doctor Oudney, *Narrative of Travels and Discoveries*, (London, 1826). This account is repeated by S. Johnson (1921), pp. 5–6; this is probably largely responsible for its modern currency. There seems to be no evidence that it is a genuine Yoruba tradition independent of Johnson. R. and J. Lander (*Journal of an Expedition to explore the Course and Termination of the Niger*, London, 1832, I, 180A recorded at Old Oyo the usual Yoruba tradition of Ife as their centre of origin.

[7] A characteristic expression of the views of a European-trained Yoruba historian will be found in *The Origin of the Yoruba*, The Lugard Lectures, 1955, Lagos, by Dr S. O. Biobaku.

[8] On the Igbo see H. U. Beier in *Odu: A Journal of Yoruba and Related Studies*. No. 3, 28 and following. On the Edi Festival see the account by the Rev. Fr M. J. Walsh in *African Affairs*, (1948) 47, pp. 231–8.

[9] Though Akinsale, the founder of Ikole in Ekiti, is said to have taken 440 gods away from Ife with him.

still very strong, even among the young people, who play, after the priests, the most active roles. Indeed a new cement temple of large size and closely resembling a Christian church is at present nearing completion on the highest point in Ife town; this is for Ifa, the divination cult, and all Babalawos (Ifa-priests), not only in Yorubaland but in the Americas too, are regularly contributing to the building costs at a fixed rate.

Many of the shrines, however, have fallen into disuse; and at others, still used, visitors are permitted. Such shrines to which anyone has access are the Opa Oronmiyon, a granite column eighteen feet high, decorated with iron nails,[10] the shrine of Ogunladin[11] in the palace, and the principal Ogun[12] shrine where the Olojo festival is celebrated. On the other hand, no stranger is permitted to enter some of the shrines, such as Igbodio, the 'tomb' of Oduduwa.

Groves in the forest play an important part in Ife ritual, as in most of southern Nigeria. In many of the groves there is nothing to see, in some cases because the antique works of art which are the foci of the worship are kept elsewhere, in some cases because they are buried after the festival and resurrected before the next, but in many cases because there are no antiquities there at all. The annual 'resurrection' of the figures, especially if they are of terra-cotta, would account for the fragmentary nature of so many of them; even the bronze head called 'Olokun' was broken in Frobenius' presence by the Ife man who was digging it up to sell it to him.[13]

The present day people of Ife, even the priests, know very little about the figures and other objects of worship in the shrines and groves. Different priests of the same cult will give different identifications of the individuals represented, and even the same priest will give different accounts on different occasions.[14] This does not appear to be due to a simple desire to mislead, but to a real confusion in the tradition. Ife was evacuated for a period of about five years up to 1854, and again from 1878 to 1894 after the Modakekes[15] had driven them out. They were finally permitted to return

---

[10] This was reconstructed by Mr Bernard Fagg and the Nigerian Antiquities Service in 1953. See Nigeria (1953–4), for an account of the staff and photographs. It is said to be the walking stick of Oronmiyon, who was begotten of the beautiful war captive Lakange by her captor Ogun and by his father Oduduwa. He is said to have been a great warrior, and the founder of the kingdom of Oyo (which became the political capital of Yorubaland) and of the Yoruba dynasty in Benin.

[11] This shrine was illustrated by Frobenius (1913), p. 303. Ogunladin is sometimes identified in the literature with Ogun the god of iron, but the present writer has usually been informed that Ogunladin was the greatest Yoruba smith, or the first Yoruba smith; Aderemi (1937) describes him as the smith of Odua. All four of these concepts are clearly compatible.

[12] It appears to be the remains of two staffs similar to the Opa Oronmiyon. See Talbot (1926), II, fig. 91.

[13] Frobenius (1913), 102.

[14] See Murray and Willett (1958).

[15] Modakeke is the twin town of Ife. It lies on the western edge of Ife and began as a settlement of refugees from northern Yorubaland during the Ilorin wars. The refugees

to Ife 'as it would never do to let the cradle of the race remain perpetually in desolation and the ancestral gods not worshipped'.[16] These interruptions, however seem to have broken the continuity both of traditions and practices, probably because many of the oldest men, the custodians of tradition and belief, died in exile. When the people returned, the groves and shrines would be difficult to locate in the overgrown town, and many alternative identifications emerged. Throughout the nineteenth century wars were raging all over Yorubaland, the Ifes being particularly engaged in many of them; this unrest, too, no doubt contributed to the discontinuity. One of Frobenius's informants told him; 'Many ... make mutual accusations of having stolen their Orishas (gods) and are therefore not descendants of the Gods upon whom they allege dependence. ... Many were not entitled in any way to make a claim to such descent, for in the earlier warlike times everything got mixed.'[17] These factors probably also explain the failure to remember the places where important antiquities lie buried. Probably there were similar periods of desertion in earlier times. Certainly many of the shrines and groves appear to have been created in the nineteenth century for antiquities, usually fragmentary, which had been found accidentally, and whose real nature was not always appreciated. Such a one is Igbo Obameri, excavated by Oliver Myers; a radiocarbon date of A.D. 1730 ± 100 (M-1686) came from a level which Myers thought antedated the establishment of the shrine.

The first European to acquire an Ife antiquity appears to have been one of the Landers at the Queen's market in Katunga (Old Oyo)[18] on 15 May 1830. He writes 'I met and purchased a very curious and singular kind of stone in the market. The natives informed us that it was dug from the earth, in a country called *Iffie*, which is stated to be "four moons" journey from Katunga, where, according to their tradition, their first parents were created, and from whence all Africa has been peopled. Ignorant of mineralogy, as I am ... I am unacquainted with the nature and properties of the stone alluded to, and therefore I grieve to say I am incapable of giving a scientific description of it. It consists of a variety of little transparent stones, white, green, and every shade of blue, all embedded in a species of clayey earth, resembling rough mosaic work.'[19] This specimen can be exactly matched in the collections of the Ife Museum. It is the incompletely remelted residue of mixed fragments of glass, looking quite opaque

---

had settled in various smaller towns in Origbo, westwards from Ife to the Oshun River, but as the Fulani continued to raid them, the Oni Adegunle (=Abeweila) permitted them to settle in a deserted and overgrown quarter of the town some time before 1849. According to Johnson (1921), he was poisoned by the Ifes for his kindness to the Oyos, who were then attacked by the Ifes. The Oyos however repulsed the attack and finally drove the Ifes right out of the city.

[16] Johnson (1921), 232.
[17] Frobenius (1913), 285.
[18] On Old Oyo, see Willett (1960).
[19] R. and J. Lander, loc. cit. under footnote 6.

as mosaic glass does, from the bottom of a crucible, found originally in the Olokun Grove on the north side of Ife.

The first example of Ife art which made some impression outside Nigeria was a ritual stool carved in quartz to an elaborate circular form with a looped 'handle'. This was given by the Oni of Ife to Sir Gilbert Carter in 1896, and by him to the British Museum (Plate IV). The Oni gave him three stools, but until a few years ago the British Museum specimen was the only one known to have survived. Sir Gilbert's widow, however, bequeathed the second to the Nigerian Museum in 1956.[20] This one is of the four-legged type, and shares with the British Museum specimen the distinction of being the only complete example of its type to have survived. The third stool was found in 1959 by Mr Kenneth Murray in the stewards' quarters of a house close to Government House, Lagos. It resembles the British Museum specimen, but the 'handle' has been broken off.

Somewhere about this time or a little later, the British Museum acquired the plaster cast of a terra-cotta head, in a style which suggests that it came from the Iwinrin Grove. It was published by Sir Hercules Read in 1910, as a counterblast to Frobenius's press releases claiming to be the first to discover this naturalistic art. Unfortunately Read does not say how the British Museum acquired the cast, nor who had the original. The original, however, was exhibited at the Brooklyn Museum in a loan exhibition of African Art in 1954.[21] It has not proved possible to trace its travels in the interim.

It was Leo Frobenius, however, who first undertook serious work in Ife in the course of the third German Inner Africa Expedition. He arrived at Lagos on 16 October 1910, and after four days proceeded to Ibadan, where he stayed until 27 November. Two days later he reached Ife, which he left a week before Christmas, after working there for barely three weeks. He was forced to return by the police, and remained there until the middle of January 1911, whilst his actions were 'tried'. He reached Mokwa in Nupe territory on 27 January. Thus he was in Yorubaland for just over three months, and was able to work relatively unhindered in Ife for only three weeks, yet in this short time he collected enough information to write a most valuable ethnographical study, which was the only work of its kind for many years, and has still not been replaced by any single work. Although we now know that it contains a number of errors, some of them important, it remains an astonishing achievement. Yet one forms a very strange view of Frobenius from his writings if one has no first-hand experience of working in Ife. We may reasonably take Hays's[22] view as typical of the general reader's impression. 'His adventures (in Nigeria) were destined to

[20] See B. E. B. Fagg (1956), and B. E. B. Fagg and W. B. Fagg (1960).
[21] Illustrated in *Masterpieces of African Art*, Brooklyn Museum, 1954, No. 113. It was lent to the exhibition by the J. J. Klejman Gallery, but is now in the collection of Alistair Bradley Martin, New York. It is also illustrated in W. B. Fagg (1963), pl. 3.
[22] H. R. Hays, *From Ape to Angel, An Informal History of Social Anthropology* (London, 1959), pp. 282–291.

increase his sense of persecution to near paranoia' (p. 285). 'Frobenius had none of the true ethnologist's patience. He did not try to gain the confidence of the people, but merely extracted their possessions by a combination of browbeating and exploitation of greed' (p. 286). (The expedition had little time and its primary purpose was to enrich the collections in German museums.) 'He ardently defended the Negroes as "culture-bearers". Yet . . . he particularly hated the semi-civilized whom he called "trouser-niggers" ' (p. 286). In fact it is the translator who provided the contemptuous tone. The German has *Neger* which is elsewhere translated as negro. But surely it is hardly fair to judge Frobenius's methods and frank reactions in 1910 by the standards of half a century later. Yet it is still true that the trouble-makers in African societies in general are neither the well-educated nor the illiterates, but the half-educated. Suffice it to say that Frobenius encountered real difficulties, not imaginary ones; that all archaeologists, ethnologists and social anthropologists who have since followed in his steps have found far more frustrations in Ife than anywhere else in their experience. In addition Frobenius eventually had Government opposing him. It is little wonder that he appears in an unflattering light to the modern reader, for he does not attempt to dissemble his annoyance, and his methods were by no means unique at that period.

The first site Frobenius visited was the Ore Grove,[23] which had earlier received partial description by Elgee (1907) and Dennett (1910). It is curious that Europeans should have been permitted to visit the grove without difficulty, so long ago. It is still the only grove to which Europeans are freely admitted, although it is the only one known to me at which individual devotees carry out their private ceremonies at all times of the year. It is possible that the stone figures[24] which it contains are older than the Yoruba occupation, and that the Yoruba have never therefore held them in as great a devotion as the shrines of their own making. Yet the fact that one of the figures has iron nails in the hair appears to conflict with this view, for the staff of Oronmiyon and two terra-cotta heads have similar nails, and it is difficult to believe that these are all pre-Yoruba. Frobenius was soon afterwards taken to a grove of Osonyin to the north-west of the palace. The main feature was a nondescript stone, but he was much more interested in two fragments of a terra-cotta face in a naturalistic style, which he and Martius, his mining engineer assistant, picked up from the ground surface. He thought them 'reminiscent of Ancient Greece, and a proof that, once upon a time, a race far superior in strain to the negro, had been settled here'.[25] Two days later a terra-cotta head was brought to him, and he bought it. He later discovered that it was the Edja,[26] which he was

[23] A detailed account of the Ore Grove is in Murray and Willett, 1958.
[24] A group of related figures has since been discovered at Eshure in Ekiti by Mr Alan Dempster, of the Nigerian Geological Survey. See Willett and Dempster (1962a).
[25] Frobenius (1913), 88–9.
[26] *Eja* appears to be the Yoruba word for a fragment. It is most likely that it was not a proper name for the head.

forced to return. It is, however, now in the Berlin Museum.[27] Satisfied
that there were worthwhile antiquities to be found in Ife, he encouraged
the local people to dig wherever there were traditions that their ancestors
had disappeared into the ground.

He soon obtained guides from the Oni to take him round Modakeke,
which had been evacuated only the year before, but was already an overgrown ruin. He was conducted to a grove with monoliths and some
unfinished figures; he at once started to dig with the help of some farmers
who were working nearby, and found a quartz crocodile, half a metre in
length. He was delighted with this success, particularly as the Oni had
agreed to his digging there. He knew that there had been long-standing
enmity between the Ifes and the Modakekes, but it did not occur to him
that, whereas the Ifes might be glad therefore to have him interfere with
sacred sites in Modakeke, they might object to his taking similar liberties
with their own shrines. He returned repeatedly to Modakeke, and found
fragments of several stone stools.[28]

Before he reached Ife, Frobenius had heard of the Olokun Grove, the
source of great wealth. He obtained the Oni's permission not only to visit
the place but also to dig there. Frobenius's own phrase was that Martius
was 'burrowing'.[29] This describes the technique very well. Two vertical
shafts were dug to a depth of fifteen feet. They were joined at this depth
by a gallery and two more galleries were dug, meeting beneath a large tree
at a depth of seventeen feet below the ground surface. At a depth of ten
feet they found pottery with a glaze on it, and at sixteen to seventeen feet
ashes and beads. He encouraged the Ifes to dig on their own account in the
grove, as he found them impossible as employed labour, and offered to pay
well for any finds. It is often obscure therefore whether finds which are
described as excavated were dug up in this way, or by Martius. At any
rate the fine series of nine terra-cotta heads[30] seem all to have been dug up
in the Olokun Grove at a depth of eighteen to twenty-four feet,[31] although
a unique quartz sculpture[32] came from the centre of the town and various
other finds, including fragments of terra-cotta stools resembling the
important group from the Iwinrin Grove, were dug up in the palace.
Frobenius conveys a clear picture of the Olokun Grove, in spite of his
haphazard methods. His many shafts revealed the following sequence:
surface down to three-quarters of a metre, very hard compact soil with
'glazed' potsherds overlying a red homogeneous laterite with decomposed

[27] Krieger (1955), 33 and 34.
[28] If these are the ones illustrated in the plate opposite p. 304 in Frobenius (1913),
they are all now in the Ife Museum.
[29] (1913), 94.
[30] Frobenius (1913), Plates VI and VIII facing pp. 318 and 320. They are now in the
Berlin Museum. Frobenius (1912), has an extra plate of these heads facing p. 346.
[31] Frobenius (1913), 313.
[32] Ibid. 292; Krieger (1955), 38, fig. 8, now in Berlin where the writer has examined it.
It is not a handle as Frobenius thought, but the leg of a circular vessel. Illustrated in
Willett (1967a) pl. 63.

quartz. At two metres was a layer of pottery, and at five metres, charcoal and ash. Through these layers there penetrated shafts, twelve to twenty-four feet deep, at the bottom of which were glass-making crucibles[33] (for Frobenius learned after he got back to Germany that this was the purpose of the 'glazed' pottery), together with other pots and terra-cottas. Here evidently had been the centre of the great glass making industry which had spread blùe glass *segi* beads across West Africa.

Frobenius's most famous find, however, was the brass head known as Olokun which appears to have been dug up in the Olokun Grove during the second half of the nineteenth century. He bought it for six pounds and a bottle of whisky. The Oni agreed that he should keep it, and send an electro-type back, but the interpreter later admitted having translated that Frobenius would keep the copy and return the original! In the end Frobenius got out of Nigeria only the piece that was broken off it when it was being dug up for him, and the head remained behind in Ife. Underwood and Fagg (1950), however, have demonstrated that the head purporting to be this one, which is now in the Ife Museum (and figured on the old Nigerian sixpenny stamp) is not an original Ife head, but a copy made by sandcasting, the technique used in modern foundries, but certainly unknown in ancient Ife. There is, however, no evidence that Frobenius perpetrated the substitution; moreover, the composition of the metal corresponds to that of the other Ife heads, which were found almost three decades after Frobenius's visit.[34] The original of the 'Olokun' head has never been found.

Frobenius thought he had found traces of a Greek colony on the Atlantic coast of Africa, founded in the thirteenth century B.C., and left without further Mediterranean influence after about 800 B.C. It no longer seems necessary to refute this.

Frobenius's discoveries brought him into conflict with the government, which seems to have decided to regulate the export of antiquities only after receiving reports of his finds. After Frobenius there followed a period of consolidation, when information collected about Ife was incorporated in works of wider ethnographical scope. Outstanding among these are Talbot's (1926) four volumes, which have descriptions and illustrations of many of the Ife antiquities. Hambly's (1935) much smaller study has particular value in that he illustrates six heads and a torso from the Iwinrin Grove (Plate 157) and the beautiful head from the palace known as Lajuwa (Plate 156).

During this time Europeans were increasingly admitted to the groves and shrines, and in 1934 the heads were brought into the Palace from the Iwinrin Grove, at the instigation of the present Oni of Ife, Sir Adesoji Aderemi, K.B.E., K.C.M.G., who ascended the throne in 1931. His

[33] Frobenius (1912) has a fine colour plate of a crucible and fragments, facing p. 337.
[34] The substitution must have been effected between 1910 and 1934 when it was brought into the palace.

sympathetic interest and understanding, together with his desire to preserve all that is best in Ife's cultural heritage, has had a beneficial effect on all the work which has been done in Ife during his reign. Indeed he himself set an example by publishing 'Notes on the City of Ife' in 1937. This included a photograph of the bronze mask of 'Obalufon' and of part of a potsherd pavement, neither of which had been illustrated before.

None of these publications seems to have prepared the art world for the discovery in 1938 of thirteen bronze heads of approximately life size in Wunmonije[35] Compound, not much more than 100 yards from the back door of the palace. A little later, in 1939, a bust (actually the upper part of a broken figure) and four more heads were found in the same compound. Immediately steps were taken by government to prevent their export, but one eventually reached the collections of the British Museum. It resembles the 'Olokun' head in general appearance but is even better. Two others were bought by Professor W. R. Bascom, who was doing ethnographical field-work in Ife at the time; after they had spent some years in the safe-keeping of Northwestern University, he gave them back to Ife when the Museum was built there (Plate I).

The publication of these finds[36] astonished the art world just as Frobenius had been astonished almost thirty years before. The heads were unlike any known African art, and being in a style of *quasi*-mensurational naturalism, had an immediate appeal to those trained in the canons of European taste. These heads could be judged without condescension as works of art in their own right; they would stand comparison with anything which Ancient Egypt, Classical Greece and Rome, or Renaissance Europe had to offer. Although no parallels to them could be found in any of these art traditions, it was assumed that they must have been made elsewhere than Ife and imported, or else, since many of the heads are clearly negroid, made in Africa by an artist working in one of these traditions. The evidence which pointed to an African origin was scarcely considered. Yet Kenneth Murray, writing in 1941, effectively demonstrated that Benin bronzes were being made before the Portuguese arrived, and that the Ife bronzes appeared to be ancestral to them. The identity of style between the bronzes and terra-cottas at Ife, showed that they could not have been made far away. He also pointed out that naturalism is much more common in African art than is usually supposed.[37]

Mr Murray undertook investigations in Ife and compiled a most valuable descriptive list of the shrines and antiquities. Many of the antiquities he brought into the palace for safety, and he was largely responsible for the provision of the Museum there. He was officially appointed Surveyor of

[35] Wunmonije was Adegunle's (=Abeweila) predecessor as Oni in the early middle of the nineteenth century.
[36] Duckworth (1938); Bascom (1938, 1939).
[37] On the purpose of these heads see Willett (1966).

Antiquities in 1943. When a Government archaeologist, Mr Bernard Fagg, was appointed to assist him, one of the first priorities was to investigate the archaeological possibilities of Ife. Consequently in 1949 a dozen small cuttings were made in various parts of the town to test the nature and depth of the occupation deposit. The mere presence of an archaeologist in the town, however, led to the notification of two important finds. One was a small gagged head in bronze from the Wunmonije Compound[38], which had washed out of the earth during heavy rain. The other was an important group of terra-cottas from the village of Abiri some miles away from Ife.[39] Like the large heads from Wunmonije, these had been discovered when digging earth to puddle for house building. The site had been disturbed, but altogether three fine terra-cotta heads were found in the naturalistic style, three conventionalized heads resembling the rook in a modern chess set,[40] one conical head, a ram's head on a platter,[41] a coiled snake and various body fragments. The great importance of this find is that it revealed that beside the naturalistic art of Ife, and almost certainly contemporary with it, there was a freely imaginative style as well.

A much more ambitous programme was undertaken during the first five months of 1953.[42] Bernard Fagg was assisted during part of this season by the late Professor A. J. H. Goodwin, of the University of Cape Town, and William Fagg of the British Museum. Their presence made possible the simultaneous working of a number of sites. Apart from the shrines and groves, there are no surface indications of antiquities in Ife. Formal excavation was therefore concentrated on certain shrines in which antiquities were thought to be buried, whilst exploration of the town as a whole was carried out by the digging of about eighty well shafts. It was hoped that evidence of bronze casting might be discovered by this method, but this aim was not achieved. On the other hand it provided an indication of the depth of occupation deposit in various parts of the town (up to twenty-eight feet) and provided a large series of potsherds recorded in one-foot layers from the whole area. The present writer studied this material in conjunction with pottery from Old Oyo in 1956, and found that it gave a consistent and useful cross-section of the Ife pottery sequence. More recent work however suggests that depths of occupation material in excess of one metre are usually old pits, not natural accumulation.

The grove of Osongongon Obamakin was investigated first. It lies right up against one of the town walls on the western side of Modakeke. A number of interesting pieces from this shrine had been taken to the palace

[38] W. B. Fagg (1950), fig. 1.

[39] B. E. B. Fagg (1949). See Plate II.

[40] Illustrated in W. B. Fagg (1951), fig. 24. This paper also adduces on pp. 114–116, cogent arguments for the indigenous character of the art of Ife. See also Willett (1967a), pl. 61.

[41] See Willett (1967a), pl. 45.

[42] My account of this season is based in part on Mr Fagg's fieldwork diaries. I am extremely grateful to him for permission to use them.

in 1943 for greater safety. They included a sculpture in granite of a calabash or pot with a sash round its neck, the terra-cotta head said to be of Osongongon Obamakin,[43] which was supposed never to see the light of day, and the incomplete representation in terra-cotta of a fettered man suffering from *elephantiasis scroti*.[44] Two minor shrines, to Eshu and Ogun respectively, were found to be mounds of fairly recent votive pots, probably for palm wine. The main shrine lay in the ruins of an old hut, and contained many fragments of terra-cotta figures. A fine head was found buried on its side next to a food bowl which appeared to be recent. All the fragments were within eighteen inches of the ground surface; the lowest level was a hard gritty layer pierced by a shaft almost fourteen feet deep, containing pottery and charcoal. At the bottom the shaft was three feet three inches in diameter, though it was narrower at the top. It seemed possible that this was a burial pit from which the bones had completely decayed.

The Ogunladin shrine[11] in the palace was also investigated. The visible antiquities, a large wrought iron 'drop', a granite mudfish,[45] and a quartz cylinder, were, and still are, arranged as in Frobenius' time. They were found to overlie a pavement made of broken pottery set on edge; set flush with the surface of the pavement was a pot, covered with a terra-cotta ram's head. Eighteen inches deeper at the back of the shrine was another potsherd pavement of better quality, arranged radially; in some places, however, the upper pavement lay on bedrock. The upper pavement, which was discontinuous, was left *in situ*, to minimize disturbance, as the shrine is closely associated with the welfare of the royal family. These potsherd pavements outcrop all over Ife. They are especially common in Ogbon Oya quarter behind the Palace, where they are frequently superimposed. Investigations here showed that the tiny discs of pottery (about three-quarters of an inch in diameter), which had been previously found associated with the pavements, were laid not flat as a top dressing, but on edge, forming a corduroy surface. Some of these pavements were provided with cement edges to prevent further erosion, and in the course of this work some fragments of terra-cotta were found; these included some incomplete rectangular stands, and a head in a rather coarse version of the naturalistic style.

The small grove of Olokun Walode was excavated. This is dedicated to the same Olokun as the Olokun Grove, under her function as bringer of wealth, rather than as goddess[46] of the sea. Walode is her priest in this grove. A few inches deep in the centre of the shrine fragments of terra-cotta were found, apparently all from different figures. One of the most delicate examples of the art of Ife—the greater part of a human face bearing

---

[43] See Willett (1967a) pl. 21.
[44] See Willett (1967a) pl. 40.
[45] See Willett (1967a) pl. 72.
[46] The sex of this deity is ambiguous, but it seems more often to be regarded as female than male.

what appear to be Nupe facial scarifications[47]—was found here, together with a small head with fantastically large ears.[48] The latter is rather eroded whereas the former is probably in fresher condition than any other Ife terra-cotta. The other finds included the foot of a bushcow, the left thighs of two different kneeling figures, two hands holding a bowl, a right hand holding a cutlass, a large fragment of a right foot, and a dozen other fragments, some with bead ornaments. Their condition suggested strongly that they had been brought to the grove from elsewhere. With them was a fragment of a glass-making crucible, which suggests that they had perhaps been dug up originally in the Olokun Grove.[49] Some inches below the terra-cotta fragments lay a much eroded patch of potsherd pavement. There appeared to have been a long gap between the laying of the pavement and the deposition of the fragments, which might well have been later than the re-occupation of Ife in 1854.

The Olokun Grove itself was re-examined. It covers an area of three-quarters of a mile by half a mile, and has been extensively disturbed, but the original bell-shaped chambers about twelve feet deep can be distinguished. Over seventy well-shafts were dug without success in the hope of locating an undisturbed chamber. After a careful examination of the evidence, Frobenius's[50] impression of these chambers as burial pits seemed the most satisfactory interpretation. The site is nowadays a mine for old glass, suitable pieces of which are now drilled in Ife to make beads, the glass industry having evidently died out long ago.[51]

However, at Elesije, near the Olokun Grove, a similar chamber was excavated; beside it was a vertical shaft. Both were filled entirely with recent skeletons, some pottery and plenty of modern beads. The chamber seems to have been one of the Olokun Grove type which had been plundered and re-used for the burial of smallpox victims.

A small amount of work was undertaken at the Iwinrin Grove, where more fragments were found of almost life-size figures of which the heads and large body fragments were already in the Museum. William Fagg established that many of the fragments came from a large pottery group representing a figure seated on a round stool (like the quartz one in the British Museum) with his feet on a rectangular stool which supported the loop of the round stool. In 1959 he was able to show that this figure was flanked by a pair of attendants of almost life size, apparently all modelled as one piece of pottery. This is probably the largest single terra-cotta object ever made in Africa (Plate V).

An interesting disc, about three-quarters of an inch in diameter, of blue-green glass with a red centre, was found during the work at the Iwinrin

[47] See Willett (1967a), pl. 31.
[48] Illustrated in B.E.B. Fagg (1959), fig. 5.
[49] The main antiquities at this shrine are a terra-cotta head and a glass-making crucible.
[50] (1913), 308.
[51] The question of exploitation of the Olokun Grove for glass is discussed in Fagg and Willett (1960).

Plate I. Bronze head, probably of a royal personage, found in Wunmonije
Compound in 1938. Presented to the Ife Museum by Prof. W. R. Bascoin

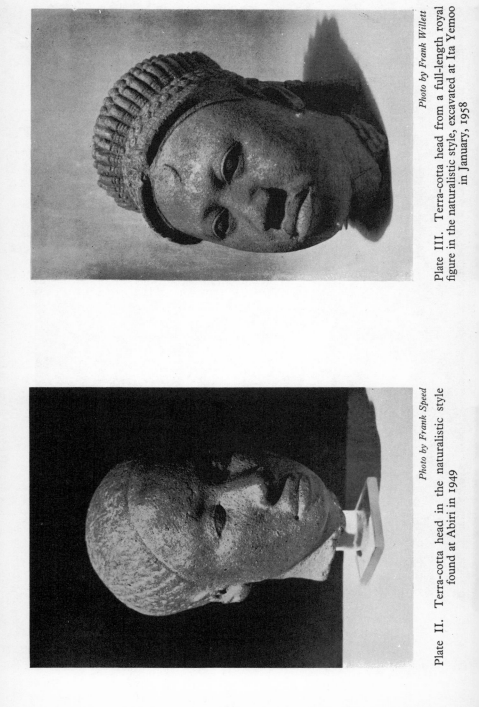

Plate III. Terra-cotta head from a full-length royal figure in the naturalistic style, excavated at Ita Yemoo in January, 1958

Plate II. Terra-cotta head in the naturalistic style found at Abiri in 1949

Photo by courtesy of the Trustees of the British Museum

Plate IV. Ritual stool in vein quartz presented to the British Museum by Sir Gilbert Carter in 1896

Photo by W. B. Fagg

Plate V. A stage in the reconstruction of the large terra-cotta group from the Iwinrin Grove. A four-legged stool supports both the loop of a stool of the type shown in plate IV, and the foot of a royal figure. No adhesive had been employed at this stage, but the reconstruction has not been carried much further as more pieces of this group are expected to be found in future excavations

Photo by Frank Willett

Plate VI. Bronze ritual vessel found at Ita Yemoo in November, 1957. Only 4¾ inches high, it shows a royal figure curled round a pot on top of two stools of the types represented in Plate V

Photo by Frank Willett

Plate VII. Bronze figure of an Oni, 18⅝ inches high, found at Ita Yemoo in November, 1957. It will be noticed that the head occupies a quarter of the overall height

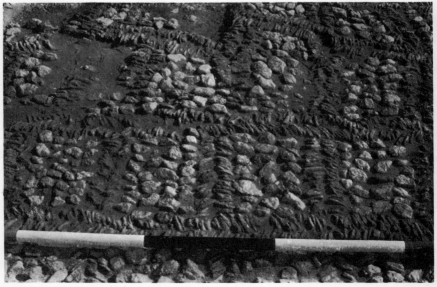

Photo by Frank Willett

Plate VIII. Detail of a pavement of potsherds and quartz pebbles, excavated in the grounds of the Catholic Mission, Ife, in 1958

Grove. Four more were found there in 1959. All are mounted in thin bronze, and appear to have been studs set in a metal strip, probably applied as decoration to a wooden structure, possibly a stool.

The most spectacular work undertaken during this season was the reconstruction of the Opa Oronmiyon,[52] which was preceded by a thorough excavation of the area round it. It was discovered that it had earlier been erected twenty feet away from its present site; no burial pit was found, thus disproving the tradition that it marked the site of Oronmiyon's grave.

Ever since 1953, casual finds of terra-cotta and stone carvings, and of fragments of glass-making crucibles have continued to be brought in to the Museum. At the end of November 1957 a particularly spectacular find of bronzes was made at Ita Yemoo, and I was invited by Mr Bernard Fagg to investigate the site. The find[53] consisted of seven objects: the figure of an Oni just over eighteen inches high (Plate VII); a royal pair with arms and legs interlocked; an elaborate small (less than five inches high) vessel in the form of a pot supported on a round stool, the loop of which is supported on a rectangular stool, whilst curled round the pot is a royal figure holding a staff (Plate VI); two staffs just under one foot in length topped with human heads (one of them gagged); and two ovoid mace-heads each bearing two gagged heads. The particular importance of this find lies in the fact that, although all the pieces are all in the naturalistic style, the four figures which are represented at full length show the proportions which are characteristic of African sculpture, with a head which is a quarter of the overall height of the figure, while the legs are somewhat shorter than in nature. This confirmed the idea that the art of Ife was largely if not entirely African in nature.

The bronzes had lain on a potsherd pavement, most of which had been destroyed by the builder's labourers who found them. A complete pavement was excavated nearby within the foundation trenches of one of the buildings which it was proposed to erect there. It was the first complete pavement to be discovered, and it has been preserved. More important than this pavement, however, was a shrine furnished with at least seven figures in terra-cotta, of about two-thirds of life size, which had been only partially destroyed by a man who was puddling mud there to build his house. These figures also lay on a potsherd pavement. Two unbroken heads were recovered, one wearing a crown; two more, almost complete, were recovered and reconstructed. Here evidently was a shrine in which there had been complete figures standing, not a shrine specially made for a few random fragments. The figures had been standing in a mud-walled house with thatched roof; the roof had been burned off (presumably in war), the figures had thus been left open to the weather for a short time which had produced slight erosion of the surface; soon the rains had brought the mud walls down on top of the figures, shattering them, and impacting part of one head into the pavement.[54]

An exploration of the adjacent land showed the existence of pavements over a very large area, and, a hundred yards from the shrine of the terra-cotta figures, a fragment of yet another royal figure was found. Steps were taken to secure the whole area as an archaeological reserve. There were legal delays, but part of the site was eventually handed over to the Department of Antiquities as a national monument.

The following season, 1958–9, was devoted chiefly to overall exploration of the Ita Yemoo site, to decide which was the minimum area which must be protected. Many pavements were located but no more formal excavation could be conducted at that time.[55] At the same time it was discovered that the Catholic Mission, which is at the northern end of Modakeke,[56] overlay an important archaeological deposit, crossed by the two town walls. About forty pavements were discovered here, one of which was immediately roofed over to preserve it. It was made of lines of potsherds laid in herring-bone, forming hollow rectangles filled-in with quartz pebbles (Plate VIII). The short ends of the pavement had 'cutaways' for the bases of shrines. From these pavements, which are clearly from inside buildings, we hope to be able to reconstruct house plans, for normal stratification is almost invariably absent from the upper levels at Ife,[57] as walls, floors and sub-soil merge into a homogenous laterite in a single rainy season, while the usual building method of puddling the soil by digging a hole and pouring in water, has produced a great deal of mixing up of archaeological material and the re-incorporation of old material in modern mud walls.

During the 1960 season on this site a shrine was excavated, consisting of a few votive pots and a very large number of domestic pots; these were found to overlie a burial in which the bones survived. Pavements were excavated close to the town walls, and it was established that the ditchless wall, which Ozanne's recent work suggests was the older of the two systems, was younger than the laying of the pavements. The pavements have been found as much as four miles from the palace in several directions, which suggests that in the 'pavement period' the town of Ife was much more extensive than it is at present. When the ditchless system was built

---

[54] Preliminary accounts written at the time of these excavations are: Willett (1958, 1959b). Some of the terra-cotta sculptures are illustrated in Willett (1967a), plates VII to IX and 12.

[55] Substantial excavations were carried out in 1962–63, preliminary accounts of which will be found in: *Council for Old World Archaeology: Surveys and Bibliographies*, West Africa, Area 11, no. 3, 1965, pp. 6–7, and *Proc. VIIth Internat. Cong. of Prehistoric and Protohistoric Sciences*, Prague (in the press).

[56] See footnote 15, page 305–6.

[57] Although a site excavated 20 miles away at Ilesha proved to be well-stratified. A preliminary account is in *Odu, A Journal of Yoruba and Related Studies*, No. 8, Ibadan, 1961, 4–20. The 1962–63 season at Ita Yemoo however discovered excellent stratification below the levels of the potsherd pavements and in the section through the town wall.

(and this may have been in more than one phase) the town appears to have been reduced in size. The younger wall system with bank and ditch is no longer to be attributed in its entirety to Abeweila, who may only have built (or rebuilt) certain sections of it. This later system covers much the same area as the earlier one, which suggests that there was a population of similar size to be defended at the time of both constructions. After the Ife-Modakeke wars the population seems to have decreased again. It has now been expanding for some time and has begun to overflow the walls in most directions. The 'pavement period', if it really is a single phase of Ife history, appears to be in part later than the introduction of maize into West Africa, for pottery decorated with the impressions of maize cobs has been found incorporated in at least one pavement.[58]

In any account of Ife, the art receives the greatest emphasis, for until 1949 no serious archaeological work was undertaken. Even since that date the existing literature emphasizes the art rather than the archaeology because it is easier to describe the outstanding individual finds in an interim report than to study the mass of potsherds in detail. The 'treasure-hunting' phase has long been over, but the vast quantities of domestic pottery from the excavations conducted since 1949[59] have not yet been sufficiently studied for publication.[60] When completed, this study will provide the basis for a detailed relative chronology at Ife, and will allow comparisons to be made across Yorubaland; at present more is known about the pottery of Old Oyo, the other important Yoruba site, than about that of Ife. Oyo and Ife appear to represent distinct ceramic traditions, probably because, even if Oyo was founded from Ife as tradition records, the settlement was chiefly of men, who married into the local population without affecting their existing style of pottery.[61] Traditions of movements of people may thus be difficult to check by archaeological means, since the pottery will show the movements of women rather than men.

Until the excavated material at Ife has been more thoroughly studied, any discussion of origins and of outside contacts must be highly tentative. European trade-goods (chiefly modern glazed pottery) have so far been excavated only from the uppermost levels at Ife. The art objects, however,

[58] This was taken to indicate a date not earlier than the sixteenth century for these potsherds for reasons indicated in Willett (1962). However the radio-carbon date recently obtained from a level above a pavement at Ita Yemoo (B.M.–262: A.D. 1060±130) suggests that some of the pavements may be substantially older. No maize-impressed pottery occurs in the pavement on this site.

[59] This paper was originally written in 1960. To have included an account of excavations conducted since that date would have required a substantial expansion of this paper. Accounts of the more recent work will be found in the references given in footnote 53, and also in *Nigeria* (1958–62); in 'The Iron Age in Nigeria' in *The Iron Age in Africa*, ed. P. L. Shinnie (O.U.P. forthcoming); and in Oliver Myers, 'Excavations at Ife; *West African Archaeological Newsletter* (1967), No. 6, 6–11.

[60] Some account of the methodology being used is given in Willett (1967b).

[61] The relations of the Ife and Old Oyo ceramic traditions are discussed in Willett (1960).

are sufficiently numerous to permit historical deductions to be made about them, and traditions elsewhere throw some light on the history of Ife.

A Benin tradition, for example, recounts that Oba Oguola sent to the Oni of Ife for a bronze-smith to instruct his people in the craft; previously bronzes are said to have been sent to Benin from Ife on certain ceremonial occasions. Examination of the Benin bronzes shows that the earlier ones are more similar to those of Ife than the later ones. As Oguola seems to have reigned towards the end of the fourteenth century,[62] bronze-working must have been established at Ife before that time. How much before is still a matter for conjecture.

All the bronzes so far known from Ife (apart from some evidently recent work) are in the naturalistic style, of which far more numerous examples have survived in terra-cotta. A study of the terra-cotta figures reveals stylistic affinities with those of the Nok Culture, already known from a large part of Northern Nigeria, but probably in reality even more widely spread. Radio-carbon samples from the type-site suggest that the terra-cotta figures began to be made some time after 900 B.C., probably by a neolithic or early metal-age people; and that the culture may have continued to produce terra-cottas after A.D. 200. The cultures of Nok and Ife are the only ones so far known in Africa which produced pottery figures approaching life-size; moreover, the stylized treatment of bodies and limbs is in many cases closely similar in both cultures; figures in both cultures wear elaborate bead ornaments; and already in the Nok culture there are elements of naturalism, whilst at Ife, of course, there are important non-representational elements. A fragment of a head found in 1956 at Ire, near Ikirun, about thirty-five miles north of Ife, appears to be intermediate between the two styles.[63] It looks very much as if the art of Ife developed from that of Nok. Moreover, as Bernard Fagg has pointed out,[64] there are many features in the art of Nok which occur not only in the art of Ife, but also in modern Yoruba sculpture. The art of Ife thus occupies its appropriate place in the sequence of evolving artistic style covering a period of approximately three millennia.[65]

Radio-carbon dates have now become available from the author's excavations at Ita Yemoo in 1962–63:

B.M.–262: 890±130=A.D. 1060. This is from a level in which there lay two sculptures in terra-cotta which were already old and fragmentary when the site was abandoned at the time indicated by this date.

B.M.–259: 790±130=A.D. 1160. This date comes from occupation material underlying potsherd pavement no. 4, beneath the town wall.

B.M.–261: 990±130=A.D. 960. This date comes from the bottom of a

[62] On 'Chronological Problems in the Study of Benin History', see R. E. Bradbury's paper in *The Journal of the Historical Society of Nigeria* (1959), I, 4, pp. 263–87.

[63] Illustrated by B. E. B. Fagg (1959), fig. 8, and Willett (1967a), fig. 27.

[64] B. E. B. Fagg (1959) and (1962).

[65] The question of the relationship between the peoples and the arts of Nok and Ife are discussed in Willett (1967a), 119–128.

pit beneath the potsherd pavement (no. 1) discovered during the first season's excavation.

Taken together these dates suggest that the period when the naturalistic art of Ife was flourishing may have been earlier than the twelfth to fourteenth centuries to which it has usually been dated on the evidence of the Benin traditions.

Other radio-carbon dates come from Orun Oba Ado, the site in the middle of Ife where the heads of the Kings of Benin were reputedly buried until 1888:

B.M.–264: 960±130=A.D. 990.

M.–2116: 1010±150=A.D. 940. Both dates come from Pit 6 and confirm each other.

Pit 3 was dated: M.–2114: 1150±120=A.D. 800

Pit 5 was dated: M.–2115: 1150±120=A.D. 800

Pit 11 was dated: B.M.–265: 1390±130=A.D. 560.

This series of dates is internally consistent, with the possible exception of Pit 11, though this could represent an eighth, ninth or even tenth century burial. All these dates are earlier than expected, but they prove beyond doubt that the present day town of Ife is the same Ife to which the traditions refer, and help to reduce the gap in time between the Nok Culture and Ife.

An isolated radio-carbon date from charcoal associated with non-descript pottery discovered by Dr Horst Folster in a trench on the University of Ife Campus urgently needs confirmation:

N.–346: 2360±120 B.P.=410 B.C.

This appears to indicate that human habitation at Ife was contemporary with the Nok Culture, but it is dangerous to assert this on the evidence of a single date. Even if we discount this date, it is still clear that the gap in time between the flourishing of the art styles of Nok and Ife is being greatly reduced.

The knowledge of bronze-casting must have been introduced to Ife from outside, for no more than traces of copper occur anywhere in Nigeria. The limited evidence at present available suggests that the naturalistic art was already fully developed by the time bronze-casting was introduced, and that it was transposed bodily into the new, more durable medium. The technical skill which this would require was great, but no greater than that required to control the successful firing of near life-size terra-cotta groups.

In Ife there are examples of terra-cottas which are almost certainly post-classical, and lead on to the modern Yoruba style. In due time we may hope to find more examples of terra-cottas to illustrate the stages of development from the Nok to the classical Ife style. Some of the sites which have produced Nok terra-cottas may be substantially later than the type-site itself, whilst we know that the apogee of the naturalistic style at Ife was probably between the tenth and fourteenth centuries. The first millennium A.D. represents a crucial phase in the history of most of the major peoples of Nigeria, to judge by traditions. In the case of the Yoruba, it seems likely that a small but influential group of people came into Nigeria during this period and established themselves as rulers over an indigenous iron-using population making something akin to the Nok terra-cottas. The newcomers may have brought with them the knowledge of bronze-casting, which was known at Igbo Ukwu by the mid-ninth century A.D.

As yet there is no direct evidence of who these people were, where they came from, or when. Speculation about whether they came from Meroe, which collapsed in the early fourth century, or a few centuries later from Zaghawa or from Christian Nubia, is idle in the present state of our knowledge. It is more profitable for the present to concentrate on recovering their history inside Nigeria, for their great cultural achievement appears to have occurred within the borders of modern Nigeria. In any case, Yoruba migration legends, both those about their origin and those of diffusion within Nigeria, almost certainly refer only to the ruling group.

Yoruba civilization appears therefore to result from the fusion of a small intrusive ruling class, bringing ideas from outside, with a highly artistic indigenous population. The resulting social pattern seems to have borne some resemblance to that of the City States of Ancient Greece, but the unique achievement of the Yoruba was to have possessed such an evolved urban civilization without the knowledge of writing.[66]

SELECT BIBLIOGRAPHY

Aderemi (1937), 'Notes on the City of Ife', *Nigeria* (Lagos, 1937), XII, 3–6.

Arriens, C. (1930), 'Die heiligen Steinfiguren von Ife', *Der Erdball*, IV, 333–41.

Bascom, W. R. (1938), 'Brass Portrait Heads from Ile-Ife Nigeria', *Man*, XXXVIII, 201; (1939), The legacy of an unknown Nigerian 'Donatello', *The Illustrated London News* (8 April 1939), 592–4.

Bertho, J. and Mauny, R. (1952), 'Archeologie du pays Yorouba et du Bas-niger', *Notes Africaines*, no. 56, 97–114.

Braunholtz, H. J. (1940), 'A Bronze Head from Ife, Nigeria', *British Museum Quarterly*, XIV, 75–7.

Dennett, R. E. (1910), *Nigerian Studies* (London).

Duckworth, E. H. (1938), 'Recent Archaeological Discoveries in the Ancient City of Ife', *Nigeria*, XIV, 101–5.

Elgee, C. H. (1908), 'Ife Stone Carvings', *Journal of the African Society*, VII, 338–45.

Elisofon, E. and Fagg, W. B. (1958), *The Sculpture of Africa* (London).

Fagg, B. E. B. (1949), 'New Discoveries from Ife on exhibition at the Royal Anthropological Institute' *Man*, XLIX, 79; (1953), 'Some Archaeological problems at Ife', *Conference Internationale des Africanistes de l'Ouest*, Ve Reunion, Abidjan, Compte Rendu, 125–6; (1956), 'Caribbean Treasure Hunt',

---

[66] This paper had to be written in hospital from brief lecture notes. I should like to acknowledge my great indebtedness to Mr James Packman, then Deputy Librarian of University College, Ibadan, who personally provided my bibliographical and secretarial requirements. I also wish to thank Mr Paul Ozanne for permitting me to use his new map of the Ife city walls and to quote some of his conclusions in this revision.

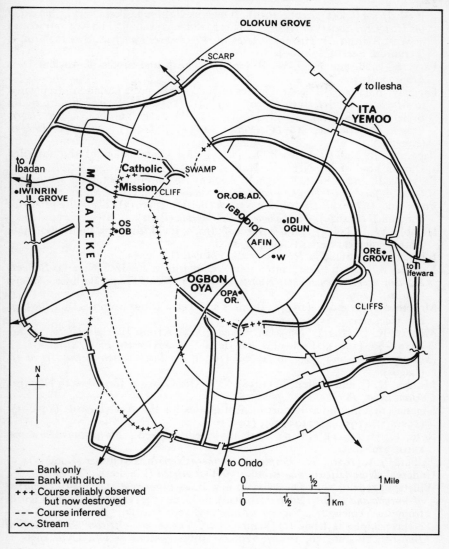

MAP OF IFE

This map is based on the detailed survey by Paul Ozanne conducted during 1967 and 1968 and is the most up to date and accurate map available. There appear to have been two major phases of construction of walls. The first consists of ditchless banks, and the second of banks with ditches. The second has partly obliterated the original system.

Afin: The palace, site of the Ogunladin shrine and of the Ife Museum; *OPA OR:* Opa Oronmiyon; *OR. OB. AD.:* Orun Oba Ado; *OS. OB.:* Osongongon Obamakin; *W.:* Wunmonije Compound, site of the discovery of bronze heads in 1938 and 1939.

West Africa (6 Oct. 1956); (1959), 'The Nok Culture in Prehistory', *Journal of the Historical Society of Nigeria*, I, part 4, 288–93; (1962), 'The Nok terracottas in West African Art History', *Actes du IVe Congres Panafricain de Prehistoire*, Tervuren, Sect. III, 445–50.

Fagg, B. E. B. and Fagg, W. B. (1960), 'The Ritual Stools of Ancient Ife', *Man*, LX, 155.

Fagg, W. B. (1949), 'The Antiquities of Ife', *Image*, no. 2 (London), (reprinted in *Magazine of Art*, XLIII (1950), 129–33); (1950), 'A Bronze Figure in Ife Style at Benin, *Man*, L, 98; (1951), 'De l'Art des Yoruba', *L'Art Negre*, Presence Africaine, 10–11 (Paris), 103–35; (1963), *Nigerian Images*, (London).

Fagg, W. B. and Underwood, L. (1949), 'An Examination of the so-called Olokun head of Ife, Nigeria', *Man*, XLIX, 1.

Fagg, W. B. and Willett, F. (1960), 'Ancient Ife, an ethnographical summary', *Odu, A Journal of Yoruba and Related Studies*, no. 8 (Ibadan), 21–35.

Frobenius, L. (1912), *Und Afrika Sprach* (Berlin), I; (1913), *The Voice of Africa* (London), I; (1949), *Mythologie de l'Atlantide* (Paris).

Hambly, W. D. (1935), *Culture Areas of Africa*, Field Museum, Publication 346, Anthropological Series (Chicago), XXXI.

Johnson, S. (1921), *The History of the Yorubas* (London).

Kreiger, K. (1955), 'Terrakotten und Steinplastiken aus Ife', Nigeria, *Berichte aus den ehem. Preussischen Kunstsammlungen*, Neue Folge, Berliner Museen (Berlin), 32–9.

Meyerowitz, H. and V. (1939), 'Bronzes and Terra-cottas from Ile-Ife', *Burlington Magazine*, LXXV, 150–5.

Murray, K. C. (1941), 'Nigerian Bronzes: Works from Ife', *Antiquity*, XV, no. 57, 71–80; (1943), 'Frobenius and Ile Ife', *The Nigerian Field*, XI, 200–3.

[Murray, K. C. and Fagg, B. E. B.] (1955), *An Introduction to the Art of Ife* (Lagos).

Murray, K. C. and Willett, F. (1958), 'The Ore Grove at Ife, Western Nigeria', *Man*, LVIII, 187.

Nigeria (1949), Annual Report on Antiquities for the year (Lagos); (1950–1); (1952–3); (1953–4); (1957–8); (1958–62).

Read, C. H. (1911), 'Plato's "Atlantis" rediscovered', *Burlington Magazine*, XVIII, 330–5.

Talbot, P. A. (1926), *The Peoples of Southern Nigeria*, 4 volumes (London).

Underwood, L. (1949), *The Bronzes of West Africa* (London).

Willett, F. (1958), 'The Discovery of new Brass Figures at Ife', *Odu, A Journal of Yoruba and Related Studies* (Ibadan), no. 6, 29–34; (1959a), 'Bronze Figures from Ita Yemoo, Ife, Nigeria,' *Man*, LIX, 308; (1959b), 'Bronze and Terracotta Sculptures from Ita Yemoo, Ife', *The South African Archaeological Bulletin*, XIV, no. 56, 135–7; (1960), 'Investigations at Old Oyo, 1956–7: an Interim Report', *Journal of the Historical Society of Nigeria*, II, 1, 59–77; (1962) 'The introduction of Maize into Africa . . .', *Africa*, XXXII, no. 1, 1–13; (1966) 'On the funeral effigies of Owo and Benin and the interpretation of the life-size bronze heads from Ife,' *Man*, N.S. 1, 34–45; (1967a), *Ife in the History of West African Sculpture*, (London); (1967b), 'Pottery classification in African Archaeology', *West African Archaeological Newsletter*, no. 7, 44–55.

INDEX

Millets (see also Digitaria, Eleusine, Finger millet, Fonio, Pennisetum, Sorghum), 49–55
Modakeke, 305, 309, 312, 320
Mogadiscio (Mogadishu), 241, 257, 260, 264, 267, 268, 270
Mombasa, 240, 241
Monomotapa, see Mwenemutapa
Mousterian culture, 17
Mulongo, 230, 233–5
Murdock, G. P., 33, 61–2, 65, 67, 70, 71, 144–5
Musingezi industry, 166
Mwenemutapa, 152, 167, 168
Myers, Oliver, 306
Mzilikazi, 170

Nabombe, 216
Nachikufu, 39
Nagana, 86
Naivasha, 30
Nakuru, 30, 39
Napier, J. R., 5
Naqada pottery, 122
Ndebele, 170, 171, 220
Ndonde, 204, 205, 206, 217, 218
Ndorobo, 64
Neanderthal type, 15, 16, 17
Nebarara, 189
Negritos, 47
Negroes and Negroids (see also Bantu), 19, 21, 28, 32–3, 38, 72–3, 101–5, 106, 119, 190
Neolithic cultures, 20, 21, 27, 28, 29–31, 60, 144, 157
Ngoni, 42, 169
Ngorongoro, 30
Nguni, 150, 178
Niger, 46, 61
Niger-Congo languages, 112
Niger-Kordofanian languages, 111–12
Nilo-Saharan languages, 111, 112
Nilotic peoples, 37, 155
Njimi, 294–5, 301
Nobatia, 278, 282, 283
Nok culture, 21, 29, 30, 71, 147, 322, 323–4
Nsongezi, 35
Nuba, 110, 112, 113–14
Nubia, 31, 71, 104, 277–87
Nubian pottery, 280–2
Nubian language, 112, 286–7
Nyamwezi, 150
Nyima, 112

Obalufon, 311
Obsidian, 30
Oduduwa, 303, 304, 305
Ogun, 73, 304, 305, 313

Ogunladin, 313
Oguola, Oba, 322
Oil Palms, 43, 144
Olduvai Gorge, 3ff., 22, 85
Olokun, 305
Olokun Grove, 309, 310, 314
Olokun Walode, 313
Olorgesailie, 11
Oranian culture, 18
Ore Grove, 308
Oronmiyon, 305, 308, 319
Orun Oba Ado, 323
Oryza, see Rice
Osongongon Obamakin, 312–13
Osonyin, 308
Oyo, 312, 321

Paranthropus, 5, 9
Pemba, 239, 257, 258, 262, 274
Pennisetum, 21, 31, 43, 51–2
Periplus, 148, 239, 240
Pietersburg culture, 17
Pilgrimage routes, 277
Pithecanthropoids, 10
Potato, Kaffir, 68, 144
Ploughs, 56, 124–5, 127–8
Population increases, 142–3
Portères, R., 33
Portuguese, 152, 154, 167–8, 242–3
Potassium/argon dating, 3, 9
Pottery, see under Chinese, Dimple-based, Gokomere, Islamic, Kangila, Kisalian, Mesolithic, Naqada, Nubian, Stamped
Ptolemy, 148
Pulses, 61
Punt, 126
Pygmies and Pygmoids, 37, 64, 119, 150

Qasr Ibrim, 279, 286
Quiha, 30

Rabat, 11
Radiocarbon dates, 151–2, 155, 169, 171, 193, 206, 237, 322–3
Rats, 207
Religious beliefs, early, 17
Rhapta, 257
Rhodesia, 157ff.
Rhodesian and Rhodesioid human types, 10, 12, 16–17, 187–9
Rice (oryza), 21, 33, 45–9
Rinderpest, 94
Robinson, K. R., 35
Rozwi, 167, 168, 169, 196

INDEX

331

Sahara, 27, 29
Saharan languages, 112, 113
Salt, 214, 215
Sandawe, 40, 150, 189
Sanga, 90, 154, 207, 223ff.
Sangoan culture, 13, 15, 16
Sanje ya Kati, 266, 271
Sankuru, 39
Sassanian, 282, 284
Sculpture (*see also* Figurines), 307ff.
Sebanzi, 216–17
Sebilian culture, 70
Seligman, C. G., 59–60, 99, 104–5
Semites, 117, 123, 124–5, 127–8
Semliki valley, 93
Semyen, 123–4
Senegambian culture, 47
Sennar, 126
Sergi, G., 101–2
Sesame, 61
Shaheinab, 65, 69
Shaka (Chaka), 42, 169
Shangaan, 170
Sheep, 38, 41, 69
Shilluk, 113, 114
Shinyanga, 95
Shirazi immigrants, 241, 255, 257, 258, 264, 267, 272, 274
Shona, 152, 164, 195–6
Sickle blades, 27
Sickle cells, 87, 106, 109, 110
Sidama, 119
Singa skull, 37
Slave trade, 73, 93
Sleeping sickness, *see* Trypanosomiasis
Smithfield culture, 20
Snowdon, J. D., 49
Soba, 278, 280, 282
Sofala, 259, 260, 262, 274
Somalis, 59
Songhai language, 112
Sorghum, 21, 30, 31, 33, 43, 49–51
Sotho, 150, 170, 182, 195
Stamped ware, 36
Sterkfontein, 9
Stillbay culture, 17
Stone Bowl culture, 31, 41, 144
Stools, ritual, 307, 309, 314
Sukuma, 150
Summers, R., 85
Suttee burial, 107
Swartkrans, 9

Tabi language, 112
Taferjit, 28
Tama language, 112
Tamaya Mellet, 28
Tana, Lake, 123, 124

Taros, 44, 67, 144
Tassili, 27
Tatog, 150
Teda, 112
Teff (Tef, T'eff), 21, 31, 53, 125, 127, 128
Telanthropus, 9
Temein language, 112
Ternifine, 10
Thonga, 152
Tié, 295–6, 301–2
Tin, 39, 161
Tonga, 189, 201, 216–20
Tools, stone, 4, 6–8, 11, 29–31, 64
Transhumance, 41–2
Trypanosomes, species of, 78–80
Trypanosomiasis, 75–98
Tsetse flies, 34, 75–98, 163
Tshikapa, 155
Tshitolian culture, 18
Tuli Kapi, 30
Tungur, 277
Twa, 189

Uganda, 65, 93–4
Uitkomst industry, 162
Umayyad Caliphs, 241, 248
Upemba, Lake, 223–4

Vaufrey, R., 29
Vavilov, N., 44–5, 48, 52, 62, 117
Veddoid, 110
Vegeculture, 27, 61, 144
Venda, 170, 196

Wadi Halfa, 279
Wells, L. H., 41
Wesa, 169
Wheat, 20, 21, 27, 31, 33, 125–6, 127
Willett, K. C., 81
Wilton culture, 20, 144, 158, 201–3
Wire drawing, 212
Woolandale, 161–3, 165
Woolega, 30
Wunmonije Compound, 311, 312

Yams (Dioscorea), 21, 30, 61, 67, 68–9, 144
Yaqut, 240
Yemen (*see also* Arabia), 124–5
Yoruba, 303ff.

Zambia, 151, 201–21
Zanzibar, 240, 241, 242, 257, 262, 265, 267, 269, 274
Zimbabwe, 21, 35, 152, 161, 163–71, 183, 195–6
Zinjanthropus boisei, 4
Ziwa, 160, 161, 237–8
Zulus, 42, 169
Zwangendaba, 169

DATE DUE